Hyderabad,



This rich examination of the formally autonomous state of Hyderabad in a global comparative framework challenges the idea of the dominant British Raj as the sole sovereign power in the late colonial period. Beverley argues that Hyderabad's position as a subordinate yet sovereign "minor state" was not just a legal formality, but that, in exercising the right to internal self-government and acting as a conduit for the regeneration of transnational Muslim intellectual and political networks, Hyderabad was indicative of the fragmentation of sovereignty between multiple political entities amidst empires. By exploring connections with the Muslim world beyond South Asia, law and policy administration along frontiers with the colonial state and urban planning in expanding Hyderabad City, Beverley presents Hyderabad as a locus for experimentation in global and regional forms of political modernity. Through state-level consideration and social analysis, Beverley recasts the political geography of late imperialism and historicizes Muslim political modernity in South Asia and beyond.

ERIC LEWIS BEVERLEY is Assistant Professor of History at State University of New York, Stony Brook.

# Hyderabad, British India, and the World

## *Muslim Networks and Minor Sovereignty, c. 1850–1950*

Eric Lewis Beverley

CAMBRIDGE
UNIVERSITY PRESS

CAMBRIDGE
UNIVERSITY PRESS

University Printing House, Cambridge CB2 8BS, United Kingdom

One Liberty Plaza, 20th Floor, New York, NY 10006, USA

477 Williamstown Road, Port Melbourne, VIC 3207, Australia

314-321, 3rd Floor, Plot 3, Splendor Forum, Jasola District Centre, New Delhi-110025, India

79 Anson Road, #06-04/06, Singapore 079906

Cambridge University Press is part of the University of Cambridge.

It furthers the University's mission by disseminating knowledge in the pursuit of education, learning and research at the highest international levels of excellence.

www.cambridge.org
Information on this title: www.cambridge.org/9781107463080



First published 2015
First paperback edition 2017

*A catalogue record for this publication is available from the British Library*

ISBN 978-1-107-09119-1 Hardback
ISBN 978-1-107-46308-0 Paperback

For Regina and Yahima Regina

# Contents

# Illustrations

## Maps



## Table



## Images

Acknowledgments

This book centers on extended and often unexpected circuits of connection through one particular place, and its completion would have been impossible without my ability to rely on connections to people spread between many places. I am enormously grateful for the hospitality, support, friendship, intellectual generosity, and critical engagement of a great number of friends and colleagues.

I began and completed the final draft of this work in Cambridge, Massachusetts. Several parts of this project and many of its broad concerns were first thought through, researched, and written up as a dissertation in the Indo-Muslim Cultures field of the Department of Near Eastern Languages and Civilizations at Harvard University, and my four committee members were critical in its formation. Ali Asani, my supervisor, taught me much about explaining counterintuitive points to audiences of all kinds. Sugata Bose offered incisive feedback at a key moment. Cemal Kafadar helped me begin to situate Hyderabad's institutional life in comparative perspective. Engseng Ho pushed me to extend some of my positions to their logical conclusions. Fellow grad students, unionists, teachers, archivists, roommates, interlocutors, and friends around Harvard and Boston made my time there enjoyable and edifying: Jessica Mulligan, Maple Razsa, Diana Allan, Justin McDaniel, Alex Keefe, Hussein Rashid, Ayesha Jalal, Wheeler Thackston, Homi Bhabha, Stephen Greenblatt, Robert Travers, Charlie Hallisey, Ilham Khuri-Makdisi, Teena Purohit, Michael M. J. Fischer, Bhrigupati Singh, Ajantha Subramanian, Maggie Schmitt, Mike Guinan, Bob Cronin, and Seth Young.

During my MA studies at the University of Texas, Austin, my advisor Cynthia Talbot showed me the ropes of academia and Deccani history, and inspired me with her rigorous and creative approach to scholarship. Courses and meetings with Akbar Hyder and Gail Minault helped stimulate my early interest in Hyderabad State. Fellow students at UT, such as Mark McClish, Gardner Harris, and Laura Brueck, made Austin an ideal place to start graduate school. As an undergraduate at New College of Florida, John Newman adeptly introduced me to the academic study of South Asia.

The History Department at the State University of New York, Stony Brook, which has been my institutional and intellectual home since 2007, has provided a supportive, stimulating, and remarkably friendly environment. My colleagues in History, and many in other departments, provided a marvelous intellectual community. I am particularly grateful for feedback, advice, or unrivaled companionship and solidarity on the LIRR to Kathleen Wilson, Paul Gootenberg, Daniel Levy, Themis Chronopoulos, Iona Man-Cheong, Ned Landsman, Gary Marker, Shobana Shankar, Larry Frohman, Young-sun Hong, Gene Lebovics, Said Arjomand, and Rowan Ricardo Phillips. Conversations and classes with the wonderful graduate students at Stony Brook in History and other departments pushed me to clarify and extend some of the arguments here, and I am grateful in particular to Erica Mukherjee, Tim Nicholson, Eron Ackerman, Andres Estefane, Froylan Enciso, Juhi Tyagi, and Andrew Ehrinpreis. Many others made New York City a stimulating and welcoming place: Manan Ahmed, Anand Taneja, Abhishek Kaicker, Bill Eidtson, Margret Knight, Tara Broughel, Erik Gheniou, Michael Gilsenan, David Lelyveld, Bhavani Raman, and Aparna Balachandran.

During my time in Hyderabad in 2002–3, 2008, and 2010 I was constantly humbled and edified by warm hospitality and stirring intellectual exchanges with Aniket Alam, Manjari Katju, Javeed Alam, and their families. David MacLean shared many memorable adventures and insights. Kavita Datla was an excellent archive buddy. Rasna Bhushan, Sonia and Amar Sirohi, Uma Maheshwari, Rayalu Rama, and K. Satyanarayana provided Hyderabadi hospitality, and K. Venkateshwarlu explored with me some remnants of the urban projects this book examines.

Shorter visits elsewhere for research or writing were extraordinarily productive and enriching, and this is thanks largely to the guidance, companionship, and hospitality of friends and members of vibrant communities of scholars living or working in various places: in London, Graeme Napier, Chinnaiah Jangam, Abhijeet Paul, Shabnum Tejani, Daud Ali, Shruti Kapila, Taylor Sherman, Clare Anderson, and Stephen Legg; in Delhi, Suzanne Schulz, Sean Pue, Elizabeth Kolsky, Amitava Sanyal, Priyo Banerjee, and Radhika Singha; in Mumbai, Rahul Srivastava, Karin Zitzewitz, Will Elison, and Sanjay Bhangar; in Berlin, M. Erdem Kabadayı, Margrit Pernau, Johann Büssow, Marina Rustow, and Gudrun Krämer.

A handful of people have formed the core of my intellectual community through all of these times and places. My uncle, John Beverley, has been a model of intellectual productivity and critical engagement. John Rogers and Doug Haynes selflessly gave extensive, challenging, and enormously productive feedback. Sunil Sharma has been an exemplary teacher and mentor, not to mention an incomparable host. Mana Kia always poses difficult questions in a manner both unforgiving and constructive. Sarah Waheed has been an unstintingly enthusiastic fellow traveler in the study of South Asian Muslim history. Svati Shah showed me the obligation we have to rigorously contextualize the politics and livelihoods of different people and places, and the potential of this project. Prachi Deshpande has been an indispensable mentor throughout my graduate studies and beyond, and read the whole of this manuscript in multiple forms and provided copious and always helpful comments. Nikhil Rao is in part responsible for my introduction to South Asian urban history, often while slowly unraveling difficult intellectual questions over leisurely walks through cities. Shekhar Krishnan has been a friend, interlocutor, collaborator, and co-conspirator for nearly two decades, and has interrogated – and helped fortify – many of the concepts and arguments in this book.

In addition to those mentioned above, many others have provided valuable comments or advice on different sections or ideas in this book, offered crucial encouragement, shared unpublished work of their own, or otherwise assisted: Seema Alavi, Sebouh Aslanian, Cemil Aydin, C. A. Bayly, Lauren Benton, Partha Chatterjee, Will Glover, Sumit Guha, Thomas Blom Hansen, Rajeev Kinra, Lara Kreigel, Julie Laut, Karen Leonard, Darryl Li, Anant Maringanti, Brinkley Messick, Lisa Mitchell, Gyan Prakash, Sunil Purushotham, Shayan Rajani, Julio Ramos, Prithvi Datta Chandra Shobhi, Eric Tagliacozzo, and Ben Zachariah. Conversations with many others surely informed the ideas here, and apologies to anyone I have inadvertently not named.

Parts of this work were presented at conferences and workshops organized by Stanford University, New York University, Princeton University, Irmgard Coninx Foundation, Freie Universität Berlin, George Mason University, Harvard University, SUNY-Stony Brook, Alam Khundmiri Foundation, Vidyasagar Art Centre, Wissenschaftskolleg zu Berlin, US National Humanities Center, Cambridge University, University of California-Berkeley, and Arizona State University; and at annual meetings of the American History Association, Association for Asian Studies, European Social Science History Association, and Urban History Association. I am thankful to organizers and participants for providing forums to present and comments.

Crucial material and institutional support for research and writing of this book was provided by the Fulbright-Hays Program, Harvard University, the State University of New York at Stony Brook, Berlin Graduate

School of Muslim Cultures and Societies at Freie Universität Berlin, and the Institute for the Study of Muslim Societies and Civilizations at Boston University.

This project would have been impossible without the assistance of archivists and librarians in Hyderabad (Andhra Pradesh State Archives, High Court Library), Mumbai (Maharashtra State Archives), London (British Library, Oriental and India Office Collection), Delhi (National Archives of India), New York (Melville Library at SUNY-Stony Brook, Butler Library at Columbia University, the New York Public Library), the Boston area (Widener and Loeb Libraries at Harvard University, Rotch Library at MIT), Austin (Perry-Castañeda Library at UT), and Miami (Green Library at FIU).

I am grateful to the MIT Aga Khan Program staff, the late Omar Khalidi, and Moacir P. de Sá Pereira for crucial assistance with maps and images. For the book's image of the Asaf Jah flag I am grateful to HEH the Nizam's Museum in Hyderabad for allowing the flag in their collection to be photographed, to the museum's chief curator Bhaskar Rao for locating the flag in storage, B. V. Ramana for his photography work, and to Raghu Cidambi, independent scholar, for his initial interest and persistence in helping track down an existing flag. Versions of Chapters 6 and 7 appeared previously as "Frontier as Resource: Law, Crime, and Sovereignty on the Margins of Empire," *Comparative Studies in Society and History* 55.2 (2013): 241–72 and "Urbanist Expansions: Planner-Technocrats, Patrimonial Ethics and State Development in Hyderabad," *South Asia: Journal of South Asian Studies* 36.3 (2013): 375–96, respectively, and thanks to the publishers of those journals for permission to use this material here. Thanks also to peer reviewers at both journals, and editors Andrew Shryock, David Akin, and Vivien Seyler.

Working with Cambridge University Press has been a wonderful experience, and I am grateful to everyone in the UK and India offices who had some part in bringing this book to fruition. I owe particular thanks to my editor Lucy Rhymer for her enthusiasm about the project and masterful guidance from the start. Thanks also for patience and adept editorial work from the production stage onwards to Sarah Green, Beata Mako, and Mary Starkey.

My parents, Diane and James Beverley, have been inexhaustible founts of love, confidence, and support of all kinds from the very beginning. My brother Mark Beverley has kept me in good spirits and provided a soundtrack for part of my writing process. My oldest friends – Adam Zwiebelman, Maggie Schmitt, Greg McGrath, and Justin Murfin – have kept me grounded and connected to home throughout this adventure.

Wanda I. Rivera-Rivera has been my closest companion and friend as I have written both dissertation and book. She has kept the home-fires burning with great patience and remarkable good cheer, and has taught me much about intellectual creativity and responsibility. Words cannot describe how grateful I am to her. Her mother, Aracelis Rivera-Lopez, and sister, Odette S. Rivera-Rivera, have provided essential warmth, love, and support throughout.

The book is dedicated to Regina Eisenman Rosin, my late grandmother, who first made me think of the many different connections, livelihoods, and migrations that make up the world we inhabit, and Yahima Regina Beverley-Rivera, who will someday know worlds and places we can hardly imagine.

# Abbreviations

| | |
|---|---|
| APHB | Andhra Pradesh Housing Board |
| CIB | City Improvement Board (Hyderabad) |
| CTA | Criminal Tribes Act (1860) |
| EIC | East India Company |
| FMS | Federated Malay States |
| FOA | Fugitive Offenders Act (1881) |
| *HSFM* | *The Hyderabad Scarcity and Famine Manual* (1938) |
| IHC | International Historical Congress |
| ITPI | Institute of Town Planners, India |
| MCH | Municipal Corporation (Hyderabad) |
| MH | Model House |
| MIM | Majlis-i Ittihad al-Muslimin |
| *RHFHHND* | *Report on the History of the Famine in His Highness the Nizam's Domains in 1876/77, 1877/78* (1879) |
| *RISC* | *Report of the Indian States Commission* |
| *RPHCIB* | Hyderabad, City Improvement Board, *Report on the Progress of the Hyderabad City Improvement Board for the Years 1322–1327 Fasli (1914–1919 A.D.)* (Hyderabad: Goverment Central Press, 1919) |
| SC&D | Slum Clearance and Development |
| T&DD | Thagi and Dakaiti Department |
| TIT | Town Improvement Trust (Secunderabad) |
| *TP* | *Town Planning in H.E.H. the Nizam's Dominions* (1944) |
| TPD | Town Planning Department |
| UMS | Unfederated Malay States |
| UN | United Nations |
| UNSC | United Nations Security Council |

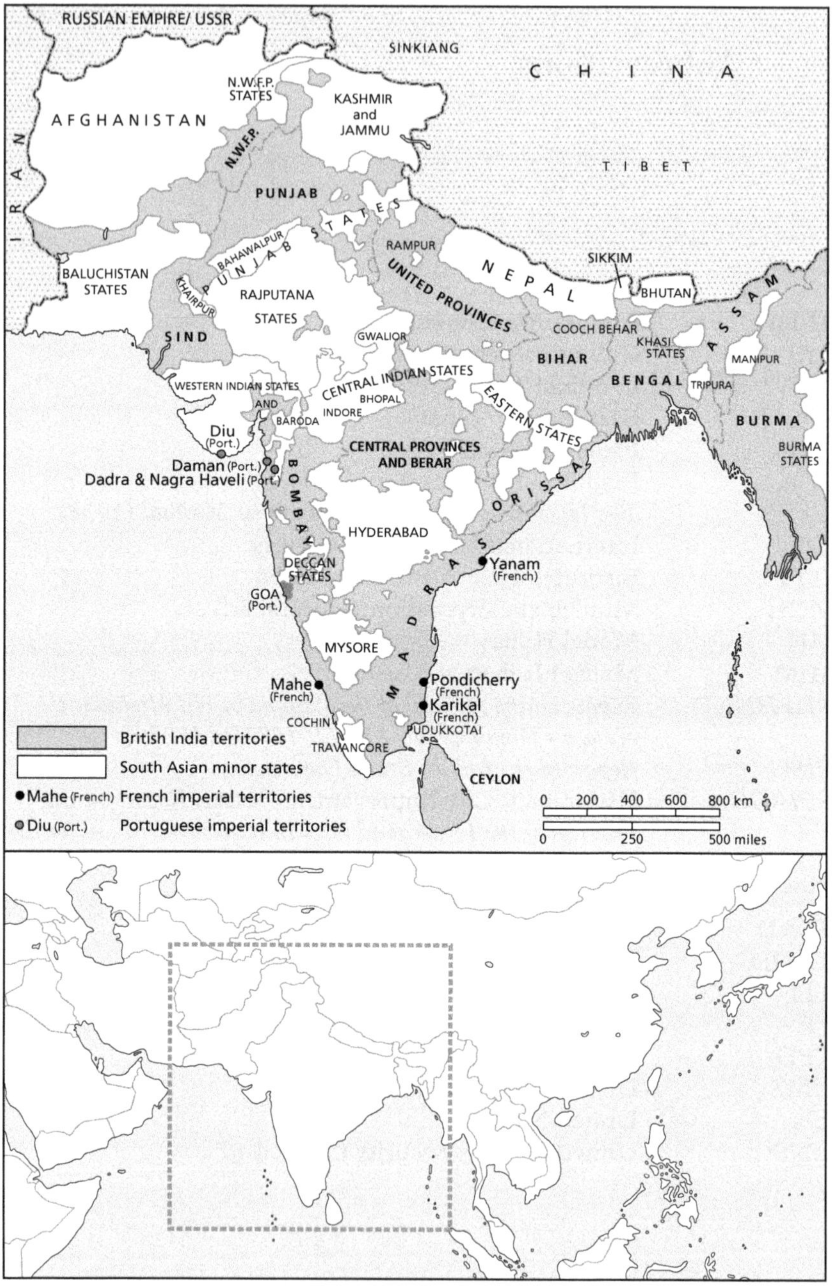


Map 1 South Asian minor states and British Indian territories prior to 1947.

Map 2 Hyderabad State within South Asia, *c.* 1900.

# Introduction: fragmenting sovereignty

As we settle into the twenty-first century it remains very difficult to conceive of political alternatives to either dominant global imperial formations or territorially bounded and autonomous states. All places imaginable can either be plotted on the map as part of one or the other of these characteristic modern geopolitical forms or envisioned in an evolutionary trajectory between subordination and independence. Viewed from the peripheries of dominant imperial or national centers, however, states appear as works in progress, and their frontiers and externalities as sites of alternative political experimentation.

This book examines politics and society in the South Asian state of Hyderabad, and its capital city of the same name, from the late nineteenth through the mid-twentieth centuries. The state, under the Āṣaf Jāh dynasty, whose Muslim rulers were known as the Niẓāms of Hyderabad, was formally sovereign and politically autonomous. For the duration of its existence, however, Hyderabad was under pressure from the dominant British colonial authority in the region, which comprised the largest component of the most powerful empire during an era of modern imperialism. Indeed, Hyderabad was surrounded on all sides by territories of the Raj and bound by treaties with the neighboring empire that limited Asaf Jahi power in certain areas (military, diplomatic).[1] Nevertheless, as this book argues, Hyderabad's sovereignty was no mere legal nicety, and it was crucial in providing scope and context for developments in the state. Administrators and intellectuals were engaged in a productive dialogue with histories of regional Muslim rule or political ideas and practices current elsewhere in the world, often creatively combining these two sources of authority. The state's formal autonomy – and institutional difference from the surrounding colonial empire – was also decisive in shaping the social worlds and lived spaces of its populations.

[1] I use 'Raj' as shorthand for the government of British India and its constituent units (Bombay or Madras Presidency, Central Provinces, and so forth). This is not to deny the considerable internal fissures between and within colonial administrative units.

This introduction elaborates some of the core concepts and contexts that frame the book, both global (the fragmentation of sovereignty in modern imperialism) and particular to Hyderabad (modernist patrimonialist statecraft and bureaucrat-intellectuals as critical figures). It then describes methodological challenges and the book's approach, the sources of the study, and the different sections and chapters of the book.

## Sovereignty and statecraft in an age of empire

The legacies of political difference in Hyderabad are often obscured by subsequent political developments and related trends in historical thinking. In focusing on Asaf Jah Hyderabad, this book examines a state that no longer exists as a sovereign political entity. The stories that are told about the past and present of state sovereignty in South Asia make it difficult to account for polities such as Hyderabad. Narratives of the unitary, highly centralized postcolonial Indian nation-state, and the legacy of forceful British colonial dominance in the region, combine to portray competing political entities as ephemeral or insignificant. Accordingly, dominant conceptual frameworks tend to fix the colonial state, anticolonial nationalism, or postcolonial nation-states as the sole modes of sovereignty worth taking seriously. This study, on the contrary, contends that there is much to be learned – about the history of the last few centuries, and the present – by taking seriously developments in polities at lower levels in hierarchies of global political sovereignty.

I use the term 'sovereignty' here in a strictly political sense: supreme and autonomous political authority of a state over a particular territory or place.[2] While Hyderabadi performance of sovereignty was important in the making of the modern South Asian political landscape, the state was not an exception. Rather, the view from Hyderabad helps to reveal the contours of the fragmented political scene in South Asia and worldwide. The nascent formulation of state sovereignty within international law served as a resource to empower states such as Hyderabad to act as autonomous and discrete fragments, even as they existed on lower rungs of the global hierarchy of states. Hyderabad's dynamism through the nineteenth century and until decolonization in the region illuminates

[2] The presumed territorial moorings of political sovereignty, and the related question of autonomy, are two thorny problems that I will address throughout this study. On the historical emergence and contextual production of sovereignty and related concepts see Kathleen Davis, *Periodization and Sovereignty: How Ideas of Feudalism and Secularization Govern the Politics of Time* (Philadelphia: University of Pennsylvania Press, 2008). On the status of Hyderabad and other similar polities as sovereign, see Chapter 3 below.

a broader condition: the enduring fragmentation of sovereignty across imperial terrain.

The focus here on the presence of minor sovereignties in an imperialized world should not be taken as an indication of the weakness of modern colonialism. European empires deliberately and knowingly deployed economic and military coercion, and the justificatory rhetoric of rule by law and order they employed hardly veiled the regular suspension or disregard of legal frameworks. As decades of scholarship have shown convincingly, the Raj (and British and other empires more broadly) asserted dominance over expansive lands in a forceful, often violent and extra-legal, fashion.[3] While fully registering the coercive nature of imperial dominance, this book approaches empire from the distinct political terrains visible in frontier zones, and manifest beyond its borders.

Even at the apex of empire's territorial spread in the early twentieth century, British imperial efforts to expand and homogenize political authority remained incomplete. Colonial language cast the entire space of the South Asia subcontinent as a consolidated imperial terrain, which integrated areas of formal 'direct' rule and informal 'indirect' imperialism.[4] Rhetorics of cohesive empire obscure a picture in which sovereignty was divided among varied imperial entities, formally autonomous states (such as Hyderabad), political entrepreneurs in frontier zones, and emerging sovereign domains in colonial space and institutions (municipalities, provincial administrations). All of these sites of sovereign assertion were loci of widely varied political improvisations informed by a range of exemplary models.

Developments in Hyderabad, because it was not a colonial territory, underscore the possibility of political difference during the height of global imperial power. As such, the view from Hyderabad puts in stark relief a broader trend of political improvisation and experimentation informed by regional and local historical precedents, other Muslim states, and examples from Europe, Asia, Africa, and the Americas. There were comparable dynamics of connectivity and political experimentation in colonized space, albeit often on smaller scales, and frequently bundled with nationalist positions. Similar possibilities were inherent in many

3 On violence and coercion see the essays collected in Ranajit Guha, *Dominance without Hegemony: History and Power in Colonial India* (Cambridge, MA: Harvard University Press, 1997). On extra-legality see Nasser Hussain, *The Jurisprudence of Emergency: Colonialism and the Rule of Law* (Ann Arbor: University of Michigan Press, 2003).

4 In colonial discourse and much subsequent historical scholarship, Hyderabad, like other South Asian states that were not formally colonized, was dubbed, diminutively, a 'Princely State.' Except in referring to sources that invoke the term I do not use the phrase here, but rather describe Hyderabad and similar polities as sub-imperial, non-colonial, or minor states.

other South Asian sub-imperial states, and particularly the larger among them, and this book develops more detailed consideration of affinities in several instances.[5] These parallels indicate that Hyderabad was not an exceptional case in the South Asian political landscape, though particular dynamics in effect there make it problematic to make detailed claims about all sub-imperial states in the subcontinent. Leaving aside the question of to what degree it was exceptional or typical within South Asia, this book is concerned with discussing Hyderabad as a window on and entity within a broader global context of state sovereignty during the period in question.

Rather than emphasizing comparisons with other South Asian sub-imperial states or British India, this book deliberately foregrounds comparisons and connections between Hyderabad and places beyond the subcontinent. This commitment to transnational analysis is intended to participate in and initiate discussions that bring places in South Asia, such as Hyderabad, other areas dominated by the British and other European empires, and places ostensibly outside the imperial web into a single analytical framework. In doing so I seek to demonstrate that Hyderabad, while particular in terms of scale and circuits of connections, is not exceptional in relation to the South Asian or global field.

Viewing Hyderabad in comparison and connection to other places in the world, I argue that state sovereignty (whether imperial or national) remained supple and fluid during the high point of European global imperialism. The ostensibly modal form of the territorial nation-state emerged as the core unit of modern political sovereignty only haltingly and unevenly in Europe itself.[6] The picture is even more complex when viewed from places subjected to colonial and imperial domination, such as Asia and Africa. There, European (and, later, North American) polities asserted political dominance. In many cases they seized territories and fabricated or extracted sovereign power. In other instances, however, they recognized, manipulated, or created sovereign entities they endeavored to control, often quite successfully, through enacting unequal treaties.

[5] Chapter 3 develops an extended discussion of Hyderabad and other sub-imperial states in colonial discourse. Parallels with such sub-imperial states as Kashmir, Mysore, Baroda, Travancore, Kalat, and Bhopal are noted in Chapters 2, 4, 6, and 7. The book's conclusion discusses the differential postcolonial careers of sub-imperial sovereigns in India and Pakistan.

[6] Derek Croxton, "The Peace of Westphalia of 1648 and the Origins of Sovereignty," *International History Review* 21.3 (1999): 569–91; Wolfgang Knöbl, "State Building in Western Europe and the Americas in the Long Nineteenth Century: Some Preliminary Considerations," in *State and Nation Making in Latin America and Spain: Republics of the Possible*, ed. Miguel Angel Centeno and Agustín Ferraro (Cambridge University Press, 2013), 56–75.

These minor states – sovereign but subordinated – occupied a vast legal gray area in which they were neither colonial territories nor full-fledged states with complete self-determination. A variety of states worldwide – Siam, Iran, the Ottoman Empire – were neither formally under colonial rule nor sovereign in the sense of possessing complete autonomy throughout their domains. Like many other 'minor' polities, Hyderabad was a key node in the circulation of a wide variety of people with diverse relationships to empire.

Conceptual and historical connections between Hyderabad and other places in the world are difficult to see when viewing South Asia's and Hyderabad's history retrospectively through the context of subsequent history and the nation-state form. The rise of nationalism in South Asia, as in other locations, generated, coordinated, and brought into conversation diverse and often conflicting political visions, some mediated through eclectic global connections.[7] Owing to the centrifugal dynamics of the nation-state form as a political unit, however, South Asian nationalist thought ultimately inscribed the boundaries of the subcontinent itself as its political horizons. Further, the widespread popular and state violence that marked Hyderabad's brief post-1947 independence, and 1948 integration into postcolonial India, solidifed the state's provincialization within a subcontinental political formation, and also had implications for the retrospective image of Muslim rule there.[8]

The late colonial and early postcolonial crisis in Hyderabad hinged upon tensions regarding the relation between religious community membership and political authority. After the formation of postcolonial India and Pakistan, a militia organized by the Majlis-i Ittiḥād al-Muslimīn (MIM, a Muslim political organization in Hyderabad) claiming to represent the Asaf Jah state took control of Hyderabad, ostensibly to preserve the state for the purpose of Muslim political dominance in the region. This occurred in a context where militant Hindu majoritarian interests both from within Hyderabad and beyond its borders were attempting to assert control in the state. The 1948 Indian military blockade and

[7] For a consideration of Hyderabad's critical role in negotiating the terms of late colonial nationalism in British India and an anticipated postcolonial nation-state see Kavita Saraswathi Datla, *The Language of Secular Islam: Urdu Nationalism and Colonial India* (Honolulu: University of Hawaiʿi Press, 2013). While its orientation is quite different, Datla's account of the potential Hyderabad's alterity and global connections had for rethinking South Asian nationalist visions of political modernity are parallel and complementary to the account of Hyderabad's alterity and its potential for moving beyond colonial and territorial nationalist political visions presented here.

[8] On Hyderabad's integration see Sunil Purushotham, "Internal Violence: The 'Police Action' in Hyderabad," *Comparative Studies in Society and History* 57.2 (forthcoming [2015]). The account in the subsequent paragraph draws in part from this source.

subsequent invasion of Hyderabad resulted in both widespread anti-Muslim violence and a dismantling of much of the Asaf Jah central political structure and disemployment of its participants. The MIM's rhetoric, and the subsequent acrimony and violence of the Hindu majoritarian and Indian official response, has left in place a historical image of Asaf Jah rule as oppressive Muslim political dominance. This impression, together with the provincializing tendencies of the nation-state form, obscure the global circuits and political experimentation that Hyderabad's Muslim stateness in previous decades facilitated.[9]

Hyderabad was, crucially, ruled by a Muslim dynasty historically loyal to the Raj in an era of pronounced imperial anxiety about the potential for transregional Muslim political engagement. This led the British to countenance not only Hyderabad's internal autonomy but also its significant international networks. Ideas of universal solidarity between Muslim states provided one key idiom of global political community for Hyderabad, and channeled many connections between intellectuals, state officials, and the rest of the world. Related political experiments were aimed at 'modernizing' institutions and spaces in the state, but were shaped by both existing 'patrimonial' state structures and political rhetorical frameworks in place in Hyderabad.

## Patrimonial modernity

In describing the experimentation and improvisation that shaped Hyderabad's political scene between 1850 and 1950, this study uses *patrimonialism* and *modernity* to describe discourse and practice in the state. These two concepts are often conceived as mutually exclusive stages in developmental teleologies in political and scholarly discourse alike. In Hyderabad, state officials and advocates intermingled the two political languages in describing, legitimizing, and disseminating to domestic and global audiences the content of official projects.

As a type of political rhetoric, patrimonialism entails personalized authority premised on relationships of reciprocity between ruler and ruled. Such ideas had a lengthy history in Hyderabad, linked to the longstanding dynastic political structure of the state and established ethical frameworks in Indo-Muslim political discourse. Patrimonialist rhetoric, however, also resonated with languages of statecraft in proximate, yet divergent, contexts in modern South Asia and elsewhere.

Patrimonialism has usually been cast as part of an evolutionary transition between forms of authority. As such, patrimonialism (personalized

[9] The term 'stateness' here indicates the contingency and scalability of state sovereignty, as opposed to 'statehood', which casts sovereignty as a zero-sum game. See J. P. Nettl, "The State as a Conceptual Variable," *World Politics* 20.4 (1968): 559–92.

authority) is viewed as an earlier stage in an inevitable transition to bureaucratic (depersonalized, normative) authority. Work on South Asia and other colonized places has largely echoed this teleological view. As such, patrimonialism is used as a sociological concept to describe pre-modern state forms or ostensibly retrograde political forms in non-colonial states outside Europe.[10] The early modern Mughal state, for example, has been seen as a "patrimonial-bureaucratic empire" that combined "pre-modern" with "modern" modes of authority, and declined with the wane of the latter.[11] A key work by Margrit Pernau has extended this framework to suggest that the first half of the twentieth century in Hyderabad witnessed the "intermingling" of patrimonialism (loyalty of officials to the ruler) with bureaucratized forms of political legitimization. Pernau described this as a "partial" transition from authority of "men of culture" within the state to that of "men of technical knowledge," and emphasized enduring mutual dependence between these groups.[12] Such 'transition narratives' about its inevitable decline or uncanny persistence treat patrimonialism as a sociological category with temporal, teleological implications.[13] My contention here is that patrimonialism as a mode of political rhetoric had important stakes for legitimization of a wide variety of political projects and states.[14] In Hyderabad patrimonialism was frequently blended with languages of technocratic, rationalist, or modernist political change. Such combinations do not necessarily indicate internal contradiction or demonstrate structural tension.

Recent scholarship on Africa has theorized patrimonialism as a mode of political authority that potentially applies to many different state forms.[15] Beginning by decoupling modes of legitimization from types of

[10] For a key use of the term for South Asia see Stephen P. Blake, "The Patrimonial-Bureaucratic Empire of the Mughals," *Journal of Asian Studies* 39.1 (1979): 77–94. On pre-modern patrimonialism elsewhere see Karen Barkey, *Bandits and Bureaucrats: The Ottoman Route to State Centralization* (Ithaca: Cornell University Press, 1994), 9–17, *inter alia.* For patrimonialism and South Asian sub-imperial states see Margrit Pernau, *The Passing of Patrimonialism: Politics and Political Culture in Hyderabad, 1911–1948* (New Delhi: Manohar, 2000); Susanne H. Rudolph, Lloyd I. Rudolph, and Mohan Singh, "A Bureaucratic Lineage in Princely India: Elite Formation and Conflict in a Patrimonial System," *Journal of Asian Studies* 34.3 (1975): 717–53.

[11] Blake, "Patrimonial-Bureaucratic Empire."

[12] Pernau, *Passing of Patrimonialism*, 59, 271, 321, 358.

[13] On the transition narrative as a historiographical entity see Dipesh Chakrabarty, *Provincializing Europe: Postcolonial Thought and Historical Difference* (Princeton University Press, 2000), 30–37.

[14] For a critique of the presumed evolutionary relationship between patrimonial and bureaucratic state forms, and an argument that the latter can often be components of effective states, see Lloyd I. Rudolph and Susanne H. Rudolph, "Authority and Power in Bureaucratic and Patrimonial Administration: A Revisionist Interpretation of Weber on Bureaucracy," *World Politics* 31.2 (1979): 195–227.

[15] Anne Pitcher, Mary H. Moran, and Michael Johnston, "Rethinking Patrimonialism and Neopatrimonialism in Africa," *African Studies Review* 52.1 (2009): 125–56.

regime, scholars argue that patrimonialism as a mode of legitimization is "remarkably adaptable" to numerous types of regimes ranging from authoritarianism to liberal democratic. Emphasizing the typological, rather than teleological, character of the designation allows for a clear elaboration of the concept itself: patrimonialism is a political relationship centered on a mutual understanding of reciprocity between ruler and ruled, with expectations of "voluntary compliance" by the subordinated and accountability by leaders.[16]

In Hyderabad, ostensibly progressive and benevolent authoritarian or autocratic state authority defined a context for patrimonial legitimization. As in several other sub-imperial states, officials in Hyderabad were largely insulated from internal political opposition and British colonial intervention. The patrimonial rhetorical framework of Hyderabad – ruler as ultimate source of legitimate authority obliged to see to the needs of subjects – was conducive to a variety of progressive modernization projects ranging from legal and revenue reforms, to state welfare for famine sufferers or marginalized communities, to urban and economic planning. The patrimonial, ethical, and explicitly modernizing character of state practice in Hyderabad was institutionally enacted and globally disseminated by a particular type of official figure that emerged in Hyderabad and worldwide during the modern period.

## Hyderabadi bureaucrat-intellectuals as Deccani *letrados*

The bureaucrat-intellectual – characterized by knowledge of putatively modern statecraft techniques, awareness of global trends, political savvy and connections, and finely honed polyglot rhetorical skills – was a key social and political actor in Hyderabad since mid-nineteenth-century political reforms in the state. These Deccani *letrados*[17] were critical in yoking Hyderabad's patrimonial loyalty networks – the framework of the state's political structure – into changing and revivified global circuits, especially between Muslim states. Officials in longstanding

16 Ibid., 127, 144.

17 Deccani, as a geographical term, refers to the Deccan Plateau in the center of the South Asia subcontinent. Hyderabad State spanned the eastern Deccan between the eighteenth and mid-twentieth centuries (this region is now divided between Indian provincial states, including Telangana, and parts of Maharashtra and Karnataka). Culturally, Deccani (or Dakkani, Dakhni) refers specifically to linguistic (especially the southern variety of Urdu–Hindi) or culinary practices of the region that comprised the erstwhile Hyderabad State. *Letrado* is a Spanish term referring as a noun or adjective to one who is, or the state of being, learned or educated (literally, 'lettered').

institutions (judiciary, police, revenue, and education administrators; *dīvāns* or prime ministers) and newer disciplines (engineering, urban and economic planning, transportation) worked to harmonize modernist administrative projects within an ethical patrimonialist framework of reciprocity between ruler and populace and obligatory official benevolence to state subjects.

The dynamic roles of bureaucrat-intellectuals in Hyderabad during the putative era of modernization provide key material for rethinking frameworks for conceiving political change in modern South Asia. Scholarship on the colonial period, in considering engagements between South Asian 'native informants' and British Raj officials, has stressed the increasing prominence of racialized European dominance in South Asian governance. Such arguments track the openness of imperial racial hierarchies and fluidity of social boundaries up to the second quarter of the nineteenth century, followed by the effective eclipse of non-British political agency until nationalism and independence.[18] According to this narrative, even if governance ideas were mined from native informant discourse and hammered into shape in dialogue with them, at the stage of their compilation and articulation of political systems, colonial officers were without question at the helm.

Recent work by Bhavani Raman identifies the key role played by South Asian scribes, as repositories of embodied knowledge, in the emergence of a political culture premised on the production of documents.[19] Her consideration of colonial consolidation from the perspective of the early colonial administrative office (*kaccheri* or cutcherry) casts the process of state-making as indelibly local. Rethinking the making of the Raj from the bottom up through textual and oral administration, and the focus on an emergent technology of documentary practice, shifts attention away from stymied debates about South Asian versus British policy agency. Examining governance practice in Hyderabad though the state's bureaucrat-intellectuals provides a means to extend this approach from the locality of the administrative office to the autonomous South Asian polity. Here, state intellectuals could function largely independent of racialized frameworks within colonial bureaucracies by drawing on global flows of administrative ideas. Conceptualizations of the political roles of intellectuals in other imperial contexts also help frame this discussion about political change in Hyderabad.

[18] For an influential version of this argument see Nicholas B. Dirks, *Castes of Mind: Colonialism and the Making of Modern India* (Princeton University Press, 2001).

[19] Bhavani Raman, *Document Raj: Writing and Scribes in Early Colonial South India* (University of Chicago Press, 2012).

Describing the relationship between literate culture and state power in colonial and postcolonial Latin America, Uruguayan scholar Angel Rama identified *letrados* as "'lettered' functionaries . . . involved in transmitting and responding to imperial directives" during the consolidation of Latin American colonial rule.[20] These figures served as cultural mediators, formulating and maintaining the "cultural dimension of the colonial power structure," meeting the "administrative requirements of the vast colonial enterprise," and "evangelizing and overseeing the transculturation of an indigenous population numbering in the millions."[21] For Rama, rather than functioning as "mere executors of orders issuing from the institutions that employ them," *letrados* were "intellectual *producers*" who elaborated ideological messages and designed cultural models.[22]

The "fluid and complex relationship between intellectuals and institutions" Rama emphasizes helps frame the state as a work in progress, and situates bureaucrat-intellectuals as critical agents in mediating between and manipulating a range of symbolic idioms. This dynamic continued into the nineteenth and twentieth centuries when *letrados* elaborated and refashioned "the ideals and myths of modernization" in Latin American contexts.[23] Similar figures in Hyderabad during this period – Deccani *letrados*, one might say – served to mediate between established idioms. These ranged from political languages linked to Muslim rule in the Deccan region and South Asia as a whole to broader cosmopolitan lexicons such as Persianate Muslim statecraft and, indeed, putatively global ideologies of modernity. Hyderabadi bureaucrat-intellectuals and their writings elaborate the complex mediations between the diverse political idioms and places encountered in the study, and recur frequently as authorizing state agents in official archival and documentary records.

## Transnational approach, fragmented sources

This book is not a conventional monograph, but an attempt to examine several linked themes of increasing global relevance – the changing international regime of state sovereignty, transnational political thought, Muslim modernist statecraft, legal jurisdictions and the social possibilities they produce, expanding cities and urbanist projects – through one empirical context located on the borderlands of empire. The fragmented character of political sovereignty the book describes is mirrored by the

20 Angel Rama, *The Lettered City*, trans. John C. Chasteen (Durham, NC: Duke University Press, 1996 [Spanish 1984]), 18.

21 Ibid., 17, 19.

22 Ibid., 22, emphasis in original.

23 Ibid., 52.

book's organization (in terms of diverse themes) and archival base (written from the perspective of numerous states and mobile intellectuals). To situate Hyderabad, the study draws upon the insights of recent scholarship in multiple disciplines covering several world areas in a wide variety of fields and sub-fields in the humanities and social sciences (British Empire and comparative colonialism, Islamic studies, South Asian history and area studies, transnational history, political anthropology, urban studies, history of political thought, historical study of law and crime, historical sociology).

The central empirical touchstone is Hyderabad, and the project seeks to engage with questions in South Asian history. It also, crucially, pushes beyond the often insular concerns of that field.[24] The book develops a transnational approach in both the connections and affinities it traces and in its methodological engagements. This entails developing grounded accounts of circuits of connectivity, and comparative discussions with reference to recent scholarship on other places in Asia, Africa, Europe, and the Americas. The multiple, often unruly connections considered here – political and infrastructural networks across the British Empire, nationalist and anti-colonialist links, Muslim internationalist circuits, ties between diverse modernizing states, global legal and urbanist ideas – suggest geographies unfamiliar to existing transnational historical scholarship.[25]

Situating Hyderabad State transnationally entails a focus on external relations, self-presentation, and transnational flows, and on the articulation between these domains and the intellectual, institutional, and social histories of Hyderabad and Hyderabadis. Developing a

24 For an attempt to write histories of South Asian politics during the colonial period from a transnational perspective see Thomas R. Metcalf, *Imperial Connections: India in the Indian Ocean Arena, 1860–1920* (Berkeley: University of California Press, 2007). For a history of global scope with extensive treatment of South Asia see C. A. Bayly, *The Birth of the Modern World, 1780–1914: Global Connections and Comparisons* (Malden, MA: Blackwell, 2004). See also C. A. Bayly, Sven Beckert, Matthew Connelly, Isabel Hofmeyr, Wendy Kozol, and Patricia Seed, "AHR Conversation: On Transnational History," *American Historical Review* 111.5 (2006): 1441–64.

25 Research centered on mobile groups of people or diffuse political movements rather than states provides a key means to rethink geographies of connections in the modern world. See Engseng Ho, *The Graves of Tarim: Genealogy and Mobility Across the Indian Ocean* (Berkeley: University of California Press, 2006); Ilham Khuri-Makdisi, *The Eastern Mediterranean and the Making of Global Radicalism, 1860–1914* (Berkeley: University of California Press, 2010); Mana Kia, "Limning the Land: Social Encounters and Historical Meaning in Early 19th-century Travelogues between Iran and India," in *On the Wonders of Land and Sea: Persianate Travel Writing*, ed. Roberta Micallef and Sunil Sharma (Boston: Ilex, 2013), 44–67; Ali Raza, Franziska Roy, and Ben Zachariah, eds., *The Internationalist Moment: South Asia, Worlds, and World Views, 1919–1939* (New Delhi: Sage Publications, 2014).

consideration along these lines requires a creative and probing relationship to sources. I draw here on a wide range of materials, varied in terms of language (English, Urdu, Persian), origin and genre (official publications from Hyderabad or British India, unofficial writings of Hyderabad officials or subject, narratives of visitors to Hyderabad, correspondence, legal records, intelligence reports, employment records), and archival location (archives of the Nizam's State, British India, and Britain in Hyderabad, London, New Delhi, and Mumbai). A focus on transnational links between Hyderabad and other places has shaped the approach to sources. Locating archival traces of these links is further complicated by the contingent and subordinated nature of Hyderabad State in relation to British India, particularly in the domain of diplomatic relations.

Many sources considered here provide evidence of the relationship between Hyderabad and the British colonial state in both broader conceptual and practical political terms. To address the ambivalent power dynamic (dominant Raj, sovereign Nizam) I engage extensively with colonial sources and Hyderabadi responses. The dominant political discourses and institutional practices of the Raj exerted enormous pressure upon Hyderabad State. On the conceptual level, articulations of the meaning and content of Hyderabad as political space often entailed direct engagements with colonial accounts of the state and its legitimacy or lack thereof. In political terms, the British sought not only to regulate Hyderabad's international relations, but also to exert control on some matters within the state or on its borders. At times this entailed attempts to subject Hyderabad to colonial political authority. Other instances suggest mundane negotiations over laws and policies ostensibly affecting both polities.

Some of the colonial sources considered here document attempts to subordinate Hyderabadi political sovereignty, and I have read them 'against the grain' in order to situate Raj dominance and its limitations. Further, materials from Hyderabad provide conceptual refutations or undertake political negotiations that begin to make legible the contours of alternative notions of sovereignty or strategies of governance. At other times, discomfort or ambivalence in colonial sources indicates the limitations of colonial authority within the fragmented geographies of sovereignty throughout the empire.

While I make a case for the limits of colonial power by reading British sources against the grain, it is also critical to note the effect political subordination of Hyderabad had on sources for studying the state. The political vision from Hyderabad was not consistent; it rarely appears as a coherent whole; and the available sources often reflect the enduring instability generated by the state's position in global political geography. As such, Hyderabadi state ideology was improvised and negotiated in relation to a dominant colonial power, and drawing on eclectic transnational sources. Even as Hyderabad's subordinated position within an emerging international order entailed instability and contingency, its 'minor' sovereignty was also productive of unexpected political dynamics and combinations from a range of influences.

## Organization of the book

This study is structured to reveal the architecture of fragmented sovereignty that characterized the period of high colonialism, and the political possibilities inherent in entities such as Hyderabad. The sections situate Hyderabad's sovereignty in relation to British India's umbrella of suzerainty, which both preserved and constrained the sub-imperial state's autonomy. Further, they emphasize Hyderabad's productive dialogue with other places in the world, which was informed by global networks of political allegiance between Muslim states and other circuits. The chapters discuss many formative events in the histories of Hyderabad, South Asia, and the world around 1850–1950, and track several particular trajectories and developments. However, the book as a whole is not organized chronologically, but around broad themes, and as such its chapters frequently circle back to the same moments encountered earlier in a recursive fashion. Further, the focus here is on structures and dynamics that develop over decades or longer. As such, crisis moments in Hyderabadi and South Asian history (the 1857 uprising, its suppression, and subsequent imperial reorganization; 1947 decolonization; Hyderabad's post-World War II decline into widespread violence and militia rule, and its violent integration into postcolonial India in 1948) form background and framing contexts rather than core concern.

Chapter 1 situates Hyderabad within the global political scene during modern European global imperialism (*c.* 1850–1950). I elaborate a geography with multiple levels. Dominant imperial formations, mostly ruled by European states, are well known. I emphasize, however, sites of political improvisation that are obscured in familiar accounts of the imperially dominated world of this era. Chapter 1 thus focuses on what I describe as 'minor' states, such as Hyderabad, defined by their being formally sovereign, but subject to intensive imperial pressures. Chapter 2 traces the emerging legal framework of Hyderabadi sovereignty in Nizam–Raj treaties and situates it within a chronology of South Asian history from the mid-eighteenth century to the early twentieth. The chapter describes an enduring legal ambiguity characterized by treaties that described Hyderabad and Britain in a language of equivalence, but which emerged in the context of rising imperial dominance. I contend that state sovereignty remained supple and fluid throughout the period, and ambiguity was less a mask of colonial power than a resource for sub-imperial empowerment. I then turn to three key arenas within Hyderabad to elaborate the state's complex relationship with British imperialism and the emerging international order, and the alternative political practices the state's autonomy allowed. Part I examines ideas, in official statist and non-state varieties; Part II traces institutions of governance; and Part III looks at the ordering of modern urban space. These three core sections (Ideas, Institutions, Urban Space) are composed of two chapters each (3 and 4, 5 and 6, 7 and 8, respectively). The first ('odd') chapter of each part lays out the context in terms of states, sovereignty, and political imaginaries (thus situating Hyderabad in relation to the British Empire and other places in the world), and the second ('even') chapter of each part looks at how this framework creates a context for alternative social worlds and political practices. The three core sections are followed by a concluding chapter, considering postcolonial transformations of state sovereignty in South Asia, and recasting the implications of the book's global history of modern sovereignty with an eye to the contemporary world.

### *Part I: Ideas*

This part examines the place of Hyderabad State in the South Asian and global intellectual history of the period from the mid-nineteenth to the mid-twentieth century. Its two chapters respectively consider Hyderabad in historiographical and political writings, and the state's connections to other places and polities in the world through writings and intellectual work of state officials and travelers to and from the state. Both chapters come back to two enduring themes integral to locating Hyderabad in British India and the world: First, the *Muslimness* of Hyderabad's rulers, in historical and temporal terms, and with respect to the state's role in global political geographies; and second, the state's status as a *modern*, progressive, and reforming polity, defined in terms of emerging notions of good governance or technological advancement. The movement between chapters, and their overlapping themes, suggest that textual representations (in historical, literary, and official political writings) were integrally tied into political relationships.

Chapter 3 considers the representation of the state in writings on the history and political ethics of South Asia during the period of British colonial dominance. The chapter traces a chronology of changing colonial policies on indigenous political authority, which framed representations of sub-imperial states such as Hyderabad. It highlights a shift in representations of the state from pre-1850s attempts to delegitimize existing political authority there (an expansive movement of the liberal colonial state) to a post-1850s trend to cast the state as a worthy ally of the British Empire and exemplar of 'native' modernity (a consolidating and pacifying moment of later imperialism). Hyderabadi officials and advocates played this shift to their advantage by claiming increased autonomy and legitimacy as a state in its own right. However, the enduring tension in colonial discourse over the role of Muslim political actors and states in the imperial project was both a severe constraint and a productive foil in history writing and political discourse in and about the state. Colonial anxieties about Muslim solidarity as a competing foundation of loyalty and countervailing global political design bolstered surveillance and oversight of politics related to the state. This trend gave an important place to potential Muslim leaders who could be cast as allies in empire, such as the Nizam.

Chapter 4 examines Hyderabad's relations to other places in the world. I look at imagined and actual connections between the state and political formations elsewhere through writings designed to project Hyderabad's achievements to international observers, and records of travelers between the state and other parts of Asia, Europe, and Africa. I suggest that two key conceptual nodes that linked Hyderabad to other places were notions of progress toward modern governance (often enabled by application of technologies associated with 'the West'), and Muslim internationalism defined as political solidarities with fellow Muslim-ruled states (similar to what some scholars have described as 'Pan-Islam'). While formal diplomatic relations were restricted by a Nizam–Raj treaty, engagements between state officials and their counterparts of other polities provide evidence of a lively arena of informal global diplomacy in which Hyderabad participated.

### *Part II: Institutions*

The second part of the book moves from the conceptual and intellectual foundations of Hyderabad considered in Part I to an examination of the everyday conduct of governance. It contrasts the working of institutions in the Nizam's state compared to those in British India by looking at the operation of the law, the police, and other representatives of state along Hyderabad's frontiers with Raj territories. This part provides accounts of a variety of attempts to extend colonial power by informal transgressions of the border. Further, it underscores the limitations of such moves by viewing the picture first from a statist perspective, and then from the angle of people living in the frontier region. The chapters together reexamine the role of colonial knowledge and power in the making of South Asia's political modernity by viewing colonial forms of racialized institutional power, and their limits, from the perspective of peoples and polities on the margins of empire. Evidence of the physical and legal limitations of imperial power presented here indicates continuity of fragmented sovereignty through the colonial period in South Asia.

Chapter 5 looks from the perspective of the state, and lays out the contentious and indeterminate character of conflicts over legal jurisdiction between Hyderabad, Bombay Presidency, and other colonial provinces or agencies. I argue that Raj modes of governmentality often met limits at imperial frontiers, and show that across Hyderabad's borders distinct internal political dynamics prevailed. I sketch contrasting state rhetoric and practice in Hyderabad, exemplified by official initiatives for the welfare of marginalized groups such as the famine-stricken, Dalits, and Adivasis. The limited reach of British disciplinary power facilitated Hyderabadi projects that were informed by patrimonialist and progressive ideologies of state. It also produced enduring political complexity amid tightly clustered jurisdictions in the frontier zone.

Chapter 6 shifts to examine everyday life in the frontier zone. The social history of the borderland world suggests that political indeterminacy served as a resource not only for states and elites (Hyderabad, Bombay, various administrators and merchants), but also for diverse populations (peasants, sex workers, smugglers) on either side of the border. People of different social statuses were able to carry out their agendas by taking advantage of jurisdictional complexity. Local rural elites were able to summon the force of the law to their advantage, and groups whose livelihoods did not fit into the colonial vision for rural society (pacified, sedentary, morally stable) were able to evade punishment.

### *Part III: Urban space*

The third and final core section of the book moves from the largely rural world of the frontier to the capital's urban terrain. The Nizam's state was a contested contact zone between colonialism and a native sovereignty informed by alternative global circuits. The capital city's development was the paradigmatic expression of this dynamism. This section casts Hyderabad City as an imperialized but not quite colonial space, in which selective appropriation of the ensemble of practices that constitute colonial urbanism resulted in the emergence of a major and distinctive South Asian city. The urban history of modern South Asia, owing in part to the rural allegiances of Gandhian nationalism, is a fledgling field, and colonial cities have provided the primary focus.[26] Hyderabad was the fourth-largest city in South Asia during the course of British colonial rule.[27] Chapters here examine Hyderabad City's rapid growth, the development of urbanist institutions, and their importance for broader visions of development. To set the context for the making of the modern twin cities of Hyderabad–Secunderabad, this part examines political and social developments in the urban area during the time when the northern Cantonment and Residency sections, previously under British control, came to be socially and politically united with the Nizam's capital to the south.

Chapter 7 describes the rise of urban space as locus of intervention, and planning as a modality of state power in the remaking of Hyderabad from the 1870s onwards. It traces a shift of the urban core from the walled city to a new political and population center located near the terminus of the railway line and the British Cantonment and Residency. This shift was enabled by the Nizam's wresting of judicial authority over parts of the city from the colonial establishment, and a physical remaking of the city by improvement projects centered on infrastructure development, slum clearance, and construction of public housing for the working class. In conceiving and describing urban changes and planning work in Hyderabad, officials articulated a particular developmentalist idiom fusing an older ideology of ethical patrimonialism with emerging technocratic rhetorics. The chapter contends that Hyderabad urbanism and state-led planning exemplify the emergence of a crucial and enduring new form of power in South Asia.

Chapter 8 considers ways in which these spatial and political changes provided a framework for urban social worlds. The chapter constitutes a micro-history of urban governance from the perspectives of two states seeking to materialize urban visions, and of people who were subjected to these discourses. To underline the simultaneously influential and imperious way the Raj made its authority felt in Hyderabad, I focus on the rapidly urbanizing fringe area outside the Cantonment, which became a zone of contestation and collaboration between the Nizam and the colonial state.

The book's core sections provide a historical ethnography of state practices around Hyderabad from the 1870s to the 1940s. The conclusion examines postcolonial closures in the narrative of Hyderabad autonomy,

[26] On concepts and trends in South Asian urban history see Eric L. Beverley, "Colonial Urbanism and South Asian Cities," *Social History* 36.4 (2011): 482–97.

[27] Hyderabad is now the sixth-largest urban area in India, with estimates approaching 8 million for the metropolitan area, after Mumbai, Kolkata, Delhi, Chennai, and Bengaluru (leaving out Delhi, which retains its name, these cities were up until recently officially known as Bombay, Calcutta, Madras, and Banglaore, respectively).

and the configuration of fragmented sovereignty in South Asia. New nation-states, such as India and Pakistan, were increasingly buttressed by dominant languages of centrist political unity, territoriality, and majoritarianism. While the chronology and consolidation of these new states differed, the early postcolonial period saw polities at lower levels of sovereignty, such as Hyderabad, squeezed out of the South Asian political scene. The conclusion then zooms out to reposition 'minor' sovereign states such as Hyderabad within the global political picture of the era, and to consider implications this revised account of historical political geography holds for thinking about the present and future of state sovereignty and the international order.

Alternate possibilities for a postcolonial subcontinent, such as the fragmented sovereignty represented by Hyderabad, were foreclosed by the transfer of power to unitary and highly centralized national units in 1947. The 1948 conquest of Hyderabad by that centralizing Indian nation-state sealed the postcolonial consolidation of formal political authority. The central focus of the book is on alternative modes and idioms of sovereignty that Hyderabad exemplifies, and which were foreclosed in the post-imperial context by the victory of nationalisms centered on visions of unitary state sovereignty. These alternative modes and idioms are obscured within conceptual frameworks that fix the colonial state, anti-colonial nationalism, or postcolonial nation-states as the sole languages of sovereignty worth taking seriously. While the unitary state triumphed in the postcolonial era, there is no good reason why its characteristic perspectives should triumph in the writing of history. This book reflects and gives texture to the historical lives of these other possible paths, and by framing Hyderabad transnationally opens the study of political discourse and practice in South Asia to comparative and connective historical inquiry.

# 1 Minor sovereignties: Hyderabad among states and empires

Many territorially sovereign polities across the globe circa 1850–1950, the so-called high colonial era, were decidedly not equivalent powers to dominant European nation-states. But neither were they colonial territories subordinated and integrated into European (or American) empires. These *minor* states – neither dominant nations nor colonial possessions – were highly productive political spaces in the nineteenth and twentieth centuries. They took up international legal sovereignty as a potent language to authorize experimentation with ideologies and institutions of governance, and to position themselves within global intellectual and political configurations.[1] British colonial discourse represented minor sovereigns as 'princely' states (and thus not quite fully sovereign 'kings' or 'monarchs') or 'indirectly ruled'

[1] My use of the term 'minor' to describe varied forms of sovereignty that were decidedly less powerful than dominant empires and nation-states follows postcolonialist and poststructuralist theory and criticism, in which 'minor' literatures, authors, and texts undermine dominant notions of belonging or canonicity. In this parallel, minor sovereigns force a reconsideration of canonical notions about the workings of power during modern imperialism. For the key elaboration of the concept of 'minor literature' see Gilles Deleuze and Félix Guattari, *Kafka: Toward a Minor Literature* (Minneapolis: University of Minnesota Press, 1986), ch. 3. For Deleuze and Guattari a minor literature emerges when a politically and culturally subordinated group composes in a major language (in his case, the Czech Jewish Kafka writing in German). This writing marks a deterritorialization (Czech Jewish distance from Czech or German territorial belonging), but is also a political act productive of solidarity. Minor literatures in turn reterritorialize the minority group in terms of the language's "sense" (20). As shall become clear below, Hyderabad and other minor states took up the emerging 'major' political language of the modern state (dominated by European nation-states and empires) as a way to assert their authority. For the use of 'minor' authors and texts to reframe the early modern literary canon see Catherine Gallagher and Stephen Greenblatt, *Practicing New Historicism* (University of Chicago Press, 2001). On 'minority culture' as a vantage point for political and literary critique, see Aamir Mufti, "Auerbach in Istanbul: Edward Said, Secular Criticism, and the Question of Minority Culture," *Critical Inquiry* 25.1 (1998): 95–125 and *Enlightenment in the Colony: The Jewish Question and the Crisis of Postcolonial Culture* (Princeton University Press, 2007).

polities.[2] Such conceptual frameworks cast states such as Hyderabad as possessors of illusory sovereignty. These marginalizing designations formed key rhetorical elements of colonial discourses that emphasized the primacy of the British Raj. However, these terms and implicit assumptions have problematically shaped scholarly accounts of the nature of modern sovereignty.[3] To understand the dynamic nature of sovereignty it is critical to look to intervening nether zones, which empires and dominant nations endeavor to liquidate, integrate, or pacify.

This chapter situates the 'minor' state of Hyderabad within the complex, multi-tiered, global political geography of the last quarter of the nineteenth century through the middle of the twentieth. Here, state sovereignty across ostensibly imperial space was heterogeneous, and a product of negotiation and contestation between numerous authorities. This position runs counter to presumptions about effective imperial consolidation of state sovereignty by about 1900.

The history of state sketched here – the condition of fragmented sovereignty, and the existence of anomalous sovereign entities such as Hyderabad – has important implications for the intellectual history of South Asian political modernity. Viewed in the context of global political geography, South Asian minor states appear as critical spaces for institutional experimentation carried out by state intellectuals. Further, the coexistence of patrimonial political structures, combined with aggressive appropriation of technical and institutional modernist forms in Hyderabad, underscores the eclecticism and dynamism that characterized sub-imperial statecraft.

In laying out this theory of fragmented sovereignty, I focus on Hyderabad's relation to other places in British India and the world in both transnational connective terms and comparative framework. The chapter sketches the splintered political geography of the world during the high colonial era, then presents examples of three key modes of 'minor' political sovereignty (uncolonized states, sub-imperial polities, and political improvisations in imperial frontier zones). It then elaborates the role of global Muslim solidarity as the foundation of a powerful political vision that provided a template for counter-colonial ideas and practices, and constituted one network for circulation of institutional and technical

[2] On the conceptual foundations and political dynamics of 'indirect rule' as imperial ideology see Karuna Mantena, *Alibis of Empire: Henry Maine and the Ends of Liberal Imperialism* (Princeton University Press, 2010), introduction.

[3] See Chapter 3 on colonial and scholarly discourse on South Asia's sub-imperial states, and the limitations posed by uncritical incorporation of value-laden concepts such as 'indirect rule' and 'princely states.'

modernist ideas.[4] Before describing the global political architecture, I begin with three anecdotes that elaborate the range of political possibilities in the state of Hyderabad.

### I

In the 1880s, after being expelled from Egypt, the anti-colonial Muslim internationalist Jamāl al-Dīn al-Afġhānī, denounced as a fanatic in colonial sources, resided in Hyderabad city.[5] Under the patronage of high nobles and state officials, including the prime minister, he penned some of his most incendiary works on the injustices of European colonialism and the means of bringing about its rapid end. He met, debated, and confabulated with several leading Muslim modernist intellectuals of Hyderabad, and was allegedly offered a post in the state administration, which he declined.[6]

### II

In June 1897, after celebrations for the Diamond Jubilee of Queen Victoria's coronation, the conservative brahmin anti-colonialist Chapekar brothers carried out the political asassination of two plague officers, Ayerst and Rand, in Pune, Bombay Presidency, British India. Colonial police quickly captured two of the brothers, but a third, Balkrishna Chapekar, slipped eastward across the British India frontier into Hyderabad state. Despite the large bounty on his head, the fugitive evaded police for more that a year. Balkrishna ranged across southwest Hyderabad state, through hills and valleys, state-administered territories and domains under land grantees who exercised police and judicial power. He hid out with a notorious robber band in the hills, and found shelter in local towns, allegedly owing to popular support for his brand of extremist Hindu nationalism. Despite difficulties sourcing reliable information from Hyderabadi rural society or the Nizam's officials, Raj police finally managed to nab the fugitive in January 1899 as he boarded a train for the Portuguese territory of Goa.[7]

4 As will become clear, this solidarity was based on Muslimness as a social and political basis for connection. What I describe here was decidedly not an Islamic solidarity based on theological or scriptural content.

5 On Muslim internationalism in Hyderabad and al-Afghani's network there see Chapter 4.

6 Aziz Ahmed, "Afghani's Indian Contacts," *Journal of the American Oriental Society* 98.3 (1969): 476–504.

7 *Source Material for a History of the Freedom Movement in India (Collected from Bombay Government Records)*, vol. II: 1885–1920 (Bombay: Government Central Press, 1958), 361–64.

### III

In the early 1920s the Scottish urban planner Patrick Geddes traveled to Hyderabad to select a site and draw up preliminary plans for a new Urdu-medium public university. During the same period planners in Hyderabad took cues from developments in Germany, Britain, the United States, and British India in drawing up a long-term plan for new infrastructures and housing in the rapidly expanding capital city and its suburbs. Simultaneously, Hyderabad State officials struggled against British attempts to prevent construction of new places of worship or eliminate 'sanitary threats' such as workers' housing and urban agriculture in the vicinity of the British military Cantonment in the capital.[8]

The experiences and productivity of people in Hyderabad – such as those sketched above – elaborate structures and developments beyond the formal borders of European empire. Hyderabad's political and geographical space provided a laboratory for experimentation with putatively modern ideas and institutions of governance, and a refuge from colonial practices in a world dominated by imperialism.[9] Intellectual and political flows pulsing through Hyderabad tied the city and state into broader conceptual frameworks of global allegiance. Some of these undermined concepts and practices that envisioned states solely as bounded territorial entities, unsettling dominant narratives of the nature and periodization of the modern state. In Hyderabad, officials took advantage of territorial sovereignty to pursue projects of governance that departed from British colonial initiatives. Hyderabad's ambivalent relationship to empire was founded on the tension between its status as an autonomous territorial state and its nodal position in diffuse, often Muslim, political networks. Hyderabad provides a key vantage point for reconsidering political dynamics in an era often presumed to be one of closure.

The prevailing scholarly consensus on South Asia is that by the late nineteenth century the British had managed to consolidate the entire region under one state, perhaps for the first time in history.[10] However,

8 On Geddes and Hyderabad see Helen Meller, *Patrick Geddes: Social Evolutionist and City Planner* (London: Routledge, 1990), 171.

9 On decentering Eurocentric genealogies of modernity by "recast[ing] metropolitan modernity as its dominant form rather than as its (self-proclaimed) universal standard" see Fernando Coronil, *The Magical State: Nature, Money, and Modernity in Venezuela* (University of Chicago Press, 1997), 8.

10 Standard textbook surveys of South Asia, produced by scholars of widely varying schools of thought, identify the period from the mid-nineteenth century through World War I as the height of modern imperialism. Their narratives describe an era of British imperial consolidation in the region, and the integration of South Asia into a worldwide colonial capitalist economy. Sugata Bose and Ayesha Jalal suggest that the high colonial period

the view from minor states suggests that political authority was not so neatly integrated as this claim implies. Hyderabad was one of several hundred sub-imperial sovereign polities in the subcontinent that occupied gaps in the map of European colonial space. Empire was organized around such units, and theoretical claims of imperial integration were in tension with explicit recognition of non-colonial sovereign power over localities or regions. The vignettes above suggest that the South Asian colonial era witnessed more political complexity than simply the generalization of imperial authority and governance, and articulation of an anti-colonial nationalist other.

From the end of the eighteenth century Hyderabad was bound by treaty to the suzerain British.[11] Nevertheless, borderlines were clearly inscribed between Hyderabad and neighboring colonial territories, which surrounded it on all sides.[12] In the late nineteenth century Hyderabad's sovereign territory and state space provided a venue for several related ideological, institutional, and developmental projects. These were possible because the subcontinent during this period was a heterogeneous entity, and sovereign sub-imperial states and unstable border zones that proliferated were key nodes in the global circulation of political ideas and practices. As such, Hyderabad and other sovereign actors in South Asia and elsewhere below the imperial level create a systemic problem for unitary understandings of empire – the imperial 'core' was perpetually unsettled by perceived or actual threats from the 'periphery.'[13] The view from Hyderabad illuminates the conceptual and political geography of a

was defined by a British imperial "monolithic, unitary sovereignty," whose foil was a "shallow, if not 'fake' authority of 'traditional rulers'" (this latter category included the 'princely states'). See *Modern South Asia: History, Culture, Political Economy*, 2nd edn. (New York: Routledge, 2004), ch. 10, esp. 83. Barbara Daly Metcalf and Thomas R. Metcalf describe the turn of the nineteenth century as the "apogee of the British imperial system," which was characterized by the integral relationship of expanding communication and transformation infrastructures and the consolidation of colonial state sovereignty. See *A Concise History of Modern India*, 2nd edn. (Cambridge University Press, 2006), chs. 4 and 5, esp. 94–99. Burton Stein claims that the Raj became a "unitary state" in 1858, in *A History of India*, 2nd edn., ed. David Arnold (Malden, MA: Wiley-Blackwell, 2010), ch. 6, 227.

11 See Chapter 2 for a consideration of the British imperial doctrine of suzerainty.

12 While these borderlines were unambiguous on maps and in the understanding of the governments of Hyderabad and of different British Indian entities, they did not always appear so clear from the perspective of those on the ground. See Chapter 5 on the limited success of colonial attempts to 'fix' the border.

13 Sameetah Agha and Elizabeth Kolsky, eds., *Fringes of Empire: Peoples, Places, and Spaces in Colonial India* (New Delhi: Oxford University Press, 2009). For an earlier critique of accounts of global systems organized on a core–periphery basis see David Washbrook, "South Asia, the World System, and World Capitalism," *Journal of Asian Studies* 49.3 (1990): 479–508.

subcontinent that remained, despite attempts at consolidation, a remarkably uneven terrain in which the power to exercise political sovereignty was fragmented between numerous entities and animated by often conflicting concerns.

## Rethinking political sovereignty in an age of empires

The familiar periodization of South Asian history runs as follows:

Formal political power was flexible, layered, negotiated, and often severely limited in scope and effectiveness from early modernity through the late eighteenth century.

After a period of imperial consolidation culminating in the middle of the nineteenth century, however, the British succeeded in rendering the entirety of the subcontinent a de facto colonial possession.

Authority was delegated within a complex and strategically designed imperial structure, and colonial rulers maintained power through a combination of military force, economic coercion, and the production of consent among subordinate leaders and various segments of the population.

Working through quintessentially modern ideological and repressive institutional forms, the Raj's ability to manipulate South Asian economy and society was unprecedented in its depth and thoroughness.

The late nineteenth century was the dawn not only of full-blown colonial rule but also of modern state sovereignty in the subcontinent.[14]

[14] This rough timeline is an abstracted composite based upon dozens of recent scholarly works on early modern and modern South Asia. On the pre-modern scenario see Muzaffar Alam and Sanjay Subrahmanyam, *Writing the Mughal World: Studies on Culture and Politics* (New York: Columbia University Press, 2011); Muzaffar Alam and Sanjay Subrahmanyam, eds., *The Mughal State, 1526–1750* (New Delhi: Oxford University Press, 1999), introduction. On the colonial transition see Stewart Gordon, *Marathas, Marauders, and State Formation in Eighteenth-Century India* (Delhi: Oxford University Press, 1994); Sugata Bose, *A Hundred Horizons: The Indian Ocean in the Age of Global Empire* (Cambridge, MA: Harvard University Press, 2006), ch. 2; André Wink, *Land and Sovereignty in India: Agrarian Society and Politics under the Eighteenth-Century Maratha Svarajya* (Cambridge University Press, 1986); C. A. Bayly, *Indian Society and the Making of the British Empire* (Cambridge University Press, 1988); Nicholas B. Dirks, *The Hollow Crown: Ethnohistory of an Indian Kingdom*, 2nd edn. (Ann Arbor: University of Michigan Press, 1993). For accounts of the precolonial past through the lens of the colonial period see Partha Chatterjee, *The Nation and its Fragments: Colonial and Postcolonial Histories* (Delhi: Oxford University Press, 1995), chs. 4, 5; Sudipta Kaviraj, *The Imaginary Institution of India: Politics and Ideas* (New York: Columbia University Press, 2010); and Chakrabarty, *Provincializing Europe*. Significant divergences and

This chronology holds for South Asia, as do variations thereof for many other places in the world.[15] Critiques of postcolonial scholarship on European imperialism have argued for greater emphasis on change over time and foundational differences between empires.[16] Notwithstanding these revisionist impulses, broad terrains subjected to imperial dominance, such as South Asia around 1900, are widely regarded as coherent and relatively homogeneous political entities.

The above chronology of colonialism and the state provides an indispensable foundation for scholarship, but is highly problematic in one respect (at least). The rise of modern power in the subcontinent the chronology centers on is undeniable. Infrastructural and institutional technologies of governance enabled unprecedented depth of state penetration, and these developments were wrought in the subcontinent during the era of British domination. The key problem with the chronology, however, is the presumption of a rapid and thorough transition from complex, multiple, and malleable forms of political power to effectively consolidated state sovereignty under unitary colonial authority.

Revisionist scholarship on modern colonialism from the last few decades has nuanced and challenged the timeline above in certain ways, but has left in place assumptions about the subcontinent-wide scope and

debates continue regarding the details and dynamics of the transition to high colonialism, especially around questions of causality. Few scholars, however, have questioned the thoroughness of de facto British political authority. Some scholarship on the colonial period, however, emphasized the weakness of certain aspects of the colonial state. See, *inter alia*, Anand A. Yang, *The Limited Raj: Agrarian Relations in Colonial India, Saran District, 1793–1920* (Berkeley: University of California Press, 1989). K. Sivaramakrishnan, *Modern Forests: Statemaking and Environmental Change in Colonial Eastern India* (Stanford University Press, 1999) has described "zones of anomaly" that existed in relation to a normative all-controlling imperial state. The current argument suggests that much of the world during the colonial era fits into the former category.

15 For other places see Barkey, *Bandits and Bureaucrats*; Richard White, *The Middle Ground: Indians, Empires, and Republics in the Great Lakes Region, 1650–1815* (Cambridge University Press, 1991); Peter C. Perdue, *China Marches West: The Qing Conquest of Central Eurasia* (Cambridge, MA: Harvard University Press, 2005); and Lauren A. Benton, *Law and Colonial Cultures: Legal Regimes in World History, 1400–1900* (Cambridge University Press, 2002). The story is somewhat different when viewed from the perspective of Europe, but nevertheless the nineteenth century there is also broadly understood as the era during which the modern national state successfully rooted out all opposition. For a classic account of the extension of state institutions and the generalization of national mentalities in rural France see Eugen Weber, *Peasants into Frenchmen: The Modernization of Rural France, 1870–1914* (Stanford University Press, 1976).

16 C. A. Bayly, *Empire and Information: Intelligence Gathering and Social Communication in India, 1780–1870* (Cambridge University Press, 1996); Frederick Cooper, *Colonialism in Question: Theory, Knowledge, History* (Berkeley: University of California Press, 2005).

stable nature of colonial power. D. A. Low sought to explain how the British Empire maintained authority despite being vastly outnumbered by subject populations, and focused on networks of collaboration.[17] Low developed a useful argument about the scale and intensity of British power, and the typology he laid out described the spectrum of "imperial authority" (from "quasi-diplomatic" to "administrative"), and in some ways corresponds to the modes of minor sovereignty described here. However, by taking the fact of imperial authority as his departure point, Low's work situated "indigenous political authorities" in a hierarchy controlled by and constitutive of colonial power. As such, the dynamism and eclecticism of minor states for themselves is squeezed out of a quintessentially *imperial* history. More recent revisionist scholarship had increasingly seen colonial domination as uneven across space, or occasionally absent in certain areas. Even when acknowledged, however, anomalous zones tend to be viewed as possessing illusory, insignificant sovereignty neatly 'nested' within a colonized terrain, or stateless.[18]

The political and legal architecture of British colonialism incorporated, in addition to an array of Raj provinces and residencies, several hundred sub-imperial, formally sovereign polities.[19] The continued existence of these states was guaranteed by accords with the British that required official colonial oversight and limitations of minor states' international and military powers. Larger states were obliged to host influential advisors known as Residents, and to provide space and funding for British Indian military cantonments.[20] Nevertheless, sub-imperial states behaved as sovereign entities in internal governance, and often in limited international diplomatic capacity.

Assessing South Asian sub-imperial states as political entities in the era of British colonial dominance requires nuance and attention to particularities. These states, individually or collectively, did not pose a serious

[17] D. A. Low, *Lion Rampant: Essays in the Study of British Imperialism* (London: Cass, 1973), ch. 1.

[18] For studies that make broader arguments see Lauren A. Benton, *Search for Sovereignty: Law and Geography in European Empires, 1400–1900* (Cambridge University Press, 2010) and James C. Scott, *The Art of Not Being Governed: An Anarchist History of Upland Southeast Asia* (New Haven: Yale University Press, 2009). On South Asia see, *inter alia*, Michael Herbert Fisher, *Indirect Rule in India: Residents and the Residency System, 1764–1858* (Delhi: Oxford University Press, 1991); Dirks, *Hollow Crown*; Sivaramakrishnan, *Modern Forests*.

[19] Barbara N. Ramusack, *The Indian Princes and their States* (Cambridge University Press, 2004).

[20] Smaller states were grouped together into agencies under particular British Indian provinces or presidencies, and were overseen by mobile political officers of different kinds. The discussion here emphasizes larger states. On the role of colonial officials in 'princely states' see Fisher, *Indirect Rule*.

challenge to British imperial power in the subcontinent after 1857. The Raj exercised dominant, coercive, and often violent authority across most of the subcontinent, but their formal legal sovereignty never spanned the whole of the region. In South Asia, as in numerous locations in which European empires were dominant powers, colonial sovereignty remained uneven in both theoretical and practical terms. Textured imperial sovereignty produced spaces for political maneuvering with emerging autonomous domains in imperial cities and provinces, anomalous frontier spaces, and among numerous colonial entities with markedly diverse interests. Formally autonomous polities such as Hyderabad were thus not exceptional: trends there put in clear relief the enduring political heterogeneity of an ostensibly colonized world. Sovereign sub-imperial states produced a complexity in the legal domain through which various actors at state level or well below could undermine the working of colonial institutions. Further, the jurisdictional complexity that set off the social and political worlds of these states from colonial territories (which were in turn offset from one another) foreshadows new configurations of 'major' and 'minor' sovereignty in the ostensibly postcolonial world from the mid-twentieth century onward.

The configuration of *fragmented sovereignty* described here carved out territories that were within the web of empire, but not entirely of it. Their sovereignty facilitated political connections and experimentations. From another perspective, these territories gave shape to empires by providing them with sustaining mythologies and threatening frontiers which authorized official colonial state violence and state illegalities within imperial boundaries. But empires also had outsides. States in Asia, Africa, and elsewhere whose authority paled in comparison to that of dominant imperial formations provided discursive and institutional spaces for the articulation of political visions including but not limited to progressive or exclusivist idioms of Muslim solidarity, anarchist internationalism, radical Marxism, Pan-Asianism, Pan-Africanism, conservative nativist varieties of anti-colonialism, and reformist ideas of liberal European empire.[21] Such political languages cut across and through political,

[21] For a general survey of 'Pan-Islamism' see Jacob M. Landau, *The Politics of Pan-Islam: Ideology and Organization* (Oxford: Clarendon Press, 1990); on Southeast Asia see Barbara Watson Andaya, "From Rūm to Tokyo: The Search for Anticolonial Allies by the Rulers of Riau, 1899–1914," *Indonesia* 24 (1977): 123–56; Anthony Reid, "Nineteenth Century Pan-Islam in Indonesia and Malaysia," *Journal of Asian Studies* 26.2 (1967): 267–83. Pan-Islamism in South Asia, the Ottoman world, and elsewhere will be discussed below. On Pan-Asianism and Pan-Islamism see Cemil Aydin, *The Politics of Anti-Westernism in Asia: Visions of World Order in Pan-Islamic and Pan-Asian Thought* (New York: Columbia University Press, 2007). On Anarchism see Benedict R. O'G. Anderson, *Under Three Flags: Anarchism and the Anti-Colonial Imagination* (London:

imperial, and regional boundaries. The scope and effect of European colonialism was thus tempered by other crosscutting geographical visions within arenas such as the British Empire or British India. These visions, and related institutional experiments, were nurtured against a background of global imperialism, but not always in formally colonized places.

## Colonial empires and a world of states

European imperialism was a dominant global force, but formal sovereignty of minor states was of central importance to changing political ideologies and institutional developments. Further, frontier zones of empires and states provided spaces for articulating political authority at lower levels, or refuges for dissidents against or people criminalized by established states. Physical geography and environment often played an important role in carving out zones of anomaly that were problematic to established political entities. However, more so than material factors, formal legal sovereignty was crucial in producing a fragmented political scene. The autonomy claimed by a range of minor states endowed a complexity to the global political geography of the nineteenth and twentieth centuries.

The distribution of sovereignty from the late nineteenth century onward was largely an effect of European imperialism. The geopolitical remaking of world power by empires combined territorial conquest with conceptual hegemony. The latter entailed the generalization of the notion of unitary and territorially defined sovereignty, as well as refashioned notions of society, culture, and the political domain. Scholarship on places beyond the realm of formal European colonial rule has effectively demonstrated the ineluctability of imperial pressures. Recent writings on formally independent states such as Siam, Iran, the Ottoman domains, China, and Japan have shown that sovereignty often meant considerably less than total independence and autonomy in relation to European

Verso, 2005); on Pan-Africanism see P. Olisanwuche Esedebe, *Pan-Africanism: The Idea and Movement, 1776–1991*, 2nd edn. (Washington, DC: Howard University, 1994); on imperial reformism see Antoinette M. Burton, *At the Heart of the Empire: Indians and the Colonial Encounter in Late-Victorian Britain* (Berkeley: University of California Press, 1998) and Catherine Hall, *Civilising Subjects: Colony and Metropole in the English Imagination, 1830–1867* (University of Chicago Press, 2002); on global radicalism see Khuri-Makdisi, *The Eastern Mediterranean*. For a consideration of global South Asian anti-colonialism see Maia Ramnath, *Haj to Utopia: How the Ghadar Movement Charted Global Radicalism and Attempted to Overthrow the British Empire* (Berkeley: University of California Press, 2011).

imperial powers, in either political or intellectual terms.[22] Scholarship demonstrating the inescapable fact of global European power provides a crucial foundation from which any discussion on world history in the age of high imperialism must begin. Notwithstanding nationalist valorization of continuous independence in places such as Thailand, Iran, and Turkey, the postcolonial scholarly consensus about the age of high imperialism envisions a map of the world conceptually and politically ordered by Western imperialism.

The fact of European global political ascendancy, and the classic modalities of capitalism and liberalism through which colonialism operated, do not exhaust the intellectual and political repertoire of the late nineteenth and early twentieth centuries. Political sovereignty in numerous non-colonial states produced contingent or enduring zones of alterity. Colonial territories surely served as laboratories for experimentation with new and increasingly invasive forms of everyday governance in the metropole.[23] But simultaneously, non-colonial polities amidst empires

[22] Imperial powers had widely varied degrees of influence and formal power in these places, with the Ottomans themselves continuing to act as an imperial force despite European pressure, and Egypt largely under British administration by the 1880s. On Siam see Thongchai Winichakul, *Siam Mapped: A History of the Geo-Body of a Nation* (Honolulu: University of Hawaiʿi Press, 1994) and Hong Lysa, "'Stranger within the Gates': Knowing Semi-Colonial Siam as Extraterritorials," *Modern Asian Studies* 38.2 (2004): 327–54. On Iran, Firoozeh Kashani-Sabet, *Frontier Fictions: Shaping the Iranian Nation, 1804–1946* (Princeton University Press, 1999) and Mohamad Tavakoli-Targhi, *Refashioning Iran: Orientalism, Occidentalism, and Historiography* (New York: Palgrave, 2001). On the Ottomans, Selim Deringil, *The Well-Protected Domains: Ideology and the Legitimation of Power in the Ottoman Empire, 1876–1909* (London: I. B. Tauris, 1998). On China, Prasenjit Duara, *Sovereignty and Authenticity: Manchukuo and the East Asian Modern* (Lanham, MD: Rowman & Littlefield, 2003). On Japan, Harry D. Harootunian, *Overcome by Modernity: History, Culture, and Community in Interwar Japan* (Princeton University Press, 2000). Sudan was jointly administered by Britain and ostensibly Ottoman Egypt from 1898 to 1856. See Eve Troutt Powell, *A Different Shade of Colonialism: Egypt, Great Britain, and the Mastery of the Sudan* (Berkeley: University of California Press, 2003) and Heather J. Sharkey, *Living with Colonialism: Nationalism and Culture in the Anglo-Egyptian Sudan* (Berkeley: University of California Press, 2003). The Ottoman Empire presents an extremely complex scenario, which I shall address in more detail below. I have excluded the Americas from the scope of comparison here, though several locations there would fit the framework. On the anomalous case of Egypt – an autonomous state within the Ottoman Empire, subjected to intensive and quasi-formal French and British imperial rule – see Khaled Fahmy, *All the Pasha's Men: Mehmed Ali, his Army, and the Making of Modern Egypt* (Cambridge University Press, 1997), esp. ch. 7; Timothy Mitchell, *Colonising Egypt* (Berkeley: University of California Press, 1991) and *Rule of Experts: Egypt, Techno-Politics, Modernity* (Berkeley: University of California Press, 2002).

[23] Technologies related to criminal identification, gender and sexuality regulation were often developed and experimented with in the context of colonial rule and then re-exported to the metropole. On the regulation of gender and sexuality see Judith R. Walkowitz, *City of Dreadful Delight: Narratives of Sexual Danger in Late-Victorian London* (University of Chicago Press, 1992) and Philippa Levine, *Prostitution, Race, and Politics:*

were staging-grounds for wide-ranging political experimentation with concepts and practice of modern governance, and imperial coercion was rarely the primary motivation. Officials who carried out these projects engaged intimately with the intellectual content and institutional manifestations of Western European and other idioms of political modernity, but appropriated and customized received ideas. European developments were neither taken as static modal templates nor did they exhaust the range of political possibilities.

### Uncolonized states

Though dwarfed by European world empires, smaller sovereign states that were not colonized provided fertile ground for refashioning political concepts and institutions in dialogue with other global examples as well as local and regional histories. States such as Siam and Qajar Iran were subject to powerful pressures from European 'informal empires,' sometimes via restrictive treaties. This was particularly so with respect to border policy, fiscal management, and external trade.[24] Even if compromised, the formal legal sovereignty and international status of these states provided shelter for autonomous development of institutions, redefining the criteria of legitimate statecraft, and strategically engaging with the emerging global system. This process involved sustained attention to political ideas and practices in the West and in colonized countries on the part of elites, administrators, and intellectuals in uncolonized states. In colonies, political and institutional change was often carried out under direct political compulsion from occupying European powers. While uncolonized states were subject to powerful political and economic pressures, officials controlled the levers of most internal reforms.[25]

*Policing Venereal Disease in the British Empire* (New York: Routledge, 2003). On criminal identification, through the technology of fingerprinting, see Chandak Sengoopta, *Imprint of the Raj: How Fingerprinting was Born in Colonial India* (London: Macmillan, 2003); and on the passport as mode of colonial control see Radhika V. Mongia, "Race, Nationality, Mobility: A History of the Passport," *Public Culture* 11.3 (1999): 527–56 and Radhika Singha, "Settle, Mobilize, Verify: Identification Practices in Colonial India," *Studies in History* 16.2 (2000): 151–98.

24 Winichakul, *Siam Mapped*; Lysa, "'Stranger within the Gates'"; Kashani-Sabet, *Frontier Fictions*. For a classic account of the economic context of 'informal empire,' cast as an apologetics for imperialism, see John Gallagher and Ronald Robinson, "The Imperialism of Free Trade," *Economic History Review* 6.1 (1953): 1–15.

25 Places where colonialism was quasi-formal and European officials shared political power with state officials, such as late nineteenth-century Egypt or early twentieth-century Morocco, were a mixed form and only partially fit this rubric. The late Ottoman Empire provides one example of internal economic pressures in which European imperial forces applied leverage via state bankers. See Edhem Eldem, "Ottoman Financial Integration

## *Siam*

Siam underwent extensive internal political change during the era of global European imperialism.[26] Out of a keen awareness of rising colonial power nearby, Siamese state officials drew upon European political concepts and institutional practices, and modified them to suit their own needs.[27] Twentieth-century Thai nationalism has generated an imaginative historical image of an uncolonized state that remained unmarked by imperial power, unlike others in Southeast Asia that fell under British, French, or Dutch control. Recent scholarship, however, has demonstrated that Siam was subject to intensive European pressure, both as economic imperialism and, from the 1890s, threat of conquest.[28] As Siamese officials began to appreciate the dire implications of regional European dominance for their own sovereignty, the state consolidated control of previously autonomous regions and centralized political authority in Bangkok. Integral to this process of 'internal colonialism' were investments in infrastructure (roads, electrification), institutional changes (new bureaucracy, law codes, courts and judicial system), and notions of etiquette reflecting changing elite aesthetic values (dress codes, hygienic practices).[29] These developments evidenced a conscious modeling of the Siamese state and elite culture on European examples. The wide array of changes was in part an attempt to shore up Siam against external threats by strengthening state institutions and to "maintain [a] semblance of sovereignty."[30] The modernization of the state apparatus, as

with Europe: Foreign Loans, the Ottoman Bank and the Ottoman Public Debt" *European Review* 13.3 (2005): 431–45; C. G. A. Clay, *Gold for the Sultan: Western Bankers and Ottoman Finance 1856–1881: A Contribution to Ottoman and to International Financial History* (London: I. B. Tauris, 2000). In earlier moments, similar techniques incorporating finance mechanisms were used to expand colonial authority into new territories, such as Bengal and the Northern Circars in British India. See Bayly, *Indian Society*.

26 I use Siam rather than Thailand here since the former was the name used internally by state officials and the international community in the period under consideration.

27 Egypt from 1800 through the 1880s presents a partial parallel, in that state officials drew on a variety of sources, primarily European, to modernize the state in the face of the threat of imperial encroachment. See Mitchell, *Colonising Egypt*; Fahmy, *All the Pasha's Men*.

28 Much of this summary on the question of colonial influence in Siam is distilled from the synthetic treatment in Peter A. Jackson, "Autonomy and Subordination in Thai History: The Case for Semicolonial Analysis," *Inter-Asia Cultural Studies* 8.3 (2007): 329–48.

29 Thongchai Winichakul, "The Quest for 'Siwilai': A Geographical Discourse of Civilizational Thinking in the Late Nineteenth and Early Twentieth-Century Siam," *Journal of Asian Studies* 59.3 (2000): 528–49. Winichakul does not use the term "internal colonialism," which is taken from Jackson's account of recent scholarship.

30 Michael Herzfeld, "The Absent Presence: Discourses of Crypto-Colonialism," *South Atlantic Quarterly* 101.4 (2002): 899–926, here 907.

Thongchai Winichakul shows, was also tied into a broader attempt to articulate Siam's place in a world defined by relative degrees of *siwilai* ('civilization'):

> Unlike the European experience, the Siamese quest for *siwilai* was a transcultural process in which ideas and practices from Europe, via colonialism, had been transferred, localized, and hybridized in the Siamese setting. [This] quest for *siwilai* was not simply a reaction to the colonial threat. Rather, it was an attempt originated by various groups among the elite, later including urban intellectuals, to attain and confirm the relative superiority of Siam; as the traditional imperial power in the region, Siam was anxious about its position among modern nations.[31]

Crucial here was "the active role of Siamese rulers in the transformation," and their capacity to localize quintessentially modern Western modes of governance to establish Siam's position within an expanded world of states. If Europe had replaced China and South Asia as the center of a new global order, "Siam had to reconceptualize itself in relation to the rest of the world."[32] Emerging civilizational discourses located urban Thai intellectuals within a spatialized hierarchy, above the jungle people and rural villagers among their countrymen, and below Europeans.[33]

In spite of largely successful efforts to consolidate authority and develop modern institutions, Siam remained marginal in elite perceptions and international diplomatic clout.[34] European imperialism – felt in the form of political pressure and an emergent elite consensus regarding the nature of civilization – played a significant role in shaping Siamese ideas and institutions. Thongchai's work suggests, however, that the thoroughgoing changes in the late nineteenth-century Siamese political domain resulted from complex and highly productive engagements between established Thai concepts and political practices and malleable Western templates. Despite a palpable degree of humiliation in attempts to behave as peers of their European counterparts, Siamese rulers and administrators retained sovereign authority and developed their state from this platform. Parallel to Hyderabad, Siam was part of a global geography of minor states, decidedly subordinate in terms of power to European empires, but with formal authority that facilitated autonomous development.

[31] Winichakul, "Quest for 'Siwilai'," 529. [32] Ibid., 533. [33] Ibid., 546.

[34] On the exclusion of non-Christian states from the community of nations see Charles Henry Alexandrowicz, *An Introduction to the History of the Law of Nations in the East Indies: (16th, 17th and 18th Centuries)* (Oxford: Clarendon Press, 1967).

### *Qajar Iran*

Qajar Iran (1794–1925), like Siam, was never directly colonized, and played a secondary role on a global stage increasingly dominated by expanding European empires.[35] While uncolonized, the Qajars "never remained immune from the European powers' all-embracing, and often intrusive, presence."[36] From the 1820s the Russian Empire and British India employed a strategy of "geopolitical containment" in Qajar northern and southeastern borders.[37] The experience of imperial pressure and threat of conquest made it imperative that state officials consolidate political authority over highly decentralized domains. The early Qajars put very little investment into fortifying their military and police or developing institutions and infrastructures such as courts, schools, hospitals, roads, and railways.[38] This left them not only vulnerable to pressure from imperial neighbors, but also in need of development paradigms to consolidate internal territories and establish a place on the world stage. This dilemma provided the opportunity for Qajar engagement with methods of statecraft employed by imperial rivals. State officials looked to reforms in Europe and the neighboring Ottoman Empire for exemplary models, but approached these with a decided ambivalence.[39]

Late nineteenth-century Qajar Iran administrators experimented with new political ideas and undertook development projects to communicate changing concepts of authority to the population. Under Nasir al-Din Shah (r. 1848–96) the Iranian state developed a royal style blending notions of Perso-Islamicate kingship, reciprocal relationships between state officials and clerics, and Western-inspired models of government and public displays.[40] Qajar political culture sought to naturalize familiar concepts keyed around established mediators of authority that dated back centuries, such as Shia *mujtahids* (jurisconsults) and the king cast as *zillullah* ('shadow of God [on earth]'). The form in which much of this content was communicated, however,

35 I use Iran, the name used internally in the Qajar state, rather than Persia. The latter name was used internationally until 1935. My use of Iran rather than Persia is not meant to imply direct continuity between Qajar Iran and the contemporary nation-state.

36 Abbas Amanat, *Pivot of the Universe: Nasir al-Din Shah Qajar and the Iranian Monarchy, 1831–1896* (Berkeley: University of California Press, 1997), 1.

37 Ibid., 15.

38 Nikki Keddie, "Iran under the Later Qājārs, 1848–1922," in *The New Cambridge History of Iran*, vol. VII: *From Nadir Shah to the Islamic Republic*, ed. Peter Avery, Gavin Hambly, and Charles Melville (Cambridge University Press, 1991), 174–212, here 176.

39 Amanat, *Pivot of the Universe*, 14.

40 Ibid., 5–18.

was derived in large part through engagements with political practices elsewhere.[41]

According to Afshin Marashi, Qajar encounters with European and Ottoman cities were exemplary for the development of "a new style of politics borrowed from an increasingly available model of state authority."[42] Based on detailed communications from consular officials in Istanbul and Paris and personal encounters with the spaces of public life in Europe, from the 1870s onwards Nasir al-din Shah dedicated extensive resources to the redesign of his capital city, Tehran.[43] His urban policy sought to create a sphere of publicity through carving out "broad boulevards and centralized open spaces in the European style," punctuated by museums and exhibition grounds that could serve as "sites for the transmission of values and meanings to an urban populace."[44] Nasir al-Din Shah utilized these staging-grounds for spectacles of royal authority and legitimacy, targeting both his subjects and the rest of the world. Speaking of Qajar, as well as the Ottoman, territories as "semicolonial zones that had escaped direct colonization but where sovereignty remained precarious," Marashi speculated on the desired effect of public display of royal authority:[45]

> For the international audience, it was intended to convey the equal status of the semicolonial states and thus discourage further imperial encroachments. For the domestic audience the new ceremonies and public spectacles enhanced the position of the state as the main focus of domestic loyalty, providing the basis of modern identity in an age when social forces were producing rival and centrifugal identifications.[46]

Qajar anxieties over loss of territory or political autonomy, then, produced both an imperative and an opportunity to develop new regimes of state authority. This project entailed engagement with models of authority from other places, and reexamining older modes of legitimacy and rule. The integration of new technologies and rhetorics of power into the Qajar system performed multiple functions. On one level, it was a means to solidify control over subject populations. Further, the new imperial style registered a proclamation of sovereign authority in a symbolic

[41] For a consideration of the role of European genres and modes of knowledge in Iran, such as travelogue writing and journalistic reportage, see Naghmeh Sohrabi, *Taken for Wonder: Nineteenth-Century Travel Accounts from Iran to Europe* (New York: Oxford University Press, 2012).

[42] Afshin Marashi, *Nationalizing Iran: Culture, Power, and the State, 1870–1940* (Seattle: University of Washington Press, 2008), 16.

[43] Ibid., 20–26. On the expansion of city services such as cleaning, lighting, trash collection, and parks see Keddie, "Iran under the Later Qājārs," 198.

[44] Marashi, *Nationalizing Iran*, 18, 26. [45] Ibid., 17. [46] Ibid., 18.

language of political modernity familiar in London, Paris, Istanbul, Cairo, and beyond.

Siam and Qajar Iran in the late nineteenth century illustrate two prevailing trends in uncolonized places. First, such states were under intensive imperial pressures that obliged them to consolidate authority over their territories and subjects. This was carried out through engagement with global political ideas and practices, and resulted in the emulation and localization of modes of governance employed by European states or empires (or emulation of other implicitly successful 'Westernized' states, such as Japan or the Ottomans).[47] Second, the threat to state territories – or sovereignty itself – posed by European colonialism engendered tremendous anxiety on the part of political leaders of uncolonized states. These leaders addressed concerns through presenting their political sophistication and degree of authority as *comparable* to that of European states. It mattered little that attempts to engage with European states as equals were ineffectual: The fact of formal sovereignty and opportunity for autonomous political development both compelled and enabled uncolonized states to experiment politically in hopes of obtaining a secure physical and conceptual location amidst empires.

## Sub-imperial states

In addition to uncolonized states, such as Siam and Qajar Iran, the era of high colonialism featured a wide array of *sub-imperial* states: polities that were not formally colonized, but whose sovereignty was guaranteed by treaties subordinating them to regionally dominant colonial powers.[48] Political configurations of this kind were prominent in different parts of the British Empire, and the imperial geographies of Asia and Africa were

47 On emulation of European legal ideas and the making of international law see Richard S. Horowitz, "International Law and State Transformation in China, Siam, and the Ottoman Empire during the Nineteenth Century," *Journal of World History* 15.4 (2004): 445–86.

48 The term 'sub-imperial' here designates sovereign states subordinate to imperial powers, and is distinct from the use of the term to designate smaller-scale imperial projects that emerge in the context of post-World War II US economic imperialism. See David Harvey, *The New Imperialism* (Oxford University Press, 2003), 185–86. There is some affinity between the roles of minor states I sketch here and the capacity Harvey identifies of smaller states to "insert themselves" into the global power matrix. However, I do not contend that the empowerment of minor states necessarily represents a parallel, if lesser, form of imperialism. My use of the term is also distinct from scholars, chiefly of South Africa, who define sub-imperial states as proxies of a larger dominant imperialist force. See Patrick Bond, "Bankrupt Africa: Imperialism, Sub-Imperialism and the Politics of Finance," *Historical Materialism* 12.4 (2004): 145–72; Melanie Samson, "(Sub)imperial South Africa? Reframing the Debate," *Review of African Political Economy* 36.119 (2009): 93–103.

composed in considerable part of native sovereign territory. The British Empire of the late nineteenth and early twentieth centuries included hundreds of 'princely states' in South Asia, several emirates in the Persian Gulf, federated and unfederated states in Malaya, and a variety of chiefdoms, emirates and sultanates in southern, western, and eastern Africa. These states ranged widely in size and autonomy relative to the empire. In the case of larger sub-imperial states, variations on political dynamics in uncolonized states, such those considered above, are visible. Owing to their presence as sovereign entities within broader imperial geographies, sub-imperial states complicated the workings of power in colonial space. Further, such states create historiographical problems by undermining the integrity of empire as a unitary object of analysis.

Recent scholarship tends to emphasize the high degree of political subordination experienced by various "princes" (Raja, Maharaja, Nawab, Maharana, Begum, Nizam, Khan), sultans, emirs, and chiefs who retained formal sovereignty within British imperial space. Colonial discourses, attempting to present imperialism as "trusteeship," at times emphasized the independent political status of subsidiary 'native rulers.' Revisionist histories of the last several decades have accordingly stressed that various forms of "indirect rule" (following the British colonial designation) veiled colonial domination equivalent in extent to that in 'directly ruled' territories.[49]

The histories of sub-imperial polities have been marginalized by the discursive power of postcolonial nation-states into whose bodies they were often integrated, and the subsequent redrawing of postcolonial provincial (subnational) boundaries.[50] 'Indirect rule,' however, for a variety of ideological and material reasons, was a key organizing principle of the British Empire from the mid-nineteenth century onward.[51] Developments in British-dominated regions of Malaya and Northern Nigeria elucidate the political complexity sub-imperial polities endowed to

49 On South Asia see Dirks, *Hollow Crown*; Fisher, *Indirect Rule*. On Africa see Mahmood Mamdani, *Citizen and Subject: Decentralized Despotism and the Legacy of Late Colonialism* (Princeton University Press, 1996). See also Chapter 3 of this book. It is worth noting that Dirks and others often use "indirect rule" to refer to a wide array of colonial policies ostensibly based on established local practice, such as land control regimes or social hierarchies of privilege. My discussion here is exclusively concerned with formal state sovereignties, not the entirety of colonial political practice.

50 For a discussion of the histories and legacies of South Asian and other minor non-colonial states after decolonization see this book's Conclusion.

51 Mantena, *Alibis of Empire*, pinpoints in 1857 a key shift from "liberal" empire, premised on the notion of "civilizing" colonized populations through reform, to an imperial ethos based on "indirect rule" through "traditional" institutions. Mamdani, *Citizen and Subject*, 62–63, traces the institutional origins of indirect rule in Africa to British Natal in the 1840s, and its codification as law to 1891.

the space of empire. Trends in these places – bureaucrat-intellectuals' roles in securing the status of states in emerging global political landscapes; developing Muslimness, if not Islam per se, as a political identity and basis for transnational solidarities; fusions of Muslim state identity with institutional and technological modernity – resembled those in Hyderabad that subsequent chapters of the book examine.

### *Johor, Malaya*

The bulk of territory in the imperial configuration of 'British Malaya' was formally under native sovereign rulers, each subject to different degrees of colonial oversight.[52] Malaya was a heterogeneous political entity composed of directly colonized enclaves (Straits Settlements), states with sovereign rulers closely managed by a British-led federation (Federated Malay States, or FMS), and largely autonomous sovereign states (Unfederated Malay States, or UMS). Both FMS and UMS were obliged to host a powerful British-appointed political advisor. This produced a tension between symbolic and de facto political authority, and "the sovereignty of the Malay Rulers became a sacrosanct principle of British rule in Malaya" in order to "legitimise the residency system and the advisory treaties which underpinned it."[53] Malay rulers' dependence on British patronage facilitated colonial economic and political penetration. The decades around 1900 saw the rapid expansion of colonial capital into lucrative tin and rubber plantations worked by migrant labor across the peninsula.[54]

British power in the Malay states was limited by sultans' authority to determine the content of 'Islamic law' and 'Malay custom.' Control over these domains embedded Malay rulers "within the institutional hierarchy of the colonial state," but gave them a degree of power both within their own states and in Malaya as a whole.[55] London designated political status and was dominant in regional economic administration, but sultans'

52 'British Malaya' was not an official designation, but administrative shorthand that came into use in the early twentieth century to describe the governing bodies in what is now western (peninsular) Malaysia and Singapore. As will become clear, British Malaya was not a uniform political terrain in de jure or de facto terms.

53 Simon C. Smith, "'Moving a Little with the Tide': Malay Monarchy and the Development of Modern Malay Nationalism," *Journal of Imperial and Commonwealth History* 34.1 (2006): 123–38, here 124–25.

54 Carl A. Trocki, "Political Structures in the Nineteenth and Early Twentieth Centuries," in *The Cambridge History of Southeast Asia*, vol. II: *The Nineteenth and Twentieth Centuries*, ed. Nicholas Tarling (Cambridge University Press, 1992), 79–130, here 113–14.

55 Iza Hussin, "The Pursuit of the Perak Regalia: Islam, Law, and the Politics of Authority in the Colonial State," *Law and Social Inquiry* 32.3 (2007): 759–88, here 784.

jurisdiction over domains designated as religious or customary produced a fluid legal terrain from the 1880s onward.[56]

Malay states' sovereignty was important in both ideological and institutional terms. Royal courts fashioned administrations, staffed departments, and carried out development projects; they also remained key participants in and subjects of broader ideological debates among political thinkers in the region. As treaties were signed and Residents took up posts in UMS, they encountered "not only the nucleus of an administrative cadre but a strong sensitivity among ruling groups to all attempts to overstep the boundaries of advice and guidance."[57] Malay officials themselves were experimenting with "bureaucratic modernization," customizing European templates to accommodate established modes of governance.[58] Willingness to collaborate with the British in certain areas allowed Malay sultans to retain internal sovereignty in their states.

A closer examination of the Sultanate of Johor, one of the more active UMS, reveals Malay rulers' political maneuvers and their results.[59] Starting as a high port official in Singapore island, in the 1850s the Temenggong of Johor extracted from the British the status of territorial ruler, and proceeded to seize political autonomy in a neighboring area.[60] Late nineteenth-century Johor rulers parlayed loyalty to the expanding empire into increased authority. The process of consolidation brought the British into conflict with the existing Malay state system, which they chose to reinforce and turn to their advantage. This strategic move secured British ascendancy by reinscribing the authority of Malay sovereignty. Abu Bakar (r. 1862–95) amplified his status to Maharaja (1866) then Sultan (1885) in exchange for agreeing to host a Resident in Johor (a post that remained vacant until 1914). Working from allegiances and intimacy with British officials, Johor established a governmental framework during the 1870s

[56] Hussin, "Pursuit of the Perak Regalia," posits legal hybridity, an alternative to legal pluralism, as an optic for describing juridical politics in Malaya as a colonized space. The coherence of Malaya as political space may appear less thorough if looked at from the perspective of state officials or the popular experience of the law in Malay states, where sultans' administrations had sovereign control over internal governance. On legal pluralism in Raj–Nizam frontiers see part II of this book.

[57] Willam R. Roff, *The Origins of Malay Nationalism*, 2nd edn. (Kuala Lumpur: Oxford University Press, 1994 [1967]), 94.

[58] Ibid., 94–95.

[59] The British officially designated the ruler of Johor "Sultan of the State and Territory of Johore." This made explicit that he was not heir to the old Johor sultanate, which thrived in the Malay region from the sixteenth to nineteenth centuries. See Carl A. Trocki, *Prince of Pirates: The Temenggongs and the Development of Johor and Singapore, 1784–1885* (Singapore University Press, 1979), 191.

[60] Trocki, *Prince of Pirates*, 119. The following summary is extracted from 150–207 of the text.

incorporating Malay and Chinese officials and hired Europeans. Subsequently, when the British were consolidating political and economic control in the Straits Settlements and the FMS, Johor undertook governmental expansion and reorganization, and developed a lucrative rubber plantation system. The Johor Sultan used his expanding sovereignty to build a state integrating new institutions constructed on the British model alongside royal legislative authority, courtly ceremony, and state support for education and intellectual production. Debates about what constituted legitimate governance in the region often hinged on the activities of Muslim Malay rulers in Johor and elsewhere.

Sultans and their official activities (patronage of scholarship and literature, development projects, representation of Malay Islam) were at the center of the emerging Malay public sphere. Institutional changes, which affected the everyday lives of Malay subjects, became wrapped up in broader debates about political legitimacy. Anthony Milner examines a series of texts that elaborate lively ideological contestations in this context, attempting to "identify elements of experimentation in ideology-making, moments, perhaps, when Malay writers sought to comprehend or reformulate alien doctrines . . . [where] we find evidence of independent momentum, of 'autonomy.'"[61] Milner details tensions within the ideological landscape between liberal nationalism (*bangsa*), textualist Islamist internationalism (*umat*), and loyalism to ruling sultans (*kerajaan*). Liberals and Islamists made the fact and practice of sultanate authority a target for critique, and royalist intellectuals attempted to placate these critiques, as well as advice from British officials, "in a creative manner."[62] Sultan Abu Bakar sought to appease those skeptical of his Muslim credentials by hosting religious scholars and assembling legal texts to be used in courts, and informed the British governor of Singapore "that he had revised his state's legal code to make it 'more comfortable to European ideas.'"[63] Johor writers in the 1890s and 1900s produced articulate works addressed to the wide range of potential critics yoking together Muslim and European idioms of political legitimacy.[64]

Educated at elite English schools in Singapore, Johorean bureaucrat-intellectuals penned texts lauding the sultanate as modernist and nationalist. A state survey officer's 1894 book emphasized advancements in road construction and police administration, surveying and boundary-making.[65] The widely influential *Hikayat Johor* (1908) highlighted the sultan's service to the Malay race, and responded to anxieties

[61] Anthony Milner, *The Invention of Politics in Colonial Malaya: Contesting Nationalism and the Expansion of the Public Sphere* (Cambridge University Press, 1994), 7.

[62] Ibid., 193, 198. [63] Ibid., 198. [64] Ibid., 204. [65] Ibid.

of international comparability by emphasizing its independence, modern institutions, and foreign policy achievements.[66] Such writings and the projects they describe suggest that Malay sultans functioned as agents of political experimentation and loci for ideological claims. Sub-imperial states attracted highly trained administrators, and remained in the spotlight of political debates carried out at the centers of British power in Malaya. Even as Islamist intellectuals in the Straits Settlements decried the Johor Sultan for his frivolous ceremonialism and focus on titles, they lauded his achievements in saving an "Islamic country" from "the jaws of a savage tiger."[67] Retaining formal sovereignty during colonial expansion, Malay sultans were key players in ideological contestations, and figures of political desire for colonized Muslim intellectuals.

The case of Johor demonstrates that sub-imperial states, while products of colonial strategy, were venues for political experimentation in concept and practice. Figures who integrated ideas into institutions, such as court circles of bureaucrat-intellectuals, played a central role in combining established and new trends, and communicating results to local critics and global observers. The anxiety of comparability, as in sub-imperial (Hyderabad) and uncolonized (Siam, Qajar Iran) states, consumed state intellectuals in Johor. Nonetheless, accommodations with imperial configurations gave minor states considerable leeway for experimentation.[68]

### *Sokoto, Northern Nigeria*

Sub-imperial political authorities ranged widely in their responsibilities and powers. Chiefs or emirs in British Africa could hardly be called heads of state. They often, nevertheless, used limited sovereign powers to transform social and political relations in imperial space in substantial ways. Lord Frederic Lugard, High Commissioner of British Northern Nigeria from 1901 to 1906, coined the term indirect rule to describe the system of delegation of political authority he established on the frontier of colonial expansion. He formalized an administrative system based on established British colonial practice in western and southern Africa, where "multifarious indigenous authorities . . . were recognized as 'chiefs' by the relevant British governor and were allowed to exercise often quite wide-ranging powers."[69] Indirect rule policies in early twentieth-century

66 Ibid., 201–2. 67 Ibid., 143–44.

68 Trocki, "Political Structures," 86, suggests that Siam during the period under study might be seen as "an extreme example of indirect rule" whose position was "quite similar to the situation of one of the unfederated Malay states, such as Johor."

69 The quotation is taken from D. C. Dorward, "British West Africa and Liberia," in *The Cambridge History of Africa*, vol. VII: *From 1905 to 1940*, ed. A. D. Roberts (Cambridge

British West Africa reoriented and politicized social cleavages, and in many cases elevated people to the formal political status of 'chiefs' where no such institution had existed previously.[70] Scholars have emphasized that indirect rule in Africa and emerging canons of 'customary law' were not so much examples of European 'invention of African tradition' to serve colonial ends, but rather arenas for complex negotiations between European administrators and African elites.[71] Sub-imperial authorities had considerable power in relation to colonial administrators, since the latter could not hope to meet imperial demand for land, labor, and taxes without availing local authorities' capacity to maintain widespread legitimacy.

'Indirect rule' in Africa may have facilitated imperial dominance with minimal investment, but it provided arenas for political experimentation that at times threatened colonial power. In the case of Northern Nigeria, British policy endowed continued legitimacy and formal political status to a Muslim dynasty that had reshaped the political terrain of the region in the nineteenth century. The Sokoto Caliphate, established by the *jihad* of Usman dan Fodio in 1804, controlled much of the Hausa and Yoruba country throughout the nineteenth century. Conquered in 1903 by the British, the Sokoto Sarkin Muslimi, or Caliph, and subordinate emirs of the cities and provinces that made up the empire, contemplated undertaking *hijra*, mandatory migration to a country under Muslim rule.[72] Sokoto leaders, faced with the difficulty of fleeing the region, and without a feasible destination given that Egypt and the Sudan were informally colonized as well, colluded with the colonial conquerors to retain formal political authority within the new dispensation. This produced the conditions for what Murray Last has dubbed a "Colonial Caliphate," where

University Press, 1986), 399–459, here 403. Dorward also notes "analogous developments" in Southern Nigeria, the Gold Coast, Sierra Leone, and the Gambia. See also Mamdani, *Citizen and Subject*, 62–63.

70 Jonathan Reynolds, "Good and Bad Muslims: Islam and Indirect Rule in Northern Nigeria," *International Journal of African Historical Studies* 34.3 (2001): 601–18; Thomas Spear, "Neo-Traditionalism and the Limits of Invention in British Colonial Africa," *Journal of African History* 44.1 (2003): 3–27; Mamdani, *Citizen and Subject.*

71 Spear, "Neo-Traditionalism"; Kristin Mann and Richard Roberts, "Law in Colonial Africa," in *Law in Colonial Africa*, ed. Kristin Mann and Richard Roberts (Portsmouth, NH: Heinemann, 1991), 3–60.

72 *Hijra* refers to the Islamic jurisprudential distinction between *dar al-Islam* ("Islamic land," implying a place under Muslim rule, but often extended to places where Islam can be freely practiced) and *dar al-harb* ("land of war"). According to dominant legal opinion it was incumbent upon Muslims to migrate from the latter to the former if they were physically capable of doing so. See Murray Last, "The 'Colonial Caliphate' of Northern Nigeria," in *Le temps des marabouts: itinéraires et stratégies islamiques en Afrique Occidentale française, 1880–1960*, ed. David Robinson and Jean-Louis Triaud (Paris: Karthala, 1997), 67–82, here 67–69.

Sokoto leaders had "institutional authority" as a sub-imperial Native Administration, staffed the government of the region with Muslims, and even presided over areas that had not previously been integrated by the conquest of the nineteenth-century Caliphate.[73] Last describes the integration of urban centers and most rural areas under expanding civil bureaucratic, judicial, and police systems, and the rise of networks of state-sponsored Sufi orders supervised by a core of emirs.[74] Northern Nigeria emirates' sovereign powers operated under severe colonial constraints. Rulers nevertheless developed a stable core of institutions that would have been impossible were the area under direct colonial administration.

Northern Nigerian emirs, as Shobana Shankar argues, have frequently been seen as "quintessential traditionalists and therefore idealized indirect rulers" in a conservative colonial system, but could also be agents of conceptions of modernity.[75] Through Christian leprosy missions in Northern Nigeria, "Emirs translated Islamic ideals of charity into governmental responsibility for medical welfare, demonstrating their modernizing impulse in matters of social progress."[76] After 1933, when missionaries were allowed access to the region, colonial medicine worked by "delimiting spaces of authority" which emirates used to control "new institutions and non-Muslim peoples."[77] Mahmood Mamdani has argued that the autonomous Native Administrations in British Africa were 'decentralized despots' within a carefully designed bifurcated imperial architecture.[78] Notwithstanding the subordination of African rulers within the imperial structure, they also carried out projects that belied the autocratic roles in which Mamdani argues that they were cast. Indeed, as Shankar shows, Northern Nigerian emirs' development of medical services promoted loyalty and interest among the population.

To keep the political structure of sub-imperial sovereignty under British oversight in place, colonial administrators were obliged to exhibit "a certain degree of respect for and deference to this [Sokoto's] particular state-centered form of Islam."[79] Nevertheless, established colonial anxieties about the threat of oppositional Islamist political visions motivated extensive British intervention into Sokoto. Colonial authorities distributed propaganda impugning the Ottomans during World War I, and removed uncooperative emirs to empower leaders they saw as more compliant.[80]

73 Ibid., 74, 69. 74 Ibid., 73, 77.

75 Shobana Shankar, "Medical Missionaries and Modernizing Emirs in Colonial Hausaland: Leprosy Control and Native Authority in the 1930s," *Journal of African History* 48 (2007): 45–68, here 47.

76 Ibid., 47. 77 Ibid., 53, 57. 78 Mamdani, *Citizen and Subject*.

79 Reynolds, "Good and Bad Muslims," 601. 80 Ibid., 605–6.

Fears of Muslim sedition in Sokoto were often expressed with respect to Sufi orders with connections to other places. The Tijaniyya – an order so prominent in Northern Nigeria that some emirs were initiates – had networks running through French African colonies, and were thought to have links to German spies, 'pan-Ottomanists,' and communists in the Arab world.[81] Emirs' popular legitimacy, based partly on their association with histories of regional Muslim authority, rendered them and the regions they controlled both integral units of and potential threats to colonial power in Northern Nigeria. Emirs' connections to broader Muslim networks rankled British authorities in Northern Nigeria throughout the colonial era there.

In everyday governance sub-imperial authorities enjoyed considerable autonomy. The modicum of sovereignty Northern Nigerian emirs held allowed them scope for political experimentation, such as advancing ideologies of Islamist political authority, or reconstructing the physical space, infrastructure, and bureaucratic architecture of the region.

## Beneath and between states: improvising sovereignty

On the lowest level of political sovereignty, below uncolonized states and sub-imperial polities, were anomalous border and frontier zones that were loosely integrated into imperial and state structures. In many contexts such spaces were productive locations for political improvisation by which bandits could expand networks of allegiance into small states. In the early modern world there was direct continuity between small-scale power based on raiding and the state-building process.[82] By the end of the nineteenth century entrepreneurial state-making on this scale was largely impossible. Political improvisation on the margins of stable state forms was not entirely extinct, though. This was exemplified in a number of locations on the fringes of imperial forms: 'statelets' that periodically emerged in the politically unintegrated zones of highland Southeast Asia; 1870s Baluchistan where authorities in Kalat claimed autonomy and eventually emerged as a sovereign sub-imperial state by playing off conflicts between Qajar Iran and British India.[83] In other places wedged

[81] Ibid., 616.

[82] See, *inter alia*, Gordon, *Marathas, Marauders*, on South Asia, and Barkey, *Bandits and Bureaucrats*, on the rise of the Ottomans. On Europe see Charles Tilly, "War Making and State Making as Organized Crime," in *Bringing the State Back In*, ed. Peter B. Evans, Dietrich Rueschemeyer, and Theda Skocpol (Cambridge University Press, 1985), 169–91.

[83] Scott, *The Art of Not Being Governed*; Arash Khazeni, "On the Eastern Borderlands of Iran: The Baluch in Nineteenth-Century Persian Travel Books," *History Compass* 5.4 (2007): 1399–1411.

between dominant imperial states, such as British Malaya and the Dutch East Indies, negotiation and improvisation were prevalent.[84] The inter-state jurisdictional complexity – legal powers and forums with overlapping or ambiguous domains of authority – produced by frontiers offered opportunities for those who wished to evade state regulations.[85]

In combination with political and juridical frontiers, physical geography played a considerable role in endowing unevenness and mutability to imperial and national sovereignty. As the cases above suggest, unstable frontier zones – while often elements of 'lumpy' sovereignty within empires – could at times be launching points for competing assertions of legal authority and territorial control.[86] In this regard, formal state sovereignty – even if subordinate to dominant imperial formations – mattered, and was a key precondition for political experimentation. Border and frontier zones, defined by geography or ambiguous jurisdiction (two factors often coinciding and synergistic), undermined the integrity of imperial formations and held out the possibility of political organization at a smaller scale, and the slim chance of improvisation of sovereign stateness.

Despite a shrinking scope for political entrepreneurship, frontier zones during the high colonial period (and into the present) provided spaces of refuge for dissidents against dominant imperial structures or populations whose livelihoods were rendered archaic or criminalized in stable consolidating states. This was not exactly political sovereignty, and hardly a workable route to state power by the dawn of the twentieth century. Nevertheless, political and geographical frontiers continued to unsettle the hold of state sovereignty over territory.

## Ottoman Caliphs, Muslim connections, and colonial anxieties

The world of states described above was linked together by complex and varied networks that provided a flexible conceptual architecture for colonial subjects and polities below the imperial level to navigate. Shared investment in anti-colonial nationalist ideas linked political thinkers

[84] Eric Tagliacozzo, *Secret Trades, Porous Borders: Smuggling and States along a Southeast Asian Frontier, 1865–1915* (New Haven: Yale University Press, 2005).

[85] On jurisdictional complexity see Benton, *Law and Colonial Cultures*, and Chapter 6 below.

[86] On geography in the making of 'lumpy' sovereignty see Benton, *A Search for Sovereignty*. On environmental friction as a precondition for the elaboration of "non-state spaces" see Scott, *The Art of Not Being Governed*.

across imperial space, and especially within formations such as the British Empire. Broadly cast regional solidarities such as Pan-Africanism and Pan-Asianism cut across terrains governed by a variety of colonial and non-colonial state forms. While such ties could provide a foundation for exchanging political strategies and ideas of world order, they did so with little consistency across space or historically grounded emotive appeal. Notions of global Muslim community, however, were frequently invoked by those advancing claims of political solidarity across the imperial world, and resonated with historical memory and, in some places, continuing practice of Muslim rule. As such, Muslim internationalism provided a flexible counter-colonial, and at times anti-colonial, political language that served as a conceptual resource for many of the smaller states below the imperial level.[87]

Ideas of global Muslim political cohesion were crucial in sourcing content for ideological and institutional experiments underway in many minor states that were obliged to accommodate themselves to imperial dominance. Ottoman Sultans actively promoted the institution of the Caliphate, or political leadership of the global Muslim community, as the core locus of Muslim internationalism. The fact that the Ottomans were also extremely active in institutional modernization projects from the mid-nineteenth century onward fixed Istanbul as a key focal point for both ideological and institutional guidance in Muslim-ruled states from West Africa to Southeast Asia. Situating Muslim internationalist politics across the world of the late nineteenth and early twentieth centuries entails some consideration of the particularities of the late Ottoman world.

By the nineteenth century the Ottomans' state or parts of their empire fell into all of the categories enumerated in the above classification of modes of sovereignty. The Ottoman Empire remained composed of territories incorporated over the course of several centuries of imperial expansion. By this time, however, their power was on the wane and the Ottoman state was under extreme pressure from European powers. Many territories were formally autonomous and exercised different degrees of sovereign power under the imperial umbrella of Ottoman rule. Of these, several, such as Egypt, Algeria, and Tunisia, were subject to different

[87] I use Muslim internationalism rather than Pan-Islam/ism to underscore that these ideas represented contingent, often improvised, political claims – often without scripturally mediated content – rather than a coherent, unified movement. It is crucial to understand these projects during the colonial period in terms of their own specificity rather than echoing colonial discourses that hinged on anxieties about an imagined 'Muslim threat' to imperial power. See Chapter 4 below.

degrees of de facto or official European colonial control.[88] Ottoman domains also included numerous loosely governed frontier zones where sovereignty could be effectively improvised, such as Iraq, Kurdistan, Yemen, parts of the Balkans, and the border with Qajar Iran.[89] The political complexity of their far-flung domains combined with European pressure to compel a series of state projects to shore up imperial power internally and on the global stage. As such, while a key player in the geography of world power, the Ottomans were in thrall to many of the dynamics acting upon the minor states considered above.[90]

Retaining power well into the age of European empire, the Ottomans were in a position to lay claim to political leadership of the global Muslim community. Since the sixteenth century Ottoman Sultans had made reference to their status as Caliphs of the Muslim world. This claim was based on their assumption of titles previously held by the Egyptian Mamluks and Ottoman political authority over Egypt, Syria, and the Muslim holy sanctuaries in the Hijaz.[91] During the reign of Abdülhamid II (r. 1876–1909) the Ottomans began to systematically deploy propaganda to publicize their status as leaders of the Muslim world for international political purposes. That this occurred after the modernizing Tanzimat reforms of the mid-nineteenth century has often been taken to indicate a dichotomy between Islamism and modernization.[92] On the contrary,

88 For an examination of contestations between the British imperial establishment, the Ottoman-appointed Khedive (viceroy or governor) of the province, and established Arab elites in late nineteenth century Egypt see AbdelAziz EzzelArab, "The Experiment of Sharif Pasha's Cabinet (1879): An Inquiry into the Historiography of Egypt's Elite Movement," *International Journal of Middle East Studies* 36.4 (2004): 561–89. EzzelArab briefly draws a comparison between the power struggle in Egypt and that in mid-nineteenth-century Hyderabad. See also Mitchell, *Colonising Egypt* and Fahmy, *All the Pasha's Men*, on Egypt. On Tunisia see L. Carl Brown, *The Tunisia of Ahmad Bey, 1837–1855* (Princeton University Press, 1974).

89 See Thomas Kühn, "An Imperial Borderland as Colony: Knowledge Production and the Elaboration of Difference in Ottoman Yemen, 1872–1918," and Isa Blumi, "Beyond the Margins of the Empire: Searching the Limitations of Ottoman Rule in Yemen and Albania," both in *MIT Electronic Journal of Middle East Studies* 3 (2003): 5–17 and 18–26 respectively. For Qajar–Ottoman conflicts see Selim Deringil, "The Struggle against Shiism in Hamidian Iraq: A Study in Ottoman Counter-Propaganda," *Die Welt des Islams* 30.1/4 (1990): 45–62.

90 Deringil, *Well-Protected Domains*, and Selim Deringil, *The Ottomans, the Turks and World Power Politics: Collected Essays* (Istanbul: Isis, 2000); Cem Emrence, "Imperial Paths, Big Comparisons: The Late Ottoman Empire," *Journal of Global History* 3.3 (2008): 289–311; EzzelArab, "Experiment."

91 Ş. Tufan Buzpinar, "Opposition to the Ottoman Caliphate in the Early Years of Abdülhamid II: 1877–1882," *Die Welt des Islams* 36.1 (1996): 59–89, here 63.

92 The relative power of the later Ottomans in various spheres and the timeline of the decline of the empire is a subject of considerable historical debate. See, *inter alia*, Donald Quataert, *The Ottoman Empire: 1700–1922*, 2nd edn. (New York: Cambridge University Press, 2005), ch. 4; Kahraman Şakul, "Eastern Question," in *Encyclopedia of the Ottoman*

as recent scholarship has argued, the Hamidian period saw a strengthening of reforms in various institutions and regions simultaneous with increased emphasis on the Muslim character of the state.[93] The Sultans' status as Caliphs of the global Muslim community *and* heads of a powerful modernizing state ostensibly on equal footing with European powers established the Ottomans as a key ally and exemplary model for Muslim political thinkers elsewhere.

The Ottoman propaganda regime was successful in stimulating a global Muslim public sphere that cut across colonized and independent states in Asia, Africa, and Europe. Their ability to mobilize this public, however, was limited. William Ochsenwald has argued that the sole successful Ottoman 'Pan-Islamic' project was their initiative to attract monetary support for railroad construction between Damascus and Mecca, Medina, and Jidda in their Hijaz province between 1900 and 1908.[94] The symbolic import of the Caliphate had greater purchase than its potential for advancing specific projects conceived in Istanbul. Widespread support in South Asia and elsewhere at crucial points in late Ottoman history such as the Crimean War and the post-World War I imperial crisis are well known, and underscore Ottoman status in global Muslim political imagination.[95]

Ottoman-centered Muslim internationalism was not only an important referent among Muslims, but was also a core anxiety that fired imperial security concerns. From 1857 onward the British imperial intelligence

*Empire*, ed. Gábor Ágoston and Bruce Masters (New York: Facts on File, 2009), 191–92. On cultural efflorescence in the Ottoman eighteenth century see Dana Sajdi, "Decline, its Discontents and Ottoman Cultural History: By Way of Introduction," in *Ottoman Tulips, Ottoman Coffee: Leisure and Lifestyle in the Eighteenth Century*, ed. Dana Sajdi (London: I. B. Tauris, 2007), 1–39.

93 On public welfare and the modernization of policing during the Hamidian period see the work of Nadir Özbek: "'Beggars' and 'Vagrants' in Ottoman State Policy and Public Discourse, 1876–1914," *Middle Eastern Studies* 45.5 (2009): 783–801; "The Politics of Poor Relief in the Late Ottoman Empire," *New Perspectives on Turkey* 21 (1999): 1–33; and "Policing the Countryside: Gendarmes of the Late 19th-Century Ottoman Empire (1876–1908)," *International Journal of Middle East Studies* 40.1 (2008): 47–67. On Abdülhamid's reign and continuities with the Tanzimat era see Benjamin C. Fortna, "The Reign of Abdülhamid II," in *The Cambridge History of Turkey*, vol. IV: *Turkey in the Modern World*, ed. R. Kasaba (Cambridge University Press, 2008), 38–61, esp. 40. On Ottoman municipal reforms in relation to local pressures and global models see Nora Lafi, "Mediterranean Connections: The Circulation of Municipal Knowledge and Practices at the Time of the Ottoman Reforms, c. 1830–1910," in *Another Global City: Historical Explorations into the Transnational Municipal Moment, 1850–2000*, ed. Pierre-Yves Saunier and Shane Ewen (New York: Palgrave Macmillan, 2008), 135–50.

94 William L. Ochsenwald, "The Financing of the Hijaz Railroad," *Die Welt des Islams* 14.1/4 (1973): 129–49.

95 See Chapter 4 below on the Ottomans in relation to Hyderabadi Muslim internationalism.

apparatus keyed in on 'Pan-Islamism' by enacting a largely clandestine policy of containment and increased surveillance of Muslims on the move between colonial territories and the Ottoman world, among other places. Colonial anxieties centered in particular on Hajj pilgrim traffic from British India to the Ottoman-ruled Hijaz, which was regarded as a key circuit for the potential exchange of anti-colonial propaganda, and the fabrication of concrete schemes.[96] Colonial intelligence officials alternately exaggerated or downplayed the coherence and threat of global Muslim sentiment as a competitor to European imperialism throughout the nineteenth and early twentieth centuries.[97]

While the colonial perception of Muslim internationalism as an ideology of resistance was unstable, the enduring anxiety on the topic compelled the British to cultivate Muslim allies whenever possible. As such, imperial officials worked to maintain harmonious relations with Muslim subjects (in British India, the Dutch East Indies, and elsewhere) and sovereign Muslim-ruled states that were either formally autonomous (Qajar Iran, the Ottomans) or ambivalently tied into the web of empire (Hyderabad and other Muslim-ruled South Asian 'princely' states, Malay states, Northern Nigerian emirates, Gulf states, Egypt, Sudan). Colonial concerns peaked during the late Hamidan era, World War I, and the early Bolshevik period, when numerous schemes of collaboration between Ottomans, Germans, communists, and Muslim political activists in North and West Africa and South, Central, and Southeast Asia were the subject of close surveillance.[98] Even after the abolition of the Ottoman Caliphate in 1924, maneuvers to reinstate caliphal authority elsewhere, sometimes via Ottoman connections, continued to occupy Muslim political activists and concern colonial observers.[99]

The Ottomans played a crucial role in infusing longstanding ties between Muslims in different places with renewed political meaning in an era of European imperial dominance. The worldwide Muslim solidarity around the Caliphate that Ottoman officials sought to stimulate though propaganda was of limited effectiveness for the purposes of resuscitating "the sick man of Europe." The Ottomans and their advocates in other locations did, however, establish Istanbul as a key node within an

[96] Michael C. Low, "Empire and the Hajj: Pilgrims, Plagues, and Pan-Islam under British Surveillance, 1865–1908," *International Journal of Middle East Studies* 40.2 (2008): 269–90.

[97] John Ferris, "'The Internationalism of Islam': The British Perception of a Muslim Menace, 1840–1945," *Intelligence and National Security* 24.1 (2009): 57–77.

[98] Ibid.; Reynolds, "Good and Bad Muslims."

[99] See Chapter 4 below on Asaf Jah–Ottoman marriage ties and their political valences.

emergent Muslim public sphere composed of participants with diverse political aspirations. This network incorporated and accentuated existing loyalties, and expanded through colonial territories of almost every European empire, and into autonomous states in search of a global political community within which to contemplate political and institutional possibilities.

Muslim internationalism during the colonial period cannot be easily defined, nor can it be reduced to mere political advocacy of the Ottomans. For minor Muslim sovereigns such as the Asaf Jahs, however, the Muslim public sphere of the late nineteenth and early twentieth centuries provided several useful things: strategies for state legitimization, exemplary models of development, routes for intellectual exchange, and intimations of a global political geography not defined by European colonialism. These were key resources through which subordinated states in a world of fragmented sovereignty could negotiate their status and relationships. The international or trans-imperial dynamic of engagement is crucial for considerations here, since a persistent tendency to consider South Asian sub-imperial states merely in relation to British India has constrained much scholarship on the topic.[100] Muslim internationalist connections provided a key framework for reconceptualizing global political geography, and it was a crucial component of Hyderabad's claims to sovereignty. The role the state's Muslimness played in political thought there was in part framed by the particular configuration of religious community and politics of colonial South Asia.

## Muslimness as reason of state and sub-imperial sovereignty

Hyderabad's status as a Muslim state seeking to obtain membership in the international family of nations made Hyderabad a key node in networks of Muslim modernist intellectuals and activists. The global dimension of political thought in South Asia is a topic that has only rarely been taken up with respect to sub-imperial states, and Hyderabad underscores the importance of considering the international relevance of these polities.[101]

[100] See Chapter 3 on colonial and contemporary historiographies of South Asian sub-imperial states.

[101] The absence of scholarly work on transnational connections in sub-imperial states is indicated by the fact that the comprehensive survey of scholarship on 'princely states' only treats officials from British India when discussing 'foreign' employees: Ramusack, *Indian Princes*, 182–86. On the international dimension of the educational development in South Asian sub-imperial states see Datla, *The Language of Secular Islam* and Manu

As Ayesha Jalal has argued in work on Muslims in colonial South Asia, "religiously informed cultural difference" served as the key site of political engagement for Muslims.[102] The colonial state marked Muslims as a permanent minority, and in response Muslim political thinkers wielded religious difference to negotiate their status vis-à-vis the Raj and other communities. Because the colonial state parceled out concessions on the basis of social categories such as religion, Muslim status was politicized. Islam or Muslimness in the public sphere, then, had little to do with religion as faith, and served rather as a position from which to voice political demands. Muslimness became useful political currency in colonial South Asia, and functioned to back up demands for concessions in negotiations over the management of the colony or the configuration of the nation-state.

In Hyderabad, Muslimness served to secure the Nizam's position of autonomy and privilege certain networks of international intellectual collaboration that animated politics in the state. The Muslim character of the dynasty became a reason of state to justify Hyderabadi sovereignty and political modernization to colonial interlocutors and international observers. Further, other Muslim states such as the Ottoman Empire, Iran, and Egypt provided a community of fellow states in dialogue with which Hyderabad could define itself. As the ideological contours of the modern sub-imperial state were sketched out, Muslimness – if not Islam – was a key component that assured its place and linked it to other entities in the world of states.

## Envisioning modern sovereignty

Comparisons between 'minor' sovereign polities such as those presented above reveal related processes as well as long-distance intellectual and institutional connections between states and people. They provide a sense of political possibilities during the era of colonialism in which power was fragmented between multiple actors. Scanning the world's political geography during this period also shows that the fragmented character of political sovereignty within imperial spaces facilitated intellectual and institutional connections between minor states. Different vantage points

Bhagavan, *Sovereign Spheres: Princes, Education and Empire in Colonial India* (Delhi: Oxford University Press, 2003).

102 This paragraph summarizes some key arguments made in Ayesha Jalal, *Self and Sovereignty: Individual and Community in South Asian Islam since 1850* (London: Routledge, 2000), 100, *inter alia*.

within the global scene produced varied foundations for affinity and solidarities.[103]

From imperial state perspectives, the multiple modes of sovereign power in the colonial era at times not only appeared to be impediments to colonial consolidation but, more often, were cast as part of a global repertoire of imperial strategy. As Thomas Metcalf has demonstrated for the British Empire, and Mamdani has argued for colonizing powers in Africa, there was extensive exchange between administrators around indirect rule as a technique of imperial expansion.[104] In many of the instances considered above – uncolonized states subject to imperial pressure, sub-imperial polities in treaties with colonizing powers – minor states reinforced broader imperial dominance. As such, colonial empires used affirmation of sovereign powers by non-colonial political actors as a strategy for extending imperial economic networks and political spheres of influence. Moreover, imperial terrains integrating native sovereigns were less costly to administer, and insulated European officials from ethical critiques of empire in metropole and colony. As such, indirect rule, from the colonial perspective, could be a key modular strategy applicable and customizable in different local and regional contexts.

From the perspective of minor states within an imperialized world, formal political sovereignty enabled prestige, international status, and wealth. Crucially, non-colonial minor sovereignty also produced the impetus and capacity to develop state structures distinct from those in directly colonized places. This is the moment where the political history of fragmented sovereignty sketched here provides critical elucidation for the intellectual and institutional history. Minor states' political experimentation entailed engagement with local and regional concepts of legitimacy and state obligation, European ideas and examples of political development, and also, significantly, with other non-Western repertoires of modern state practice. Experimentation on the part of states, statelets, and other political actors amidst empires availed of and fostered the expansion of emerging counter-colonial – and at times anti-colonial – geographies of power. As Cemil Aydin has demonstrated, putatively anti-Western political visions such as Japanese Pan-Asianism and Ottoman 'Pan-Islam' emerged in the context of global European imperialism. These movements, while informed by the same "global constellation of

103 This account of perspectives borrows some ideas and structural elements from that in the section entitled "The effect of indirect rule on the principles" in Fisher, *Indirect Rule*, 7–18.

104 Metcalf, *Imperial Connections*; Mamdani, *Citizen and Subject*, 86–87.

ideas" in which European empires were situated, articulated competing visions of international politics.[105] It is no mistake that many key minor sovereigns and their administrative elites looked to these counter-colonial configurations for exemplary political ideas and institutional practices, and to advance their own agendas.

From the perspective of subject populations and potential administrators amidst these varied empires and states, levels of sovereignty below the imperial were significant since they provided opportunities for mobility of many kinds. Administrators and intellectuals – European, Asian, African – unable to find lucrative employment or moral peace in the context of racialized colonial domination, or seeking international experience, obtained postings or patronage in non-colonial places. Al-Afghani and Geddes, mentioned earlier in this chapter, provide examples. Minor states often employed intellectuals trained in languages or administrative methods phased out by colonial policies. Activists, such as al-Afghani and Chapekar, disseminating political ideas not permitted or supported under colonial regimes, could organize or seek shelter in places insulated from colonial surveillance by jurisdiction and sheer distance. Such figures were sometimes linked to state projects, or found social support to assist them in advancing agendas and avoiding incarceration. Peasants or groups whose livelihoods were under threat from colonial policies could flee across borders into non-colonial terrain, or play off the jurisdictional complexity of abutting states to continue their work.

The vantages considered above suggest a political geography of the era of high imperialism radically different from that which frames most current scholarship. Conventional chronologies of modern empire – in South Asia and globally – hold that, by the second half of the nineteenth century, older multiple and malleable configurations of sovereignty were thoroughly contained by a stable, overarching, and unitary colonial authority. Global empires, such as the British, were supple formations that integrated widely dispersed domains within a symbolic and institutional imperial framework. Scholars have articulately and extensively debated the conceptual and political 'shape' of empire.[106] However, as this work shows, other enduring and indelible sinews of solidarities and political imaginaries – such as Muslim internationalism and institutional and technocratic modernity – tied the nineteenth- and twentieth-century world

105 Aydin, *The Politics of Anti-Westernism*, 14.

106 On the British Empire see Metcalf, *Imperial Connections*; Tony Ballantyne, "Rereading the Archive and Opening up the Nation-State: Colonial Knowledge in South Asia (and Beyond)," in *After the Imperial Turn: Thinking with and through the Nation*, ed. Antoinette Burton (Durham, NC: Duke University Press, 2003), 102–21.

together and helped officials and intellectuals conceive political experiments. The conjuncture of global imperial pressure, new technologies for state development, and potential for participating in and articulating the terms of an emergent international order created a place in the world for minor states such as Hyderabad.

# 2 The legal framework of sovereignty

> Hyderabad was an independent state, waging war and entering into relations with other powers in India, including the French and the British, without reference to Delhi. When, for example, the Mogul Emperor did purpose to cede territory within the State to the British without the consent of the Nizam, the cession was contested by the Nizam, and the territory was recognized by the Treaty of Paris in 1783, as being under the Nizam's sovereignty.[1]

In 1951 Moin Nawaz Jung, Representative of Hyderabad to the United Nations, published a tract outlining and providing supporting documentation for Hyderabad's 1948 complaint to the UN Security Council. The appeal cast Hyderabad as a sovereign international political entity, and pleaded for a response from the global community of nations to India's invasion and integration of the Asaf Jah state into newly independent India. Nawaz Jung described the takeover as an act of aggression in violation of international law, and sought UN intervention. Notwithstanding the legal status of India's actions, the invasion and liquidation of the Nizam's state was a fait accompli by 1951. In practical terms, Moin Nawaz Jung's quixotic overtures document a lost cause, a failed claim to untenable sovereignty. The fact that officials of a defunct state had the imagination and diplomatic traction to petition the UN, however, underscores the indeterminacy and contingency that characterized the global state system during the period of decolonization. Hyderabad's ambivalent political status during the colonial period, as this chapter will argue, conditioned its continuing indeterminacy, and underscores the protean nature of the very concept of state sovereignty throughout the modern era.

Hyderabad's complaint, lodged in September 1948 and debated by UN delegates for the next several months, hinged on the question

[1] Hyderabad, Delegation to the United Nations, *The Hyderabad Question before the United Nations: Documents and Other Materials* (Karachi: Civil and Military Gazette, 1951), 13.

of whether the Nizam's polity was "a State in the international sense."[2] Domestic matters internal to existing, recognized nation-states were beyond the purview of UN consideration, so Hyderabad's 'stateness' was a critical consideration. Representatives from a variety of countries – India, Pakistan, Argentina, Syria, China, Colombia, Canada – commented on whether the matter should be placed on the agenda for UN Security Council consideration.[3] Hyderabad's advocates argued its claim's legitimacy from a number of tacks, ranging from comparisons to instances where other entities whose sovereign status was in question had appeared before the UN, to descriptions of how the Nizam's state met the UN's baseline requirements for statehood, to considerations of the major impact of this particular case on international peace.

Narrating the history of Hyderabadi statehood in the colonial era and earlier was a key component of arguments for the state's sovereignty in the middle of the twentieth century. As the epigraph above indicates, Moin Nawaz Jung traced Hyderabad's sovereignty from its early eighteenth-century independence from the Mughal Empire in Delhi through the political ascent of the British later that century.[4] As the British consolidated their South Asian empire during the late nineteenth century, they developed the doctrine of paramountcy to mark their supreme position above other political entities. Nawaz Jung described this expression of "the over-rising suzerainty of the Crown" as markedly ambivalent, having "never been precisely defined," and exaggerated in British accounts.[5] During the colonial era, he contended, Hyderabad's "international personality . . . although dormant, was not extinct and the original basis of its status was international in character."[6] In his estimation Hyderabad's subordination to Raj dominance did not undermine its sovereign claims, and decolonization should result in increased autonomy and independence. However unrealistic, Nawaz Jung's arguments highlight two key ideas that shaped Hyderabad's history in the period of colonial domination and afterwards. First, Hyderabad's sovereignty rested on sound legal foundations in the form of treaty relations with the British Crown. Second, Hyderabad, even while limited by British oversight, was an entity in the international community.

The legal structures and political dynamics that emerged during the period of British colonial dominance in South Asia provided the

[2] Indian UN Representative Sir Benegal Rau in May 1949, quoted in Clyde Eagleton, "The Case of Hyderabad before the Security Council," *American Journal of International Law* 44.2 (1950): 277–302, here 280.

[3] This book's Conclusion below returns to this debate on the status of Hyderabad after British India's decolonization.

[4] Hyderabad, Delegation, *Hyderabad Question*, 13. [5] Ibid., 14. [6] Ibid., 11.

conditions of possibility – and constraints – that framed Moin Nawaz Jung's advocacy of Hyderabad before the UN. This chapter provides a sketch of Hyderabad's emergence in legal terms as a 'minor state' and a player within the global framework of fragmented sovereignty described in the previous chapter. As such it outlines the formal international legal structure that conditioned Hyderabad's relationship to British India and the world. An ambivalent legal framework – parity and commensurability without equality – subordinated Hyderabad to British control while facilitating pretensions to membership in the emergent international community.

This chapter traces the making of Hyderabad's ambivalent legal position, first sketching the global scene in the era of modern empires, by which non-European polities were gradually marginalized within an emerging international legal order. Second, it locates South Asia in this picture, developing a rough chronology of legal sovereignty over the period of rising British colonial power, culminating in the late nineteenth-century articulation of the doctrine of British imperial suzerainty (or paramountcy) in relation to lesser sovereignties. Third, to complicate this account of the victorious career of British paramountcy, I zoom in to examine the legal framework of Hyderabad's sovereignty through close analysis of treaties governing Hyderabad–Britain relations. In these I highlight the enduring international character of this relationship, the ambivalence of colonial legal control, and the constructed nature of sovereignty as a contingent bundling and unbundling of different components.

## The making of the global state system and international law

Recent work on the formation of the modern global legal order, and the role and meaning of sovereignty therein, has emphasized the divergence between developments in Europe and elsewhere. Scholars have highlighted the systematic disempowerment of non-European states in an international order designed to bolster colonial and imperial domination. As such, it is possible to distinguish multiple histories of the practice of legal sovereignty. One of these, written from the perspective of Europe, defines sovereign states as unambiguously independent, equivalent entities that function in reciprocity with one another. A Eurocentric history of this kind would describe a continuous thread from the seventeenth-century Peace of Westphalia through contemporary international relations mediated by governance bodies such as the UN.[7] Another history of sovereignty, written from a postcolonial perspective, emphasizes the experience of colonization, imperialism, and continuing political and economic marginalization in much of the world, and historicizes the global state system and international law as vehicles for normalizing relations of political dominance.[8] This section considers the second of these histories of sovereignty, and the location of sub-imperial states (such as Hyderabad and the Indian 'princely' states) therein.

In his recent "alternative history of sovereignty" Antony Anghie argues that, outside Europe, international law never promoted a Westphalian equivalence between states, but represents an imperial project for codifying structural inequality in the legal domain.[9] During the era of modern imperialism European empires justified political dominance or takeover of ostensibly commensurable sovereign entities (often through violation of treaties) by deploying notions of civilizational difference. In describing sub-imperial states and protectorates, Anghie emphasizes the strategic function of legal fluidity and ambiguity: "Colonial jurists self-consciously grasped the usefulness of keeping sovereignty undefined in order that it could be extended or withdrawn according to the requirements of British interests."[10] For Anghie, sovereignty was a "flexible instrument" that empowered European empires to, by turns, assert formal control or expand informal economic or political influence.

Discussing the formation of the global state system, Edward Keene comes to conclusions compatible with Anghie's view of international law. He describes the predominant understanding of a system "of mutually independent states who recognize each other's territorial sovereignty" as a deceptive, conservative ideology designed to contain threats to the extant

7 Books considered in this section provide extensive descriptions and critiques of the 'Eurocentric' or 'orthodox' accounts of legal sovereignty, international law, or global governance bodies. See Antony Anghie, *Imperialism, Sovereignty and the Making of International Law* (Cambridge University Press, 2004), introduction; Edward Keene, *Beyond the Anarchical Society: Grotius, Colonialism and Order in World Politics* (Cambridge University Press, 2002), ch. 1; Mark Mazower, *No Enchanted Palace: The End of Empire and the Ideological Origins of the United Nations* (Princeton University Press, 2009), introduction.

8 In addition to the works considered below, for attempts to approach contemporary law from a postcolonial perspective, see Balakrishnan Rajagopal, *International Law from Below: Development, Social Movements, and Third World Resistance* (Cambridge University Press, 2003), and works by other scholars associated with the Third World Approaches to International Law (TWAIL) movement, *inter alia*, B. S. Chimni, "Third World Approaches to International Law: A Manifesto," *International Community Law Review* 8 (2006): 3–27.

9 Anghie, *Imperialism, Sovereignty*, quoted phrase from 310.

10 Ibid., 89.

European political system.[11] Further, he contends that the ostensibly global system of sovereign states only historically included Europe. It was paralleled by an imperial world order of European dominance legitimized by rhetoric of foundational civilizational inferiority and incapacity for good governance of non-European peoples.[12] In discussing British and Dutch treaties with South and Southeast Asian polities, Keene argues that "flexibility" in defining sovereignty empowered colonizers to intervene or seize power in certain domains or locations.[13] While he indicates the need to understand "international dimensions" of sub-imperial states (which he describes as "semi-sovereign"), the thrust of Keene's narrative is that sovereignty never actually meant equivalence and reciprocity for non-European states.

Other accounts of international legal history written from a postcolonial vantage point have emphasized how global institutions facilitated imperial expansion. C. H. Alexandrowicz's pathbreaking work described the shrinking of the domains of international law and the "Family of Nations" from the seventeenth to the nineteenth centuries, and the ousting of South Asian polities from the ostensibly universal world of states.[14] Martti Koskenniemi has argued for the Eurocentric character of international law, tracing post-1850 consolidation of imperial dominance through the colonization, exclusion from international legal jurisdiction, or unequal treatment of non-European states.[15]

The scholars discussed above have emphasized the subordination of most of the world to European empires by about 1900. Such interventions challenge accounts that present historical and contemporary international law as apolitical and founded on global equality rather than hierarchy. Even as revisionist histories lament the uneven legal terrain it veiled, these accounts confirm that modern European empires sustained the illusory notion of international law's universality and equality.

These histories also grapple with the fact that, along with numerous formal incorporations of heretofore sovereign territories into empire, many non-European states remained sovereign, at least in legal terms. Flexible definitions of sovereignty, as Anghie and Keene maintain, surely often facilitated European imperial marginalization (or conquest) of such states, and perhaps were structured to do so. But even if various non-European minor states were lesser entities in the international legal scene,

[11] Keene, *Beyond the Anarchical Society*, 13, 26.
[12] Ibid., 77–78, *inter alia*. [13] Ibid., 91.
[14] Alexandrowicz, *Law of Nations*; see also Charles Henry Alexandrowicz, *The European–African Confrontation: A Study in Treaty Making* (Leiden: Sijthoff, 1973).
[15] Martti Koskenniemi, *The Gentle Civilizer of Nations: The Rise and Fall of International Law, 1870–1960* (Cambridge University Press, 2002), ch. 2.

dominant states' need to maintain the language of commensurability created a productive ambivalence.

The potential implications of the tension between the view of modern political sovereignty as equivalence and the fact of unequal power are visible in Mark Mazower's work on the United Nations. Mazower demonstrates that the newly formed post-World War II global governance body was devised as an instrument for the preservation of empire. But, as an unintended consequence of global decolonization, colonial powers quickly became a minority in the UN. Spurred on by independent India's prime minister, Jawaharlal Nehru, the UN quickly became a venue for facilitating the dismantling of formal empires. Even if European powers sought to marginalize non-Western polities via international institutions and flexible definitions of sovereign powers, formal legal sovereignty allowed for mobilization through these channels.

In a fashion less dramatic than Mazower shows for the early UN, minor states during the era of modern imperialism were at times able to utilize the productive ambiguities of sovereignty in international law. In the South Asian context this ambivalence was a historical legacy of the braiding together of two languages of formal sovereignty.[16] The first was reciprocity between equivalent states; the second, political subordination along lines of racial or 'civilizational' difference. These languages of legal sovereignty were overlaid in the course of Britain's rise to political dominance from the late eighteenth century, and adjustment of colonial strategy from the mid-nineteenth.

## Periodizing sovereignty in British-dominated South Asia

Britain's extensive global empire was patched together through conquest and formalized through diplomatic transactions and legal declarations over five centuries. This era, roughly from the late sixteenth century through World War I, was also shaped by profound change in technologies of governance, economic production, and global political structures. As considered above, in the era of modern empires non-European states were subordinated in legal arrangements devised to structure and regulate sovereignty. Shifts in British colonial strategy and capacity over the long period of imperial formation had important implications regarding the nature and stability of state power. This section describes distinct eras

[16] On the enduring fact of residual and never abrogated sovereignty of South Asian sub-imperial states see Sudipta Sen, "Unfinished Conquest: Residual Sovereignty and the Legal Foundations of the British Empire in India," *Law, Culture and the Humanities* 9.2 (2013): 227–42.

of British imperialism in South Asia – from conquest, integration, and expansion to consolidation, pacification, and subordination – and the way these two phases shaped and were shaped by the sovereign claims and powers of minor states such as Hyderabad.

### *Conquest, integration, and expansion*

Founded in 1600, the English East India Company (EIC) cobbled together political sovereignty in the Indian Ocean region from a combination of English Crown charters and grants from Asian rulers.[17] Chartered by newly unified Britain, the eighteenth-century EIC expanded by asserting sovereignty over people, economic transactions, and coastal urban settlements rather than landed territory. Aggressive expansion into new markets entailed perpetual negotiation and alliances with political actors and financiers in South Asia. By the second decade of the eighteenth century Mughal authority was fragmenting – with regional governors breaking away from Delhi and new rulers asserting sovereign claims – and the South Asian political scene became increasingly decentralized. The protean character of state power and the fluid definition of sovereignty the EIC traded upon facilitated the rapid expansion of its political networks in this context.

Regionalization of power in the second quarter of the eighteenth century opened new vistas and possibilities for the expansion of British commerce and political influence.[18] By seizing control of territory – starting in the eastern Ganjetic plain in the 1750s and 1760s – the EIC inserted itself firmly into political networks. Access to land revenues allowed the EIC to expand its army. South Asian sovereigns, increasingly protective of their domains in a time of instability, turned to the EIC for military support against opponents or cash influxes to maintain the loyalty of their own troops. For its part, the EIC depended on constant cash infusions to secure its position in a political scene that it was beginning to dominate. Thus EIC military forces were forged into a machine for territorial conquest to take advantage of land revenue sources, and hem in or eliminate other expansive states.

Growing EIC power, and continuing aspirations and concerns of existing rulers, set the stage for a variety of treaty relations between the British and existing South Asian political actors. The British depended on allies

17 This paragraph summarizes Philip J. Stern, *The Company-State: Corporate Sovereignty and the Early Modern Foundations of the British Empire in India* (New York: Oxford University Press, 2011).

18 Bayly, *Indian Society*.

to assure success in conquests, and to secure peaceful and stable commercial and political frontiers. The legal language of treaties indicates voluntary agreements between states in a reciprocal relationship, as evidence from Hyderabad considered below shows.

As EIC territory and military might expanded over the second half of the eighteenth century, subcontinental politics remained unstable. The British grappled with frequent rebellions within and on the frontiers of EIC domains, and machinations of the French in the Deccan. Expanding South Asian powers, such as Mysore and various Maratha sovereigns, posed a threat to the ambitions of the British and their South Asian allies. By the last decade of the eighteenth century the British deployed a particularly effective diplomatic mode to turn the enduring instability to their benefit.

Subsidiary Alliance treaties were a legal mechanism by which the EIC deepened its influence and resource base in South Asia. They supplied guarantees of military support, including permanently stationed troops, to South Asian rulers.[19] In exchange, the British required periodic cash tributes, control over revenues of productive agricultural lands (usually amounting to cession of territories), and eventually diplomatic restrictions and political controls. Developed by the French in the 1740s based on South Asian governmental practice, the Subsidiary Alliance mechanism was used by the British as a diplomatic means for expanding their financial and territorial base across the subcontinent, and asserting their primacy and propriety as dominant military force in the region. Relying on a widespread system of alliances, often pitting South Asian states against one another – and against the competing French – the British eliminated threats to their power in the Deccan. Between the 1790s and 1810s the EIC and its allies defeated Mysore and various Maratha rulers, then incorporated some territories from these states, and brokered the rise to power of subordinate collaborators in the remainder.

The first half of the nineteenth century saw the widening of the British alliance system, continued renegotiation of treaties to limit military and diplomatic powers of South Asian rulers, and periodic spates of annexation or conquest for territorial expansion.[20] The EIC began to elaborate a doctrine of sovereignty founded on restriction of the powers of native rulers, and expectations of British non-intervention for those who obeyed the rules. While the dominance of the British Raj was increasingly clear, the legal language of reciprocity and equivalence continued to frame

[19] On Subsidiary Alliance Treaties see ibid., ch. 2, esp. 58; Ramusack, *Indian Princes*, 59–65.

[20] Ramusack, *Indian Princes*, ch. 3.

treaties and agreements. Annexations and conquests of rulers in treaty relations with the British (along with a host of other economic, political, social, and cultural factors) triggered a massive, inter-regionally coordinated, armed insurrection against colonial rule in 1857.

## *Consolidation, pacification, and subordination*

The 1857 uprising fixed the foundational instability of the South Asian empire into clear view, and subsequently the British reworked their political system to undermine opposition and assure continued dominance. Stabilizing the colonial state was a process. It entailed, first, violent and exemplary suppression and disenfranchisement of communities and leaders associated with anti-colonial resistance; second, Crown takeover of EIC sovereignty and restructuring of institutions from military to legal to fiscal to infrastructural; and, third, increasing focus on consolidating imperial power in formally colonized regions, while pacifying frontiers with other states via alliance and containment.

The process of imperial recalibration had profound implications for remaining South Asian rulers. The fluid meaning of sovereignty and loose relation to territoriality the EIC deployed had long corresponded poorly with the ambitions of the increasingly centralized British nation-state.[21] The post-1857 imperial makeover provided an opportunity for developing a consolidated imperial structure and hierarchy in which roles and obligations of different rulers in the region were clearly defined. Colonial centralization and securitization required pacification of potential competitors and frontiers. This was done through assuring sovereignty to South Asian rulers and attempting to yoke them in as subordinate collaborators in the imperial system. The third quarter of the nineteenth century thus saw a move to assure loyalty and formalize relations between the Raj and South Asian sovereigns.[22] After 1857 imperial boundaries were virtually frozen into place, with formal recognition of territorial claims for hundreds of non-European sovereigns across the subcontinent.

The stabilization of South Asia's political geography was a strategic compromise. It eschewed further expansion, but enabled the Raj to focus on internal stability within its domains and the pacification of remaining frontiers and borders. Guaranteeing the sovereignty of a vast number of South Asian rulers – now referred to, condescendingly, as 'princes' – was a move calculated to provide the British with ready justification for the imperial project and a circle of influential and highly visible South Asian

[21] Stern, *The Company-State*, 208. [22] Fisher, *Indirect Rule*.

collaborators. This system of 'indirect rule' represented a shift from earlier imperial liberal reformist frameworks to a new rhetoric wherein ruling through sovereigns and institutions that instantiated 'native' culture became a critical "alibi of empire."[23] This turn to a vision of a culturally sensitive, non-interventionist empire that "accommodated and contained" instead of attempting to reform depended upon an increasingly conciliatory relation to South Asian sovereigns.[24]

While the British legally guaranteed the sovereignty of non-European states across South Asia, they also attempted to subordinate these polities within the imperially dominated political system. The Raj, now directly under the British Crown, sought to exercise increased informal influence, often through colonial political officers known as Residents.[25] Scholars of political relations between the Raj and sub-imperial sovereigns during the late colonial period have emphasized the enduring fluidity of the scenario after 1857.[26] British Indian moves to dictate terms to now-stabilized sub-imperial states were consistently opposed in those states, and Raj officials were compelled to back off by Crown officials increasingly anxious about imperial stability. If clearly subordinate to the British, as spelled out within the doctrine of imperial 'suzerainty' or 'paramountcy,' sub-imperial sovereigns periodically managed to expand their powers between the late nineteenth century and the end of empire.

In legal terms, Raj relationships with sub-imperial states continued to be expressed in a language of reciprocity that had framed earlier treaties. The complex articulation between British imperial suzerainty and other sovereignties remained productively ambiguous.[27] Though its dominance across the subcontinent was clear, Raj attempts to expand influence in the states were restricted by broader British imperial and domestic concerns. The language of commensurability between states enshrined in foundational legal documents sheltered sub-imperial sovereignty even as Raj officials sought to exert political pressure. The late-period Raj, in a mode of political consolidation, endeavored to subordinate sub-imperial South Asian sovereigns by overwriting a legal framework devised

23 Mantena, *Alibis of Empire*. Mantena's book discusses 'indirect rule' exclusively in the context of colonial governance through ostensibly 'native' institutions (caste, religious community, land revenue systems) in 'directly ruled,' hence British Indian, territories. Her work does not address state spaces of formal non-European sovereignty, such as Hyderabad or other sub-imperial states.

24 Ibid., 12, 52.

25 Bayly, *Indian Society*, 197.

26 Ramusack, *Indian Princes*; Fisher, *Indirect Rule*.

27 Keene, *Beyond the Anarchical Society*; Anghie, *Imperialism, Sovereignty*; Jane Burbank and Frederick Cooper, *Empires in World History: Power and the Politics of Difference* (Princeton University Press, 2010), 306.

in a less secure era of colonial alliance and expansion. The interbraiding of languages of legal sovereignty – reciprocity and subordination – are visible in diplomatic treaties and enactments between the Raj and Hyderabad.

## Sub-imperial sovereignty in Hyderabad

Early treaties between the East Indian Company state and Hyderabad dating to the mid-eighteenth century suggest negotiation on the basis of equivalence between the two states. British officials during this period functioned from an expansive and inclusive understanding of membership in the "family of nations."[28] In keeping with global trends that Alexandrowicz has traced, the British began attempts to restrict the powers of non-European states such as Hyderabad during the eighteenth century, in an era when state sovereignty as such was still in the process of being defined. Hyderabad retained, and fortified, its status as a state and certain sovereign powers through the mid-twentieth century in the context of the emergence and consolidation of a global regime of international law.

Classic studies on Hyderabad's relationship with the British center on political relations, and in emphasizing rising British dominance tend to treat sovereignty as an absolute quantity. In these accounts Raj power either forced the Nizam's hand, and eroded state sovereignty there, or Hyderabad managed to push the British into a policy of non-interference.[29] Treaties and negotiations between Nizam and Raj over the state's legal status, however, suggest shifting hierarchical relations in the political domain, but persistence of the language of reciprocity in the legal sphere.

[28] See Alexandrowicz, *Law of Nations*, on the "family of nations." For treaties I draw from several editions of the multi-volume compilations periodically produced by the British Government in India. The first edition, C. U. Aitchison, *A Collection of Treaties, Engagements, and Sunnuds, Relating to India and Neighbouring Countries*, 8 vols. (Calcutta: J. L. Kingham, Foreign Dept. Press, 1862–66), includes vol. V, *The treaties, &c., relating to Hyderabad, Mysore, Coorg, the Madras presidency, and Ceylon* (1864). Subsequent revised editions, all published in Calcutta, are attributed to India, Foreign and Political Department, C. U. Aitchison, and A. C. Talbot. The title remains the same, though the spelling of 'sunnud' is modernized to 'sanad' for the third edition. The volumes cited here – 1876 (2nd edn., vol. V), 1892 (3rd edn., vol. VII), 1909 (4th edn., vol. IX), and 1929–33 (5th edn., vol. IX [1929]) – will be referenced as *Treaties*, with the year of the relevant edition or volume provided.

[29] Sarojini Regani, *Nizam–British Relations: 1724–1857* (New Delhi: Concept, 1963); Nani Gopal Chaudhuri, *British Relations with Hyderabad, 1798–1843* (University of Calcutta Press, 1964); Bharati Ray, *Hyderabad and British Paramountcy, 1858–1883* (Delhi: Oxford University Press, 1988).

Raj–Nizam treaties over the second half of the eighteenth century demonstrate a gradual formulation of the terms of the relationship between the two states, in a context of intra-European imperial rivalries. The earliest treaties, beginning in 1759, were produced during moments of British instability, particularly in the Deccan, in the era of colonial expansion. Hyderabad, for its part, was immersed in political and financial crises, facing frequent internal uprisings, challenges from other Deccan powers, and the threat of British takeover. The earliest Raj–Nizam treaty reflects British military ascendancy. The document gave the EIC control over the coastal areas around Masulipatnam as *inam*, defined as "free gift." It also explicitly banished from Hyderabad territory soldiers from France, a state that was clinging to a foothold in India via Hyderabad ties. Both Raj and Nizam agreed to neither assist nor protect their counterparts' enemies.[30] This initial treaty demonstrates two enduring features of Raj–Nizam relations: first, the language of reciprocity and free choice; and second, British attempts to restrict alliances, and thus Hyderabad's international status.

Subsequent treaties, such as British attempts to certify their hold on territories known as the Northern Circars (or Sarkars), repeated similar elements, with previously French territories granted by Hyderabad to the British as "free gift."[31] Between two enactments in 1765 and 1766, however, negotiation is visible. The British initially relied on the Mughals, under whom the initial Nizam had been a regional governor, to decertify Hyderabad's grant of the territories to the French. The second treaty – of "honor, alliance and friendship . . . and mutual assistance" – recognized Hyderabad's sovereignty as independent from the Mughals, reserved some lands and features (a fort and diamond mines) to Hyderabad, and guaranteed permanent stationing of British troops, ostensibly for Hyderabad's security. The shifting political balance and negotiation of terms characterizes an era of widespread insecurity, with numerous South Asian competitors for power in the Deccan, and both Raj and Nizam eager to secure territories and revenue streams.

Later eighteenth-century Raj–Nizam treaties continued to work from a framework of military alliance, and indicate mutual dependence between the two states, as well as shared land acquisitions from joint conquests. Treaties accompanied successive British campaigns against Mysore (1790, 1799) and Maratha rulers in the Deccan, Central India, and in regions on the east and west coasts of the subcontinent (1804, 1818,

30 Until otherwise noted, treaty information is taken from *Treaties* 1864.

31 These territories later comprised coastal regions of Madras presidency, and now constitute portions of the Indian provincial states of Andhra Pradesh and Odisha.

1822). In several instances the British developed three-way pacts including various Maratha allies, signing separate treaties exclusively with each party to hedge bets in case alliances broke down (1790, 1799, 1800). Even as the EIC at times claimed territories from Hyderabad to compensate for its military support (1768, 1789, 1800), the Nizam often shared in the territorial spoils of conquest (1799, 1804, 1802). By the turn of the century the EIC began to expand its position as the dominant military force in the subcontinent, a trend visible in the 1798 Subsidiary Alliance treaty.

Treaties around the turn of the eighteenth century suggest stabilization of Hyderabadi sovereignty around control over state subjects and lands, along with British imposition of economic and diplomatic restrictions. A 1779 agreement guaranteed jurisdiction for the Nizam over his own subjects even in conflicts with EIC military forces. In exchange, the British asserted jurisdiction over EIC troops and officers there, and required expulsion of the remaining French troops in Hyderabad. Later treaties (1803, 1831) guaranteed diplomatic relations and British recognition of Hyderabad "until the end of time."[32] The extensive commercial treaty (1802) agreed between the states advanced EIC economic hegemony. It was cast in the language of peer states and granted Hyderabad "most favoured nation" status and free use of British port facilities at Masulipatnam. However, it also bound Hyderabad to EIC trade regulations and limited duties on imports into Hyderabad, producing a favorable – and captive – market for British Indian export commodities.

Also visible in treaties from this period are British restrictions of Hyderabadi power, and colonial land grabs for non-payment of tribute. A 1789 letter from the Governor-General (certified in the House of Commons as legally binding in 1792) upheld the Nizam's right to diplomatic exchanges with other Deccan powers, but forbade him from entering into treaties independent of British intermediation.[33] The EIC continued to assert control over Hyderabad's employment of Europeans in official capacities (1798). Hyderabad obtained lands upon the fall of some Maratha states and Mysore, but many of these territories were 'assigned' to the British under the auspices of the renewal and reorganization of the subsidiary military force agreement in 1853. Herein the EIC, during an era of colonial expansiveness, increased the number of regiments to be stationed in Hyderabad and asserted control over extensive territories constituting the northwestern, western, and southwestern boundaries of the state. British land grabs from Hyderabad included the 1853 seizure of the lucrative

[32] Phrase quoted from 1803 treaty.

[33] A subsequent 1798 treaty, however, required both Nizam and Raj to approve any diplomatic exchanges for either state with the Maratha Peshwa.

cotton-growing region of Berar, which the Nizam had claimed in 1803 after the fall of a Maratha ruler.[34]

Hyderabad supported the British during the conflicts of 1857, putting down local insurrections and serving as a buffer zone between sites of insurgency in other corners of the subcontinent. Accordingly, Asaf Jahi sovereignty was guaranteed anew by the British in 1860, with the south-western region of Raichur, which the British had appropriated in 1853, being returned to the Nizam as a 'reward' for loyalty. In a move designed to allay fears of colonial seizure of states owing to lapse of succession – a frequent alibi for colonial expansion in the 1840s and 1850s – the Raj granted permission to sub-imperial sovereigns to adopt heirs to state thrones (1862).

The period from 1860 through the end of empire saw a change in tenor of legal agreements between Raj and Nizam. This was in accordance with the renewed British focus on stabilizing their empire in regions under formal colonial rule through solidifying alliances with South Asian rulers. Formalizing sovereignty for these figures facilitated cooperation in pacification of borders and expanding regional infrastructures for both economic and security purposes.

Several of the treaties of this period involved apportioning out legal powers, such as the 1861 grant of jurisdiction over Europeans and foreigners in Hyderabad to the British Resident.[35] Still others (1867, 1887, 1910) fixed or adjusted procedures for extradition between Hyderabad and British India.[36] While these enactments guaranteed "strict reciprocity" (1867), they fitted neatly into Raj policies of the era to contain alleged rampant criminality in the frontier zones between colonial and sub-imperial territories.[37] Also suggestive of concerns regarding economies that were being criminalized in British India was the 1883 prohibition of the cultivation of poppy and manufacture of opium in Hyderabad (in exchange for guaranteed colonial supply to Hyderabad officials for "licit home consumption"). Restrictions from 1875 on the transit of another key excisable commodity, salt, further indicate colonial attempts to control commercial flows between Hyderabad and surrounding colonial territory.

34 The sovereign status of Berar remained a bone of contention between Nizam and Raj until decolonization and the integration of Hyderabad into the Republic of India in 1947–48. See Vasant K. Bawa, *The Nizam between Mughals and British: Hyderabad under Salar Jang I* (New Delhi: S. Chand, 1986), ch. 5.

35 Though never formally rescinded by legal treaty, these jurisdictional claims, at least in the capital city, seem to have been short-lived, as shown in Chapter 7 below.

36 On these agreements see *Treaties* 1876, 1892, 1929.

37 *Treaties* 1876 on Extradition. See Chapters 5 and 6 below on criminal law in Nizam–Raj frontier zones.

Beyond enactments related to implicit legal or security questions, a number of post-1857 treaties related to increasing governmental efficiency for both Hyderabad and British India, and to expanding the network of infrastructures connecting the regions. Treaties in these categories seem to have been of mutual benefit to the two polities. In many places the Hyderabad–British borders were irregular and punctuated with isolated enclaves, and pacts for exchange of villages (1871, 1872) represent attempts to 'rationalize' borders.[38] Agreements regarding railway or light rail developments (1883, 1885, 1897, 1909, 1910), or postal and telegraph connections (1882, 1897) linked the Nizam's territories into subcontinental circuits. These developments suited British concerns to extend infrastructures for circulation of commodities, troops, and intelligence. Hyderabad, focused increasingly from the 1870s on industrial development and economic expansion, stood to benefit from access to imported materials and outlets for manufactures to the British Indian market.[39]

Treaties between British India and Hyderabad during the era of Crown Raj do not reveal an active colonial attempt to subordinate the Nizam's state. In political terms, the decades around 1900 saw unprecedented stability and dominance for the British Empire. In legal relations with Hyderabad, however, the Raj continued to deploy the language of reciprocal relations between two commensurable states. Indeed, the 1928–29 *Report of the Indian States Committee* (*RISC*) – regarded as a key instantiation of the doctrine of British paramountcy, upholding Raj suzerainty over and above minor sovereigns such as Hyderabad – does little more than reiterate the restrictions of power noted above (diplomatic relations, military defense).[40] Moreover, articulations of paramountcy, such as the *RISC*, have been widely described by scholars and South Asian political agents alike as imprecise accounts of actual powers, or exaggerations of overriding colonial power.[41] Over the dynamic career of Britain's empire in South Asia and beyond, legal relations with sub-imperial sovereigns provided a relatively stable framework, even as political relations shifted to and fro.

38 *Treaties* 1876. 39 See Chapter 7 below on industrial development.

40 Great Britain, Indian States Committee, and Harcourt Butler, *Report of the Indian States Committee, 1928–1929* (London: His Majesty's Stationery Office, 1929).

41 On imprecision of the paramountcy doctrine see Anghie, *Imperialism, Sovereignty*; Burbank and Cooper, *Empires*; Keene, *Beyond the Anarchical Society*. For a critique of the *RISC* position see Hyderabad Delegation, *Hyderabad Question*, 14. For an earlier instance in which the meaning of suzerainty was contested see the account of Hyderabad *divan* Salar Jang I's protest at Queen Victoria's 1877 coronation as Empress of India: Bawa, *Nizam between Mughals and British*, 186–90.

## Ambivalent stateness

Treaty relations between Hyderabad and Britain established an enduring legal foundation of equivalent sovereignty between the two state entities. As it expanded its South Asian empire the Raj outright conquered or otherwise violated standing treaties on various pretexts (lapse of line of rulership, misgovernment, unpaid debts). Eighteenth-century colonial conquests required firm alliances with South Asian states such as Hyderabad, but by the early nineteenth century the Raj increasingly attempted to subordinate these states through restricting their diplomatic and military powers. This did not entail a fundamental shift from the legal language of commensurate sovereignties, as treaties invariably began by recognizing existing agreements. By the mid-nineteenth century, following the 1857 challenge to colonial power, Britain renounced additional formal political expansion within South Asia, and fortified the sovereignty of sub-imperial states. After 1860 the Raj began asserting its suzerainty or paramountcy in relation to South Asian rulers, but in ambivalent terms. This facilitated, at times, exercise of imperial pressure on minor states to do the Crown's bidding in matters related to imperial security, economic stability, or infrastructure development. However, the ambivalent terms of the sovereign–suzerain relationship could also be productive for sub-imperial states seeking to expand their powers within South Asia, or even internationally.

This chapter has historicized and described the framework that produced Hyderabad's sub-imperial sovereignty in relation to British imperial power. Colonialist legal thinkers, such as John Westlake, attempted in the early twentieth century to portray claims to sovereignty such as Hyderabad's as empty rhetorical flourishes in an empire exercising thoroughgoing legal power across the entire subcontinent.[42] As considered above, scholars of international law and the state system such as Anghie and Keene have seen the ambivalence of sub-imperial sovereignty as a strategy for British coercion of lesser states. Likewise, Lauren Benton, discussing the positions of Westlake and others and the politics framing legal authority, has emphasized the "quasi-sovereign" nature of states such as Hyderabad. The political landscape she describes is thoroughly defined by imperial power, even if her nuanced account depicts empire as more uneven than historians or legal scholars have tended to recognize.[43] The picture from Hyderabad suggests that the persistence of sovereignty there produced a legal terrain that was not quite part of imperial space. Law was increasingly important in British rhetorics of empire starting in

[42] Benton, *A Search for Sovereignty*, 239–41. [43] Ibid.

the eighteenth century, and shortly afterwards international law was to emerge as a key global institutional framework for structuring relations between states.

If a political history of empire reveals sub-imperial sovereignty as partial and limited (as indexed by prefixes such as 'semi' and 'quasi,' or modifiers such as 'dependent' or 'delegated'), a legal history, such as above, suggests a consistency in the language of commensurability and equivalence.[44] The productive ambivalence of the actual terms of legal relations facilitated sub-imperial mobilization and negotiation about, and experimentation with, state sovereignty. The marked thinness of the doctrine of suzerainty failed to contain and render inert Hyderabad's sovereign status. And the endurance of legal stateness provided a lexicon within which sub-imperial states could attempt to defend their interests internationally, even, as in Hyderabad's UN case, after they ceased to exist as territorial entities.[45] As subsequent chapters will show, Asaf Jah officials made use of Hyderabad's ambivalent status, undertaking informal international diplomacy and projecting Hyderabad's comparability with other states in the world (Chapters 3 and 4); defending their prerogatives to jurisdiction over state subjects, and control over extradition arrangements or frontier policing (Chapters 5 and 6); and asserting autonomy in urban governance and economic development in the capital city (Chapters 7 and 8). Thomas Metcalf has emphasized the centrality of sovereignty as such, even if subordinated in some respects, on the part of sub-imperial rulers in defining their relations to the British.[46] D. A. Low has argued that British colonial rhetoric stressed "the legal basis of authority at the expense of its political basis."[47] The legal basis, and the fact of stateness, was a fount of productive ambivalence – forged from sub-imperial sovereignty's divergent meanings, and the persistence of commensurability between states in legal language – that facilitated non-colonial statecraft in and for Hyderabad State.

44 For a parallel argument about the analytical importance of taking EIC sovereignty seriously rather than falling back on suffixes or modifiers of this kind to depict the Company as merely "state-like," see Stern, *Company-State*.

45 Hyderabad Delegation, *Hyderabad Question*.

46 Assessing the position in Dirks, *Hollow Crown*, on the illusory status of sub-imperial sovereignty, Metcalf contends: "The British had hollowed out the crown of princely sovereignty. But that the crown was hollow mattered less than that it existed" (Thomas R. Metcalf, *Ideologies of the Raj* [Cambridge University Press, 1994], 199).

47 Low, *Lion Rampant*, 18.

*Part I*

# Ideas

# 3 A passage to another India: Hyderabad's discursive universe

"I have decided to have nothing more to do with British India, as a matter of fact. I shall seek service in some Moslem State, such as Hyderabad, Bhopal, where Englishmen cannot insult me any more." – Dr. Aziz[1]

"The Muslims" come to appear as group with a paradoxical social existence – on the one hand as local and particularistic, caught in a time warp outside the temporalities of the modern world, and, on the other, formed by loyalties and affiliations that violate and exceed the territorial structure of the (colonial) state.[2]

Hyderabad is the last ray of the sun of Delhi . . . The flame of the Mughal State was extinguished in Delhi, but illuminated Hyderabad.[3]

This chapter considers Hyderabad State's place in the world of modern South Asian political ideas. The two previous chapters situated Hyderabad within global political and legal configurations of the nineteenth and twentieth centuries. This one shifts to locate the state within moral and conceptual geographies articulated by intellectuals associated with Hyderabad State and British colonialists in historical narratives and other genres of representation. These imagined geographies intersected with and at times drew extensively from colonial discourse as a literary and political formation, as well as from South Asian nationalist rhetoric of different kinds (pan-subcontinental visions, regional 'patriotism' or 'subnationalism,' linguistic or religious community solidarities). However, ideas of Hyderabad are not contained by or explicable with exclusive reference to the reified scholarly understandings of South Asian colonial or nationalist thought. I argue that writings and representations of Hyderabad, its ruling dynasty, and past history produced a particular *discursive*

[1] E. M. Forster, *A Passage to India* (San Diego: Harcourt Brace Jovanovich, 1954 [1924]), 280.
[2] Mufti, *Enlightenment in the Colony*, 93.
[3] Mirzā Ẓafarulḥasan, "Tamhīd" (Preface), in Sibṭ-i Ḥasan, *Shahr-i nigārān* (Karachi: Dāniyāl, 1984 [1966]), 7–8.

*universe* for the sub-imperial state.[4] Henry Louis Gates elaborated the concept of the "discursive universe" to describe the "parallel" or "perpendicular" domain occupied by African-American literature in relation to a dominant conceptual field, the "larger white discursive universe."[5] The black literatures Gates described staked their claims in vernacularity. Hyderabad's discursive universe was similarly perpendicular to, and partly embedded in, a larger dominant field: British Indian colonial discourse. In addition to particularity and locality, Hyderabad's discursive universe embraced transregional non-colonial circuits. As a dynamic concept, it authorized and provided a context for the political engagements, experiments, and alternative social worlds Hyderabad produced and contained.

Hyderabad's discursive universe had several defining characteristics. It relied on the notion that the Asaf Jahi domains occupied a temporality of its own, and as such was distinct from colonially ruled British India in conceptual, moral, and political terms. One of the key impediments for thinking about Hyderabad, or other sub-imperial states, as discrete spaces in modern South Asia is the existing historiography of 'princely states.' Accordingly, the first section of the chapter unpacks recent scholarship on sub-imperial South Asian states, which cast polities such as Hyderabad within a unitary history of a thoroughly colonized subcontinent, or in terms of colonial and nationalist categories ('traditional,' 'progressive') with moral and teleological implications. As such, the existing historiography of sub-imperial states integrates them into dominant narratives, and obfuscates dynamic internal developments and engagements with transnational flows. The chapter then turns to historicize and describe Hyderabad's distinct discursive universe. In doing so it details the *acolonial temporality* ascribed to Hyderabad in historiography and other representations, such as E. M. Forster's iconic British Indian novel. Writings on Hyderabad centered on the Muslim character of historical and contemporary political authority in the state and region, and deployed this association to a variety of ends. While Hyderabad's Muslimness served for some colonial authors to undermine its legitimacy, it also facilitated the narration of exceptional, exemplary benevolent Muslim governance by advocates of the state.[6] Subsequent sections trace moral valuations

[4] On colonial South Asia as discursive space see the concepts "late imperial culture" in Mufti, *Enlightenment in the Colony*, ch. 2; and "English India" in Sara Suleri, *The Rhetoric of English India* (University of Chicago Press, 1992).

[5] Henry Louis Gates, *The Signifying Monkey: A Theory of Afro-American Literary Criticism* (New York: Oxford University Press, 1988), xxii, 49.

[6] Chapter 4 considers ways in which Hyderabad's Muslimness fostered extra-territorial Muslim solidarities.

and political implications attributed to Hyderabad's acolonial temporality. First, in colonial historiography, which follows the post-1857 shift from an expanding conquest state, in which polities such as Hyderabad were derided as potential targets for colonial 'civilizing,' to a consolidating and pacifying empire that lauded sub-imperial states as critical allies or venues where functioning alternatives to colonial rule could be examined. And second, in histories written by Hyderabadi intellectuals or supporters. These accounts cast Hyderabad as measuring up to British India in terms of colonial rubrics ('good governance,' institutional 'modernization'), but also emphasized legacies of regional political legitimacy. In concluding, I consider how these narratives of historical and contemporary ethical Muslim rule in Hyderabad incorporated openings to global frameworks of Muslim political solidarity in the late imperial world.

## Situating sub-imperial states: beyond colonial and nationalist frames

The discursive universe of Hyderabad existed in relation to, but was not contained by, the field of British Indian colonial discourse. Scholarship on 'princely' states, often uncritically replicating colonial rhetoric, has tended to characterize sub-imperial polities as either 'progressive' (such as Baroda, Mysore, and Travancore) or 'traditional' states. The latter category, a euphemism for autocratic governance and lack of social or political development, implicitly encompassed all states not specifically marked as 'progressive.' Representations of Hyderabad's temporal dislocation had important stakes in shaping the conceptual universe of the state, and enabled the articulation of histories distinct from larger colonial or nationalist narratives. Disaggregating these accounts from totalizing colonial or national historiographies requires a consideration of how scholarship has submerged sub-imperial historical difference.

Standard works have presented sub-imperial polities as client states of the Raj with merely nominal sovereignty. Writing on the Residency system under Company Raj, Michael Fisher argued that British political officers in sub-imperial states, known as Residents, were imperial levers of varying effectiveness for manipulating rulers.[7] Fisher emphasized the nominal character of native sovereignty in the context of what he, using a colonial designation, termed "indirect rule." Leaving power in the hands of native sovereigns was a means for the Raj to minimize imperial expenditures, and to fabricate a public image in Britain and the empire of congenial relations with indigenous authorities. Fisher concluded by

[7] Fisher, *Indirect Rule*.

suggesting that after the post-1858 transition to Crown rule, indirect rule was refined as an imperial technique for asserting de facto power while withholding practical sovereignty, and became a modular form deployed across colonial empires.[8]

Nicholas Dirks's work on social and political relations in the South Indian state of Pudukkottai conveyed a picture of 'princes' as wielders of illusory, theatrical power that complements Fisher's account.[9] Pre-modern kingship, Dirks argued, was enacted as a political process through ritual forms structured by caste relations. In the nineteenth century, however, royal authority was stripped of political efficaciousness and severed from the public sphere by an ostensibly secular colonial civil society. In Dirks's view the 'native prince' in colonial South Asia was a shadow of his former self, an absurd figure performing the old regime's political rituals, but bereft of real power.

Critiques of arguments about the illusory nature of sub-imperial sovereignty, and particularly Dirks's position, have come in subsequent scholarship focused on particular states or regional groupings of small sub-imperial states.[10] Mridu Rai's book on the state of Kashmir and Jammu directly contested Dirks's claim that sub-imperial rulers were disempowered.[11] While allied to the imperial British, they also commanded immense authority when it came to governing their subjects, and in the high politics of colonialism.[12] In Kashmir, Rai argues, the Dogra Maharajas fashioned themselves as autocrats with powers undersigned by the Raj, who in turn were little concerned about governance within states. This enabled an ensemble of despotic state initiatives, such as the dissolution of the landholding structure through confiscation of granted parcels long held by Muslims, and the ramping up of tax demands on the peasantry.[13] Later the Dogra leadership placed increasing emphasis on their Rajput pedigree, and fashioned Kashmir into a 'Hindu state,' marginalizing the predominant Muslim population there.[14] Despite the emergence, under colonial pressure, of a discourse of rights, the

8 Ibid., ch. 10. 9 Dirks, *Hollow Crown*.

10 Mridu Rai, *Hindu Rulers, Muslim Subjects: Islam, Rights, and the History of Kashmir* (Princeton University Press, 2004); Bhagavan, *Sovereign Spheres*. See also Hira Singh, *Colonial Hegemony and Popular Resistance: Princes, Peasants, and Paramount Power* (New Delhi: Sage, 1998); John McLeod, *Sovereignty, Power, Control: Politics in the States of Western India, 1916–1947* (Leiden: Brill, 1999).

11 Rai, *Hindu Rulers*.

12 On the role of the princes in the high politics of decolonization see Barbara Ramusack, *The Princes of India in the Twilight of Empire: Dissolution of a Patron–Client system, 1914–1939* (Columbus: Ohio State University Press, 1978); Ian Copland, *The Princes of India in the Endgame of Empire, 1917–1947* (Cambridge University Press, 1997).

13 Rai, *Hindu Rulers*, ch. 1. 14 Ibid., ch. 2.

Maharajas' heavy-handedness toward the Muslim masses continued through the state's integration into Hindu-majority and intensively centralized postcolonial India.[15] Contrary to Fisher and Dirks, then, Rai suggested that in Kashmir colonial acquiescence facilitated autocratic rule.

While Rai argued that sub-imperial autonomy sheltered despotism, comparative work on the states of Mysore and Baroda by Manu Bhagavan held that autonomy led to progressive developments in the field of education.[16] Describing them as "non colonial," Bhagavan took these developments to represent resistance to colonialist ideologies or projects via hybridization of colonial imperatives (modern education) with native interests and ideologies. As such, the author presented these 'progressive state' histories as lesser-known chapters in the history of Indian nationalism.

Along with other contemporaneous scholarship on South Asian 'princely' states, these works represent important contributions to scholarly understandings of the subcontinent during an era of colonial dominance. Fisher developed a nuanced framework for understanding British power in what had been uncritically regarded as isolated places of native authority. Dirks extended this perspective into the domain of the everyday reproduction of power, arguing that boundaries between 'princely' and British India were highly permeable in the context of the colonial makeover of the subcontinent.[17] Rai's work, contrarily, contended that rulers' positions as collaborators allowed them to exercise control over internal developments, producing a political terrain distinct from British India. Bhagavan suggested that states could be venues for challenging and modifying projects central to colonial rule, which anticipated the nationalist remaking of institutions.

All of these works, however, cast sub-imperial states firmly within the problematic of colonialism (as false sovereigns under de facto colonial control, or collaborating client states) or nationalism (as autocrats

[15] Ibid., chs. 3–5. For an account of sub-imperial Kashmir that situates the state firmly within late colonial politics and describes Dogra state-building as a far more ambivalent enterprise than Rai does, see Chitralekha Zutshi, *Languages of Belonging: Islam, Regional Identity and the Making of Kashmir* (New York: Oxford University Press, 2004).

[16] Bhagavan, *Sovereign Spheres*.

[17] It is notable that both of these scholars were students of Bernard Cohn, who wrote early in his career about the sovereign authority of "little kingdoms" in the eighteenth century, but shifted in later years to emphasize the penetration of colonialism into all areas of South Asian social, cultural, and political life during the nineteenth century. For examples of his earlier and later work, respectively, see Bernard S. Cohn, *An Anthropologist among the Historians and Other Essays* (Delhi: Oxford University Press, 1987), and *Colonialism and its Forms of Knowledge: The British in India* (Princeton University Press, 1996).

whose modes of rule needed phasing out, or precursors of postcolonial nationalist institutional projects). Polities appear as part of functionally homogeneous terrains of colonial power and knowledge, or of nationalist state-making. Sub-imperial states are thus assimilated into either broader narratives of colonial historiography, in which claims to sovereignty are of little significance either empirically or analytically, or unitary nationalist teleologies.[18] Further, scholars who recognize some degree of sub-imperial autonomy within the broader framework of British India, such as Rai and Bhagavan, implicitly reproduce colonial distinctions between 'traditional' (autocratic, despotic, 'backward') and 'progressive' (modern, democratic) states.[19] The arguments below demonstrate that a critical component of Hyderabadi historiography was simultaneous emphasis on pre-modern political legacies of the state (especially underscoring Muslim histories and connections) and consciously modern and putatively 'progressive' state development. To situate the conditions of possibility for this historiography, it is first necessary to consider how Hyderabad occupied a discursive universe contiguous with, but distinct from, that of British India.

### An acolonial temporality

Key threads within British Indian thought sketch a conceptual space of sub-imperial alterity distinct from that proper to colonized places. Early colonial rhetoric about 'native states' tended to be derogatory in character, and served to authorize colonial conquest and expansion through the mid-nineteenth century. However, these visions of difference also lent themselves to reversal and inversion of the implicit moral geographies that colonial reformists and Hyderabadi intellectuals articulated. The idea of Asaf Jahi alterity was founded on the notion that the state, like other

[18] See, for example, Aya Ikegame and Andrea Major, eds., "Princely Spaces and Domestic Voices: New Perspectives on the Indian Princely States," *Indian Economic and Social History Review*, special issue, 46.3 (2009), and Waltraud Ernst and Bishwamoy Pati, eds., *India's Princely States: People, Princes and Colonialism* (London: Routledge, 2007). Both of these collections of articles provide valuable revisionist scholarship on sub-imperial states, but tend to treat their subjects as regional iterations of the histories of colonialism and nationalism that frame scholarship on 'directly ruled' parts of South Asia. For a literature survey that makes the case for different conditions of possibility in polities outside British Indian rule, see Fiona Groenhout, "The History of the Indian Princely States: Bringing the Puppets Back onto Centre Stage," *History Compass* 4.4 (2006): 629–44.

[19] For another example of this tendency, see an otherwise critical and highly nuanced survey of work on 'princely states,' that nonetheless frequently uses the term 'progressive' to mark certain states, implicitly reinforcing the unmarked 'traditional' nature of governance in other states: Ramusack, *Indian Princes*.

sub-imperial polities, occupied a different temporality than the one colonial rule had put in place in British India.[20] In the case of Hyderabad, this concept was closely tied to a prevalent notion of Muslim political difference, often connected to stereotypes about rulers' despotism and recalcitrance in the face of colonial intervention. Hyderabad's rulers, as Muslims and 'native princes,' figured in colonial discourse as both yoked to non-modern Mughal political legacies and linked into threatening extra-territorial Muslim networks of political loyalty. Scholarship on colonial ideology, and the particular place of Muslims and 'princely states' therein, sketches a conceptual space for Hyderabad, and E. M. Forster's canonical British Indian novel indicates political possibilities associated with this space apart.

In "late imperial culture," as Aamir Mufti put it, the figure of the Muslim exemplified South Asia's "supposed impermeability to such forms of modern political and cultural experience as citizenship and nationality." The Muslim was "local and particularistic, caught in a time warp outside the temporalities of the modern world."[21] If the temporal dislocation of Muslims as colonial subjects posed a problem, so too did the intractability of Muslim political sovereignty in the late imperial geopolitical landscape.

Colonial intellectuals and administrators developed articulate and dynamic stereotypes about many aspects of South Asian society, culture, and politics, and deployed them as adjuncts to colonial projects and conquests. These shaped British policies toward subject populations, but also relations with sub-imperial states. Nineteenth-century colonialist writings depicted South Asia as a perpetually 'medieval' mirror of Britain's past which competing Raj factions sought to either preserve or 'civilize.' Native sovereigns, and particularly Hindu Rajputs, were often seen as potential targets of preservation, and a useful group of pliable subordinate collaborators in the imperial enterprise.[22] Muslim-ruled states, on the other hand, were cast as heirs to an important legacy of political progress, but in deep decline, and moreover endemically despotic.[23] Colonial ideologues described the enduring "medievalism" of the Raj's Muslim subjects, and of Muslim-ruled states in the region, as either a threat to law and order and colonial stability or a potentially helpful ally in colonial endeavors to connect the fading legacies of Mughal political morality with British modern governance.[24] Shifts in colonial

[20] On the practice and articulation of "countertemporality" in Egypt as a mode of "carving out counterhegemonic modernities" within the context of hierarchical colonial modernity see On Barak, *On Time: Technology and Temporality in Modern Egypt* (Berkeley: University of California Press, 2013), 144.

[21] Mufti, *Enlightenment in the Colony*, 93.

[22] Metcalf, *Ideologies of the Raj*, 72–73.

[23] Ibid., 88–89.

[24] Ibid., 139–40, 196.

ideology and policy, as discussed below, created productive dynamism in Raj visions of states such as Hyderabad. There were, however, other potential ways in which the Muslim state, occupying a temporality distinct from British India, figured in emerging twentieth-century visions of South Asian political legitimacy.

In the interwar era, in the context of increasing challenges to Raj authority in South Asia, and a weakening reputation in the global public sphere, British critics of empire began to envision sub-imperial states as potential alternatives to majoritarian and often explicitly anti-colonial nationalism. E. M. Forster's 1924 novel *A Passage to India* closed with an emotionally charged meeting between the characters Cyril Fielding, an earnest colonial liberal, and Dr. Aziz, a South Asian Muslim physician wrongly charged with molesting an Englishwoman.[25] The novel's conclusion, set after Aziz's departure from British India, called into doubt the possibility of real human intimacy between South Asians and British under conditions of colonial rule. Forster's work described the structures that generated these tensions. *A Passage to India* was also shot through with fleeting gestures toward sub-imperial states as islands of autonomy where colonial racism could not impede South Asian progress.

Transformations of characters in the novel underscore the integral nature of colonial racism to empire, and its particular effect on Muslims. Initially, Aziz regarded himself as a member of a hybrid class of South Asians with British education and modern technical skills, but he later found his racial difference indelibly marked him as a second-class subject. The novel depicted a racially polarized social landscape, with his support of Aziz resulting in Fielding's ostracism from polite British Indian society, which in turn created new tensions between them. Despite the two friends' desire for intimacy, the boundaries produced by colonial racism pervades the plot.

Aziz contemplated possible places in the subcontinent where he might pursue his patently modern livelihood as a medical doctor beyond the reaches of colonial racism. During these moments, Aziz turned to a blurry vision of a space outside Raj territory, and envisioned a life "in some Moslem State, such as Hyderabad, Bhopal, where Englishmen cannot insult me any more."[26] Aziz further spelled out the foundations of political difference he envisioned, underscoring the importance of the Mughal legacy and contemporary Muslim sovereigns: "I do want to get away from British India, even to a poor job . . . I wish I had lived in Babur's time and fought and written for him . . . We need a king . . . it would make our lives easier . . . My notion now is to try for some post as doctor in

[25] Forster, *A Passage to India*. [26] Ibid., 280.

one of their states."[27] These shadowy and remote utopias that provided a projection screen for Aziz's political desires were separated by spatial distance and political difference, but also by their temporal alterity from British India. The theme of nostalgia for the just rule of monarchs in bygone eras infused South Asian Muslim political thought during this era. The novel explicitly connected the Mughal past with Muslim sub-imperial states of the colonial present. Such polities appeared as the Raj's ineluctable doppelgangers in South Asia, spaces for pursuing modern livelihoods in polities informed by a Mughal legacy of ethical governance, and beyond the pale of colonial racism.

Read in the context of the author's own experiences, Forster's novel appears as a meditation on alternative moral and political geographies represented by actual sub-imperial states. While often seen as indicative of his sympathy to emerging nationalist politics, Forster's own life and personal connections suggest that his novel entailed a deliberate and adulatory focus on sub-imperial states.[28] Forster spent the greater part of his few years in South Asia working not for the Raj or the British Crown, but for the Hindu Maharaja of the tiny sub-imperial state of Dewas (Senior).[29] Dr. Aziz's political desire, however, was projected upon *Muslim* states in the novel. Syed Ross Masood, to whom the novel was dedicated, is a likely source for Forster's ideas about these polities. Indeed, there is a broad consensus that the character Aziz is based on Masood, and Fielding on Forster himself.[30] Biographical materials on the author reveal that Forster and Masood were intimate friends throughout their lives, starting when the latter was a young elite Muslim in England for a Cambridge education, and the former his Latin tutor. The international student was the grandson of the nineteenth-century loyalist Muslim educationist Sir Syed Ahmad Khan, whose Muslim Anglo-Oriental College at Aligarh was a key laboratory for modernist Muslim thought in North India. Masood later become the Director of Public Instruction for Hyderabad State.[31]

The idea of an empowered Muslim world played a key role in Forster's political thought and ethical orientation toward empire. His critique of

27 Ibid., 299.

28 On Forster and Gandhian nationalism see Frances B. Singh, "A Passage to India, the National Movement and Independence," *Twentieth Century Literature* 31:2/3 (1985): 265–78.

29 For the novelist's writings during his employment there (1912–13, 1921) see E. M. Forster, *The Hill of Devi* (San Diego: Harcourt Brace Jovanovich, 1953).

30 On Forster's sexuality, including his love for Masood, see Robert K. Martin, ed., *Queer Forster* (University of Chicago Press, 1997).

31 On Syed Ross Masood's educational work in Hyderabad see Datla, *The Language of Secular Islam*, ch. 2.

colonialism was often articulated with regard to the Ottoman Empire. He supported the South Asian Khilafat movement in demanding a guarantee of political sovereignty for the Ottoman Sultan, as leader of the Muslim world, and lamented the dismantling of Ottoman domains following World War I. During the same period he advocated British military action against Italy to oppose their conquest of Ottoman territories in North Africa.[32] He corresponded with British critics of imperial practices, such as Wilfrid Scawen Blunt, Muhammad Marmaduke Pickthall, and T. E. Lawrence, over the ethics and practice of European imperialism in Muslim-ruled lands.[33] According to private correspondence, Forster and Masood had planned a trip together in 1910 to Constantinople.[34] It is notable that several passages in his novel implied that friendship between colonizers and colonized (such as that of Fielding/Forster and Aziz/Masood) may be possible in other Muslim lands (West or Central Asia, North Africa), against which South Asia was contrasted.[35] These connections between Forster's thinking about colonialism and Muslim states, his novel, and Hyderabad show how the latter potentially fit into alternative geographical visions during the period of high colonialism. Further, the novelist's own engagements, noted above, with the Muslim world as a venue of global political connections allude to another key element of Hyderabad's acolonial temporality, to which we shall return in the next chapter. The idea that Hyderabad occupied a political and moral space distinct from that of British India, and that its Muslimness was a key reason for this difference, provided an outline for the state's discursive universe, to which writers during late imperialism gave content.

## Colonial histories of Hyderabad

Before Forster penned his novel, sub-imperial states had long been a frequent preoccupation of British Indian writers.[36] Shifts in the

32 David Roessel, "Live Orientals and Dead Greeks: Forster's Response to the Chanak Crisis," *Twentieth Century Literature* 36.1 (1990): 43–60.

33 Muhammad Shaheen, "Forster's Salute to Egypt," *Twentieth Century Literature* 39.1 (1993): 32–46. See Chapter 4 below on Blunt and Pickthall in Hyderabad.

34 Roessel, "Live Orientals," 51–52.

35 This contrast reflected powerful orientalist stereotypes about the egalitarian nature of Arab Islam in contrast to caste-ridden South Asian society.

36 One recent example is William Dalrymple, *White Mughals: Love and Betrayal in Eighteenth Century India* (London: HarperCollins, 2002). This work of popular history uses a fictionalized account of a historical love affair between the British Resident of Hyderabad and a Muslim noblewoman to celebrate the possibility of interracial intimacy during the

conception and configuration of South Asian political sovereignty corresponded to changing representations of these states. As described in the previous chapter, a critical transition in the nature of British rule in South Asia – from Company Raj as expansive conquest state to the consolidating and pacifying rule of Crown Raj – occurred in the mid-nineteenth century. These two imperial phases shaped the treatment of sub-imperial sovereigns in colonial historiography. During the expansive first phase South Asian sovereigns were cast as illegitimate and despotic rulers inimical to the realization of the colonial civilizing project. The representation of Muslims as emphatically problematic owed much to the Mughals' role as the Raj's imperial predecessors. During the consolidating second phase the British ceased territorial expansion, and perforce sought to cultivate support networks and present their empire as a collaboration with South Asians. As such, sub-imperial states were increasingly cast as complementary political entities, preserved museums of precolonial South Asian society, or spaces for native political advancement. These dynamic representations, all premised on the alterity of sub-imperial temporalities, were foundational components of Hyderabad's discursive universe. While shifts in imperial strategy at times entailed clear breaks with the past, the kind of representational shifts considered here were less thorough. The persistence of numerous strands of representation endow an ambivalent and productive character to Hyderabad's conceptual space as it appears in colonial, Hyderabadi, and nationalist, communist, subnational, or other histories.

### *Hyderabad in early colonial historiography: tales of Muslim misrule*

In the first half of the nineteenth century sub-imperial sovereigns appeared as negative counterpoints to the Raj's vision of civilizing empire. Comparing them with British India, 'indirectly ruled' regions were shown as frozen in the past, and filled out a synchronic vision of South Asia's possible histories. This mode of representation downplayed the robust exchanges between the suzerain British and other sovereigns of South Asia. Nevertheless, it provided a key organizing principle for describing 'princely states,' and a narrative framework with scope for a broad spectrum of views. Sub-imperial states were cast as stagnant backwaters to modernizing British India, and figured as a potential menace to directly

early colonial period, and particularly in sub-imperial states. On postcolonial representations of sub-imperial states see Barbara Ramusack, "The Indian Princes as Fantasy: Palace Hotels, Palace Museums and Palace on Wheels," in *Consuming Modernity: Public Culture in a South Asian World*, ed. Carol A. Breckenridge (Minneapolis: University of Minnesota Press, 1995), 66–89.

ruled regions.[37] Some colonialists sought to justify Raj territorial expansion by presenting competing rulers as security threats and oppressive 'Oriental despots.'

Hyderabad's dynastic line originated when a Mughal regional *ṣūbahdār* (provincial governor) declared independence in the early eighteenth century. The British formally deposed the Mughal sovereign following the insurgencies of 1857, though the Nizam, possessor of a separate treaty, retained formal sovereignty. In keeping with the image of the late Mughals in colonial historiography, the Nizam's state was often cast as an example of despotic, medieval, and backward Muslim rule.

Early British colonial discourse on Muslim rule in South Asia was inflected by the Raj's attempt to cast itself as superior to existing polities. This entailed writing the histories of 'native' rulers as stories of oppression and ineffective government, to legitimize colonial seizure of sovereignty from non-European competitors. The strategy was especially prevalent with respect to Muslim rule. In 1833 EIC officer John Clunes published an influential study that was to shape later colonial discourse on sub-imperial South Asian states.[38] He rendered as historical objects "for the general reader" states that had entered into alliance with the British in the subcontinent in exchange for continued sovereignty.[39] Clunes's narrative glossed the remaining non-British rulers in South Asia derisively: "Of the states, whose histories form the subject of the following pages, few are of ancient date. All the Mahomedan have been founded in rebellion, crime, and usurpation. None of them can claim the antiquity of one century."[40] He thus defined the princes en bloc as illegitimate by dint of their recent and dubious sovereign claims. In an environment where the colonial state claimed to be protecting legitimate rulers, such an assault on the 'antiquity' of dynasties served as condemnation and justification for conquest.

Clunes's description of "Mahomedan" states emphasized particularity of Muslim political illegitimacy. Different states were classed first of all by the community of their rulers: "Abyssinians, Brahmins, Hindoos etc., Mahomedans, Mahrattas, Rajpoots, protected Seiks."[41] Viewing the subcontinent's people as a conglomeration of different ethnic and religious units, Clunes organized rulers in these terms as well. In his model each group had its own characteristic essence, and Muslim

[37] Such representations framed later contestations over legal jurisdiction on Raj–Nizam frontiers. See Chapter 5 below.

[38] John Clunes, *An Historical Sketch of the Princes of India: Stipendiary, Subsidiary, Protected, Tributary, and Feudatory; with a sketch of the origin and progress of British Power in India* (Edinburgh: Shortrede, 1833).

[39] Ibid., vii. [40] Ibid., 18. [41] Ibid., ix–xii.

sovereigns were given to "rebellion, crime, and usurpation."[42] In keeping with this essentialist vision, Clunes described Hyderabad: "The present dynasty of Hyderabad originated with the Nizam-ool-Moolk, a crafty and ambitious Ameer of the rigid school of Aurangzeb, who was deputed from Delhi as soobehdar of the Deccan, in 1713."[43] Late Mughals were cast as "rigid" despots, and the Nizam–Mughal connection thus shaped the political space of Hyderabad. Clunes's lack of discrimination between Hyderabad as Mughal province and as independent state provides a key to the logic of his presentation. Distinct phases – Mughal imperial rule, the Nizam's secession, consolidation of an independent Asafi Jahi state – were assimilated into a unitary narrative of Hyderabad's history. For Clunes these changes were proof of the internal instabilities of the polity. What sub-imperial Hyderabad's official historians would present as disjunctures within a regional history of ethical Muslim governance were for Clunes evidence of an antique, continuous history of misrule. Legitimizing the Raj in this way entailed debasing Muslim sub-imperial states such as Hyderabad. Clunes figured these polities as future victims of the forward march of British 'progress' and 'civilization.'

Belittling the Hyderabadi line was facilitated by established colonial stereotypes about the later Mughal state: unabated decline, barbarism, disorder. The ostensible nadir of Oriental despotism under Aurangzeb (r. 1658–1707) and his successors served as prelude to and justification of the British entry into the South Asian political scene. Under the expansive Company Raj such rhetorical thrusts against the Mughals were commonplace, and provided justification for nineteenth-century colonial consolidation.[44] The latent authority, political culture, and popular memory of Mughal rule were to remain productive figures in South Asian political discourse. Anticipated restoration of Mughal sovereignty was a rallying point for 1857 challenges to colonial rule, and the Raj mined Mughal iconography of power to articulate a ritual vocabulary for their self-presentation as a South Asian empire.[45] Later colonial writings on Hyderabad, however, inverted Clunes's derisive account.

42 Ibid., 18. 43 Ibid., 81.

44 On ambivalent early Raj attitudes toward the Mughal state and its institutional forms see Robert Travers, *Ideology and Empire in Eighteenth Century India: The British in Bengal* (Cambridge University Press, 2007); Jon E. Wilson, *The Domination of Strangers: Modern Governance in Eastern India, 1780–1835* (Basingstoke: Palgrave Macmillan, 2008).

45 Bernard S. Cohn, "Representing Authority in Victorian India," in *The Invention of Tradition*, ed. Eric Hobsbawm and Terence Ranger (Cambridge University Press, 1983), 165–209.

### *Hyderabad in late colonial historiography: seeing alternatives to imperial rule*

> There still survive many native States independent as to their internal action, which afford now, and for years to come will continue to afford, some opening for native talent and ambitions, some opportunities for solving the general problem of native advancement.[46]

After the post-1857 shift in imperial strategy and discourse, sub-imperial states often served as examples of amicable British relations with South Asian polities, and reference points for critiques of colonial governance. 'Native states' were often depicted as key locales for modern governance beyond the domains of an empire under mounting internal and external pressure. The emergence of this discursive space enabled colonial officials to articulate accounts of legitimate Asaf Jahi statecraft, which paralleled arguments by Hyderabadi officials.

In 1875 Bengal Army colonel G. B. Malleson published what was to become a standard history of South Asian sub-imperial states. In contrast to Clunes's account, Malleson's writings cast these polities as venues for revising the failures of the colonial project by legitimizing native political ideas and institutions within the framework of British imperial protection. This representation was in tune with the 'culturalist' turn of imperial discourse from the mid-nineteenth century onward, after the Raj guaranteed perpetual sub-imperial sovereignty and increasingly cast 'native states' as allies in empire.[47] Malleson's project deployed a dynamic reading of past and present South Asian history, and revised depictions of Muslim rulers as despotic which had become a commonplace of colonial historiography. This rereading of the history of cultural difference, however, did not go so far as to challenge the colonial social theory that posited cultural difference as the primary political problem of South Asia.

Malleson began by drawing the lines between who was actually 'Indian' and who was not by speaking of the subcontinent as a coherent unit subjected to "foreign rule" for the five hundred years between 1206 and 1707, the period during which Muslim states wielded political power in much of South Asia.[48] The narrative thus established a religious and ethnic distinction between Hindu and Muslim as an essential,

[46] G. B. Malleson, *An Historical Sketch of the Native States of India in subsidiary alliance with the British Government; with a notice of the Mediated and Minor States* (London: Longman, 1875), 6.

[47] On the culturalist turn in imperial political thought see Mantena, *Alibis of Empire*.

[48] Malleson, *Native States*, 2.

ahistorical condition. Nevertheless, the author brought to bear a dynamic reading of the moral status of Muslim rule. Rather than present all historical Muslim states as degenerate, as did Clunes, Malleson highlighted particular rulers:

Though belonging to an age which had but scarcely emerged from barbarism, he [the Mughal Emperor Akbar] recognized that a good Government must rest on the affections of the people. The measures which he adopted for breaking down the barriers between the conquering and conquered races are worthy of all praise.[49]

Parsing the monolithic representations of Muslim rule in South Asia, Malleson cast Akbar as an exemplary ruler, in contrast to his predecessors. This rhetorical move was grounded in the assumption that good government entailed managing Hindu–Muslim relations. Thus cultural difference between ethnic and religious groups was inscribed as a basic social fact of South Asia, and Akbar's tolerance provided a model to be emulated.

Malleson subsequently drew connections between the "good Government" that prevailed in Akbar's domains and sub-imperial states, and contrasted it with with British colonial practice as a way to critique the latter:

The superior science and civilisation of the British nation have annihilated whatever native arts or manufactures had been in existence, and have introduced nothing in their stead, whilst the exclusiveness of their national character and the still more exclusive nature of the administrative machinery adopted in India; have shut out the people from all share in the political administration of their affairs.[50]

If Muslim rule in South Asia was a kind of medieval colonialism, Malleson enumerated distinct moments and personae in this older imperial history. Some figures, such as Akbar, could be exemplary for the British, imperial heirs to the Mughals. Rather than upholding a static picture of European advancement and Muslim degeneracy, Malleson envisioned a polity blending the best from each.

Sub-imperial states held great potential for Malleson, and he saw in them "opportunities for solving the general problem of native advancement."[51] His program entailed a revised vision of the British role in organizing empire in South Asia, and emphasized the centrality of managing cultural difference:

49 Ibid. 50 Ibid., 3. 51 Ibid., 6.

> [Native states] are peopled by almost all nationalities into which the country is divided. They thus form so many centres, where the Sikh, the Mahomedan, the Rajput, the Marhata, and the Dravidian can each bring out to the best advantage whatever may be particular and excellent in his national character and national institution, under the generalising principle of English principles and English civilisation.[52]

Sub-imperial states, then, stood in both as bearers of unsullied South Asian legacies ("national character"), and as workshops for the molding of modern polities informed by the "generalising principle" of "English civilisation." Malleson's vision of empire reflected British ideas of imperial trusteeship, but also emphasized the potential import of these distinct temporal spaces.

Malleson's influential sense of sub-imperial states' roles in late imperial South Asia broke down constituent elements of earlier colonial stereotypes. Muslim rulers, while often 'barbaric,' could also be exemplary ethical sovereigns, as in the case of Akbar. Sub-imperial states were also critical sources for crystalizing visions of South Asia's past and possible futures, and revising prevalent colonial designs. Malleson's history cast sub-imperial states, as confluences of distinct temporalities, within the discourse of post-1857 imperial reform. Echoes of the potential Malleson envisioned are visible in Forster's novel, considered above, which forms an apogee of imperial narratives. Hyderabad's historians took up similar threads, toward different ends, in crafting a history of the state.

## Hyderabadi historiography

Histories written from Hyderabad shared key elements with colonial historiography, but made important departures. Sub-imperial difference – constituted by formal sovereignty, geographical distance, and temporal alterity – was marked in Hyderabadi historiography in ways related to views in Clunes and Malleson. Historians within Hyderabad also adopted genres of writing (empirical, enumerative, ethnographic) and references to the 'modern' institutions (census, surveys, development projects) that animated colonial historiography and governance. However, by simultaneously recasting the particular past of Deccani Muslim states and producing equivalents of the regional nationalist histories emerging in British India, Hyderabadi historians presented the Nizam's state as a legitimate and indeed desirable modern alternative to British rule in South Asia. While the horizon of political aspiration for nationalist historiography

52 Ibid.

was the unitary territorial nation-state form, Hyderabadi historiography, owing to the state's particular political status, was more ambivalent. Hyderabadi stateness was often envisioned within a broader subcontinental and global configuration of fragmented sovereignty rather than situated within the abstract territorial logic of nation-states. As such, the state was a discrete and autonomous entity constituted by patrimonial networks of loyalty, oriented to the monarch, yet coursing through and beyond its physical territory. Hyderabadi histories cast the Nizam's state at once as a historically grounded polity in the South Asian historical landscape and as a constituent element of a shared global modernity, linked with Muslim states elsewhere, British India, Europe, and other ostensibly modern polities. This section examines, first, a British Civil Service officer's history of Hyderabad that developed a regionalist history in defense of the state, and, second, a key "official history" of Hyderabad oriented toward internal and global readerships. Considerations of other historical narratives and fragments by various intellectuals connected to the state further demonstrate the ways the state's discursive universe emerged as a space for fusing ideas of regional particularity and Muslim transregionalism, and recasting colonially and globally mediated categories such as good governance and political modernity within this framework.

### *Muslim regionalism: Gribble's Deccan*

Recent scholarship has drawn on evidence of regional political consciousness in South Asia during the colonial period, such as vernacular historical narratives and linguistic nationalist rhetoric, to point to the diversity of conceptions of state and community.[53] Works in this vein have shown that, rather than being framed within homogenizing colonial or national conceptual frameworks, histories and political positions were often framed from the perspective of particular regions. Such accounts demonstrate how ideas of place, language, and other forms of solidarity textured and regionally differentiated the world of political ideas in late imperial South Asia.[54] Scholarship on regional and linguistic domains

[53] Prachi Deshpande, *Creative Pasts: History, Memory and Identity in Western India* (New York: Columbia University Press, 2007); Zutshi, *Languages of Belonging*; Rai, *Hindu Rulers*; Sugata Bose, "Nation as Mother," in *Nationalism, Democracy and Development: State and Politics in India*, ed. Sugata Bose and Ayesha Jalal (Delhi: Oxford University Press, 1997), 50–75; Yasmin Saikia, *Fragmented Memories: Struggling to Be Tai-Ahom in India* (Durham, NC: Duke University Press, 2004).

[54] Many scholars have emphasized the centrality of regional linguistic communities in the formation of modern South Asian political solidarities. The 'literatures project' coordinated the work of numerous scholars of South Asian literary texts from various regions

have resulted in nuanced accounts of the heterogeneous composition of modern South Asia, but situate their objects within unified overarching 'colonial' or 'nationalist' discursive and political terrains and trajectories.[55] Earlier histories written in or about sub-imperial states present a different vision of possible political geographies. Autonomous, parallel polities in South Asia that were outside the jurisdictional domain of the Raj, such as Hyderabad, have defined distinct targets of political desire or aspiration. Hyderabadi histories refashioned the image of the state visible in colonial histories, and developed narratives about regional political legitimacy.

J. D. B. Gribble's 1896 *A History of the Deccan* described a long legacy of morally virtuous regional rulers from the medieval period to the present in the Hyderabad Deccan, and wrote the controversial Mughals out of the picture.[56] Gribble, a former British Indian Civil Service officer who entered into Hyderabad employment, dedicated his book to the current Nizam. The introduction to his two-volume work made clear that, rather than "Akbar, Aurangzebe, Clive or Warren Hastings," icons in Mughal and British Indian history, Hyderabadis should have been learning about the regional history of political sovereignty, just as "a Poonah boy should be thoroughly grounded in the history of the Mahrattas, and a Bangalore boy in that of Mysore."[57] Accordingly, Gribble's project existed in parallel to other regional political visions, and took up older Hyderabadi legacies of asserting difference from pan-subcontinental historical narratives that prevailed in imperial historiography.[58]

and periods: see Sheldon Pollock, ed., *Literary Cultures in History: Reconstructions from South Asia* (Berkeley: University of California Press, 2003). Studies focused on specific languages in the modern era include Sumathi Ramaswamy, *Passions of the Tongue: Language Devotion in Tamil India, 1891–1970* (Berkeley: University of California Press, 1997); Lisa Mitchell, *Language, Emotion, and Politics in South India: The Making of a Mother Tongue* (Bloomington: Indiana University Press, 2009); Farina Mir, *The Social Space of Language: Vernacular Culture in British Colonial Punjab* (Berkeley: University of California Press, 2010).

55 Histories of South Asian sub-imperial states, such as those discussed in the above section, also tend to intervene by recasting and broadening scholarly understandings of colonialism or nationalism, not situating sub-imperial states in broader contexts.

56 J. D. B. Gribble, *A History of the Deccan*, edited and completed by Mary Gribble Pendlebury, vol. I (London: Luzac, 1896).

57 Ibid., ii.

58 Gribble's work was produced in an environment where British colonial historiography dominated the scene. He continued a long-established historical practice in the Deccan of writing against historiography looking south from political centers in Delhi, Agra, or Calcutta. For an early seventeenth-century example of Deccani regionalist historiography see Muḥammad Qāsim Hindū Shāh Astarābādī Firishtah, *Tārīkh i Firishtah* (Lucknow: Navil Kishore, 1864).

Gribble's book drew up a back-story for Deccani regional political consciousness, and as such his project bore a close affinity to nationalist historiography produced in other regions of South Asia. Owing to the Nizam's loyalty to the British, such writings produced in Hyderabad State were typically not explicitly anti-colonial nationalist in orientation. Hyderabadi histories often shared techniques with colonial histories, such as positivist narrative style, reference to 'antique' primary source texts to assure 'authenticity,' and emphasis on empirical grounding.[59] Gribble drew extensively from Bombay Presidency Gazetteers and colonial translations of South Asian language sources, and from Bilgrami and Willmott (a key Hyderabadi official history, discussed below). Borrowing well-worn tropes from colonial genres he drew from, Gribble described autonomous and timeless villages in a world unaffected by state politics; inherent animosity between Hindus and Muslims which periodically erupted into violence like a force of nature; and eighteenth-century decline and Mughal brutality.[60] To this grim picture he posed Hyderabad as exception.

Whereas the early colonial sources considered above took the regime's Mughal roots as indicative of barbaric governance, Gribble disassociated Hyderabad's rulers from the Mughals. He did so through emphasizing the legacy of the early modern Deccani sultans conquered by the Mughals in the seventeenth century, and particularly the Quṭb Shāhs of Golkonda, who founded Hyderabad City. Gribble described the Mughal ruler Aurangzeb's "feelings of detestation" for the Qutb Shahs and other autonomous Deccani rulers as almost equal to his hatred of the Hindu Marathas. The bigoted Aurangzeb, he maintained, opposed both the Shia piety of the various Deccan sultans and their practice of "allowing infidels [non-Muslims] to thrive in their domains," specifying Qutb Shah's Hindu prime minister and the "tolerance . . . shown toward Christians, such as was not to be found elsewhere in the Mahomedan world."[61] In detailing the reasons for Mughal "detestation," and reifying colonial stereotypes about general Muslim intolerance, Gribble asserted a distinct and exceptional character to Muslim rule in the Deccan. In his account, the Adil Shahs of Bijapur, another Deccani sultanate that ruled parts of what became Hyderabad State, were exemplary, behaving with

59 For a detailed account of regionalist South Asian history-writing during the colonial period see Deshpande, *Creative Pasts*, esp. chs. 3 and 4 on the formative impact of colonial education on Marathi historical consciousness.

60 Gribble, *History of the Deccan*, 205, 293, 357–58, *inter alia*.

61 Ibid., 293.

"singular moderation" and declaring "'My faith for myself and your faith for yourselves' [as] his tolerant maxim."[62]

Having narrated a particular ethical political history for Deccani Muslim rule, Gribble downplayed Mughal–Asaf Jah links. He connected the Hyderabad regime to the Qutb Shahs, suggesting a regional moral and political continuity. In contrast to the "bloodshed and intrigue" of Mughal conquest, the first Nizam, initially a Mughal-appointed *subahdar*, behaved with "caution [in] . . . all his actions" and "did his best to bring the Deccan into order and repose."[63] Qutb Shahi Golkonda played an "important and lasting part in Indian history," though "under a different dynasty [Asaf Jahi Nizams] and another name [Hyderabad]" up to Gribble's "present day."[64]

Gribble's intricate tracing of historical connections between early modern and late nineteenth-century Hyderabad entailed positing a composite image of the Deccan sultans and contrasting them with the Mughals. His narrative referenced physical locations to illustrate the exceptional character of Hyderabad's ethical Muslim rulers. Writing places in this manner was a technique taken up by other writers in other, more explicit attempts to tie notions of past ethical governance to arguments about the contemporary Nizam's political legitimacy, such as one by Hyderabadi official historians.

### *Ethical Muslim rule, past and present in Hyderabadi historiography*

During the 1880s Syed Hossain Bilgrami and Charles Willmott, two state officials, authored an exhaustive two-volume compendium of information on Hyderabad under the title *Historical and Descriptive Sketch of His Highness the Nizam's Dominions*.[65] Describing their work as inspired by the recently instituted British Indian census, the authors drew on standard colonial histories, translations from Persian and Arabic, travelers' accounts, archeological survey reports, statistical data, and official correspondence. Similar in format to British colonial gazetteers, the text covered physical and historical geography, history, economy, government, and culture of Hyderabad territories. Bilgrami and Willmott's monumental text functioned as a venue to collect and display the various projects of knowledge that had been instigated in the Nizam's endeavor

62 Ibid., 147. 63 Ibid., 354. 64 Ibid., 171.

65 Syed Hossain Bilgrami and C. Willmott, *Historical and Descriptive Sketch of His Highness the Nizam's Dominions*, 2 vols. (Bombay: Times of India Steam Press, 1883–84). Willmott was later to claim that he was in fact the sole author of the text. For a discussion of his life and work see Chapter 4 below.

to modernize Hyderabad.[66] The emphasis on enumeration and exhaustive cataloging of people, places, and developments in the state suggests that the notion, shared by colonial thinkers, of empirical knowledge as guarantor of authority to rule was current among Hyderabadi bureaucrat-intellectuals. The text was referenced internally in the governing of Hyderabad State. Colonial political practice and expectations informed the contents and emphasis, and indeed the Nizam had begun to employ numerous European officers from the mid-nineteenth century in the process of modernizing state institutions.[67] One function of the text was to serve as a manual for European officers, many of whom (unlike Willmott, who was literate in Urdu and Persian) would not have been able to read state documents in Urdu or Persian. The text showcased projects of institutional and technical modernization in a manner approachable by global audiences.[68]

Narrating Hyderabad's history from medieval times to the present gave the authors the opportunity to reframe regional legacies to meet contemporary ideological ends. While not yoked to a coherent nationalist movement as such, official histories such as Bilgrami and Willmott's resemble nationalist historiography produced elsewhere. In such sources, selective and embellished narrations of a region's past, often fuzzily conceived, conveyed the present coherence and legitimacy of an existing or imagined state form or geopolitical unit.[69]

66 The similarities of this project to contemporary developments in the presentation of colonial knowledge are considerable, and indeed Bilgrami and Willmott's work shares a conceptual framework with late nineteenth-century genres of 'scientific' and empirical writings on South Asian society produced by the colonial state. For discussions of the changing forms of knowledge in colonial South Asia see Bernard S. Cohn, "The Census, Social Structure and Objectification in South Asia," *Folk* 26 (1984): 25–49; Gyan Prakash, *Another Reason: Science and the Imagination of Modern India* (Princeton University Press, 1999); and Carol A. Breckenridge and Peter van der Veer, eds., *Orientalism and the Postcolonial Predicament: Perspectives on South Asia* (Philadelphia: University of Pennsylvania Press, 1993), esp. contibutions by Arjun Appadurai, Nicholas Dirks, and David Ludden. Other major late Asaf Jah-era texts that share elements of this empirical framework include A. C. Campbell, *Glimpses of the Nizam's Dominions* (London: William Watson & Co., 1898) and K. Krishnaswamy Mudiraj, *Pictorial Hyderabad*, 2 vols. (Hyderabad: Chandrakanth Press, 1929–34).

67 Shamim Aleem, *Personnel Management in a Princely State* (New Delhi: Gitanjali Publishing House, 1985).

68 The weighty two-volume work was distributed internationally, as suggested by multiple copies of the original 1883–84 edition in libraries in Europe and North America. The function of such texts, and the roles of bureaucrat-intellectuals, in comparing Hyderabadi modernity to other states, and projecting it to world audiences, is considered in Chapter 4 below.

69 In many regards, official histories of Hyderabad, such as the one considered here, bear similarities to those examined in what remains a key work on global nationalism: Benedict Anderson, *Imagined Communities: Reflections on the Origin and Spread of Nationalism*, new edn. (London: Verso, 2006 [1983]).

Like Gribble, Bilgrami and Willmott portrayed Muslim rulers of the Hyderabad Deccan as being inherently different from other Muslim states of South Asian history. Crucially, however, they combined these historical narratives of legitimacy with explicit invocations of contemporary Asaf Jahi political legitimacy. The form and content of the book – emphasis on empirical data, enumeration of various products of the state, social groups, transportation, and administrative infrastructure – present a modernizing state commensurable with, but historically and territorially distinct from, British India.

Hyderabadi historiography legitimized the Nizam's rule by positing a continuous practice of ethical rule on the part of past and present Deccani Muslim polities. Bilgrami and Willmott devoted considerable space to descriptions of Qutb Shahi monuments in the region of the capital city. Architectural remains served as vehicles for describing the practices of just governance by the Qutb Shahi builders, and then of bringing this history to bear on the contemporary discourse about government in Hyderabad. Many of the buildings discussed were still standing, and extensive photographs accompanied the text, which provided visceral material supplements to arguments about past–present linkages. In the lengthy portion devoted to Hyderabad City, Bilgrami and Willmott described Qutb Shahi buildings and their social functions in detail.[70] Included here were a pavilion where the sovereign could display the "efficiency" of state military chiefs and troops and dole out corresponding rewards, and a state hospital staffed by "native physicians and hakims to minister to the sick."[71] Such accounts allowed free rein for the authors to reconstruct benevolent policies of Qutb Shahi rulers toward subject populations. The materiality of architectural monuments in the contemporary city gave these accounts a ring of factuality, bringing bygone kings to life in the remains of their institutions. The text sketched out a progressive character of the early modern state in its arrangement of public services and reward systems for their subjects and employees. In describing the Dād Maḥal ("Palace of justice"), Bilgrami and Willmott invoked the easy access subjects had to rulers: "Any person desiring to make a petition or to complain against any of the officers had but to ring the bell, when he was admitted to the presence of the king."[72] This conveyed an idealized image of the accessibility of government in the early modern state. Like Gribble, Bilgrami and Willmott also contrasted Hyderabadi Muslim

[70] Bilgrami and Willmott, *Historical and Descriptive Sketch*, vol. II, 555–69.
[71] Ibid., vol. II, 562, 565.
[72] Ibid., vol. II, 562. To provide further "evidence" for their claims, the authors cross-referenced the seventeenth-century French traveler Tavernier's favorable description of the justice system in Qutb Shahi Hyderabad. Ibid., vol. II, 564.

rulers with the ostensibly bigoted Mughal Aurangzeb, and emphasized the key roles of non-Muslim officials and subjects in Hyderabad.[73]

In yoking the early modern past to the present, Bilgrami and Willmott described a "typical street scene" in Hyderabad, scrambling references to the authors' own observations and early modern sources in creating an inventory of the many different ethnicities of the city with orientalist detail: "Arab, Sidi, Rohilla, Pathan, Afghan, Rajput, Persian, Bokhariot, Georgian, Turk, Dekhani Muslim, Sikh, Mahratta, Brahmin, Parsi ('Anglo-Saxons of the East'), Madrassi, [and] Chinese."[74] Crucially, the state's management of cultural diversity – here explicitly speaking of the current Nizam's Hyderabad – provided proof of the ruling government's legitimacy and aptitude: "This imperfect sketch of a street scene in Haidarabad will afford a slight idea of the cosmopolitanism that pervaded the place, to keep all the elements of which in order is no easy task."[75] This jumbling of times – through references, architectural description of old and new buildings in the city, associations between early modern Qutb Shahs and late nineteenth-century Nizams – articulated a distinct, layered temporality that characterized Hyderabad's discursive universe. These linkages across time, and the overarching notion of political legitimacy they conveyed, hinged upon Hyderabadi Muslim rulers' benevolent, patrimonial relationship with diverse subject populations and "progress" toward modern governance.

The historical legacy of modern Hyderabad, stretching back to the Qutb Shahi dynasty centuries before, was to remain a key point of reference for writers who sought to emphasize the legitimacy of the Nizam's rule. From the 1930s onward the subcontinent's decolonization was on the horizon, and this expectation generated a Nizam loyalist discourse that advocated Hyderabad's future as an independent state. Scholarship on the history and literature of the early modern Deccan took on new implications and political valence. The Urdu writings of Muḥīuddīn Qādirī Zor, a key early twentieth-century scholar of Qutb Shahi Hyderabad, exhibits the interweaving of contemporary political aspirations into narratives of early modern history. Zor's popular history *Sair-i Golkunḍah* (A walk through Golkonda) is a brief text, designed to be accessible to a wide readership. Zor presented the Qutb Shahi capital as a veritable utopia of benevolent patrimonial governance:

> [The Qutb Shahi] emperors obtained such success in the making of one common culture (*ek mushtarik kalchar*) of Shia and Sunni, Muslim and Hindu – in short, inhabitants of all religions (*ġharaz har mażhab-o millat ke bāshindon*) – that the

[73] Ibid., vol. II, 567. [74] Ibid., vol. II, 552–55. [75] Ibid., vol. II, 555.

mutual closeness and unity of this country's residents was a source of others' envy.[76]

Like Bilgrami and Willmott, Zor took up the technique of writing about architecture as a means of conveying in a tangible fashion the ethical rule of the Qutb Shahs. One metaphor he employed to convey this was the rulers' egalitarian optic from the vantage point of the *bālā ḥiṣār*, the highest point of the hilltop citadel of Golkonda:

To reach here, one must ascend hundreds of hard and lengthy steps, and when someone manages to reach the peak descent and ascent are united (*niṣāb-o farāz yaksān*) in their vision. No wonder Muslim and Hindu, Shia and Sunni were equal in the gaze of Sultan Muḥammad Qulī [fifth Qutb Shah and Hyderbad's founder, r. 1580–1612] and Abul Ḥasan Qutb Shah [eighth and last Qutb Shah, r. 1682–87], since they were in the habit of looking out from a place where high and low, ascent and descent, appeared unified.[77]

Zor's imaginative metaphor linked the kings' view from on high to equanimity toward diverse state subjects. The *bala hisar* was a vista that would have been familiar to many of his readers in Hyderabad, and endowed its sweeping view of the city with clear political implication.

The claim for egalitarianism matched Zor's broader emphasis on the progressive character of Qutb Shahi rule, and the relevance of this history for contemporary Hyderabad. The city's founder, Muhammad Quli Qutb Shah, was accordingly described as concerned less with military expansion than "the progress of the education of his subjects (*rā'āya kā ta'līmī taraqqī*)."[78] For Zor this history had implications for reforms in the Nizam's Hyderabad:

Those concerned with the prosperity and well-being of this country and the improvement and progress (*iṣlāḥ-o taraqqī*) of the children can never forget the fact that, without our own self-reliance and mindfulness, progress (*taraqqī*) will be impossible.[79]

Emphasizing the exemplary, and explicitly progressive, ethics of the Qutb Shahs, Zor cast the region's distinctive early modern Deccani Muslim legacy as a critical source of guidance for Hyderabad administrators. His use of Urdu terms *iṣlāḥ* and *taraqqī* represented a conceptual translation of the ideas of "improvement" and "progress," two key touchstones in both colonial rhetoric and global modernist discourse. Emphasizing the continuity of these political values from the distant past to the contemporary

[76] Muḥīuddīn Qādirī Zor, *Sair-i Golkunḍah* (Hyderabad: Idārah-yi Adabiyāt-i Urdū, 1940), 6.
[77] Ibid., 87. [78] Ibid., 9. [79] Ibid., 13.

in the capital city, Zor elucidated the meaning of Hyderabad's distinct temporality.

In highlighting the productivity of Hyderabad's jumbled temporality, its historians stressed the particularity of Muslim rule in the region. They continued an established pre-modern historiographic practice of arguing for political and cultural Deccani difference from imperial powers to the north. In late imperial iterations this entailed assertion of the ethical status of Muslim rule in Hyderabad in contrast to the early modern Mughals as well as contemporary British rulers. Hyderabadi historiography was resolutely regionalist in the sources considered above, and indeed this was a practical way of asserting difference from colonial stereotypes about Muslim misrule for which the late Mughals often provided a site of enunciation.

The Mughal connection played an ambivalent role in the Hyderabadi discursive universe.[80] As future chapters will elaborate, while colonial descriptions of Hyderabad as "Moglai" may have implied political disorder, the jurisdictional difference the attribution signaled also facilitated political experimentation within an autonomous political space. Others regarded the Mughal legacy as a critical source of Hyderabad's importance and attraction. South Asian Muslim intellectuals, such as the leftist activist and writer Sibṯ-i Ḥasan, who was employed in Hyderabad state during the interwar era, celebrated links between the Nizam's Hyderabad and the storied ethical culture of the Mughal Empire. During the postcolonial period, after the state's dissolution, Sibt-i Hasan and other Urdu-speaking intellectuals remembered the Nizam's Hyderabad as "illuminated" by "the flame of the Mughal State" long after it had been extinguished in Delhi.[81] One of his companions described Hyderabad as a "*s̱aqāfatī markaz* [center of knowledge] not only for the residents of the Deccan," but for all South Asian Muslims.[82] The Nizam's government was already facing "the question of life or death" in the 1930s when Sibt-i Hasan was there.[83] Nevertheless, Hyderabad's status as a vital intellectual and cultural resource remained a subject of profound nostalgia decades after its integration into India.

80 On the politically productive use during the nineteenth century of the Mughal legacy to advance the status of Bhopal, a smaller Muslim-ruled sub-imperial South Asian state to the north, see Hannah L. Archambault, "Becoming Mughal in the Nineteenth Century: The Case of the Bhopal Princely State," *South Asia: Journal of South Asian Studies* 36.4 (2013): 1–17. On the 'Mughal Renaissance' there and 'neo-Mughal' policies in the late nineteenth century see Claudia Preckel, "The Roots of Anglo-Muslim Co-Operation and Islamic Reformism in Bhopal," in *Perspectives of Mutual Encounters in South Asian History: 1760–1860*, ed. Jamal Malik (Leiden: Brill, 2000), 65–78.

81 Sibṯ-i Ḥasan, *Shahr-i nigārān*, 7–8. 82 Ibid., 8. 83 Ibid., 112.

Hyderabadi histories selectively combined emphasis on Deccani particularity and regional ties with openings to a subcontinent-wide Mughal legacy to highlight the Nizam's status as a legitimate and ethical Muslim ruler. These writings reframed ideas present in colonial historiography about the history and essence of Muslim rule in South Asia, or the necessity of state-led intervention to stem conflict between communities and foster 'progressive' change. The complex, dynamic formation of Hyderabadi historiography functioned to create a discursive, conceptual space for the state in a colonially dominated world in which the Nizam's dominions constituted a sovereign fragment.

## Locating Hyderabad

Hyderabad's acolonial temporality, and the discursive universe it characterized, was situated parallel with, or perpendicular to, the larger British colonial world of political ideas.[84] These discursive configurations corresponded to and enabled political relationships, such as the legal enactments considered in the previous chapter, or the jurisdictional boundary-making, institutional and technological negotiations, and political experiments considered in subsequent chapters. As such, the conceptual work that Hyderabadi historiography and related genres performed was critical to securing the state's place in the modern South Asian political scene, after the Raj's mid-nineteenth-century shift from expanding conquest state to consolidating and pacifying imperial entity. Not only did distinct sub-imperial temporalities such as Hyderabad's correspond to separate state spaces within the conceptual and political geography of late imperial South Asia, they also provide a departure point for interventions into the history of political ideas in the modern subcontinent.

Hyderabad's foundational difference from British India that historical narratives about the state convey implies a need to revisit totalizing scholarly understandings of South Asian history. Recent research, noted above, has emphasized the importance of regional historical consciousness in the articulation of anti-colonial and nationalist political assertions, as well as postcolonial sub-nationalist movements.[85] Such approaches help disaggregate particular regional visions of political community from narratives of uniform colonial domination or unitary nationalism. The view from Hyderabad sketched above helps push such analysis further by

[84] Forster makes visible the role in colonial thought of sub-imperial states as figures of political desire for many who were scandalized by the enduring racist underpinnings of colonial rule.

[85] On sub-national movements and sub-imperial legacies, see Conclusion, below.

presenting a political vision of a sub-imperial state outside the colonial box or nationalist teleology. Its officials and advocates presented Hyderabad's past and present as neither an episode in the history of colonial domination nor a future component of a unitary, territorial postcolonial nation-state. As the narratives above suggest, Hyderabad provided a distinct discursive universe from which to rethink South Asia's present and future, which entailed a reframing of the past. The key defining element of this universe, which shaped narrative possibilities and opened particular circuits of connectivity, was the state's Muslim rulership.

In articulating the discursive universe of Hyderabad, state bureaucrat-intellectuals and their allies recast the polity's Muslimness as a sound ethical foundation for legitimate political authority. As the ambivalent relationship with the Mughal legacy suggests, however, political Muslimness in Hyderabad was a highly complex element with numerous potential implications and connections. Hyderabad's indelibly Muslim discursive universe was temporally scrambled – with pre-modern elements reflecting distinct Deccani or Mughal legacies and affinities with modernist ideas combining to render a 'patrimonial modernist' vision of state. It also situated the state amidst a series of overlapping geographies ranging in scale from local and regional (Deccani), subcontinent-wide (Mughal), to global. Hyderbadi historiography combined Muslim (and at times Mughal) ideas of political ethics with ostensibly progressive or modernist ideas, all presented as generated from a dialogue with the region's historical past. The centrality of Hyderabad's political Muslimness provided an opening out to broader vistas, global in scope, in the form of networks of Muslim modernist political thought. Hyderabad's discursive universe, and the political autonomy of the state to which it corresponded, channeled Hyderabad's engagement with the world beyond South Asia along lines of Muslimness and institutional or technocratic modernity. The following chapter turns to examine these connections through considering official correspondence and travel writings, genres intimately linked to historiography.

# 4 Hyderabad and the world: bureaucrat-intellectuals and Muslim modernist internationalism

Infrastructures for mobility and communication – steamship, railway, telegraph, print – proliferated globally from the mid-nineteenth century. By the dawn of the twentieth the world was linked together with unprecedented thoroughness and complexity. These developments brought different places in contact with one another, providing the frame for expanded political and intellectual geographies and exchanges of technical or political knowledge. Global connectedness also relied upon the expanding role of certain core nodes, and many cities became concourses on circulation routes of people, ideas, and things. This chapter considers how Hyderabad, as capital of a sovereign South Asian sub-imperial state, fit into global networks, and contends that these connections – and the need to communicate them to global audiences – provided a conceptual framework for changes in the state. Scholars of transnationalism in the subcontinent increasingly conceive South Asian places in circuits transgressing the British Empire.[1] Viewing the world from Hyderabad reveals connections that exceed British imperial transnational matrices, illuminating crosscutting connections across and beyond imperial domains.

The Nizam's capital served as a key concourse for transnational connections between global networks linking South Asia not only to Britain and other parts of their empire but to fellow Muslim-ruled states, other

[1] For recent examples, Metcalf, *Imperial Connections*; Bose, *A Hundred Horizons*; James Onley, "The Raj Reconsidered: British India's Informal Empire and Spheres of Influence in Asia and Africa," *Asian Affairs* 40.1 (2009): 44–62; Sana Aiyar, "Anticolonial Homelands across the Indian Ocean: The Politics of the Indian Diaspora in Kenya, c. 1930–1950," *American Historical Review* 116.4 (2011): 987–1013. Recent works that consider connections through other imperial spaces, such as the Ottoman, include Seema Alavi, "'Fugitive Mullahs and Outlawed Fanatics': Indian Muslims in Nineteenth Century Trans-Asiatic Imperial Rivalries," *Modern Asian Studies* 45.6 (2011): 1337–82 and "Siddiq Hasan Khan (1832–90) and the Creation of a Muslim Cosmopolitanism in the 19th Century," *Journal of the Economic and Social History of the Orient* 54.1 (2011): 1–38; Radhika Singha, "Passport, Ticket, and India Rubber-Stamp: 'The Problem of the Pauper Pilgrim' in Colonial India (c. 1882–1925)," in *The Limits of British Colonial Control in South Asia: Spaces of Disorder in the Indian Ocean Region*, ed. Ashwini Tambe and Harald Fischer-Tiné (London: Routledge, 2009), 49–83.

European polities, and other locations seen as exemplary models for institutional modernization projects in the state. Two key ideas that infused Hyderabadi official discourse and statecraft during the decades around the turn of the nineteenth century supplied the logic and content of intellectual and human connections.

The first was a protean *Muslim internationalism*: the idea of solidarity between Muslim-ruled polities within the emerging global state system, at times playing off the claims to universal Muslim sovereignty of the Ottomans or the Caliphate concept in general, and not always conceiving of states in a fixed territorial fashion. The terminology here requires some explanation. *Internationalism* refers to political connections between different places and people that are flexible enough to move between scales (local, regional, global), types of spaces (imperial, national), and movements or sensibilities (anti-colonial, feminist, anarchist, fascist; scientific, literary; Muslim, Asian, African).[2] The term is used here to highlight the way connections continued to exist between different and often distant formal political entities (states, but not necessarily nation-states). This included unambiguously sovereign places such as the Ottoman capital, as well as places under colonial rule such as British India, and places that did not fit neatly into either of these categories, such as Hyderabad or Egypt. Rather than describe these networks and political visions as Pan-Islam/ism, I have preferred *Muslim* (a descriptor of groups of people), as it does not imply consistent scripturally or mystically mediated ethical content as does Islam/ic. In much scholarship, like British and Ottoman imperial discourse, 'Pan-Islamic' implies solidarity of Muslims centered on the Ottoman Caliphate as coordinating institution over and against Western European imperial powers. While often important, Muslim internationalism was not always mediated by the idea of the Ottoman Caliphate.[3]

2 This definition of internationalism is informed by the considerations in Raza et al., eds., *The Internationalist Moment*, "Introduction: The Internationalism of the Moment: South Asia and the Contours of the Interwar World."

3 For a discussion of the importance of other circuits in Southeast Asian 'Pan-Islam' see Reid, "Nineteenth Century Pan-Islam"; R. Michael Feener, "New Networks and New Knowledge: Migrations, Communications and the Refiguration of the Muslim Community in the Nineteenth and Early Twentieth Centuries," in *Muslims and Modernity: Culture and Society since 1800*, ed. Robert W. Hefner (Cambridge University Press, 2010), 37–68; Michael Francis Laffan, *Islamic Nationhood and Colonial Indonesia: The Umma Below the Winds* (London: RoutledgeCurzon, 2003). For a critique of the use of the term 'Pan-Islam' in reference to South Asian Muslim politics on the grounds that the term uncritically reflects colonial discourse, and obscures other types of connections that informed "Islamic universalism," see Jalal, *Self and Sovereignty*, 66–67, 192–95. For an examination of Muslim Indian Ocean networks through Bombay, including overland

The second key idea was the notion of institutional and technocratic political *modernity*. Here, and throughout this book, the term *modern* and its derivatives (modernize, modernization, modernist, modernity) refer primarily to material technologically enabled processes related to economic and political institutions, particularly industrialization of production, global expansion of capitalism (including agrarian capitalism), urbanization, infrastructures for mobility and communication (railways, metaled roads, steamship, telegraph, telephone), and increased capacity for state regulation and control of populations. Two outcomes of these developments are the globalization of the nation-state form as sole foundation of political legitimacy and the development of the global capitalist economy, both of which reflect the dominance of the global north (primarily Western Europe, later North America) in setting the template for global interactions from the nineteenth century onward.[4] The focus in Hyderabad on achieving modernity produced a connected internationalism, routing connections into networks of expertise spanning British India and Western Europe, but also, critically, to other Muslim-ruled states undertaking modernizing reforms, such as the Ottomans.

Accounting for the interbraiding, overlapping, and at times mutual constitution of these two strands in Hyderabad's transnational life, this chapter maps a geography stretching well beyond the bounds of imperial space. Hyderabadi bureaucrat-intellectuals and others who mediated between the state and the world fueled these connections, and I begin with three anecdotes about such figures.

## I

In the early 1880s the Muslim internationalist modernist, educationist, and anti-colonial activist Jamal al-Din al-Afghani visited Hyderabad, kept under close surveillance by colonial authorities during his visit. Later the same decade an English follower of his, Wilfrid Scawen Blunt, came to the Nizam's state and frequented many of the same circuits of modernist Muslim intellectuals there to advance Afghani-influenced political and educational projects. Blunt complained bitterly of the difficulties posed by the constant presence of the Raj's security apparatus.

connections to Hyderabad, see Nile Green, *Bombay Islam: The Religious Economy of the Western Indian Ocean, 1840–1915* (Cambridge University Press, 2011).

4 Considerations of the ways in which modernity entailed key epistemological shifts are not the focus of consideration here. For a useful broad survey of modernity in material, institutional, and epistemological terms see Anthony Giddens, *The Consequences of Modernity* (Cambridge: Polity Press, 1990). For a wide-ranging consideration of its epistemological effects, Marshall Berman, *All That is Solid Melts into Air: The Experience of Modernity* (London: Verso, 1982).

## II

In January 1904 Charles Willmott wrote the Nizam's prime minister a carefully worded, deferential plea for a pension, supplemented by an account of his sixteen years of loyal service to Hyderabad State. In presenting his case, Willmott described his employment as a high bureaucrat in several key administrative departments in Hyderabad (including political, financial, and municipal posts), and his initial position as Assistant Compiler of the State Gazetteer. Willmott's letter emphasized "literary duties" he performed as a Hyderabad employee consisting of producing English publications detailing institutional and technical "modernization."

## III

In 1931 the former pro-Ottoman nationalist organizer Maulana Shaukat Ali traveled to the eastern Mediterranean in connection with his continuing attempts to establish institutions for advancing global Muslim political solidarity. The former khilafatist took a side-trip to the French Riviera, where he met the deposed Ottoman Sultan–Caliph, who was in exile there. At these meetings Shaukat Ali arranged marriages between the former ruler's daughter and niece to two sons of the Nizam, in hopes of leveraging the prestige of the Caliphate to advance Hyderbad's status as a leading Muslim state.

People such as al-Afghani, Blunt, Willmott, and Shaukat Ali performed the work of mediating between Hyderabad and other places in the world. Their activities demonstrate connections between several seemingly distinct dynamics (intellectual labor and bureaucratic work, modernization and Muslim solidarity) and places (domestic and international domains, Western Europe and West Asia). Compared with other subcontinental locations, global circulation through the Nizam's dominions was different in degree, but not in kind, and one can trace similar processes in major colonial cities and along other circuits. However, the non-colonial character of Hyderabad's state-building project, the polity's sovereign status, and its historical connections rendered the contexts of transnationalism distinct from what prevailed in British India.

Transregional Muslim circuits – with genealogies stretching back centuries, and continuous patrimonial connections within the state's political structure – infused the intellectual world of Hyderabad. These solidarities often dovetailed with the indelibly Muslim character colonialist and Hyderabadi histories, such as those traced in the previous chapter, ascribed to the Nizam's state. Reinvigorated Muslim networks in Hyderabad and new transnational political idioms worked through the infrastructures for mobility that the British Empire maintained and regulated. Hyderabad's intellectual scene, characterized by transregionally mediated discourses about modern Muslim statecraft, was often perceived by colonial officials as threatening to British designs. By the interwar era shifting geopolitical dynamics began to constrain connective circuits and the internationalist visions they sustained. As such, mid-twentieth-century Hyderabad became in many regards a venue for the contemplation of the future of Muslim power in a segmented and provincialized world of nation-states.[5] Hyderabad's transition from a cosmopolitan space for political experimentation into an isolated polity, and eventually a part of a new nation-state built on very different political–conceptual foundations, is coterminous with more ambivalent transformations in the realm of ideas. Muslim internationalism, and global modernist political imaginaries and connections, continued to resonate through the later imperial era and after. The anecdotes above track an internationalist moment between the 1870s and the interwar era. They also highlight the global framework that connected Hyderabad to South Asia as a whole, Europe, and the larger Muslim world, among other locations.

Hyderabad's global connections produced a configuration of intellectual contacts and affinities that framed the institutional experimentation and social changes traced in subsequent chapters of this book. The chapter begins by characterizing the Muslim internationalist moment, then goes on to describe Hyderabad's institutional developments and the increasingly important roles of state bureaucrat-intellectuals. Subsequent sections examine particular people to consider how global connections were constituted through discourses of international comparison and Muslim stateness, and by informal diplomatic practice. In concluding, it accounts for increasing constraints on Muslim internationalist connections, and their resonances.

## Muslim politics in an internationalist moment

From the last quarter of the nineteenth century to the second quarter of the twentieth, extraterritorial visions of political futures pulsed through expanding transnational circuits. This period saw increasing challenges to global European political and intellectual primacy. Muslim modernist

[5] On the prominence of Hyderabad intellectuals in debates over the terms of South Asian postcolonial nationalism see Datla, *The Language of Secular Islam*.

ideas and networks, particularly the Ottoman framing of Tanzimat administrative reforms as reflective of Muslim political ethics, produced a loose framework for solidarity between Muslim-ruled polities. In Hyderabad bureaucrat-intellectuals devised a political template integrated with transnational circuits by yoking state-led modernist reforms to an emphasis on the regime's Muslimness.[6] Situating Hyderabad's internationalism within global trends, and distinguishing its features from developments in British India, underscores the state's particular relation to the world.

The chronology of the British Indian colonial state – from an expanding and volatile conquest state to a consolidating and pacifying entity – intersected and articulated with global political dynamics. Technological changes of the nineteenth century, combined with the pressures of global imperialism and mounting resistance, contributed to a crisis in the international state system. Retrospectively, it appears that this crisis was resolved by a global political shift: a Europe-dominated world, organized by large empires with fuzzy boundaries, gave way to a new, still predominantly West-dominated, global system of ostensibly equivalent nation-states. The broadly effective consolidation of this shift via institutions of international governance has obscured the uncertainty of outcomes, and power of broader imaginaries and connections in defining the intellectual landscape.

Scholarship on the decades around 1900 has emphasized the central role of internationalisms in framing political debates in a world that was either colonized or subjected to intense European imperial pressure.[7] The emergence and spread of the nation-state is now broadly understood as a transnational development.[8] Other internationalisms, with ambivalent

6 The term Muslimness, as opposed to Islamic, is used to indicate a vision or configuration premised on solidarity between people who happen to be Muslims, but without the necessary presence or consistency of 'religious,' thus explicitly scripturally mediated ethical or legal, content (which would be denoted by Islamic).

7 Khuri-Makdisi, *The Eastern Mediterranean*; Raza et al., eds., *The Internationalist Moment*; Aydin, *The Politics of Anti-Westernism*; Ramnath, *Haj to Utopia*; Stephen Legg, "An International Anomaly? Sovereignty, the League of Nations and India's Princely Geographies," *Journal of Historical Geography* 43 (2014): 96–110; Manu Goswami, "Imaginary Futures and Colonial Internationalisms," *American Historical Review* 117.5 (2012): 1461–85. Many of these works rely on different periodization schemes, all of which nevertheless overlap with the one presented here.

8 A classic work on nationalism, Anderson, *Imagined Communities*, makes an early move in this direction, and subsequent scholarship has consolidated this shift: see Duara, *Sovereignty and Authenticity*; Selçuk Esenbel, "Japan's Global Claim to Asia and the World of Islam: Transnational Nationalism and World Power, 1900–1945," *American Historical Review* 109.4 (2004): 1140–70; Erez Manela, *The Wilsonian Moment: Self-Determination and the International Origins of Anticolonial Nationalism* (Oxford University Press, 2007).

relationships to parochialized territorial political sovereignty, have more recently come into scholarly focus.

Cemil Aydin's comparative work on Pan-Asianism and 'Pan-Islam' historicizes these ideologies as responses to a widespread legitimacy crisis of the existing Eurocentric world order starting in the 1880s.[9] Nineteenth-century non-Western empires – Japanese and Ottoman – invested extensively in Western-modeled institutional modernization projects based on acceptance of the putative universalism of the European civilization concept and its implications for state development.[10] European civilization's universalist status came into crisis with the continuing exclusion of non-Christian empires from the Eurocentric international community and European imperial expansion. These empires responded to the persistence and deepening of uneven power relations – particularly following Egypt's colonization and the 'Scramble for Africa' – by promoting and situating themselves within competing, explicitly non-European and anti-imperial, political geographies.[11]

Hyderabad pursued extensive institutional reforms, often referencing European models. Because of the particular circumstances whereby the state was assured sovereignty in the post-1857 imperial order, a parallel disillusionment with the false pretensions of European universalism did not have the direct political implications of fueling anti-imperial official ideologies as in the Ottoman or Japanese cases. This crisis, and the Ottoman response, was to influence the intellectual world of Hyderabad nevertheless.

The Ottoman articulation and global promotion of their vision of Caliph-centered Muslim solidarity during the Hamidian era (Abdülhamid II, r. 1876–1909) was on one level a means to shore up increasingly unstable imperial status, both domestically and imperially.[12] Nevertheless, Muslim internationalist ideology was refashioned to different uses and purposes by various state powers, movements and intellectuals. Muslims invoked the authority of the Ottomans in hopes of obtaining

9 Aydin, *The Politics of Anti-Westernism*.

10 Ibid., ch. 2. Earlier scholarship described nineteeth-century institutional modernization on Western European models as "defensive modernization."

11 Ibid., chs 3–4. On the "club of states" in international law see Alexandrowicz, *Law of Nations*.

12 Selim Deringil, "Legitimacy Structures in the Ottoman State: The Reign of Abdulhamid II (1876–1909)," *International Journal of Middle East Studies* 23.3 (1991): 345–59. On the concept of the Muslim world and the politics of 'Pan-Islam' as part of a post-1880s Ottoman bid to generate support to retain sovereignty see Cemil Aydin, "Globalizing the Intellectual History of the Idea of the 'Muslim World'," in *Global Intellectual History*, ed. Samuel Moyn and Andrew Sartori (New York: Columbia University Press, 2013), 159–86.

diplomatic intervention or military support to aid in struggles to avoid colonization or obtain autonomy within imperially dominated regions.[13] The idea of Muslim internationalism gained widespread political currency, and different parties invoked it in ways that envisioned neither the Ottoman capital of Istanbul, its ruling Caliph–Sultan, nor even the idea of the Caliphate, as core issues.[14] Further, Ottoman Muslim internationalism provided a framework for re-historicizing mid-nineteenth-century administrative reforms, known as the Tanzimat, as part of a distinctive Muslim modernity, not a universalist Eurocentric narrative.[15]

Its global salience and dynamism made Muslim internationalist ideology important in Hyderabad, but very differently than was the case in British India. As Faisal Devji has argued, South Asian Muslims were ruled by the British as a demographic minority.[16] This led them, he argues, to abandon "the idea of territorial nationality," and occupy "an imagined space situated at an angle to the sovereignty of the state" in assessing their status and contemplating political futures.[17] In the context of Hyderabad, the 'deterritorialized' component of Muslim sovereignty was present, owing both to the influence of British Indian Muslim thought and the rising global visibility of the Ottoman Caliph. Bureaucrat-intellectuals in Hyderabad, however, also envisioned the Nizam's state as a territorial arena for Muslim sovereignty. The coincidence of territorial and transregional political visions framed the Hyderabad context. Muslim internationalism was one of a varied array of political resources deployed by Hyderabad officials and advocates from a foundation of territorial sovereignty.

Seema Alavi's work on political itineraries of South Asian Muslim exiles during the late nineteenth century underscores the eclectic combinations the transregional Muslim political imagination facilitated. Alavi shows how "little men," specifically "men of religion," moving in the interstices of "big empires" along older circuits of connectivity, performed "international relations" as "ordinary individuals" pursuing their own interests in advancing claims over territory, disseminating Muslim monist or cosmopolitan universalist scriptural interpretations.[18] The figures Alavi tracks worked between states, articulating ambivalent and

[13] On Aceh in the late nineteenth century see Reid, "Nineteenth Century Pan-Islam."

[14] Laffan, *Islamic Nationhood*; Alavi, "'Fugitive Mullahs'"; Feener, "New Networks."

[15] Alavi, "'Fugitive Mullahs'," 1364–65 and "Siddiq Hasan Khan," 2–3. On initial Ottoman conception of Tanzimat as "liberal civilizationism" see Aydin, "Globalizing," 166.

[16] Faisal Devji, "A Shadow Nation: The Making of Muslim India," in *Beyond Sovereignty: Britain, Empire and Transnationalism, c. 1880–1950*, ed. Kevin Grant, Philippa Levine, and Frank Trentmann (Basingstoke: Palgrave Macmillan, 2007), 126–45.

[17] Ibid., 126. [18] Alavi, "'Fugitive Mullahs'."

often instrumentalist relations to sources of political authority such as colonial empires, the Ottomans, and other alliances or territorial moorings. Nevertheless, the Muslim modernist ethical currency of Tanzimat-style reforms, expanding internationalist networks, and patronage by Muslim-ruled states offered mobility and empowerment. Muslim exiles' flexibility and shrewdness as political brokers and clients illustrates the range of possibilities late imperial Muslim internationalist circuits produced.

Examining distinctions between the circulating people Alavi tracks and the bureaucrat-intellectuals considered here helps highlight Hyderabad's contextual particularity. First, Hyderabad bureaucrat-intellectuals worked, not only as 'individuals,' but from a firm foundation in a sovereign, territorial entity.[19] Second, the Asaf Jah state did not officially promote concrete ethical claims regarding the implication of the state's Muslimness for political practice. When performing their dual roles as administrators and intellectuals presenting the state's legitimacy to global (often Anglophone) publics, explicitly scripturally mediated ('religious') components of Hyderabadi bureaucrat-intellectuals' internationalist discourse was peripheral or absent.[20] Third, Hyderabadi figures were simultaneously constituent elements of Asaf Jahi state structure and ensconced within longstanding patrimonial loyalty networks stretching across the Indian Ocean.

Muslim internationalism in Hyderabad was extraterritorially connected but centered on an existing sovereign state, political and official in focus without overriding scriptural–ethical content, frequently Anglophone in character, and often integrated modernist internationalist ideas. The remainder of this chapter will focus on exemplary figures to parse the different streams and themes that constituted Hyderabadi internationalism: institutional and technical administrative modernization; international comparability with other states; and global solidarity between Muslim states.

[19] Despite being designated as 'individuals,' however, there are some indications that Alari's subjects played constituent roles in materializing and extending the Ottoman and other political formations or economic and social systems. See Alavi, "Siddiq Hasan Khan" on a Bhopal royal's leveraging of these networks.

[20] Muslim intellectuals also devised legal or ethical frameworks from scriptural or mystical authoritative sources, and at times cast them as critical to Muslim internationalism. However, not in official writings oriented toward state politics such as those considered here. For an account of the "Muslim International" as a movement in British Indian ethical thought without clear political linkages see Francis Robinson, "The Islamic World: World System to 'Religious International'," in *Religious Internationals in the Modern World: Globalization and Faith Communities Since 1750*, ed. Abigail Green and Vincent Viaene (Basingstoke: Palgrave Macmillan, 2012), 111–36.

## Bureaucrat-intellectuals and Hyderabadi modernity

The composition and training of Asaf Jah officials changed significantly starting in the mid-nineteenth century. The presence of new groups and types of administrators, along with rising emphasis on globally informed, technical knowledge in governance, shaped the contours of Hyderabad's global engagement. The push to modernize state institutions and to describe progress to global audiences resulted in state officials functioning both as bureaucrats, performing specialized administrative labor, and intellectuals, analyzing and disseminating ideas.

Hyderabad launched a self-conscious widespread process of institutional reform under Mīr Turāb 'Alī Ḳhāṅ, Sālār Jang I, Hyderabad *divan* from 1853 to 1883.[21] The variety of institutional and technological changes that characterized this era also provided substance for descriptions of Hyderabad designed for global consumption.[22] The backdrop featured expanding transportation and communication networks, increased presence of technically skilled foreign laborers in the state, and unprecedented levels of travel abroad for education and experience by Hyderabad officials.

The reformist program initiated by Salar Jang I, and carried on after his unexpected death by his sons Lāyiq 'Alī Ḳhāṅ (Salar Jang II, *divan* 1884–86), and Yūsuf 'Alī Ḳhāṅ (Salar Jang III, *divan* 1912–16), among others, occasioned a steady influx of administrative specialists. Labor opportunities in Hyderabad combined with disemployment in British India of Urdu

21 Sheela Raj, *Mediaevalism to Modernism: Socio-Economic and Cultural History of Hyderabad, 1869–1911* (Bombay: Popular Prakashan, 1987); Ray, *Hyderabad and British Paramountcy*; Regani, *Nizam–British Relations*; Bawa, *Nizam between Mughals and British*; Karen Leonard, "Cultural Change and Bureaucratic Modernization in 19th Century Hyderabad: Mulkis, Non-Mulkis and the English," in *Studies in the Foreign Relations of India, from the Earliest Times to 1947: Prof. H. K. Sherwani Felicitation Volume*, ed. P. K. Joshi and M. A. Nayeem (Hyderabad: Government of Andhra Pradesh, 1975), 442–54. On internal changes to Hyderabadi social structures and kinship networks during this period see Karen Isaksen Leonard, *Social History of an Indian Caste: The Kayasths of Hyderabad* (Berkeley: University of California Press, 1978).

22 Bilgrami and Willmott, *Historical and Descriptive Sketch*, discussed in Chapter 3 above, is one such description. Regarding institutional developments in a range of areas see Mīr Bāsiṭ 'Alī Ḳhāṅ, *Tārīḳh-i 'Adālat-i Āṣafī* (Hyderabad: Shams al-Islām, 1937); M. A. Muttalib, *Administration of Justice under the Nizams, 1724–1948* (Hyderabad: Andhra Pradesh State Archives, 1988); Omar Khalidi, ed., *Memoirs of Cyril Jones: People, Society and Railroads in Hyderabad* (New Delhi: Manohar, 1991); B. K. Narayan, *Agricultural Development in Hyderabad State 1900–1956: A Study in Economic History* (Secunderabad: Keshar Prakashan, 1960); M. A. Nayeem, *Hyderabad, Philatelic History* (New Delhi: Philatelic Congress of India, 1980); Y. Vaikuntham, *State, Economy and Social Transformation: Hyderabad State 1724–1948* (New Delhi: Manohar, 2002); and the studies in the previous note.

and Persian scribal experts to attract many to the state.[23] The increasingly bilingual use of Urdu and English in Hyderabad administration, in place from the late nineteenth century, favored officials adept in both Persianate Indo-Muslim and Anglophone-European governance methods.[24] Urdu and Persian knowledge allowed new officials to connect into established structures and rituals of authority, and to access existing Asaf Jahi records and documents. Official zeal for institutional and technical modernization and expansion of state functions created demand for specialists trained in the Anglophone political lexicon. Hyderabad became a destination for elite labor migration, primarily of British Indian administrators (of diverse British, South Asian, or European backgrounds), or South Asian Muslims schooled in Europe or British India.[25]

Asaf Jah administrators and nobles of this era traveled to British India, Muslim countries to the west, and Europe to observe and familiarize themselves with institutional and technical developments underway there, or for specialized education. Officials launched higher education

[23] On the 1864 dismissal of 'native law officers' see Michael R. Anderson, "Islamic Law and the Colonial Encounter in British India," in *Institutions and Ideologies: A SOAS South Asia Reader*, ed. Peter Robb and David Arnold (London: Routledge, 1993), 165–185, see 173. This change, the culmination of a long process of administrative Anglicization under the Raj, led to the exodus of textual specialists to sovereign subimperial states where skills in particular languages (Persian, Urdu, Marathi, Gujarati) or scripts (Shikastah, Modi) were the basis for employment or patronage: see Riho Isaka, "Language and Dominance: The Debates over the Gujarati Language in the Late Nineteenth Century," *South Asia: Journal of South Asian Studies* 25.1 (2002): 1–19. On mobile Marathi scribes and Modi literacy see Prachi Deshpande, "Scripting the Cultural History of Language: Modi in the Colonial Archive," in *New Cultural Histories of India: Materiality and Practices*, ed. Partha Chatterjee, Bodhisattva Kar, Tapati Guha-Thakurta (Delhi: Oxford University Press, 2014), 62–86 and "Maratha-Marathi in Madras: Thanjavur and Beyond" (unpublished manuscript, 2012); Rosalind O'Hanlon, "Letters Home: Banaras Pandits and the Maratha Regions in Early Modern India," *Modern Asian Studies* 44.2 (2010): 201–40; Sumit Guha, "Serving the Barbarian to Preserve the *Dharma*: The Ideology and Training of a Clerical Elite in Peninsular India c. 1300–1800," *Indian Economic and Social History Review* 47.4 (2010): 497–525; David Washbrook, "The Maratha Brahmin Model in South India: An Afterword," *Indian Economic and Social History Review* 47.4 (2010): 597–615.

[24] After Salar Jang I's death Urdu replaced Persian as Hyderabad's official central administrative language. This represented a culmination of the increasing power in the state of Urdu speakers from British India, many of whom were also fluent in English. The shift coincided with the arrival of increased numbers of British administrators into Hyderabad employment, and by the start of the twentieth century many state documents were bilingual Urdu and English.

[25] Particularly significant were South Asian Muslims trained at the Mohammedan Anglo-Oriental College in Aligarh, from whence Salar Jang I recruited a number of top graduates, establishing connections that were to continue to supply Hyderabad State with administrators well into the twentieth century. On Aligarh–Hyderabad connections see David Lelyveld, *Aligarh's First Generation: Muslim Solidarity in British India* (Princeton University Press, 1978), 60, 93, 141, 156; Bawa, *Nizam between Mughals and British*, 113–15.

schemes in the state and secured positions at universities in British India and abroad for potential state employees. This entailed the implementation of scholarship programs for study in universities outside Hyderabad, and the posting of a state official in England "to supervise the education and look after the interest" of the numerous Hyderabadis studying there.[26] These itineraries linked Hyderabad into a transnational education circuit, which in turn plugged future officials into intellectual networks.

Bureaucrat-intellectuals repositioned Hyderabad as a node in global Muslim modernist education networks with the 1918 foundation of Osmania University.[27] An Urdu-medium research university with scientific and technical faculties, as well as humanities curricula, Osmania drew interest, support, and faculty members from British India, Europe, North America, and Hyderabad itself. The state assembled an administrative core to develop and govern Hyderabad drawing from foreign-educated Hyderabadis, skilled emigrants, and Osmania graduates. The changing education–employment nexus was shaped in part by competition for patronage between 'insider' (*mulkī*) and 'outsider' (*ġhair-mulkī*) groups in Hyderabad.[28] The focus here on production of state bureaucrat-intellectuals and their work supplements perspectives focused on internal struggles or Hyderabad's place in British Indian and nationalist cultural politics. Asaf Jah officials – irrespective of regional, ethnic, or community origins – disseminated the image of Hyderabadi modernity to an increasingly global public. Many officials who served the Nizam and were instrumental in shaping the state's international image were neither Hyderabadis, Muslims, nor even South Asians.

### *A British employee in a 'native' state*

In 1879 Salar Jang requested a reference from the British Resident of Hyderabad regarding "One Mr. Willmott of Bombay," whom he

26 "Proposed appointment of Col. Fitzgerald, CB to supervise the education of Hyderabad students in England," APSA 7/1/355, 1904. For an example of the workings of scholarship programs see the case of Syed Ameer Ali, who was granted a "scholarship in lieu of service" in 1898 after completing his BA at Nizam's College in Hyderabad, APSA 7/1/262.

27 Datla, *The Language of Secular Islam*.

28 Karen Leonard, "Hyderabad, the Mulki–Non-Mulki Conflict," in *People, Princes and Paramount Power: Society and Politics in the Indian Princely States*, ed. Robin Jeffrey (New Delhi: Oxford University Press, 1978), 65–106. This formulation, central to internal debates in Hyderabad, has shaped scholarship on cultural dynamics of Hyderabad in the era of modernization. For an example of an ostensibly comprehensive discussion of employment centered upon this question see Aleem, *Personnel Management*, ch. 4.

hoped to employ to produce an English-language gazetteer for one of the state's districts.[29] Obtaining a favorable reference for Willmott, and in the absence of competing applications from South Asians, Hyderabad hired the former *Times of India* journalist on a temporary basis. Charles Willmott stayed on, and served the Nizam until his retirement nearly a quarter-century later in 1903.[30] Willmott and other Europeans integrated into the state administration combined with 'on-loan' British Indian officials to form a large body of outsiders with technical expertise in areas such as public works engineering, agricultural, forestry, and revenue administration, and police departments.[31]

Along with Anglophone South Asians and Europeans, Willmott played a key role in the international projection of Hyderabad as a legitimate, progressive, and modern state by composition of texts for Anglophone reading publics. After initial caution in employing Willmott – records suggest that he would not have been taken on had any 'natives' applied – by 1883 the Nizam's government considered him so indispensable that they rebuffed attempts by the British Residency to dislodge him from employment.[32] He rose to the post of Private Secretary, first to Syed Hossein Bilgrami (a leading state intellectual and Private Secretary to Salar Jang), and later to the Nizam, Mahbub Ali Khan. While Willmott was Bilgrami's secretary the two co-authored their encyclopedic *Historical and Descriptive Sketch*.[33] As noted in Chapter 3 above, the text rendered for international audiences Hyderabad's modernization as the culmination of a centuries-long legacy of progressive Muslim rule.

In spite of British obstacles to Hyderabad retaining European employees in permanent service, Willmott, E. E. Speight (considered below),

[29] "Entertainment of Mr. C. Willmott," APSA 7/1/5, 1879.

[30] Ibid. Neither his own published work nor subsequent scholarship mentions Willmott's first name. A number of documents from the era of his employment in Hyderabad, including this one, bear his full signature.

[31] The 'Europeans' section of the Hyderabad Public Services Department reported yearly on the number and occupations of these employees. APSA 7/1/204, 1895, for example, listed Europeans in the noted departments. For a later, more formalized, example of official data on the Europeans employed and their salaries see "Returns of Europeans and Eurasians in H.H.'s service for 1900 & 1901," APSA 7/1/298.

[32] Sub-imperial states were obliged to submit applications for "non-temporary" employment of Europeans, and failed to do so for Willmott. Replying to a colonial rebuke, the Nizam's officials insisted that Willmott had "proved his efficiency" and should "not have to suffer for this omission and that he may be allowed to continue in the position he now occupies," 29 March 1883, APSA 7/1/5.

[33] Willmott's claim: "Although the name of Moulvie Syed Hossain Bilgrami is associated with mine on the Title Page as joint compiler, the whole of the two Volumes were written by me": "Public Service, Pensions and Gratuities, Civil, Mr. C. Willmott (Late Assistant Financial Secretary)," APSA 7/1/350, 1904.

and numerous others made themselves indispensable by mediating to European audiences the idea of Hyderabadi progress in ways that were agreeable to participants in the state's patrimonial political structure. Willmott, who knew Persian and Urdu, was a counterpart to Anglophone Muslim Hyderabad officials from the north such as S. H. Bilgrami.[34] Hyderabad's administrative world in this era provided potential for mediations moving in multiple directions and blurring the racial boundaries that characterized the political context in British India.

Willmott's writings underscore the importance of ideological work in Hyderabad's era of modernization. His most detailed written account of his service to Hyderabad came some months after his retirement, in the form of a typewritten letter requesting the pension due to him for his years of service.[35] Willmott emphasized his "literary and personal" duties in mediating "important matters at different periods between His Highness' Government, the Government of India and various individuals." As proof, the petitioner listed official writings he had produced in the Nizam's employ: several gazetteers; the *Descriptive Sketch* (claiming sole authorship); a biography of Salar Jang published under Bilgrami's name.[36] In a subsequent letter of 1911 Willmott noted the numerous articles he published "in the Madras and Bombay papers," communicating "the marvellous prosperity and progress of the State under the personal control of His Highness . . . [to] the Government of India and the public generally."[37] The implicit justificatory criteria in Willmott's pension request, coming as it did from an official who spent decades in core Hyderabadi bureaucrat-intellectual circles, suggest an overriding concern within the state about outside perceptions of administration there.

## The anxiety of comparability

The ability to set certain developments in Hyderabad alongside those elsewhere was a way of asserting political legitimacy, and claiming a

34 Justifying Willmott's transfer to the Financial and Political Department, another Hyderabadi official noted: "He is the only European in His Highness' service who can discharge the duties of the position satisfactorily as he has a fair knowledge of both Hindustani and Persian," 19 May 1885, APSA 7/1/5.

35 The anecdote at the beginning of this chapter summarizes this letter: Willmott to Maharaji Sir Kishen Pershad [Divan], 12 January 1904, APSA 7/1/350, 1904.

36 APSA 7/1/5. Bilgrami and Willmott, *Historical and Descriptive Sketch*; Syed Hossain Bilgrami, *A Memoir of Sir Salar Jung, G.C.S.I.* (Bombay: Times of India Steam Press, 1883).

37 Willmott to Faridoonji [Jamshedji, the Private Secretary to the Divan], 28 February 1911, APSA 7/1/5.

place among states in the world.[38] This was particularly critical given the crisis in the global state system the late imperial era occasioned, the enduring power of European states in dictating the terms of global interaction, and the promise of change the internationalist moment held. Hyderabad's institutional modernization projects both relied on global circuits of expert knowledge in emerging disciplines and served as raw material for invoking comparisons with other places. New genres that gained prominence, and comparisons Hyderabadi bureaucrat-intellectuals made, reveal changing discursive strategies and political formations. Comparative work on state legitimization in the same era helps situate Hyderabad in the broader context.

Discussing internal and external threats to Ottoman imperial sovereignty, Selim Deringil highlighted increasingly prominent official attempts to legitimize political authority to world powers.[39] Comparing with other late nineteenth-century empires, Deringil detailed Ottoman strategies in a time where state legitimization had become a widespread imperative. He described, among other approaches, emphases on presenting the civilized character of the state to competing empires, often within a framework of modernist reform of Muslim institutions. Unlike in the Ottoman case, territorial sovereignty was relatively secure in late Asaf Jah Hyderabad. Legitimization provided, however, a means of bypassing colonial trusteeship claims to envision Hyderabad as an international entity. Herein, modernization represented a transregional exchange between peers rather than an example of unidirectional technology transfer. Asaf Jah officials pursued parallel legitimization strategies to the Ottomans, invoking ideas of modernization within a Muslim political framework in hopes of securing the state's place in the emerging global political system.

New genres of writing proliferated in late nineteenth-century Hyderabad, the historical coverage of which was discussed in the previous chapter. Texts, often state patronized, described the Nizam's implementation of modern institutional forms. Many of these, such as gazetteer-style texts, census capsules on places in the state, and progress reports, were modeled on genres produced during this era in the colonial state, and featured a similar emphasis on empirical or visual presentation. Administrative reports detailing progress in areas ranging from public works and education to the state archaeological survey and the agricultural,

[38] On similar projects, and justificatory strategies, in other minor states, see Chapter 1.
[39] Deringil, *Well-Protected Domains*.

revenue, and judiciary administration were regularly published in English by the early twentieth century.[40]

## *Reporting progress*

The 1929 "Progress Report of the Hyderabad State" exemplified the fully developed discourse of Hyderabadi modernity for global consumption.[41] The report was authored by Najaf Ali Khan and E. E. Speight, the latter a professor at Osmania University and a British writer and educationist who had spent the previous two decades at a preeminent Japanese university. The report's production indicates the continued importance of Anglophone state employees as advocates of Hyderabad in the colonial public sphere, and Osmania's role as coordination point for official self-presentation. The text's content demonstrates the centrality of the idea of comparability in presentations of state modernization.

Khan and Speight presented to readers "the moving finger of progress" and its doings "in Hyderabad today." The report described the state's administrative structure ("President and Executive Council . . . Constitutional instrument . . . Legislative Council . . . independent judiciary headed by a High Court . . . Civil Service") and broader departmental organization. Laying out these structural features, the authors claimed that Hyderabad was in many areas applying "the British Indian model," but was also "in advance of British India." Comparability with the colonial state indexed Hyderabad's modernity.

The polity's mirroring of, but distinctness from, British India in state functions was a central rhetorical feature, and Khan and Speight noted Hyderabad's separate but comparable monetary system and communication and transportation infrastructures. They further lauded the Nizam for following "time-honoured traditions of his family" in assisting the British in World War I, fostering scientific collaborations with British domestic and imperial institutions (astronomical, geophysical, and seismological), and allowing duty-free commerce across Nizam–Raj borders.

40 The first of such translations available in the Andhra Pradesh State Archives is "Report on the Administration of His Highness the Nizam's Dominions for the year 1322 Fasli (6th October 1912 to 5th October 1913)," Published by the Order of Government. Hyderabad-Deccan, 1915, APSA.

41 Political Secretary's Office, His Exalted Highness the Nizam's Government, "Progress Report of the Hyderabad State, compiled by Messrs. Speight and Najaf Ali Khan" [draft text], APSA 71/32/67, 1929. Subsequent quotations in this section are taken from this source, the pages of which are unnumbered.

"Officials with British training" were cast as critical to "efficient carrying out of [Hyderabad's] advanced and broad-minded schemes." But so were people and ideas from "further afield." As such, familiarity and affiliation with the colonial state shaded into a broader narrative about Hyderabad's particularity and status.

Beyond demonstrating affiliation and loyalty to British India, Khan and Speight's text presented Hyderabad's progress as matching yet surpassing the accomplishments of colonial rule in the subcontinent. Discussing "the modernization of Hyderabad . . . from the time of Salar Jang," the authors emphasized that "the modern age in Hyderabad" had given "a lead in Indian reform, and not least in the great matters of communal harmony, mutual forbearance and freedom of opportunity for all." The state's political ethics, and institutional developments, compared favorably to those of the Raj. Progress, then, entailed more than simply reshaping extant institutions after those in the colonial state. Hyderabadi modernity, informed by colonial technologies, could provide exemplary "ideals of Government" for the subcontinent as a whole.

Intimating reciprocity and parity between Hyderabad and British India, Khan and Speight gestured to more ambitious notions of international political affiliation. Inventories of specific projects underway intimate these aspirations:

> By irrigation, reclamation and afforestation of the largest advisable scale, by the application of chemical and electrical processes to agriculture and manufactures, by ameliorative work and hygienic provision, wise town-planning and colonization, by comprehensive systems of vocational training and development of industry and by rejection of extravagance in public and private life, a new Hyderabad is beginning to evolve, in which we are likely to see the fostering of much that is best in East and West, and a determination to equip our citizens for worthy companionship in the comity of nations which are leading civilization at one of the most crucial moments of transition in human history.

Irrigational and hygienic advancements were not ends in themselves here, but appeared in the rhetoric of the progress report as signposts indicating Hyderabad's ascension to the global stage.

Full membership "in the comity of nations," in light of Raj–Nizam treaties and their enforcement, seems more an expression of political desire than a description of circumstances. Informal arenas of global mediation such as the composition of progress reports allowed for the articulation of these aspirations, in the hope, perhaps, of influencing colonial officials and publics and international observers. As the authors suggested later in the text, however, there were other spaces outside the jurisdiction of subsidiary alliance treaties in which this nascent internationalism could incubate:

The influx of visitors from all parts of the world is steadily increasing, and by the development of commerce and encouragement of local industries, and through academic activities, relations with the outer world are becoming more numerous and intimate.

As in this description of the state's international life, Khan and Speight's discourse on Hyderabad's progress consistently gestured beyond Hyderabad's borders.

## Transregional connections and informal diplomacy

Hyderabad was situated at the intersection of several global publics, and the itineraries of travelers to and from the state elucidate the meanings of these connections. State bureaucrat-intellectuals employed a variety of strategies to forge affinities with other states in the world. English-language texts by Khan and Speight, Bilgrami and Willmott, and others were aimed outward to different segments of the international community: the Raj and emerging colonial publics in India; the broader British Empire and the imperial metropole itself; other potential allies in securing Hyderabad's international status. These sources paralleled writings in languages with more limited potential readerships, but which nevertheless mediated the idea of Hyderabad to still other publics. Texts in Arabic, Persian, and Urdu presented the Nizam's state to readers in Muslim West Asia, North Africa, and elsewhere in South Asia: regions with longstanding and more recent connections with Hyderabad that were also in the throes of similar dynamics of institutional change. Textual geographies of comparison and mediation mapped onto travelers' itineraries.

Records of official visitors to Hyderabad, and their reception in the state, show Asaf Jah attempts to position the state in international networks. Numerous British India and domestic British nobles and administrators visited the state, as did officials and aristocrats from other parts of Europe. As Alison Shah shows in her research on architecture in the state, visiting officials were hosted and entertained in Asaf Jah nobles' palaces, and toured through monumental urban landscapes.[42] These experiences were designed to emphasize to visitors the combination in Hyderabad of architectural and developmental idioms including transregional Muslim

42 Alison Mackenzie Shah, "Constructing a Capital on the Edge of Empire: Urban Patronage and Politics in the Nizams' Hyderabad, 1750–1950," Ph.D. thesis, University of Pennsylvania, 2005, ch. 5. Hyderabad's positioning itself within a transnational circuit of political dispensations composed of patrimonial loyalty networks comprising nobles and aristocrats was in some regards a strategic move. This mode of political capital had been globally under increasing threat since the eighteenth century.

and regional Deccani, British imperial Indo-Saracenic and Greek, international and modernist. The juxtaposition of diverse idioms manifested another angle on the transregional circuits of connectivity that infused Hyderabad. Further, the orientation of official state visitors in this manner represented an attempt to integrate them into the loose and expansive circuits of patrimonial loyalty and affiliation that constituted the Hyderabad political system. This kind of informal diplomacy provided a means of defining the terms of international relations and establishing Hyderabad's position as a peer to other states in the world.

Hyderabadis who traveled abroad performed informal diplomacy of a fashion by linking into circles of political discourse elsewhere, and by drawing comparisons between Hyderabad and other places. Young officials or students went on state-supported educational peregrinations to British India, Britain, Europe, or the United States.[43] Writings of bureaucrat-intellectuals about their voyages illustate the loose political connections and dialogues they opened up while traveling.[44] Two memoirs from several decades apart illustrate some of these dynamics, one by an erstwhile official, and the other by a state intellectual.

### *Hyderabad abroad*

During the late nineteenth century the second Salar Jang, Mir Layia 'Ali Ḵhan, traveled through Europe and West Asia. The narrative of his 1887–88 trip, *Vaqāyi'-i musāfarat*, suggests the transferability of political knowledge from one place to another, and the importance of comparing Hyderabad to other places.[45] Salar Jang II had recently been dismissed from his position as *divan* under mysterious circumstances, but expected

[43] See Chapter 7 below on urbanist and planning officials who traveled internationally for training. On Syed Ross Masood's travels to Japan as Hyderabad's Minister of Public Instruction see Datla, *The Language of Secular Islam*, ch. 2; Nile Green, "Forgotten Futures: Indian Muslims in the Trans-Islamic Turn to Japan," *Journal of Asian Studies* 72.3 (2013): 611–31.

[44] In addition to sources considered here, extant memoirs or reports document over a dozen separate voyages of nobles, officials, or students from Hyderabad to Europe, West Asia, North Africa, the United States, and the Horn of Africa in the period from the 1870s to the 1940s. These include writings by or about all three Salar Jangs, several other high officials, a major South Asian Muslim left intellectual, and a group of Osmania University students. On the Cambridge circle of future sovereigns and high officials of South Asian sub-imperial states see Zahir Ahmed, *Life's Yesterdays: Glimpses of Sir Nizamat Jung and his Times* (Bombay: Thacker, 1945), 13.

[45] Mīr Lāyiq 'Alī Ḵhān, Sir Sālār Jang II, *Vaqāyi'-i musāfarat-i Navvāb-i mustaṭāb-i ashraf-i arfa'-i vālā Mīr Lāyiq 'Alī Khān 'Imād al-Salṭanah Sar Sālār Jang Kī. Sī. Āy. Ī. baṣawb-i Farangistān* [The Travels in Europe of Nawab Mir Laik Alikan Imadul Saltane], ed. Omar Khalidi and Sunil Sharma (Tehran: Nashr-i Tārīḵh-i Irān, 2008). (English title from back cover of book.)

to return to his post. He traveled to Europe in hopes of "learning from observing the political situation and turmoil (*ḥālāt-o ḥarakāt-i pulitikiyah*) that was prevailing across all of Europe at that time, and from meetings with political figures (*arbābān-i siyāsat*) in whose capable hands the situation lay."[46] This opportunity for observation and meetings, for Salar Jang II, might provide a basis for reclaiming his position and making himself useful to the Nizam's state in an era when "all manner of progress (*har gunah taraqqī*) comes from travel (*safar*)."[47] Lauding the global infrastructure constructed by the British Empire, the second Salar Jang narrated his travel by steamship from Bombay via Aden and the Suez Canal to Cairo, Istanbul, Athens, Paris, and London. Descriptions of happenings in places he traveled often segued into comparisons between the political situations in the subcontinent in general and Hyderabad in particular. His admiration of Europe was tempered by reflections on such matters as the superiority of Hyderabad's system of taxation to that of Greece, and the relatively stable political situation in South Asia compared to that in Ottoman Turkey.[48] Salar Jang II noted explicitly that colonial networks and technologies such as the steamship had made intellectual exchanges between Hyderabad, West Asia, and Europe possible. He was never to return to the service of the Nizam and apply the knowledge he had gleaned abroad to his duties, but there were other figures from this era whose lives as state servants were informed by transnational connections.

H. K. Sherwani, Professor of History at Osmania University, resided in England and Switzerland for his studies from 1907 to 1914, supported by state funding. He published, first serially in a Hyderabadi literary journal and later as a book, an Urdu memoir of his return to Europe in 1938 as a delegate at the International Historical Congress (IHC), an academic conference.[49] Writing to convey for Urdu readers the conditions in "the security-assuring Europe of pre-war times," Sherwani made clear that he was producing knowledge for a transitional historical moment. Europe, once the center of global empire and civilization, was now merely one unstable part of a world "turned upside down" in an era of "intellectual confusion."[50] The production and publication of the text implies that knowledge from the now-bygone Europe was critical to the political future of South Asia – both as cautionary tale and template. His narrative indicates a concern with spreading word about the Nizam's achievements

46 He noted that these trends were causing connected geopolitical tensions in northwest South Asia: ibid., 21.

47 Ibid. 48 Ibid., 53–55, 75–78.

49 Harūn Ḳhāṅ Sherwānī, *Yūrup Jang Se Pahle* [Europe before the War] (Hyderabad: Idārah-yi Adabiyāt-i Urdū, 1944).

50 Ibid., "Tamhīd" [Preface].

in developing Hyderabad State to interlocutors in Europe, and describes meetings with state intellectuals in England and post-Ottoman Turkey, and with ordinary people.

In France Sherwani shared a berth with a traveler from the United States. The Osmania professor elaborated "the importance of Hyderabad and its numerous advances (*gūnagūṅ taraqiyyoṅ*)," but found his interlocutor more interested in British Indian matters. The "American itinerant" wanted to hear about the colony's political status, casteism and Hindu–Muslim conflict, and Gandhi, whom he saw as a metonomy for all of South Asia. Sherwani assessed the situation: "In his opinion Gandhi-ji's meaning was Hindustan's, and Hindustan's meaning was India's. And he had no idea that aside from Gandhi-ji's politics, other politics was possible."[51] Sherwani seemed to lament this limited perspective, and stubborn ignorance about the breadth of political possibilities in his homeland.

Sherwani's memoir detailed meetings with intellectuals and officials in post-Ottoman Turkey and Britain, and scholars from around the world at the IHC. In Turkey he met Cemil Bilsel, a historian who was at the time Rector of Istanbul University and was later to become a national parliament member and international representative of Turkey in global diplomatic fora.[52] Sherwani described a long discussion about history and politics with Şemşettin Günaltay, another state intellectual, who headed the Turkish Historical Society, was a founding member of the Kemalist party that ruled Turkey during its first years of the republic, and later served as Prime Minister.[53] Sherwani also met with important state intellectuals in England. He held meetings with the first South Asian member of the British Indian High Council in London, Sir Feroz Khan Noon; Harold Temperley in Cambridge, a British delegate, preeminent diplomatic historian, IHC officer, and national political advisor; and Alfred Hazel in Oxford, a Member of Parliament and constitutional legal scholar who had been Sherwani's college drillmaster.[54] These figures

51 Ibid., 151–52.

52 Ibid., 57–58. In the same section Sherwani described a meeting with another major historian, Mükrimin Halil Yinanç, a scholar of Islam in pre-Ottoman Anatolia who studied with German professors and was a member of the French Société Asiatique. I am indebted to M. Erdem Kabadayı for biographical details on Bilsel, Yinanç, and Günaltay.

53 Ibid., 69.

54 Ibid., 113, 120, 132. Brendan Simms, "Temperley, Harold William Vazeille (1879–1939)," in *Oxford Dictionary of National Biography*, online edition, ed. H. C. G. Matthew, Brian Harrison, and Lawrence Goldman (Oxford University Press, 2004). On the role of Temperley, and the IHC more broadly, in fashioning an internationalism of academic historians during late imperialism, Karl Dietrich Erdmann, *Toward a Global Community*

occupy the intersection of the halls of the academy with the corridors of state power. Sherwani's meetings with them suggest informal diplomatic connections Hyderabadi bureaucrat-intellectuals could forge, even in the context of Raj-mandated controls on formal diplomacy.

Writing during the denouement of empires, and of the Muslim internationalist moment, Sherwani echoed earlier Ottoman (and Japanese) rejections of European universalist pretensions to global modernity.[55] His narrative ascribed special importance to Muslim connections in Europe, and is replete with Ottoman nostalgia.[56] He sought out Ottoman cultural, toponymic, and architectural remains in republican Turkey and the Balkans, visiting wonder-houses (*navādir-ḳhānahs*) in Belgrade and Zagreb to view Ottoman artifacts.[57] He also intimated a series of historical and contemporary links between South Asian and post-Ottoman Muslims, including familial connections between medieval kings, and Central Asian imperial security networks.[58]

Writings of Hyderabadis abroad reveal travel as a venue for spreading information about the Nizam's state and forging connections with common people and state officials elsewhere. Abiding interests in administrative modernization, the structural importance of imperial infrastructures for mobility, and expansion of international contacts describe overlapping webs of connection. The narratives considered above suggest an enduring concern with the Ottoman state, even after its fall, as a key node in the Muslim internationalist circuit that ran through Hyderabad. Combined with the rising disillusionment with the universalist claims of a crisis-stricken Europe, as seen in Sherwani, this suggests that Muslim connections had a critical place in the Hyderabadi internationalist vision. Other modes of informal diplomatic relations in this era confirm the importance of Muslim links.

### *Philanthropy, military entrepreneurship, and patrimonial ties*

Hyderabad State initiatives, and independent activity of officials, at times constituted small-scale attempts to influence politics or extend networks beyond the subcontinent. The Nizam's state had significant philanthropic

*of Historians: The International Historical Congresses and the International Committee of Historical Sciences, 1898–2000* (New York: Berghahn, 2005).

55 Aydin, *The Politics of Anti-Westernism*.

56 See also his description of the Paris mosque and an Iranian exhibition in the city: Sherwani, *Yūrup Jang Se Pahle*, 143, 145.

57 Ibid., ch. 3 on Turkey, 81–82 on Bulgaria, 84 on Sofia, 90–98 on Yugoslavia, 96 and 98 on Belgrade and Zagreb wonder-houses, respectively.

58 Multiple connections emerge via some strange encounters in Edirne: ibid., 76.

involvement in Ottoman lands. Further, officials or military elites in Hyderabad's patrimonial political structure used the state as a base for advancing initiatives elsewhere. These activities constitute international political engagement through formal and informal channels.

Recent scholarship has established that in a world of increasingly restrictive international governance, philanthropy and charitable aid served as a means of forging connections and bringing influence to bear via alternative channels.[59] Hyderabad State, and high officials and nobles, including the Nizam, funded wartime medical relief in Ottoman lands through the Red Crescent Society, maintained *waqfs* in Palestine, and were critical in consolidating support for the late nineteenth-century Hijaz Railway project.[60] The latter was a showcase early twentieth-century Ottoman state project that connected infrastructural modernization with state focus on Arabian pilgrimage sites. The Nizam also provided substantial donations and maintained properties for lodging pilgrims and scholars in Mecca, Medina, and Jeddah.[61] Muslim philanthropy, even if routed through allied states, often attracted colonial suspicions.[62] Aid and investments helped produce alternative infrastructures for Muslim mobility to European imperial networks. The highly public movement of funds assured some degree of Hyderabadi presence, influence, and visibility in Ottoman lands, historical Muslim cities, and the international public sphere. Participants in Hyderabad's political system also performed more direct interventions.

In the late nineteenth century military entrepreneurs in Hyderabad routed funds and weapons from the Nizam's state to fuel a play for landed sovereignty in their Arabian peninsular homeland. The composition of Hyderabad's military elite, consisting of personal guard corps for the Nizam and state regiments that fought alongside British imperial forces, reveals transregional features of the state's patrimonialist networks. While modernization projects, educational travel, and Muslim internationalism

59 Work on the Cold War provides examples: Volker R. Berghahn, *America and the Intellectual Cold Wars in Europe: Shepard Stone between Philanthropy, Academy, and Diplomacy* (Princeton University Press, 2002), chs. 7 and 8; Young-sun Hong, *Cold War Germany, the Third World, and the Global Humanitarian Regime* (Cambridge University Press, 2015); Timothy A. Nicholson, "A Cold War Education: The Role of the Peace Corps in Creating a Tanzanian Identity," in *African Culture and Global Politics*, ed. Danielle Sanchez (New York: Routledge, 2014), 381–409.

60 Margrit Pernau-Reifeld, "Reaping the Whirlwind: Nizam and the Khilafat Movement," *Economic and Political Weekly* 34.38 (1999): 2745–51, 2748 on Hyderabad Red Crescent; Omar Khalidi, "Indian Muslims and Palestinian Awqaf," *Jerusalem Quarterly* 10.40 (2009): 52–58; Ochsenwald, "The Financing of the Hijaz Railroad," 139, 142; Low, "Empire and the Hajj," 280.

61 Alavi, "'Fugitive Mullahs'," 1374; Khalidi, "Palestinian Awqaf."

62 Low, "Empire and the Hajj."

generated new networks, Hyderabadi military elite often embodied older Indian Ocean maritime linkages. In this era they reactivated these old ties to serve new ends. Prominent in Hyderabad military ranks as soldiers or armed guards of elites were Hadramis, an "old diaspora" who for centuries had developed connective webs of prestige and power from Southeast Asia to East Africa that tracked back to their homeland on the Yemeni coast.[63] From the 1860s to the 1880s competing tribes, claiming sultanate status and aspiring to sub-imperial autonomy in the British South Aden Protectorate, clashed over territorial claims.[64] The two dominant empires in the region, the Ottomans and the British, attempted to turn the conflict to their advantage through strategic proxy alliances. Well established in Hyderabad's political structure, different Hadrami military entrepreneurs there supported three competing groups: the powerful Al Qu'aiti and Al Kathiri sultanates, and Abdallah al-Awlaqi's short-lived movement. One Qu'aiti-aligned group of Hyderabad Hadrami military officers gained the support of Salar Jang I. The Nizam's *divan* managed, for a time, to influence the British to tacitly support the Al Qu'aiti, while funds and armed Hyderabadi Rohilla troops flowed into the region.

The complex and protean political situation in South Arabia created potential for Hyderabadi elites with connections and designs there to pursue their own political advantage, either through routing funds or instigating quasi-official diplomatic or military action. Such developments prompted some Raj officials to accuse Hyderabad of attempting to set up a sphere of influence in the western Indian Ocean, even as Salar Jang was able to convince other British officials to facilitate movement of troops and ammunition from Hyderabad.[65] The fact of Hyderabadi sovereignty and the state's limited military power provided a basis for intervention into other global conflicts. Patrimionial and quasi-official international alliances with Muslims elsewhere were not always aligned

63 On Hadramis as an "old diaspora" see Ho, *Graves of Tarim*, preface.

64 Ulrike Freitag and W. G. Clarence-Smith, eds., *Hadhrami Traders, Scholars, and Statesmen in the Indian Ocean, 1750s–1960s* (Leiden: Brill, 1997), chapters by Freidhelm Hartwig ("Expansion, State Foundation and Reform: The Contest for Power in Hadhramaut in the Nineteenth Centry," 35–50), Omar Khalidi ("The Hadhrami Role in the Politics and Society of Colonian India, 1750s to 1950s," 67–81), and Ulrike Freitag ("Hadhramis in International Politics c.1750–1967," 112–30). Details of political developments in the remainder of this paragraph are drawn from these sources, along with Bawa, *Nizam between Mughals and British*, 181–86. On an 1876 attempt by a Hadrami exile from Malabar (the southeastern coast of the subcontinent) based in Istanbul to seize territorial sovereignty in a border region between Yemen and Oman see Alavi "'Fugitive Mullahs'," 1344.

65 On Raj accusations see Bawa, *Nizam between Mughals and British*, 186; on Salar Jang's role see Freitag, "Hadhramis in International Politics," 117.

with the Ottomans (indeed in this instance, they went directly against Istanbul's agenda).

This example from Yemen is suggestive of other potential informal diplomatic links between Hyderabad and places connected to the state by other participants in the Asaf Jahi patrimonial political system. Like Yemenis, Muslim East African military entrepreneurs known as Habshis or Siddis held high status in Hyderabad as soldiers or armed guards, and maintained connections to homelands in Ethiopia, Kenya, Somalia, or Zanzibar.[66] Habshis played important roles in quasi-sovereign territorial entities within Hyderabad State, such as the Hindu-ruled Wanaparthy Samasthan, and ruled over two other significant sub-imperial South Asian states, Sachin and Janjira, on the western coast of the subcontinent. There is evidence of connections between these minor sovereigns and Hyderabad elites, and nobles of both Habshi states served in the Hyderabad military and married into the state nobility.[67] The important role of Muslim Habshis in Hyderabadi military circles may also have influenced state participation in imperial armed mobilizations. The Nizam's forces were prominent in the 1868 British suppression of the uprising in Ethiopia led by a charismatic Christian modernist minor sovereign, Tewodros II, who fashioned himself an opponent of Muslim rule in surrounding regions.[68]

Like modernist connections and official or unofficial assistance, military aid from Hyderabad officials demonstrates the expansion and intensification of transregional networks, whether through new ties or older ones reinfused with vitality. Because of scholarly focus on Hyderabadi relations with British India, links between elites in the Nizam's state and political circles in Raj territory are well known.[69] The transregional ties of

66 Ababu Minda Yimene, "Dynamics of Ethnic Identity among the Siddis of Hyderabad," *African and Asian Studies* 6.3 (2007): 321–45. Yimene notes that many of these groups traced their descent to or via Yemeni port towns, often intermarried with Yemeni groups in Hyderabad, and identified themselves as at once Somali, Yemeni, Indian, African, Arab, and Habshi (among other designations).

67 Hyderabad official Nizamat Jang was a close companion of the son of the Sachin ruler when both were at Cambridge. Ahmed, *Life's Yesterdays*, 13. On the brother of the Janjira ruler's enlistment in the Hyderabad army and marriage into the nobility, see John McLeod, "Marriage and Identity among the Sidis of Janjira and Sachin," in *India in Africa, Africa in India: Indian Ocean Cosmopolitanisms*, ed. John C. Hawley (Bloomington: Indiana University Press, 2008), 253–72.

68 On Hyderabad participation see Muḥammad Aḥmadullāh Ḳhāṅ, *Savāniḥ-yi ʻumrī: Navvāb Akbar Jang Akbaruddaulah Akbarulmulk bahādur marḥūm Sī. Es. Ī. Sābiq kotwāl-i Ḥaidarābād Dakan, jismeṅ kotwāl sāḥib marḥūm ke ḥālāt-i zindagī ibtidā se intihā tak daraj kiʾe gāʾe haiṅ* (Agra: Maṭbaʻ-yi Shamsī, 1907), chs. 6–8.

69 On links between the state and Muslim loyalist or nationalist politics, in late British India and later in Pakistan, on Aligarh and Osmania, Lelyveld, *Aligarh's First Generation* and Datla, *The Language of Secular Islam*. On Muslim League connections to Hyderabad,

state elites, however, suggest broader circuits of connections, frequently linked to internationalist visions of Muslim solidarity.

## Hyderabad as Muslim state

Hyderabad's image as a Muslim state provided a flexible rubric for coordinating a variety of different webs of solidarity. Philanthropic and older patrimonial links served as informal instruments of international relations. State patronage of writers in Urdu, Persian, and Arabic, and employment of Indo-Persianate textual specialists in the bureaucracy, increased Hyderabad's reputation as a node in Muslim intellectual circuits. Its close relation to British India, together with the Nizam's status as Muslim ruler, situated the state at the center of Anglophone discourse about Muslim politics. More so than institutional substantiation, which was highly limited, the Asaf Jah Nizams' image as Muslim rulers was central to South Asian and global discourse about Hyderabad. This section considers the dynamic Muslim stateness generated by simultaneously empowering Hyderabad and subjecting it to surveillance, and the range of ways thinkers politically situated Hyderabad's Muslimness.

The context for seeing Hyderabad as a Muslim state was shaped by increasing British imperial concerns about Muslim solidarity. During the late nineteenth century and the first half of the twentieth, officials and advocates of the Nizam's authority sought to present him as leader of South Asian Muslims. The specter of Ottoman mobilization against British imperial interests in a wide range of places, and of Islamic ethical frameworks in the production of anti-colonial insurgency, provided an alibi for the direction of colonial counter-insurgency or surveillance against Muslims in particular.

In South Asia, so-called wahabi Islam – a term used to describe all manner of Muslim political ideology from agrarian protests to revivalist and reform movements – justified colonial intervention throughout the nineteenth century.[70] The putative radical militant Islamist

Ayesha Jalal, *The Sole Spokesman: Jinnah, the Muslim League, and the Demand for Pakistan* (Cambridge University Press, 1985).

70 The groups to whom the term was applied in nineteenth-century South Asia tended to have at most very loose affinity, and few if any direct connections, with the reformist movement in the Arabian Peninsula named for the late eighteenth-century conservative Islamist thinker Muhammad ibn Abd al-Wahhab, who was allied to the Saud dynastic family, whose descendants consolidated the Saudi Arabian state in the twentieth century. On colonial fantasies of Muslim radicalism and critical global responses, Julia Stephens, "The Phantom Wahhabi: Liberalism and the Muslim Fanatic in Mid-Victorian India," *Modern Asian Studies* 47.1 (2013): 22–52. For an account of the dynamic intellectual and ethical foundations of Muslim political protest, many incidents of which were dubbed

component in the 1857 anti-British mobilization, and the rise of the Ottomans after the 1870s as a touchstone across the Muslim world, stoked colonial suspicions.[71] As such, Muslim political organizing, mobility, or discourse about the implications of Muslimness for state practice and political futures became potential targets for surveillance or interdiction.[72] This focus increased with the World War I emergence of the Khilafat movement, opposing British actions against the Ottoman ruler, in alliance with the Gandhian Non-Cooperation movement as a widespread anti-colonial mobilization.[73] Raj officials pushed for the Nizam to act as leader of South Asian Muslims and encourage their loyalty to the British war cause, even as the Ottomans fought on the other side.[74] The Nizam provided the declaration, but Hyderabad officials quickly used connections through khilafatist networks in the Urdu press to circulate trenchant critiques of Raj policy in Hyderabad, prompting a colonial response.[75] The incident demonstrates the political potency and volatility of the Nizam's active cultivation of Muslim solidarity beyond the state.

The British Indian Khilafat movement collapsed following post-Ottoman Turkey's 1924 decision to abdicate the Caliphate. This victory of territorially bounded Wilsonian nationalism – to the exclusion of internationalist and collective political visions – also signaled the denouement

by colonial officials 'wahabi' mobilization, Ayesha Jalal, *Partisans of Allah: Jihad in South Asia* (Cambridge, MA: Harvard University Press, 2008).

71 For a reading of 1857 as a "religious" uprising, ideologically driven largely by rhetoric of Muslim armed *jihad*, see William Dalrymple, *The Last Mughal: The Fall of a Dynasty: Delhi, 1857* (New York: Vintage, 2008). On colonial suspicions about Muslim ties see Aydin, "Globalizing"; Saul Kelly, "'Crazy in the Extreme'? The Silk Letters Conspiracy," *Middle Eastern Studies* 49.2 (2013): 162–78; and references to Northern Nigerian networks in Chapter 1 above.

72 On colonial attempts to control Hajj pilgrim traffic, Low, "Empire and the Hajj"; Singha, "Passport, Ticket"; Valeska Huber, *Channelling Mobilities: Migration and Globalisation in the Suez Canal Region and Beyond, 1869–1914* (Cambridge University Press, 2013). On British ideas about Muslim radicalism, Stephens, "The Phantom Wahhabi"; and fears of anti-British propaganda in the Ottoman press, Alavi, "'Fugitive Mullahs'," 1380.

73 On the subcontinental importance of the Ottoman Sultan as Caliph see Gail Minault, *The Khilafat Movement: Religious Symbolism and Political Motivation in India* (New York: Columbia University Press, 1982); M. Naeem Qureishi, *Pan-Islam in British Indian Politics: A Study of the Khilafat Movement, 1918–1924* (Leiden: Brill, 1999); Min Kemal Öke, *The Turkish War of Independence and the Independence Struggle of the South Asian Muslims: "The Khilafat Movement" (1919–1924)* (Ankara: Republic of Türkiye Ministry of Culture, 1991); Syed Tanvir Wasti, "The Political Aspirations of Indian Muslims and the Ottoman Nexus," *Middle Eastern Studies* 42.5 (2006): 709–22. On historical contexts and developments leading up the Khilafat Movement of the interwar era, Azmi Özcan, *Pan-Islamism: Indian Muslims, the Ottomans and Britain (1877–1924)* (Leiden: Brill, 1997).

74 Pernau-Reifeld, "Reaping the Whirlwind."

75 Ibid., 2746–47.

of Hyderabadi Muslim internationalism.[76] But this did not prevent continuing colonial concerns about the Nizam's potential role in Muslim anti-colonial uprisings.[77]

Hyderabad's involvement in Muslim internationalist networks generated friction with the Raj. But emphasis in official discourse on the Nizam's role as a Muslim leader could also be cast as a bulwark to imperial stability. In colonial circles Hyderabad's fealty to the British Crown was often understood as a means to secure loyalty among subcontinental and global Muslim populations. Despite the pressure it attracted from the colonial state, Hyderabad's image as a Muslim state generated political and intellectual connections. Bureaucrat-intellectuals, in official and unofficial writings, as well as advocates of the state, linked the idea of its Muslimness to a variety of projects.

### *Muslim modernity in a loyalist frame*

In 1883 Maulavī Chirāġh 'Alī, a major Muslim modernist intellectual and Hyderabadi administrator, published an English-language text defending the possibility of progressive reforms in Muslim states, which he dedicated to "His Imperial Majesty; Sultan-us-Salatin [King of Kings] . . . Khalifa [Caliph]; va Sultan Abd-ul-Hameed Khan, The Sultan of Turkey and its dependencies."[78] Introducing his work as a response to an article by Malcolm MacColl, part of a rapidly accumulating archive of works which the author claimed "suffer under a delusion that Islam is incapable of any political, legal or social reforms," Ali sought to offer a corrective on the nature of Muslim statecraft.[79] The book portrayed Muslim states as progressive and republican, backing up these claims with interpretations of early Muslim history and jurisprudence, accounts of Muslim societies in South Asia and elsewhere, and, critically, references to contemporaneous Ottoman reforms. The author peppered his narrative with testimonies from various European scholars about Muslim societies, and comparisons with European institutions, arranged to highlight the benevolent character of Muslim rule. Moving seamlessly between events and institutions separated by several centuries, Ali's work

76 Aydin, "Globalizing."

77 On the surveillance of Abdulla Khan Khasmandi, a pro-Nizam British Indian journalist with alleged radical anti-colonial designs, during the mid-1920s see "Hyderabad Situation," OIOC L/P&S/10/1140, P.906/1925.

78 Moulavi Cheragh Ali, *The Proposed Political, Legal, and Social Reforms in The Ottoman Empire and other Mohammedan States* (Bombay: Education Society, 1883).

79 Ibid., i–ii.

developed an ahistorical reading of Muslim governance as tolerant, progressive, republican, and democratic. The narrative cast Ottoman and early Muslim history in the light of contemporary criteria for good governance in the Anglophone world, much of which was deployed by the British to justify their global empire. The book situated an ahistorical image of Muslim politics as a model for for modern democratic state-building.

Chiragh Ali's status and location were not part of the text's subject matter, and only the front matter and introduction indicated his position ("H. H. the Nizam's Civil Service") and date and place of the book's composition ("Hyderabad, Deccan; 27th December 1882").[80] He underscored the importance of British–Muslim alliances, and the empire's obligation toward Muslim subjects: "the British Empire is the greatest Mohammedan Power in the world, *i.e.* the Queen of England, as Empress of India, rules over more Mohammedans than any sovereign, not excepting His Imperial Majesty the Sultan of Turkey."[81] Chiragh Ali defended the ethical nature of historical and contemporary Muslim states, especially the Ottomans, and implicitly urged the British to safeguard the status and sovereignty of the Ottoman Caliph–Sultan on behalf of loyal British subjects, such as himself.

The circumstances of the text's production, viewed within Chiragh Ali's scholarly and bureaucratic career, help situate Hyderabad within the Muslim internationalist public sphere. Ali, born probably in 1844, spent the first three decades of his life moving between cities and towns in the Ganjetic plain. Educated in several languages including Urdu, Persian, English, Arabic, Hebrew, and Aramaic, the teenage Ali was pushed by the early death of his father to begin bureaucratic labor in district administration in Gorakhpur, Lucknow, and elsewhere.[82] During the 1870s he came under the influence of Syed Ahmad Khan, the Raj loyalist Muslim educationist and founder of the university at Aligarh. This association led Ali to begin composing Urdu and Arabic tracts. After Syed Ahmad Khan recommended him to Salar Jang, Ali began administrative work in Hyderabad from 1876, rising to revenue minister (*muʿtamad-i mālguẓārī*) then district governor (*subahdar*).

Chiragh Ali's writings before and after his move to Hyderabad differ markedly in subject matter and content, as well as target audience.

80 Ibid., title page and introduction. 81 Ibid., i.

82 Biographical data from Munavvar Ḥusain, *Maulavī Chirāġh ʿAlī kī ʿilmī Ḳhidmāt* (Patna: Ḳhudā Baḳhsh, 1997).

His early work, written in North India, combined commentaries on the Quran and the lives and ethics of Muhammad and other prophets with refutations of European critiques of Islam.[83] These publications are in Urdu and Arabic, oriented to South Asian (and possibly broader Arabophone) Muslim readerships. His early writings provided an abstract template for rethinking Muslim statecraft in light of contemporary intellectual developments. Ali's writings in Hyderabad, largely in English, featured strong political components in addition to ethical content. His advocacy of the Ottomans showcased this combined technique, as did his influential liberal reading of the Islamic concept of *jihād*.[84] These works present explicit interventions into debates in the global public sphere. The other major work he produced after coming to Hyderabad was an exhaustive compendium of Salar Jang's administrative reforms.[85] His Salar Jang book neatly complements the arguments and examples in his book on Ottoman reformism by providing a dense mass of raw material on kindred projects in Hyderabad. Ali's later works take the conceptual ethical framework for viewing Muslim statecraft developed in earlier writings, and detail existing states to present Muslim political modernity as comparable to European modernity.

The shift in Chiragh Ali's productivity suggests decisive contextual differences within the South Asian Muslim political world. As Faisal Devji has shown, Muslim thought in British India was deterritorialized and disjointed from the idea of state sovereignty.[86] Ali's early abstract ethical writings indicate an ambivalent relationship to states, similar to what Devji describes. His Hyderabad work, however, suggests a firm grounding within a sovereign polity with both territorial statist features and robust connections to Muslim internationalist circuits. Hyderabad's status as a Muslim state framed this dual – transregional and territorial – conceptual framework, which Chiragh Ali addressed in ethical–political writings simultaneously stressing loyalty to the British and the need for enduring Muslim political sovereignty.

83 Ibid., 29–30.

84 Cheragh Ali, *A Critical Exposition of the Popular "Jihád" Showing That All the Wars of Mohammad Were Defensive; and That Aggresive War, or Compulsory Conversion, Is Not Allowed in the Koran* (Calcutta: Thacker, Spink & Co., 1885). In a context where colonialist thinkers were increasingly defining Muslims as warlike and barbaric, and militant Muslim readings of *jihad* were gaining adherents, Ali argued that Islamic sources of authority presented armed warfare as a last resort to be avoided at all costs.

85 Cheragh Ali, *Hyderabad (Deccan) under Sir Salar Jung*, 4 vols. (Bombay: Education Society, 1885).

86 Devji, "Shadow Nation."

### *Scholarly publishing and Muslim visitors*

Hyderabad's stature in the global landscape of Muslim states loomed large in the Anglophone world of letters. English writings of bureaucrat-intellectuals such as Chiragh Ali and S. H. Bilgrami did much to establish the state as a landmark, and the itineraries of Anglophone Muslim travelers indicate the capital's nodal status. Closely related was the journal *Islamic Culture*, founded and published from Hyderabad starting in 1927 to carry English-language writings on Muslim culture and history.

*Islamic Culture* became a key organ for writings from many authors, Muslim and non-Muslim alike, but particularly prominent in its formation and activity were Anglophone converts. The founding editor of the journal, Muhammad Marmaduke Pickthall, was an English scholar of Islam who converted and moved to British India shortly afterwards.[87] He worked as an editor of the English newspaper *Bombay Chronicle* in the early 1920s, until the paper was censured by colonial authorities for allegedly false reporting on violent Raj counter-insurgency. Pickthall, who had previously collaborated with nationalist leaders including Gandhi, went to Hyderabad in 1925, disillusioned with draconian colonial rule and mourning the recent end of the Caliphate. Starting as a teacher at a prominent school in Hyderabad, Pickthall went on to obtain state funding to publish *Islamic Culture*, and later for producing an English translation of the Quran. Extensive official support for Pickthall indicates state interest in enhancing the Nizam's image in the Anglophone world as a patron of Muslim learning.

Pickthall, for his part, used his position in Hyderabad to develop Muslim internationalist connections and schemes. He proposed to Hyderabad bureaucrat-intellectual Nizamat Jang a "great Islamic project" for "wielding together, consolidating and strengthening in zeal the large Muslim population left in Hungary, Poland, and Yugoslavia," suggesting a focus on Budapest, which could form "the point of a wedge into Europe."[88] Writing about the political geography of the Muslim world, Pickthall described Hyderabad as "a sort of capital city for all Muslims." He envisioned the city as a headquarters for a "benevolent Islamic policy" to be enacted by England in reparation for colonial injustice against Muslims. Hyderabad, he argued, was pro-British, retained Mughal prestige, was "dear in the hearts of all the Indian Muslims," and provided a reputable

87 For biographical information on Pickthall see Peter Clark, *Marmaduke Pickthall: British Muslim* (London: Quartet Books, 1986).

88 Ahmed, *Life's Yesterdays*, 36–37.

"example of Islamic government."[89] In addition to these ambitious proposals, Pickthall cultivated far-reaching connections to thinkers from Malaya, South Asia, and the Arab world.[90]

*Islamic Culture* itself served to coordinate intellectual networks through Hyderabad, with Pickthall, and his successor as editor, the Eastern European Muslim convert Muhammad Asad (formerly Leopold Weiss), hosting visitors and calling upon them to supply articles.[91] The journal published important pieces by such figures as the prominent Canadian scholar of religion Wilfred Cantwell Smith, and the British Muslim convert, promoter of Islam, and critic of empire Abdullah Quilliam (formerly William Henry Quilliam, also known as Henri Leon and Harun Mustafa Leon). Networks through *Islamic Culture* and its editors, and Hyderabad's expanded role in Anglophone discourse about Islam, brought other intellectuals and activists to the state.[92] These connections overlapped with other circuits that brought British Indian Muslim thinkers to the state via patronage or employment, and mobile Indian Ocean groups (East Africans, Arabs, Persians) via older patrimonial connections. Some articulated explicit critiques of colonialism and cast Hyderabad within schemes for fortifying Muslim political sovereignty.

### *Hyderabad in Muslim internationalist visions*

By the late nineteenth century Hyderabad was an important destination for mobile Muslim thinkers from South Asia and beyond, and a nodal point in expanding Muslim intellectual networks. Some visitors were loyal to the Raj, but more radical figures also spent time in Hyderabad.

Anti-colonial Muslim internationalist Jamal al-Din al-Afghani lived in the state, most likely with the support of officials, between 1879 and 1882, after his expulsion from Egypt for criticism of European

89 Marmaduke Pickthall, "The Muslims in the Modern World," *Journal of the Royal Central Asian Society* 23.2 (1936): 221–94, quoted passages on 230.

90 Peter Clark, "A Man of Two Cities: Pickthall, Damascus, Hyderabad," *Asian Affairs* 25.3 (1994): 281–92.

91 On Asad see Sarah Waheed, "Islamic Thought and Travel in the Decolonizing World: Muhammad Asad's Orientalisms" (unpublished manuscript, 2013).

92 For example, the US journalist, ambassador to the Philippines, and Muslim convert Alexander Russell Webb visited Hyderabad in 1892, and Turkish intellectual and feminist Halide Edib traveled there in the 1930s. For their accounts of Hyderabad, Alexander Russell Webb, *Yankee Muslim: The Asian Travels of Mohammed Alexander Russell Webb*, ed. Brent D. Singleton ([Rockville, MD]: Borgo, 2007), 161–96; Halide Edib Adıvar, *Inside India*, ed. Mushirul Hasan (Oxford University Press, 2009), 141–51.

powers and their allies.[93] Colonial intelligence reports state that al-Afghani frequented Aligarhi intellectual circles in Hyderabad.[94] The Nizam's capital was also, however, where he composed and published scathing critiques of Syed Ahmad Khan's collaborationist politics and related ethical discourse.[95] Scholars debate the extent to which al-Afghani's and Aligarhi positions overlapped, and whether he even met key followers of Ahmad Khan there, such as Chiragh Ali.[96] In any case, the depth of engagement with Aligarhi arguments in al-Afghani's articles reveal that Hyderabad was an intellectual meeting-ground for competing modernist Muslim thinkers. Writings by members of al-Afghani's circle in Hamidian Istanbul a decade later show that their debates on similar topics (caliphal authority, Muslim sovereignty, colonial rule) were framed by terms from liberal discourse (liberty, justice, constitutionalism) common to Aligarhi thinkers.[97] This convergence suggests a shared discursive space emerging among Muslim modernist thinkers that borrowed terminology from dominant European rhetorics of legitimacy. Al-Afghani did not write explicitly about the Nizam's state, but one of his acolytes situated Hyderabad within Muslim internationalist visions.

Wilfrid Scawen Blunt, a minor English nobleman and poet, traveled to Hyderabad in 1883–84 after passing along the old Indian Ocean trade route through southern Arabia and Ceylon. A follower of al-Afghani and Muhammad Abduh, Blunt spent much of his life protesting excesses

93 There is no consensus on al-Afghani's dates for this trip to South Asia, including his time in Hyderabad. This is due, in part, to the possible unreliability of colonial intelligence reports upon which several scholars based their accounts. See Ahmed, "Afghani's Indian Contacts."

94 Ahmed (ibid., 478–79) cites an 1896 report authored by A. S. Lethbridge, General Superintendent, Thagi and Dakaiti Department, Government of India, which stated that al-Afghani's chief associates in Hyderabad were followers of Syed Ahmad Khan.

95 See discussion, ibid., 480, 487, and translations in Nikki R. Keddie and Jamal al-Din al-Afghani, *An Islamic Response to Imperialism: Political and Religious Writings of Sayyid Jamal al-Din "Afghani"* (Berkeley: University of California Press, 1983 [1968]).

96 Ahmed, "Afghani's Indian Contacts"; Keddie and al-Afghani, *Islamic Response*, 70–71; Elie Kedourie, *Afghani and 'Abduh: An Essay on Religious Unbelief and Political Activism in Modern Islam* (London: Cass, 1966). Al-Afghani did, however, meet S. H. Bilgrami, whose letter to the Resident about al-Afghani warned that he was "a free thinker of the French type, and a socialist" and was sending to Bilgrami and other Hyderabadi intellectuals his anti-British publications. Quoted in Ahmed, "Afghani's Indian Contacts," 481–82.

97 Fariba Zarinebaf, "From Istanbul to Tabriz: Modernity and Constitutionalism in the Ottoman Empire and Iran," *Comparative Studies of South Asia, Africa and the Middle East* 28.1 (2008): 154–69. For an account of al-Afghani as an example of late imperial Muslim cosmopolitanism, citing his mobility between different places, social practices, and conceptual lexicons, see Sami Zubaida, "Middle Eastern Experiences of Cosmopolitanism," in *Conceiving Cosmopolitanism: Theory, Context and Practice*, ed. Steven Vertovec and Robin Cohen (Oxford University Press, 2002), 32–41.

of British imperialism in Egypt and Ireland.[98] In 1882 Blunt published his major work, *The Future of Islam*, advocating full independence from colonial rule for Muslims.[99] Unlike al-Afghani he explicitly rejected the Ottoman Sultan's claim to the Caliphate in favor of Arabian leadership. Despite differences with thinkers such as Chiragh Ali, Blunt shared the notion that Muslim institutions and connections were crucial to a post-imperial international order.

On a series of trips to meet and collaborate with Muslim internationalists, Blunt visited many British-ruled portions of the Muslim world. He arrived in Hyderabad some months after the 1883 death of Salar Jang I. For Blunt British India, Hyderabad, and other sub-imperial states were key theaters of the global struggle for just government.[100] He lambasted colonial policies that marginalized Hyderabad officials brought in by Salar Jang, which he claimed isolated the state from "what happened in the outer world" and kept it "in ignorance of modern thought."[101] The Nizam, as "leader of the Mohammedans in India," and his officials had an important place in Blunt's vision for a Muslim global public.[102] For him Hyderabad both indicated South Asian "capacity for self-government" and maintained older forms of ethical South Asian political practice that colonial rule had effaced elsewhere.[103]

If European rule over Muslims was a general problem for Blunt, and Muslim internationalism a solution, his encounters with Hyderabadi bureaucrat-intellectuals reveal his strategies for developing this alternative. Lunching with Chiragh Ali, Syed Hossein Bilgrami, and the latter's brother Syed Ali Bilgrami, Blunt clarified the importance of "public opinion at home [in England]" as a counterweight to the Foreign Office, whose policy was "encroachment [and to] annex every independent State."[104] He advocated self-presentation by Hyderabadi intellectuals in the Anglophone public sphere as critical to empowering Hyderabad in a British-dominated region and wider world.[105]

According to Blunt's vision, in a seeming contradiction, an increased presence in the Anglophone public sphere would be a means for Hyderabad to break out of British imperial networks into a broader Muslim internationalism. This entailed tapping into reformist trends circulating

98 Blunt also criticized British actions in South Asia, Sudan, and Burma, among other locations. For a reckoning of Blunt as the sole "European 'expert'" on the Arab world who did not express "the traditional Western hostility and fear of the Orient" see Edward Said, *Orientalism* (New York: Pantheon, 1978), 237.

99 Wilfrid Scawen Blunt, *The Future of Islam*, ed. Riad Nourallah (London: Routledge Curzon, 2002 [1882]).

100 Wilfrid Scawen Blunt, *India under Ripon: A Private Diary* (London: Unwin, 1909).

101 Ibid., 67–70. 102 Ibid., 133. 103 Ibid., 299.

104 Ibid., 196. 105 Ibid., 73.

widely across the terrain of the Muslim world. Over "a very pleasant breakfast" with Syed Ali Bilgrami and Salar Jang II, Blunt discussed Hyderabad's place in this new geography. The diners agreed that reversing the British-led coup that had recently occurred in Egypt was crucial, as was establishing Arab sovereignty in Mecca, two centers they saw as more important touchstones for Muslim internationalism than Istanbul.[106] Describing a conversation with Chiragh Ali about his book on Ottoman governance, Blunt noted that similar reforms had been supported and defended by Muhammad Abduh. The key difference of opinion with Ali was Blunt's view that Istanbul was not a reliable leader in global Muslim reform, and that if the former was relying upon the Ottomans "he was leaning on a broken reed."[107]

Encounters between Blunt, critic of British rule and Ottoman leadership, and Chiragh Ali, supporter of Raj and Caliph, underscore the nodal role of Hyderabad in networks of Muslim political thinkers. The internationalist moment, elite employment opportunities, and Muslim sovereignty made the Nizam's capital a vibrant space for intellectual exchange. In a state that was territorially sovereign and closely connected to resonant transregional ideas of authority, thinkers with divergent positions contemplated the future of Muslim statecraft. Even if visions of Muslim sovereignty differed, intellectuals in Hyderabad found common ground around idioms of modernist institutional reform (the Ottoman Tanzimat as non-Eurocentric model), terms of discourse (Muslim ethical concepts framed in modern liberal thought), and the need for Muslim solidarity.

The productivity of the Muslim internationalist moment in Hyderabad depended largely on imperial infrastructures. C. A. Bayly described Wilfrid Scawen Blunt's use of colonial channels to criticize empire and advance competing causes during "early colonial wars of publicity."[108] Increased imperial surveillance during the last quarter of the nineteenth century put pressure on mobile Muslim internationalists, and Blunt consistently complained about the spies who shadowed him in Hyderabad and British India.[109] Departing in 1884, he never returned to the subcontinent, seeing too many obstacles to political organization there. Blunt continued to use internationalist networks to advance territorial

[106] Ibid., 62. [107] Ibid., 70.

[108] C. A. Bayly, "Representing Copts and Muhammadans: Empire, Nation and Community in Egypt and India, 1880–1914," in *Modernity and Culture: From the Mediterranean to the Indian Ocean*, ed. Leila Tarazi Faraz and C. A. Bayly (New York: Columbia University Press, 2002), 158–203, here 162, 164.

[109] Blunt, *India under Ripon*.

sovereignty movements in Egypt and Ireland, but his new focus represented a turn to what are recognizable as statist nationalist projects. The broader shift in this direction boded poorly for political visions, such as Hyderabad's Muslim internationalism, invested in transregional connections. Transformations in the British Empire, and the global public sphere, during the second quarter of the twentieth century left little political space for the kinds of projects and connections sketched above.

## The exhaustion of internationalism: provincializing Muslim politics

Beginning between the two World Wars, several factors converged to close down transregional political connections constitutive of the internationalist moment that started in the 1870s. This trend – and particular forces working against Muslim internationalism and connections through South Asia – portended a grim future for the dynamic networks described above. This section sketches the closure of the conjunctural global internationalist moment and its particular impact in Hyderabad, and examines the provincialization of Muslim politics in the Nizam's state though the life of one key figure.

The internationalist channels that proliferated in the decades around 1900 constricted in the late imperial era. Resulting parochialization or provincialization of regions, places, and people set the tone for the emergent international system of bounded states. The interwar era is a watershed in these processes, owing to the rise of nationalist ideologies, and colonial attempts to regulate mobility and secure territorial holdings (or at least maintain control over decolonization processes). The dominance of the Wilsonian doctrine as a template for post-imperial states framed political aspirations in terms of discrete territorial units defined by cultural (linguistic, ethnic, religious) consistency.

Global processes had particular manifestations in South Asia, surrounding regions, and the Muslim world. Thomas Metcalf has established British India's role as a secondary imperial center within the British Empire, with a sphere of influence spanning the Indian Ocean.[110] He traced the gradual closing down of "imperial connections" during the interwar years with increasing colonial emphasis on the British (rather than Indian) character of the larger empire, and the rise of political and economic nationalism. World War I and anti-colonialist agitations precipitated global tightening of borders, with Britain establishing passport regimes across the empire in hopes of stymying nascent internationalisms

[110] Metcalf, *Imperial Connections*.

(khilafatism, Bolshevism, anti-colonialism, anarchism).[111] The late colonial period saw the consolidation of political–economic "state space" in British India, which fixed territorial national horizons to political aspirations, and moved toward economic protectionism and isolationism, in part spurred on by wartime economic regulation.[112]

Hyderabad, landlocked and hemmed in by Raj territories, was affected by imperial trends. Tighter colonial restriction of mobility strained connections that had been cultivated by Muslim internationalist and modernist bureaucrat-intellectuals. The abolition of the Caliphate in post-Ottoman Turkey removed the symbolic lodestone of transregional Muslim solidarity. Rising South Asian nationalisms envisioned the Nizam's domains within bounded territorial state schemes. Emerging political idioms in British India also inflected Hyderabadi developments.

Religious community membership became a key structural framework for political organization in British Indian territory. Colonial knowledge forms conceived Raj subjects in terms of ostensibly fixed social categories, such as tribal or caste status, linguistic identity, or religious community. These categories in turn shaped political processes. Religious community became the preeminent category for the organization of late colonial representational schemes on a colony-wide scale.[113] When the colonial state began to concede electoral power to subjects, they defined constituencies based on religious community. The majority status of Hindus in the subcontinent, however diverse and disarticulated a community, loomed as a potential impediment to Muslim power in a contemplated postcolonial government. This dynamic led Muslim politicians to seek a variety of solutions, with both shared power schemes and claims for separate political bodies discussed seriously from the 1930s onward.[114] The rise of majority–minority politics combined with the breakdown of international connections to reshape the Hyderabad political landscape.

Activists launched political movements with conflicting visions of Hyderabad State's future. Varied Nizam loyalist positions, republican or

111 Ibid., 220. On passport regimes and South Asia see Mongia, "Race, Nationality, Mobility"; Radhika Singha, "The Great War and a 'Proper' Passport for the Colony: Border-Crossing in British India, c. 1882–1922," *Indian Economic and Social History Review* 50.3 (2013): 289–315.

112 Metcalf, *Imperial Connections*; Manu Goswami, *Producing India: From Colonial Economy to National Space* (University of Chicago Press, 2004).

113 The literature on social categories in colonial knowledge and governance is vast. See, *inter alia*, Dirks, *Castes of Mind*; Sandria Freitag, *Collective Action and Community: Public Arenas and the Emergence of Communalism in North India* (Berkeley: University of California Press, 1989); Gyanendra Pandey, *The Construction of Communalism in Colonial North India* (Delhi: Oxford University Press, 1990); Cohn, *Colonialism*.

114 Jalal, *Sole Spokesman*.

majoritarian pushes for union with British Indian territories, and communist radical movements emerged with popular or political support in Hyderabad or across British Indian borders.[115] Visions of Hyderabad as a Muslim state, severed by intensified colonial security regimes from diminished Muslim internationalist circuits, were provincialized and compressed into bounded territorial containers.

### *Bahadur Yar Jang and Muslim power in the Deccan*

The life of Bahādur Yār Jang provides a pointed epitaph for Hyderabadi Muslim internationalism. Scion of a *jāgīrdārī* (land-grant-holding) family, the young Yar Jang was a charismatic figure and gifted orator who fashioned himself as a Muslim political leader for cosmopolitan Hyderabad. He began his organizational work by leading a coordinating group for Hyderabad Mahdavi Muslims (a small community of interpretation to which his family belonged) and taking charge of a lobby organization for state *jagirdar* interests.[116] In the mid-1930s he was a key member of the Nizam's Subjects' League, a loyalist organization composed, like Hyderabad's political system, of Hindus and Muslims in the state's dense web of patrimonial loyalties. This group advocated political reforms based on international models, and equitable redistribution of political authority between classes and communities in hopes of undermining internal and external challenges to Asaf Jah sovereignty.[117]

Yar Jang's political life was supplemented by his work with the Anjuman-i Tablīgh-i Islām (Society for conversion to Islam), starting in 1927, through which he facilitated the conversion of numerous Hyderabadi Dalits to Islam.[118] The Tabligh initiative was an attempt to hedge bets against the rising tide of cross-border anti-Nizam Hindu majoritarian solidarity against Muslim rule. Like bureaucrat-intellectuals considered above, Yar Jang combined diffuse Muslim ethical and modern statist elements into political discourse. His work emphasized Muslim solidarity, invoking Islamic sources of authority (scripture, law) with support

115 Pernau, *Passing of Patrimonialism*; Lucien D. Benichou, *From Autocracy to Integration: Political Developments in Hyderabad State, 1938–1948* (Chennai: Orient Longman, 2000).

116 Naẓīruddīn Aḥmad, *Savāniḥ-yi Bahādur Yār Jang*, 3 vols. (Hyderabad: Bahādur Yār Jang Akaiḍīmī, 1986), vol. I, 134–37, 152–56.

117 Ibid.

118 Some accounts suggest that he was responsible for tens of thousands of conversions: ibid., 137–44; Benichou, *Autocracy to Integration*, 59; Pernau, *Passing of Patrimonialism*, 252; Ian Copland, "'Communalism' in Princely India: The Case of Hyderabad, 1930–1940," *Modern Asian Studies* 22.4 (1988), 783–814, here 806. See Chapter 5 below on Dalit–Nizam alliances in late Asaf Jah Hyderabad.

of Hyderabad State institutions premised on loyalties stretching across community boundaries.

Bahadur Yar Jang went on Hajj to the Hijaz in 1931, and during the time toured several Muslim countries west of the subcontinent, including Egypt, Palestine, Turkey, Lebanon, Iran, Iraq, and Afghanistan. He published a *safarnāmah* (travel narrative) recording his peregrinations between the subcontinent and *bilād-i islāmiyyah* (Muslim cities).[119] In several regards Bahadur Yar Jang's text reflected the features and concerns of earlier bureaucrat-intellectuals considered above. He described in detail administrative and political reforms and modernization projects in places he visited. A recurrent feature of his narrative was comparisons between technological and infrastructure development across the Muslim world. The young activist met other thinkers and discussed politics during his voyage. Describing the Nizam of Hyderabad while in Cairo, he praised "his master and bountiful lord" for knowledge of Arabic, Persian, Urdu, and English; the mutual admiration between ruler and subjects based on his egalitarian treatment of Hyderabadis of all communities and charitable assistance to the poor; and the success of modernization projects carried out independently of the British. He enumerated projects that were the stuff of Hyderabadi modernization: railroads; military, police and judiciary reforms; postage and minting.[120]

In 1932, following his return to Hyderabad, Bahadur Yar Jung took on leadership of what became the state's foremost exclusivist, later militant, Islamist party, the Majlis-i Ittihad al-Muslimin (MIM).[121] Continuing his work in negotiating institutional reforms through the Nizams's Subjects' League and other activities, by the mid-1930s Yar Jang's vision and tactics became increasingly strident. The MIM sought to preserve Muslim power in the Deccan through maintaining the sovereignty of the Asaf Jahs, even as the Nizam disassociated himself from the movement.[122] After Bahadur Yar Jang's death in 1944 the MIM developed a powerful and violent militia known as Raẓākars in hopes of preventing integration

[119] Bahādur Yār Jang, *Bahādur Yār Jang kā safarnāmah: bilād-i islāmiyyah (1931)*, ed. Naẓīr al-dīn Aḥmad (Hyderabad: Qaʾīd-i Millat Akaiḍīmī, 1969), 312–13.

[120] The article was published, reportedly, in *Al-Muqaṭṭam*, Cairo (Egypt) on 27 June 1931: ibid., 312–13.

[121] On the late twentieth-century emergence of the MIM as a populist platform linking Muslim and Dalit interests see Javeed Alam, "Composite Culture and Communal Consciousness: The Ittehadul Muslimeen in Hyderabad," in *Representing Hinduism: The Construction of Religious Traditions and National Identity*, ed. Vasudha Dalmia and Heinrich von Stietencron (New Delhi: Sage, 1995), 338–57.

[122] On the MIM militia and connections with British Indian Khaksar movement see Pernau, *Passing of Patrimonialism*, 254; Benichou, *Autocracy to Integration*, 91.

into postcolonial India after 1947. For the MIM and Yar Jang, Muslim solidarity was not a flexible framework through which to forge international allegiances, but a populist idiom justifying Muslim dominance within the territorial framework of Hyderabad imagined as a Muslim nation-state.[123]

Bahadur Yar Jang's mid-1930s militant, exclusivist turn serves to underline the fall of Muslim internationalism in Hyderabad. Imperial networks and infrastructures – critical for global connectivity – were canalized by bounded nationalist aspirations and imperial security regimes in the interwar era. Muslim politics was parochialized, rendering irrelevant widespread comparisons and connections that powered Hyderabadi internationalism. Provincialization of Muslim sovereignty ideas in South Asia did not, however, extinguish all ideas of Hyderabad's place in a wider political world.

## Resonances

Well into the interwar era, Muslim internationalist ideas continued to infuse Hyderabad. In some instances these were merely ways to conceptualize related political changes across distinct states. But in other cases activists envisioned Hyderabad as a site for remaking Muslim institutions, such as the Caliphate.

For H. K. Sherwani Ottoman sovereignty and the Caliphate were not the potent political resources they were for thinkers such as Chiragh Ali, or even critics of the Ottomans such as Blunt. By the time of his interwar travels the Ottoman Empire provided for Sherwani an archaic map for tracing small-scale connections between Muslims in different places. Thinking back to his student days in England before World War I, Sherwani declared, "Europe was no longer that Europe, Asia was no longer that Asia."[124] The universalist pretensions of European modernity – the justificatory edifice for empire – were in shambles, and counter-imperial internationalisms were figures of nostalgia.

For others, Ottoman sovereignty and the idea of the Caliphate remained a basis for political claims. After the dissolution of the British Indian Khilafat movement one of its key activists, Maulana Shaukat Ali, persisted in attempts make global Muslim solidarity a foundation for political empowerment.[125] A primary organizer for the World Islamic Congress (then called the World Muslim Congress) in Palestine during

123 Benichou, *Autocracy to Integration*, ch. 4, on populist ideology 108–9.
124 Sherwani, *Yūrup Jang Se Pahle*, "Tamhīd" [Preface].
125 His elder brother, Maulana Muhammad Ali, died in 1931 after years in Raj prisons.

December 1931, Shaukat Ali sought to use the meeting as a workshop for planning the remaking of the Caliphate.[126] Debates on the topic among participants broke down over disagreements as to the basis for nominating and selecting a new leader of the Muslim world. Foreshadowed in the divergent views of Blunt and Chiragh Ali a half century earlier, delegates were divided between Ottoman and Arab candidates. Further, Turkish opposition, European wariness, and the emerging global state system's canalization of internationalist connections made the prospect of reviving the institution difficult.

Even as efforts at the Palestine conference toward remaking Caliphate-centered Muslim sovereignty were ineffectual, Shaukat Ali was pursuing an alternate approach. With the 1922 fall of the Ottomans, Sultan–Caliph Mehmet VI was deposed and exiled by the new, territorial nationalism-oriented Turkish state. Turkey abolished the Ottoman Sultanate as an institution, but Abdül Mecid II succeeded Mehmet as Caliph, and assumed, from exile in France with his family and retainers, what had become a ceremonial status. In 1924 the Turkish parliament voted to abolish the Caliphate. During the 1920s and early 1930s several claimants to the Caliphate emerged in various locations, some supported by European powers as potential collaborators.[127]

In 1931, just before the Congress was held, Shaukat Ali negotiated marriage alliances between the Hyderabadi and Ottoman royal families. Visiting the deposed Ottoman Caliph in Nice, France, he brokered matches between the Nizam's sons Azam Jah and Muazzam Jah, and two Ottoman princesses, Dürrüşehvar and Nilüfer, daughter and niece of Abdül Mecid II, respectively. Both patriarchs had rejected other marriage proposals: the ex-Caliph with minor sovereigns of Iran, Egypt, and Iraq; and the Nizam with sub-imperial Muslim rulers elsewhere in South Asia.[128] The alliances proposed by Shaukat Ali conjured greater

126 Pernau-Reifeld, "Reaping the Whirlwind," 2749.

127 Hussein ibn Ali al-Hashimi, Sharif of Mecca and King of the Hijaz, sought the Caliphate through overtures to Kemalite Turkish republicans and via British collaboration. He saw the position as a means of securing suzerainty over other post-Ottoman sovereigns. Through his son Abdallah, Hussein declared himself Caliph in 1924, a claim not widely recognized. See Joshua Teitelbaum, "Sharif Husayn Ibn Ali and the Hashemite Vision of the Post-Ottoman Order: From Chieftaincy to Suzerainty," *Middle Eastern Studies* 34.1 (1998): 103–22 and "'Taking Back' the Caliphate: Sharīf Ḥusayn Ibn 'Alī, Mustafa Kemal and the Ottoman Caliphate," *Die Welt des Islams* 40.3 (2000): 412–24; Saad Omar Khan, "The 'Caliphate Question': British Views and Policy toward Pan-Islamic Politics and the End of the Ottoman Caliphate," *American Journal of Islamic Social Sciences* 24.4 (2007): 1–25.

128 On the Nizam's rejection of matches with royal families in small Muslim states on the west coast of South Asia (Junagadh, Mangrol, Manavadar) and the Caliph's rejection of marriage to a figure who seems to have been Abdallah of Iraq (described as son

possibilities. Whether or not this reflected "dynastic ambitions" to claim the Caliphate on the part of the Nizam, it is clear that these ties appeared from Hyderabad, and to Shaukat Ali, as a means of empowering Hyderabad by association with the Ottoman legacy.[129]

Close British surveillance of Shaukat Ali's trip to the World Islamic Congress suggests that the meeting, and the marriage alliances, were of great concern. Intelligence reports before the conference described Ali's designs to secure South Asian Muslim support for his "scheme for a Pan-Islamic Federation" and attempts to "revive the Caliphate."[130] His marriage-brokering came as a surprise to British spies. London warned that news of the marriages would be exploited by "Pan-Islamic propagandists" to damage British interests. Raj officials echoed concerns that the Nizam was being made a "cats-paw" in Ali's "elaborate scheme for dragging Indian Princes into revival of Khilafat."[131] The Turkish Embassy in Britain objected to the "Caliphate intrigue" they saw in the alliance.[132]

Marrying his sons into the Ottoman family may have worked to "strengthen [the Nizam's] position with Muslim world," but the strategy also held potential risks.[133] Post-wedding plans for appearances by the newlyweds in Mecca and Medina suggest an attempt to further associate the Asaf Jahs with symbols of Muslim sacral authority.[134] Shaukat Ali's attempts to generate publicity in Bombay among the Muslim public there in support of the alliances reveal conflicting political agendas. The Nizam's officials were apparently wary of arousing popular Hindu resentment in Hyderabad or Muslim mass political action in British India.[135]

of Hussein and brother of Faisal), see "Marriage of the sons of HEH the Nizam (Sahibzadas Azam Jah and Muazzam Jah) to Turkish princesses – daughter and niece respectively of the ex-Khalifa," in Hyderabad Residency, 316 of 1931, NAI R/2/73/101.

129 Clark, "Man of Two Cities," 288. The article also notes Pickthall's role in assisting Shaukat Ali in negotiations.

130 India Office to R. T. Peel, Under-Secretary of State, Foreign Office, 28 October 1931, in NAI R/2/73/101.

131 Telegram to His Majesty's Secretary of State for India, London, 14 December 1931 and Telegram from Resident, 7 December 1931, in "Report on the sons of His Exalted highness the Nizam of Hyderabad and their Turkish wives. Behaviour of Sahibzada Muazzam Jah during his stay in Europe." Foreign and Political Department, Government of India, 202-P. (Secret) of 1932, NAI R/1/1/2260.

132 Telegram from Political Secretary to Resident, 1 November 1931, in NAI R/2/73/101.

133 Telegram from Resident to Foreign Office, 3 October 1931, in NAI R/1/1/2260.

134 The visits were canceled after cholera and plague forced quarantine of the area. Extraordinary Jarida, 30 November 1931, in NAI R/2/73/101.

135 After letters appeared in Hyderabad and Bombay newspapers announcing the marriage and impending return of the newlyweds via Bombay, the Nizam sent an "angry telegram" to Shaukat Ali chastising him for "breach of confidence" in trying to launch a popular movement. Resident to Political Secretary, 24 November 1931, in NAI R/2/73/101.

Negotiations over the Ottoman–Asaf Jah marriages suggest that Muslim internationalism had become subordinate in importance to provincial, territorial conceptions of sovereignty in South Asia. Reportedly the ex-Caliph, after rejecting proposals from Arab sovereigns, consented to the alliances out of his "love and regard for Hyderabad which is the premier State in India."[136] Colonial advice, no doubt reflecting concerns about revived Muslim internationalist threats to British interests, advocated similar provincial aspirations:

> It is advisable in my opinion to inform Khalifa that he should give up all idea of the match unless he and his daughter are prepared for her to throw in her lot unreservedly with her husband's State and to inform Azam Jah that it would be fatal to his future career and happiness for him to marry a Turkish Princess whose heart and interests lie outside India.[137]

Far from consolidating transregional Muslim political solidarity, the Hyderabad heirs' marriage into the Ottoman family was cast as merely a means to advance the state's status within the subcontinent.

The Caliphate remained a potent symbol in the modern Muslim political lexicon. But provincialization of political horizons, combined with colonial manipulation of transregional Muslim mobilizations, reined in the conceptual power of the Caliphate in the late imperial world. Ultimately, British officials raised no objections to the Ottoman–Asaf Jah marriages, risks from his increased status and fortified claims to sovereignty being outweighed by the Nizam's usefulness as a loyal Muslim ruler. The internationalist moment had shaped Hyderabad's intellectual and institutional life, and the political force of transregional Muslim solidarity left ideological resonances and institutional presences.

## Internationalist connections and Hyderabad's institutions

The interbraiding in Hyderabad of globally mediated modernist discourses and ideas of Muslim solidarity is visible in the work of bureaucrat-intellectuals and others who envisioned the state's international life. Ottoman Tanzimat reforms of the mid-nineteenth century, and the state promotion of Caliph-centered Muslim internationalism there, served as touchstones for Hyderabadi political thinkers. Further, the Tanzimat were reframed in the Hamidian era as part of the Ottoman template for

136 "Note of necessary information supplied by Shaukat Ali to the Nizam (on his request) regarding the ex-Khalifa Abdul Majid's family," [n.d.], in NAI R/2/73/101.
137 Resident to Political Secretary, 17/18 October 1931, in NAI R/2/73/101.

Muslim modernist governance. Elements of this template were taken up and reworked to suit particular conditions in Hyderabad, as in Muslim polities elsewhere.[138]

The thematic alternation back and forth in this chapter between modernist, putatively secular international relations (informal diplomacy, institutional and technological development, 'progress' discourse) and explicitly Muslim internationalism (links between Muslim states or populations, Ottoman or other Caliphal leadership, patronage of scholarship on Muslim ethics and history, aid for pilgrimage facilities or places of worship) mirrors one of the core arguments here. Namely, that Hyderabadi internationalism tightly integrated ideas of global solidarity between Muslim states with political modernization that would make the Nizam's state a peer to other states in the world. This productive dual formation prevailed during the internationalist moment from the last quarter of the nineteenth century to the interwar era.

Provincialization of political horizons in South Asia, combined with constriction of transregional circuits, diminished ties between Hyderabad and the world. Notions of the state's Muslimness and its globally comparable modernity, however, had become deeply ingrained in the institutional life and political discourse of Hyderabad. The interbraiding of these streams animated Hyderabad's internationalist moment, but they began to come apart during the interwar era. As Bahadur Yar Jang's transformation suggests, Muslim stateness came to signify the repudiation of administrative modernization processes oriented toward official benevolence toward all segments of the population. Yar Jang's turn resulted, at least in part, from the rise of a politics that conceived political dominance in terms of community membership (whether majoritarian-democratic or, as in Hyderabad, through historical arguments for sovereignty).

In the institutional life of Hyderabad the modernist dynamic continued, into the mid-twentieth century, to facilitate internationalism, whether merely through looking outward, or via continuing connections. In this regard, Hyderabad's role as a space for wide-ranging exchange and experimentation endured from the mid-nineteenth century through Hyderabad's integration into postcolonial India (and possibly after). This was often, owing to Hyderabad's patrimonialist political structure or through abstract ethical ideas, tied back into notions of the Muslimness

138 On reframing the Tanzimat see Alavi, "Siddiq Hasan Khan," 2–3. On Tanzimat influence on legal reforms in Malaya, Iza Hussin, "Textual Trajectories: Re-Reading the Constitution and Majalah in 1890s Johor," *Indonesia and the Malay World* 41.120 (2013): 255–72.

of the Nizam's political sovereignty, as we shall see in subsequent chapters (though rarely via explicit Muslim internationalist connections after the interwar era).

The ideas traced above, articulated by bureaucrat-intellectuals, provided an enduring conceptual template for Hyderabad's institutional life, which in turn framed social worlds within the state. Accordingly, the intellectual histories traced in this chapter provide the context for the institutional experiments in rural and urban Hyderabad that the remainder of this book examines.

*Part II*

# Institutions

# 5 Moglai temporality: institutions, imperialism, and the making of the Hyderabad frontier

Raj Khosla's 1958 film *Kālāpānī* is a story of injustice and redemption, set in a Hyderabad rendered as an archaic externality to postcolonial India.[1] The film's hero, after learning that his father is not dead as he had believed, sets out from a quintessentially modern and ordered Bombay for an outmoded and inscrutable Hyderabad. The action takes place primarily in 1958, a decade after Hyderabad's integration into the decolonized Republic of India. The hero's father had been wrongly imprisoned for murder in Hyderabad fifteen years earlier when the city was capital of the Nizam's state. The film's Hyderabad, during both historical moments, is dominated by corruption and collusion between police and judicial officials, magnates and underworld figures; both bureaucracy and aristocracy are implicated. Miscarriage of justice appears as an unavoidable effect and constituent element of the social and political structure of the place. The hero and his allies manage to exonerate the innocent father by film's end. They do so only by navigating an orientalized world of dilettante poets, drunken itinerants, and sympathetic courtesans, inhabiting the fabulous estates, enchanting brothels, and dark alleys of the labyrinthine city. Despite an implicitly liberating change of regime from dynastic state to nation-state, Hyderabad remains in a temporality apart from that of Bombay and other postcolonial Indian places. 'Kala Pani,' the film's title (literally: black waters), indicates the experience of exile, which was historically carried out by 'transportation' to penal colonies across bodies of water, and refers by extension to life imprisonment.[2]

[1] *Kālāpānī*, dir. Raj Khosla (India, 1958).

[2] On penal transportation in colonial South Asia see Clare Anderson, *Legible Bodies: Race, Criminality and Colonialism in South Asia* (Oxford: Berg, 2004) and *Convicts in the Indian Ocean: Transportation from South Asia to Mauritius, 1815–53* (New York: St. Martin's Press, 2000); Satadru Sen, *Disciplining Punishment: Colonialism and Convict Society in the Andaman Islands* (New Delhi: Oxford University Press, 2000); Aparna Vaidik, "Settling the Convict: Matrimony and Domesticity in the Andamans," *Studies in History* 22.2 (2006): 221–51; Anand A. Yang, "Indian Convict Workers in Southeast Asia in the Late Eighteenth and Early Nineteenth Centuries," *Journal of World History* 14.2 (2003): 179–208.

Playing on both of these meanings, the film rendered Hyderabad as a remote place in temporal as well as geographical terms, whose distance is manifest in the endemic corruption of law and policing.

This chapter seeks to historicize *Kalapani*'s powerful image of Hyderabad as a place where rules do not operate as usual, and with it designations of the state as 'Moglai,' which marked political disorder as a function of temporal difference. Taking up the question of temporality considered in historiographic terms in Chapter 3 above, this chapter examines the implications of ideas of temporal difference for political practice in Hyderabad. It considers the production of the border – conceptually, juridically, institutionally – and the kinds of political spaces it divided from one another. Raj concerns with pacifying internal frontiers and eliminating threats to colonial security and economic stability drove border-regulation initiatives. However, the Nizam's assertion of sovereignty, combined with changing British fiscal concerns, fixed geographical limits on the extension of Raj authority. Hyderabad's frontier practices and policies, and strategies for defending state sovereignty, reveal traces of particular political structures and ethics operative there: a broadly non-interventionist relationship with provincial matters in the state, patrimonial networks of loyalty between the regime and nobles or officials, and protection and cultural accommodation of the subject population.

## Jurisdiction, geography, and temporalities

Even at the height of British rule in South Asia, the subcontinent abounded with frontiers where colonial territories jostled against enduring spaces of native sovereignty. Raj officials often cast sub-imperial polities as barbaric and archaic, contrasting them with British India's ostensibly ordered, civilized, and modern governance institutions. These strategic representations were used to justify expanding colonial power. Extraterritorial jurisdiction was invoked to encroach on political boundaries.

Raj jurisdictional transgressions into Hyderabad were part of several related processes. They facilitated the more powerful colonial state's bid to subordinate sub-imperial states' powers even as they recognized formal sovereignty. By the late nineteenth century the Raj was invested in consolidating formally colonized territory, and yoking these regions closely into a globalized capitalist economy. This required pacifying internal frontiers and regulating cross-border flows of commodities and ostensibly criminal communities who posed a threat to commerce or to colonially engineered social transformations. The market-oriented program for South Asia advanced by the Raj was centered on the agrarian economy, and entailed integrating the subcontinent into global capitalist relations by sedentarization and peasantization of the rural population, coerced cash-crop cultivation, stimulation of demand for European manufactures, and infrastructure development for extracting raw materials and importing consumer goods. The capitalization of the agrarian scene required containment of 'feudal pockets' and zones of legal anomaly such as Hyderabad. As such, colonial discourse about archaic governance in Hyderabad was a technology designed to accomplish goals both political (subordination or bypassing of state sovereignty) and economic (capitalist integration and transformation).[3]

Recent scholarship has emphasized the unevenness of imperial legal and political sovereignty owing to physical geography or the gradual nature of the spatial consolidation of the British Indian political economy.[4] The view from the Hyderabad–Bombay frontier suggests that state sovereignty, and not merely geography or lag time in capitalist expansion, generated enduring friction, contestation, and political difference.

Frontier relations reveal that Hyderabad officials deployed a variety of strategies for defending state sovereignty. They brought to bear claims voiced in the emergent language of territorial state authority and international law, and inverted the values enshrined in the colonial rhetoric about the archaic 'Moglai' temporality that constituted the Nizam's state. Officials of a sovereign Hyderabad State thus emphasized the regime's obligation to honor ties of loyalty and kinship that left provincial officials and land-grant holders with legal and policing powers unmediated by the political center. As such, the retention and defense of forms of 'disorder' in Hyderabad formed a bulwark against colonial intervention, and enabled the state to govern and develop on its own terms.

A key concern that will emerge in this consideration is the role that ethnographic and enumerative systems, often described as colonial knowledge or colonial sociology, played in the governance of Hyderabad and its border regions. Scholarship on colonial South Asia has emphasized the central role that colonial forms of knowledge – censuses, gazetteers, linguistic surveys, ethnography, historiography – played in the

[3] On sub-imperial states as posing "spatio-temporal limits" to Raj sovereignty and the resulting legal ambivalence and quest for legitimacy see Sen, "Unfinished Conquest," 240.

[4] Benton, *A Search for Sovereignty*; Goswami, *Producing India*.

making of South Asia's political modernity.[5] 'Colonial knowledge' provided conceptual building-blocks for what has been evocatively dubbed an "ethnographic state": a polity that categorized communities under rubrics of ethnicity, caste, or religion, and governed on the basis of these categories. Scholarship has tended to presume effective instrumentalization of racialized governance discourses in British India and in sub-imperial states. The view from Hyderabad suggests, first, that Raj officials often faced insurmountable limits to their authority at the boundaries of sovereign states, and that these limitations adversely affected the progress of colonial projects even in formally British-ruled regions. Second, knowledge forms developed in Hyderabad that correspond to British Indian colonial knowledge were only loosely yoked into projects of political control and economic transformation.[6] Further, in Hyderabad there was an enduring tension and interplay between performance of ostensibly modern state practices (such as those represented by 'colonial knowledge' genres) and alternative visions of political ethics that were instantiated in structures of state authority. As such, the career of colonial knowledge in Hyderabad reveals gaps between proliferation of texts, development of political ideologies, and conduct of governance.

This chapter is organized to show how Hyderabad signaled a limiting boundary or potential impediment to the colonial project in South Asia, and to suggest ways in which this boundary carved out a space for alternative, explicitly non-colonial political ethics and practice. I begin by describing the conceptual production of the Hyderabad–British India border. First, by Raj officials, for whom spatially and temporally situated notions of disorder were closely tied to the deployment of extra-legal colonial violence, often through extraordinary legal dispensations. I analyze specific colonial discourses about misrule in Hyderabad, referred to as 'Moglai,' indicating its implicitly enduring relationship to the bygone Mughal Empire. I then move from analysis of concepts to examining the colonial projects these discourses underwrote in the frontier zone. The case of a British Indian survey team allegedly attacked, imprisoned, and tortured in Hyderabad reveals the territorial limits of the colonial state and its counter-insurgency discourses. Raj initiatives for regulating cross-border movement of commodities and populations further

[5] See especially Cohn, *Colonialism*; Dirks, *Castes of Mind.*

[6] See discussion of divergences between Hyderabadi and colonial historiographies and state ideologies as they reflect in Chapter 3 above. For an ethhographic survey including identification of ostensibly criminal communities see Syed Siraj ul Hassan, *Castes and Tribes of H.E.H. Nizam's Dominions*, 2 vols. (Bombay: Times of India Press, 1920).

demonstrate the limits of colonial power, and the unintended consequences of attempts to pass costs of frontier policing on to Hyderabad. Negotiations over frontier policy begin to reveal contours of the strategy, ethics, and practice of Hyderabadi sovereignty. The remainder of the chapter describes the non-colonial political subjectivity visible in the above cases and in Hyderabad policies on famine relief and marginalized communities. Through juxtaposing colonial discourse and projects, and Hyderabadi policies and institutional developments, the chapter as a whole calls for a rethinking of political possibilities on colonialism's internal frontiers.

## Colonial terror, extra-legality, and the black legend of 'Moglai' justice

Rudyard Kipling's story "The Strange Ride of Morrowbie Jukes" narrates the harrowing tale of a British officer who slips outside the comfort zone of ordered imperial terrain into a desert netherworld of fearsome beasts, virulent and mendacious natives, and degenerate Europeans confined by the same morass.[7] The protagonist, trapped between a rushing river and a wall of sand, is rendered powerless and devotes himself to "a struggle against the inexplicable terror that threatened to overwhelm" him. The story embodies a familiar allegory, in which Britain's overseas empire is constantly haunted by the presence of incomprehensible barbarity in its midst. It takes all of the resources available to the Englishman – calculated deceit, ingenuity, violence, bribery, physical striving – to escape from this intractable uncivilized domain back to a place and time ordered by British imperial governance. Even this effort does not erase the constant specter of savagery within the heart of the empire, as indicated by the proximity of the nether realm and the fact that other European officials remained trapped within the barbaric temporality.

In her work on imperial rhetoric in South Asia, Sara Suleri has suggested that notions of British disempowerment in the unruly subcontinent were expressed through the trope of "colonial terror." This terror of the unknown and ungovernable was, she argued, a highly productive political language in the context of violent and racially ordered colonial governance.[8] Kipling's narrative, through utilizing this trope, implied

7 Rudyard Kipling, "The Strange Ride of Morrowbie Jukes," in *The Phantom 'Rickshaw and Other Eerie Tales* (New York: J. W. Lovell, 1890 [1888]), 76–125.
8 Suleri, *The Rhetoric of English India*, 7.

that British imperialism failed in generating progress toward civilized state and society. The persistence of archaic temporalities, such as the one that drives Morrowbie Jukes to violence and deceit, was thus a defining anxiety of empire.

Tropes of colonial terror facilitated the deployment of 'special' laws. As Nasser Hussain has argued, imperial concerns to maintain law and order in the subcontinent were met with coercive extra-legal violence. Colonial governance was thus characterized by episodic resort to emergency rule and special laws rather than consistent exercise of authority under legal mandate.[9] While Hussain treats "the jurisprudence of emergency" as a general characteristic of colonial South Asian politics, there were also particular, spatially situated notions of disorder and misrule within the subcontinent.

If Kipling located colonial terror in a vague and fictionalized desert of Rajputana between outposts of colonial civilization, state officials were clearer in assigning geographical locations to threatening disorder. As Chapter 3 showed, an enduring colonial discourse on Hyderabad cast the Muslim-ruled state as an archaic polity inimical to the rules of ostensibly civilized colonial territory. Used by colonial officials to describe Hyderabad territory, the designation 'Moglai' implied a specific connection to the pre-modern Mughals, and a political disorder more generally. The term Moglai likely entered the colonial lexicon following its use in the eighteenth-century Maratha state to describe their own frontier with Mughal territories in the Deccan, of which Hyderabad had been one, and more broadly to signify enemy territory and the implicitly chaotic political regime that prevailed there.[10]

These representations cohered into a relatively consistent orientalist rhetoric that could be invoked to justify interventions on the part of the colonial state. Hyderabad's role as a *conceptual* frontier within the colonized subcontinent was complicated by the fact that it was also a sovereign territory. Hyderabad's status as a *legal* frontier of the Raj generated a different equation between knowledge about the subcontinent and disciplinary power than obtained in colonial territory.

Colonial constructions of Hyderabad as both conceptual and legal frontier are visible in a journalist's account of a late nineteenth-century murder trial in the border district of Parbhani:

9 Hussain, *The Jurisprudence of Emergency*.

10 I owe information on the use of the term in historical and contemporary Marathi to Prachi Deshpande. On *moṇglāi* (Moglai) in Maratha usage as referring to enemy sovereignty or formerly Mughal lands held by Marathas see Wink, *Land and Sovereignty*, 33, 44, 97–98, 101, 323.

The procedure adopted by Mr. Hafiz Ahmed Raza Khan [a judge in the Hyderabad High Court] in the trial of the murder case might well make the civilized world 'gasp and stare,' and set the peace-loving Hyderabadee thinking as to whether his life and property are safe within the Moglai limits even in this century and within sight of the British flag.[11]

The state's justice system was cast as appalling to the entire "civilized world," virulent and threatening to "the peace-loving Hyderabadee," and aberrant to British accomplishments in neighboring Bombay Presidency. The rendering was also profoundly racialized, with Hyderabad administering justice "worthy only of the rulers of the Darkest Africa" in open defiance of "the most enlightened people on the face of the earth, the English . . . whom Providence had put in charge of the destinies of India."[12] The barbaric space presided over by "Moglai judges" of Hyderabad, assigned to a different temporality by association with the pre-colonial Mughal Empire, appears as irredeemably backward in comparison with a modernized British India.[13] Such images played a key role in frontier governance.

The term black legend (or *leyendra negra*) refers to self-interested northern European imperialists' dramatic portrayals of the Spanish colonial empire as fanatically Catholic, unjust, and barbaric.[14] The term was coined in a 1914 book by Spanish historian and state employee Julián Juderías in an attempt to redeem the reputation of Spain's colonial empire and deny British claims to moral superiority.[15] The recurrence of 'black legends' underscores both the consistency of British demonization of competing polities and their function in legitimizing inter-imperial encroachment.

The colonial black legend of Hyderabad portrayed governance in the state as personalized, nepotistic, and insufficiently regulated or systematized. Attempts to assert cross-border control, however, reveal

[11] Letter of 3 January 1891, in *Hyderabad in 1890 and 1891: Comprising all the Letters on Hyderabad Affairs Written to the Madras "Hindu" by its Hyderabad Correspondent during 1890 and 1891* (Bangalore: Caxton Press, 1892), 49. One can surmise that the author is a 'Westerner,' and probably British, given the cultural distancing indicated in his characterization of a letter from Nawab Mushtak (Maulvi Mushtaq Hussain), Revenue Secretary of Hyderabad, which acknowledged the latter's "great consideration for [the author] *in the usual Oriental terms*" (emphasis added), ibid., 2.

[12] Ibid., 45, 10. [13] Ibid., 47.

[14] This was applied especially by the English and to a lesser extent the Dutch and other European imperial powers.

[15] Julián Juderías, *La leyenda negra y la verdad histórica* (Madrid: Revista de Archivos, 1914). The black legend has remained politically productive as a frame for Anglophone demonizing of Iberians, and later Hispanics: María DeGuzmán, *Spain's Long Shadow: The Black Legend, Off-Whiteness, and Anglo-American Empire* (Minneapolis: University of Minnesota Press, 2005).

limitations posed by state boundaries on post-1850 British Indian consolidation attempts, and suggest a disconnect between knowledge forms and institutional power. Responses from Hyderabad to Raj frontier policy indicate opposition to particular projects, and a rhetorical inversion of negative colonial accounts of Hyderabad's decentralized, personalized form of governance.[16]

## Surveying Moglai

In January 1889, while performing triangulation work, a Topographical Survey of India team based in British Bombay Presidency entered the village of Malapur in Hyderabad State, and a conflict ensued with local authorities there. Several survey team members were imprisoned and allegedly tortured by Hyderabad police, and legal–political wrangles between Raj and Nizam officials ensued. Colonial writings on the incident cast Hyderabad as a menacing remainder of the ungovernable and unknowable subcontinent the British had largely subjected to their reign of 'law and order.' This case featured moral valuations of geopolitical space that were integral to colonial sociologies about South Asia. Hyderabadi reversals of this valuation triggered breakdowns in colonial codes of pacification, and illuminate shatter lines in the complex, fragmentary jurisdictional geography of the subcontinent.[17]

The Survey of India was critical in constructing the edifice of colonial knowledge that scholars have shown to be instrumental to British expansion in South Asia.[18] Carried out over the course of the nineteenth century, the Trigonometrical Survey of India entailed extensive overland travel across the subcontinent by teams of surveyors and intensive labor with heavy instruments such as theodolites and leaden chains. Triangulations, topographic information, and resulting cartographic renderings provided the foundation for the subsequent overlaying of maps with land revenue figures, census data about populations, and ethnographic

[16] On 'Moglai' in the historical imagination of the Dangs (western Indian Adivasis) as a temporal designation for "a time of freedom" and Dang political sovereignty, and which was "extra-colonial rather than only pre-colonial," see Ajay Skaria, *Hybrid Histories: Forests, Frontiers and Wildness in Western India* (Delhi: Oxford University Press, 1999), 15–17.

[17] The phrase "code of pacification" is from Ranajit Guha's work on the functioning of colonial knowledge, discussed below: Ranajit Guha, "The Prose of Counter-Insurgency," in *Subaltern Studies II: Writings on South Asian History and Society*, ed. Ranajit Guha (Delhi: Oxford University Press, 1983), 1–42, here 27.

[18] Matthew Edney, *Mapping an Empire: The Geographical Construction of British India, 1765–1843* (University of Chicago Press, 1997). On the "Survey Modality" in colonial knowledge formation see Cohn, *Colonialism*, 7–8.

descriptions of various cultural groups.[19] Surveying also required the passage of teams into regions where they had no formal political status, often across sensitive borders.[20]

In documents produced during a year-long correspondence, colonialists worked the Malapur incident into a full-blown illustration of the absence of justice in Hyderabad. The leader of the survey team laid out the events to his superior officer:

A number of my men have been badly beaten and four of them taken prisoners, also my theodolite officer so that I am quite unable to go on with my work. It happened this way – I was riding to work, going from Nasgani to Jalihal, on my way as I was passing the village of Malapur I met a Mussalman Chaprassi [low-level state employee or messenger] looking fellow standing just outside the village. I asked him to go into the village and tell the Patel to send a guide, he replied in a very impertinent manner and said "Go and do it yourself" or words to that effect. I rode up to him to ask him what he meant, when he at once took hold of my horse by the reins and commenced pushing him back . . . using bad language. I could not get away from him, so I hit him with my fly beater on the hand, but it was too small and light and had no effect. One of my men came up and took his hand off the reins, then he turned upon that man and tried to drag him off to the village. The villagers 50 or 60 now turned out with the Patel and took his part, so in a few minutes my men were all thrown down and kicked and beaten for nothing at all and were marched off to the village prisoner . . . These villagers ha[ve] thrown away all semblance of law and order and had I been on foot I believe I should have received a severe mauling; if not killed altogether. I got to Badami [in British Bombay] and found out that the village in question is in the Nizam's Dominions . . . after the lawlessness and wanton brutality I witnessed this morning I did not feel safe . . . The Mamlatdar [head of taluka, administrative division within district] of Kushigi (Nizam's) has been written to and I hope my men and theodolite will soon be released and that these people will be punished.

On my return from Badami this evening these villagers were all waiting for and attacked me again and caught hold of my horse, although I had policemen with me, in fact: they did their best to try to get up a row. I feel rather nervous about being in these parts and hope you will do all you can for my protection.

There is a liquor shop in the village of Malapur and this is the only way I can account for the behaviour of these people. The Musalman went on like a madman, he attacked every man I had with me in turn and finally myself, had he got hold of me with the assistance of the villagers and got me off my horse, I cannot imagine what would have happened.

[19] On the census see Cohn, "Census, Social Structure and Objectification."

[20] On the need for special arrangements in sub-imperial polities, early surveyors' claims to jurisdiction across these borders, and violence against survey teams, Edney, *Mapping an Empire*, 168–69, 209, 253, 326–27.

These people were all awfully excited and all for nothing. My men never attacked any of them, we were all the time doing our best to get away but were not allowed to.[21]

The author's shock, verging on terror, at the refusal of "the Mussalman Chaprassi looking fellow" to follow his orders and the subsequent attack by a mob of villagers is palpable, and gives the narrative an unsettled quality.

In an authoritative account of the relationship between colonial discourse and coercive state intervention, Ranajit Guha identified multiple strata of writings and their political and ideological functions. Guha described "primary discourse" produced immediately after an event, such as the passage cited above, as "official in character" and "meant primarily for administrative use – for information of the [colonial] government, for action on its part and for the determination of its policy."[22] The immediacy of such accounts written by participants in the events or contemporaries mark them as "raw, primordial," and not yet refined into the highly ideologized product of colonialist historiography.[23] Dickinson's representation of a "madman" Muslim official presiding over lawless, violent villagers was part of a document designed to secure the return of the survey team from imprisonment in Moglai and the punishment of Hyderabad officials and thus constitute primary discourse.

Subsequent communications regarding the 1889 incident resemble Guha's description of "secondary discourse," or "processed product" ensconced in an "aura of impartiality."[24] Hutchinson, the Survey Superintendent, wrote to Bombay eleven days later to seek assistance with the matter, stating that he hoped Dickinson would not himself have to return to Hyderabad and "risk his safety amongst such lawless people."[25] Hutchinson noted that colonial border policy regulating liquor sale was likely the point of contention, and categorically dismissed any charges against the surveyors and the legitimacy of the Hyderabadi justice system.[26]

21 R. Dickinson Esq, Assistant Surveyor, Survey of India to Colonel H. S. Hutchinson, Department Superintendent, Survey of India, 13 January 1889, MSA Political Department, Hyderabad vol. II, 64/298, 1889.

22 Guha, "The Prose of Counter-Insurgency," 3.

23 Ibid., 6–7.

24 Ibid., 7–8.

25 Lieutenant-Colonel H. S. Hutchinson, Department Superintendent, Survey of India, In-Charge to 10 Bombay Topographical Party to I. Monteath Esq., C.S., Private Secretary to His Excellency, Governor of Bombay, Bombay, 24 January 1889, MSA Political Department, Hyderabad vol. II, 64/298, 1889.

26 Hutchinson to Monteath, 24 January 1889, MSA Political Department, Hyderabad vol. II, 64/298, 1889. The Survey Superintendent credits Mr. Ebden, Collector of Kaladgi, for information on the contemporaneous tensions over liquor regulation. I will consider below the key role of Abkari (liquor) regulation in the making of the border.

In this and other cases colonial officials responded to perceived challenges from Hyderabad by attempting to extend their authority across the border in both informal and formal ways. They called upon English employees of the Nizam's government or sought to manipulate appointments in the state. In this case, Raj officials called upon Hyderabad's English Inspector General of Police, Colonel Ludlow, to take punitive action against local and provincial officials in Hyderabad.[27] When Ludlow refused to do their bidding, Hutchinson bemoaned "the lack of English Spirit shown by the European officials of the Hyderabad Government."[28] Despite expectations to the contrary and their readiness to invoke the black legend of Hyderabadi governance to encourage punitive and extra-legal colonial action, the case was not resolved in the manner the survey officers advocated.

The Malapur Survey Team case languished in the Hyderabad justice system for several months, and while no charges were formally brought against the Malapur *chaprasi*, local villagers, or any other Hyderabad officials or subjects, the survey team was also eventually exonerated and released.[29] Attempts such as these by British officials to exercise extraterritorial jurisdiction or exert pressure on Hyderabad officials were legion, but rendered ineffectual by Hyderabadi sovereign claims or British intra-imperial tensions. Bombay officials sought to extend their authority in various ways, but higher British authorities were wary of broader geopolitical consequences that might be set in motion by transgressing the Nizam's fiercely protected legal sovereignty. Hyderabad, after all, was a prominent Muslim loyalist state in an era of colonial anxiety about Muslim anti-colonialism. In the unruly frontiers of empire the Raj occupied a delicate and tenuous position. Colonial knowledge also had limited capacity to translate itself into state violence.

For Guha, documents that constitute primary discourse on anti-colonial insurgency "make no sense except in terms of a *code of pacification* which, under the Raj, was a complex of *coercive intervention* by the State and its protégés, the native elite, with arms and words."[30] As

[27] Hutchinson to Ludlow, 8 April 1889. Also noted in G. S. Forbes Esq., First Assistant Resident in charge of Hyderabad Residency to Secretary of Government of India, Foreign Department, 28 March 1889. Both references MSA Political Department, Hyderabad vol. II, 64/298, 1889.

[28] Lieutenant-Colonel H. Hutchinson, Deputy Superintendent, Survey of India, In-Charge, Bombay Topographical Party (Camp Kulkumbi office) to Secretary, Bombay Government Political Department, 18 May 1889, MSA Political Department, Hyderabad vol. II, 64/298, 1889.

[29] Hutchinson to Monteath, 30 October 1889, MSA Political Department, Hyderabad vol. II, 64/298, 1889.

[30] Guha, "The Prose of Counter-Insurgency," 15, emphasis added.

primary gave way to secondary discourse, the form and rhetoric shifted from contemporaneous dispatches with clear agendas to memoirs and histories written from an ostensibly depersonalized and positivist perspective. The function of the colonialist writings, however, continued to be "to instigate official violence" against insurgents.[31] In Guha's work, colonial rule was kept in place not by the generation of consent (hegemony) but by the exercise of material coercion (dominance) upon the colonized masses.[32] In border relations with Hyderabad the Raj encountered a sovereign, often intractable polity whose provincial and local officials showed little regard for British ascendancy. This dynamic broke down the tight articulation between colonialist knowledge and disciplinary power that Guha's prose of counter-insurgency relied upon. The uncertainty of the geographic and legal terrain for Raj officials across the Nizam's frontier is visible in the testimony of a survey employee who was imprisoned in Hyderabad.

A. M. Rodrigues, a Portuguese theodolite operator, was one of four British Indian subjects on the survey team.[33] His description of the incident and his treatment while in custody was included in a letter from Hutchinson to Bombay in hopes of instigating punitive action against Hyderabad officials.[34] Rodrigues's testimony described the initial confrontation upon their arrival at the outskirts of Malapur, and fruitless attempt to procure a guide through local officials. Rodrigues also provided detail on his subsequent experiences as a detainee, describing the climate ("sun and heat"), local language ("Canarese . . . which I do not understand"), total distance of marches (approximately 140 miles), and provisions they were offered (stipends for the purchase of food, occasional tea, and at one point "some liquor to drink"). In contrast to the petitions of the two British survey officers considered above, Rodrigues's testimony confined itself to dispassionate description in a serial documentary

31 Ibid., 20.

32 Ranajit Guha, "Dominance without Hegemony and its Historiography," in *Subaltern Studies VI: Writings on South Asian History and Society*, ed. Ranajit Guha (Delhi: Oxford University Press, 1989), 210–309.

33 Hutchinson's description: "Mr Rodrigues a Portugese [*sic*] (recorder of angles) who was with Mr Dickinson." Hutchinson to Monteath, 24 January 1889, MSA Political Department, Hyderabad vol. II, 64/298, 1889. It is unclear whether Rodrigues was born in Europe or South Asia, possibly among longstanding Indo-Portuguese communities in in Bombay or Goa, and moreover, whether his racial or ethnic status was relevant to his experience in Hyderabad.

34 "Written Statement of A. Rodrigues, Sub-Surveyor, submitted to Colonel Ludlow" (undated), appended to Hutchinson (Deputy Superintendent, Survey of India of the No. 10 Bombay topographical party) to Warren (Secretary to Bombay Government Political Department), dated Camp Idar, Gujarat Dist, 11 February 1889, MSA Political Department, Hyderabad vol. II, 64/298, 1889.

mode. Despite his status as a British Indian subject and Raj employee, Rodrigues's narration eschews implicit or explicit moral claims. Its documentary character reveals a subject position corresponding neither to raw and practical primary discourse nor to ostensibly neutral yet demonstrably politicized secondary discourse, which together rehearse Guha's codes of counter-insurgency.

Colonial discourse and state violence may have been neatly intertwined in British domains, but the capacity of representations to enact and naturalize violence in maintaining the rule of colonial difference were exhausted at the border of Moglai. Seen from the frontier, the ideological apparatus of colonial knowledge was disconnected from repressive institutions of colonial state power.[35] Late nineteenth-century imperial technologies, manifest in British India via territorial sovereignty, broke down in the borderlands. Guha's penetrating method of discourse analysis demonstrates colonial dominance and implies its generalized character. Such certainties were not applicable in Moglai, and Hyderabad reveals the ambivalent structural condition of colonial sovereignty across jurisdictions.

## Regulating cross-border traffic

Hyderabad's proximity to British territories, such as Bombay, constituted both a conceptual problem ('Moglai' governance amidst Raj domains) and a practical threat to the generalization of British material and institutional power across the subcontinent. The presence of the Nizam's state as a sovereign entity that was often intransigent in the face of colonial pressures undermined colonial agendas for regional economy and security. The British Resident in Hyderabad applied diplomatic pressure, and informally attempted to manipulate appointments and recruit collaborators. Operations of this kind were of limited effectiveness, and border politics provides a critical lens on the playing out of political tensions, conflicts, and negotiations between empire and sub-imperial state.[36] British attempts to regulate the flow of excisable goods and criminalized communities across the frontier demonstrate the limits

35 Althusser's distinction between Ideological and Repressive State Apparatuses (ISA and RSA) is instructive in assessing the working of colonial knowledge and material power. These two discrete levels of power are often read as simultaneous and indistinguishable in South Asia during the colonial period. On the ISA and RSA see Louis Althusser, "Ideology and Ideological State Apparatus (Notes Towards an Investigation)," in *Lenin and Philosophy* (New York: Monthly Review Press, 1971), 85–126.

36 For summaries of files regarding border matters see MSA Political Department, List of Volumes and Compilations No. I-5, P-4, 1887–1913.

of colonial power there. Moreover, Asaf Jah strategies for retaining sovereignty reveal a distinct structure and ethics of governance across the border in the Nizam's state.

### *Commodity flows*

The Raj sought to extend its state apparatus across the Hyderabad frontier through initiatives to regulate traffic of controlled substances such as salt, firearms, opium, ganja, and alcohol. The last two decades of the nineteenth century saw a focus of colonial energies on controlling the sale of alcohol in areas near the border. In 1886 the Nizam signed a treaty with Bombay to close "all liquor shops situated within 3 miles of the British Frontier."[37] During this period Bombay repeatedly pushed Hyderabad to bring their Abkari (alcohol regulation) policies into conjunction with those of the Bombay Presidency, which itself had recently raised the price of liquor in several districts. The rash of smuggling whittled away at colonial revenues in frontier districts of Khandesh, Nasik, Ahmednagar, Sholapur, Bijapur, and Dharwar. Delays in implementing the three-mile dry zone resulted in a spate of insistent communications from Bombay to Hyderabad.[38] The Bombay Commissioner of Customs, Salt and Abkari wrote in an 1887 letter to the Hyderabad Resident: "Though the shops within three miles of the British Frontier were withdrawn more than a year ago, the Moglai shops *have not yet been withdrawn.* The continuance of the shops is causing loss to the British government and the British farmer is likely . . . to claim compensation for his losses."[39] This missive is typical of exchanges over the Abkari issue during the period. The Commissioner's claim to speak on behalf of the British Indian revenue farmer veiled a push to safeguard government tax incomes on more expensive Bombay liquor.

Responses from Hyderabad to Bombay's border alcohol policies reveal a defense of decentralized administrative power. The confrontation over Abkari regulation dragged on for years, and despite officials' claims that Hyderabad was striving to comply with Bombay's demands, the matter was viewed with little urgency there. In 1899 Hyderabad's *divan* wrote

[37] Agreement cited in letter from Commissioner of Customs, Salt, Opium and Abkari, Bombay to Hyderabad Resident, 1 May 1888, APSA 7/2/13, 1887. See also "Enforcing 3 mile frontier zone at Ahmednagar," MSA Political Department, Hyderabad vol. 1, 57, 1888.

[38] See APSA 7/2/13, 1887 on Dharwar and Khandesh; APSA 7/2/10, 1887 on Ahmednagar; APSA 7/2/9, 1887 on Bijapur and Sholapur.

[39] Commissioner to Resident, 17 December 1887, APSA 7/2/10, 1887, emphasis in original.

to Bombay that the objectionable liquor shops near the Ahmednagar frontier were in villages under the jurisdiction of *jagirdars*, and that the 'owners' had been urged to comply with the new policy.[40] Rather than exercising coercion, as Bombay requested, Hyderabad allowed autonomy to state land-grant holders, legal or police authorities, and even merchants within a decentralized political system.[41]

As with alcohol, so with other excisable colonial commodities. In 1908 and 1909 "habitual smuggling" of marijuana into Bombay frontier districts provided cause for reassignment of colonial police from interior districts to the frontier in hopes of staunching the flow.[42] The Nizam's council contemplated adopting the "hemp drug rules" in force in Bombay, which might have both reduced incentive to smuggle and increased Hyderabad excise revenues.[43]

Critical to earlier Raj expansion, opium remained a major source of colonial revenue into the twentieth century. The need to protect this trade incited complaints from Bombay against Hyderabad's lax frontier governance:

> In the beginning of January 1897, three carts filled with smuggled opium, started from Indore and passing through the Central Provinces and Berar, sold their contents in Moglai ilaka [Hyderabad] . . . Large quantities of opium involving loss of thousands of rupees to the British Government are illicitly imported into Moglai ilaka, and the person who purchased most of such opium is Pestonji Parsi of Jalna [Aurangabad district, Hyderabad]. The persons arrested as well as the informers, through whom the case was detected state that about 100 maunds of smuggled opium were purchased by Pestonji Parsi during the last year . . . It is felt very necessary that either the Nizam's State should give this Agency [the Thagi and Dakaiti Department, Indore] a special force for the work, or appoint some special officers of theirs through whom action could in future be taken in the State.[44]

40 His Highness' Minister to Captain Severs, 28 December 1899, APSA 7/2/10, 1887. It is unclear whether 'owners' referred to *jagirdars* or liquor-shop proprietors.

41 Note the parallel with frontier relations between early British Burma and Siam: "For the Siamese court, it was hard to imagine why the question of boundary should be so important; it should have been a matter for the local people, not those in Bangkok" (Winichakul, *Siam Mapped*, 64).

42 "Smuggling of ganja from Hyderabad territory into adjoining districts of Bombay Presidency," APSA 7/2/332, 1909.

43 Moulvi Mhd Abdur Rahim, Hyderabad Revenue Dept. to Hyderabad Political Secretary and Private Secretary to Hyderabad Prime Minister, 8 September 1909, APSA 7/2/332, 1909.

44 "Confidential letter from Extra Assistant to the General Superintendent, Thagi and Dakaiti Department, Indore to the First Assistant to the Resident, Hyderabad," 13 February, 1897, APSA 7/2/61, 1897.

This case demonstrates colonial concerns with preventing leakage of excisable opium across porous frontiers, and the security implications of commodity movements. Significantly, communication in this instance came not from the Customs, Salt, Opium and Abkari Commissioner for Bombay – nor from any official within British India – but from the head of an extraterritorial colonial policing agency functioning out of the sub-imperial state of Indore. The opium-smuggling case above also reveals two approaches alternately pursued in colonial frontier policy: assertion of extraterritorial jurisdiction; or pressuring Hyderabad to adopt parallel regulatory institutions. Colonial frontier policy on matters related to Raj political security – cross-border movement of criminals, insurgents, and armaments – reveals shifting colonial strategies and their consequences.

### *'Criminal' mobility*

By the late nineteenth century the Raj had established a network to control the movement of commodities and people in internal frontier zones. This network linked colonial officers and agencies between Hyderabad, Indore, Berar (formally Hyderabad's sovereign territory, but British administered from 1853), key colonial provinces (Bombay and Madras Presidency, Central Provinces), and other colonial and sub-imperial locations. Frontier policy entailed extending extraterritorial jurisdiction into sub-imperial states, often via agencies such as the Thagi and Dakaiti Department (T&DD).[45] Hyderabad's officials defended legal sovereignty and the prerogative of local nobles within a decentralized state apparatus to enforce laws.

Consolidating agricultural production and trade were vital aspects of the colonial project. Peripatetic groups not integrated into the sedentary agrarian world were tagged as criminals in colonial sociology, initially by T&DD jurisdictions, and after 1860 by the related Criminal Tribes Act (CTA).[46] The T&DD functioned in British India by criminalizing

[45] On the T&DD in Hyderabad territory, and the central role of colonial pressure in the Nizam's frontier policy, focused on the experience of one key community that was criminalized in colonial sociology, see Bhangya Bhukya, *Subjugated Nomads: The Lambadas under the Rule of the Nizams* (New Delhi: Orient BlackSwan, 2010) and "'Delinquent Subjects': Dacoity and the Creation of a Surveillance Society in Hyderabad State," *Indian Economic and Social History Review* 44. 2 (2007): 179–212. See also Chapter 6 on thagi and dacoity policing in Hyderabad and British India.

[46] On the contexts and moral panics produced by pre-1857 anti-thagi campaigns see Radhika Singha, "Providential Circumstances: The Thuggee Campaign of the 1830s and Legal Innovation," *Modern Asian Studies* 27.1 (1993): 83–146 and *A Despotism of Law: Crime and Justice in Early Colonial India* (Delhi: Oxford University Press, 1998), ch. 5; Parama Roy, "Discovering India, Imagining Thuggee," *Yale Journal of Criticism* 9.1 (1996): 121–45; Tom Lloyd, "Thuggee, Marginality and the State Effect in Colonial

itinerant groups that did not fit into a colonial economic vision centered on settled agriculture and cash-crop production.[47] And dacoits were said to abound in Hyderabad.[48] The colonial state addressed this threatening frontier presence by extending the work of the T&DD across colonial borders. It was an agency whose "special jurisdiction" functioned parallel to British Indian law, and allowed for political discretion in deploying state violence or imprisoning suspects without observing existing legal procedures. From the second quarter of the nineteenth century the T&DD worked as a proxy for extending colonial police power across frontiers. In Hyderabad during the late nineteenth century the British Resident presided over a special tribunal, hearing cases of prisoners nabbed in Hyderabad State under the T&DD's extraterritorial jurisdiction. Despite the systematic character of colonial legal encroachment, Raj–Nizam frontiers continued to be flashpoints of criminal activity and sites of policing focus over the next several decades.

The colonial state took on a streamlined and pragmatic visage across frontiers. The act of sedentarizing mobile groups in British India was couched in the rhetoric of the colonial civilizing mission, and economic utility cast as moral project. Unadorned economic and security concerns overwhelm civilizing rhetoric in the workings of the T&DD across Hyderabad's borders. There the agency's work was centered on protecting the Raj's excise and taxation regimes and maintaining law and order on British Indian frontiers. The Department carried out limited actions across Hyderabad's borders, in part owing to questions over jurisdiction, since the 1830s heyday of the agency.[49] Beginning in the 1840s,

India, circa 1770–1840," *Indian Economic and Social History Review* 45.2 (2008): 201–37; Kim A. Wagner, "The Deconstructed Strangler: A Reassessment of Thuggee," *Modern Asian Studies* 38.4 (2004): 931–63. On post-1857 developments in Thagi, Dacoity, and Criminal Tribes legislation and enforcement, Sanjay Nigam, "Disciplining and Policing the 'Criminals by Birth,' Part 1: The Making of a Colonial Stereotype – The Criminal Tribes and Castes of North India" and "Part 2: The Development of a Disciplinary System, 1871–1900," *Indian Economic and Social History Review* 27.2 and 3 (1990): 131–64 and 257–87; and Meena Radhakrishna, *Dishonoured by History: "Criminal Tribes" and British Colonial Policy* (Hyderabad: Orient Longman, 2001).

47 On the linkage between criminalization and colonial economic agendas, identifying dynamics of both sedentarization and regulated mobilization, see Singha, "Settle, Mobilize, Verify." On the colonial-period rise of peasant farming and sedentarization, Bayly, *Indian Society*, 175.

48 A classic fictionalized account of a criminal community in Hyderabad State is Phillip Meadows Taylor, *Confessions of a Thug* (London: Bentley, 1839). Taylor was a civil administrator in Asaf Jah Hyderabad.

49 W. H. Sleeman, famed for his role in early colonial operations against thagi and his foundation and commissionership of the Thagi (later Thagi and Dakaiti) Department, worked in sub-imperial states. On his work, and English police officers employed by Hyderabad such as Ludlow and Hankin, see R. Jayaram, *Administrative System under*

and increasingly from 1857 onward, Hyderabad and its frontier with Bombay became a hot zone on the colonial map of criminal activity. Military entrepreneurs disenfranchised from the colonial military or Hyderabad forces, described as Rohilla Pathans, threatened provincial authorities in the Nizam's dominions.[50] The specter of sub-imperial states, as Sandria Freitag argued, loomed large in the eyes of colonial officials by the mid-nineteenth century when dacoit bands "had largely been forced out of British India."[51] Hyderabad's reluctance to surrender or prosecute state subjects identified or handed over by the T&DD limited the effectiveness of colonial extraterritorial policing, and called for alternative strategies.

### *From extraterritoriality to legal sovereignty*

Through much of the nineteenth century the Raj operated extraterritorial outposts for colonial institutions of governance in Hyderabad, but by 1900 policing the frontier increasingly became a responsibility of the Nizam. The Hyderabad branch of the Raj's T&DD was presided over by British Indian civil servant A. C. Hankin, who departed for a post in the Hyderabad Police in 1896.[52] In a letter sent to the Residency shortly after Hankin began working for the Nizam's government, his successor W. F. Gayer forecast the eventual obsolescence of the Raj agency within Hyderabad:

> The [Hyderabad] police, hitherto renowned for their impotence, suddenly became infused with energy. They captured Kallia [Multani; a dacoit leader who led raids across the border from Amba, near Auragabad]; and broke up a large

*the Nizams (1853–1935)* (Bangalore: Ultra, 1998). On the ambivalence of the early T&DD's jurisdiction, including an 1838 incident in which Sleeman opposed taking action "against the Bairagis in the Hyderabad territory" owing to its being outside the department's jurisdiction, see Singha, *Despotism of Law*, 221–22.

50 On the 1859 establishment of the Hyderabad "Court for the trial of Thuggee and Dacoity Cases" as "a special court . . . for the trial of Rohillas and others who were guilty of heinous crimes" see Muttalib, *Administration of Justice*, 128–29. On the changing importance of cultural designations in the making of South Asian armies, see Dirk H. A. Kolff, *Naukar, Rajput and Sepoy: The Ethnohistory of the Military Labour Market in Hindustan, 1450–1850* (Cambridge University Press, 1990). On the political and military status of Pathans, see Robert Nichols, *A History of Pashtun Migration, 1775–2006* (Oxford University Press, 2008), especially chs. 2, 3.

51 Sandria Freitag, "*Sansiahs* and the State: The Changing Nature of 'Crime' and 'Justice' in Nineteenth-Century British India," in *Changing Concepts of Rights and Justice in South Asia*, ed. Michael R. Anderson and Sumit Guha (Delhi: Oxford University Press, 1998), 82–113, here 84.

52 Hankin served as Inspector General of Police for Hyderabad from 1898 until 1919. For details, couched in a laudatory account of Hankin's accomplishments in Hyderabad, see Jayaram, *Administrative System*, 133–42.

and formidable gang of Bhils, which has newly sprung up in the hills near the Nasik and Khandesh border; they began reporting crime; and captured numbers of dakaits and other criminals, and recovered large quantities of stolen property. Under these circumstances, our presence seemed unnecessary, as anything we did appeared unwarrantable interference. Dreading, therefore, that we might do more harm than good, and impede the progress being made, by causing friction, I discouraged any excess of zeal on the part of my men until I could instill into them that the Moglai Police were no longer the nonentity they had been, and that our only chance of doing good work was to go with them, helping them when possible, but never to force our assistance on them, nor interfere in cases they were working unless asked to.[53]

Acknowledging Hyderabad's increasing effectiveness in controlling frontier criminality, the new Raj T&DD head rehearsed the logic of a new British frontier policy. Herein, Hyderabad would become responsible for frontier policing; British India would roll back extraterritorial claims to avoid "friction" with Hyderabad's territorial and legal sovereignty.

The Resident concurred that dismantling the Hyderabad branch of the Raj T&DD would decrease political tensions and reduce British costs.[54] By the turn of the century Hyderabad bore the lion's share of expenses for policing cross-border thagi and dacoity, the imprisonment of convicts in special 'thagi jails' at Hyderabad and Jalna, and even the transportation of particularly 'threatening' subjects of the Nizam to British Indian penal colonies.[55] In exchange for Hyderabadi legal sovereignty in T&DD policing, the Raj insisted that the post of the Hyderabad Inspector General of Police be assigned a British police officer.[56] In this manner, British

53 W. F. Gayer, Assistant to the General Superintendent for the Suppression of Thagi and Dakaiti, Hyderabad to the First Assistant Resident, 2 November 1897 in "Working of the rules in the Manual of the Thagi and Dakaiti Dept and trial of cases prosecuted by the Dept in Hyderabad," Letters from India 1898, 153–423, OIOC L/P&S/7/381.

54 Resident Trevor Chichele-Plowden, Esq., C.S.I. to Secretary of Government of India, Foreign Department, 16 November 1897, Letters from India 1898, 153–423, OIOC L/P&S/7/381. Cf. other Raj arguments that maintaining an extraterritorial policing presence in Hyderabad would "act as incentive" to Hyderabad to improve the quality of policing. "Various members of the Foreign Department, writing from Fort William to Right Honorable Lord George F. Hamilton, Her Majesty's Sec of State for India," 3 March 1898, Letters from India 1898, 153–423, OIOC L/P&S/7/381.

55 On policing costs see ibid. Two special British-administered, Hyderabad-funded thagi jails were in the capital city and Jalna (Aurangabad district), located between Ahmednagar, Nasik, Khandesh, and Berar. His Highness the Nizam's the Judicial, Police and General Depts (signed by Emad Jung, Secretary to Government), 20 July 1897/13 Shahrawar 1306/19 Safar 1315, Letters from India 1898, 153–423, OIOC L/P&S/7/381. On transportation see Bhukya, "'Delinquent Subjects'," 203 and C. Beadon, Secretary to Government of India to the Resident at Hyderabad, 4 May 1860, Tamil Nadu State Archives, Judicial, 29 May 1860, 51–52. I am grateful to Clare Anderson for sharing with me archival files on Hyderabadis transported by the Raj.

56 Resident Trevor Chichele-Plowden, Esq., C.S.I. to Secretary of Government of India, Foreign Department, 16 November 1897, Letters from India 1898, 153–423, OIOC

officials managed to sidestep the costly and controversial endeavor of expanding extraterritorial jurisdiction. The colonial state ceded frontier legal sovereignty to Hyderabad in exchange for the Nizam bearing the cost and responsibility for carrying out the Bombay-mandated task of securing the border. As such, the T&DD shift in the late nineteenth century served Raj fiscal interests while strengthening Asafi Jahi territorial control.

Later in the twentieth century the new frontier policy was to cause intractable difficulties for the Raj. Hyderabad frequently failed to hand over to Raj police fugitive offenders who had fled across borders. British Indian officials often remained unable to press Hyderabad officials to act rapidly (or at all) despite a reciprocal extradition treaty in 1867, and a subsequent 1906 Act designed to facilitate cross-border apprehension and surrender of alleged criminals or gangs.[57]

Sources from the decades around 1900 document frequent flight of alleged dacoits from jurisdiction on both the Madras and Bombay frontiers.[58] The 1881 British Indian Fugitive Offenders Act (FOA) was extended to sub-imperial states in 1915, but continued to be a topic of concern for the next two decades because of continuing flight of fugitives and difficulties in securing extradition.[59] British officials pursued two approaches to cross-border flight. One involved rendering laws in sub-imperial states identical to those in Raj territories, where surrender of suspects to other British colonies was a matter of course. This was possible in states where the exercise of sovereignty was more constrained by Raj oversight, and was accomplished, for example, in Mysore State in 1930.[60] In other states, such as Hyderabad, bringing laws into alignment was a complex process that had to be pursued piecemeal through delicate negotiations. The second solution was to compel FOA adoption in sub-imperial states. This proved to be a far more difficult proposition

L/P&S/7/381. As seen above in Ludlow's role in the Malapur survey team case, British police officers employed by the Nizam could not always be counted on to advance colonial agendas.

57 On the 1867 Extradition Treaty (and 1887 modification) see *Treaties* 1892, vol. VIII, and Bhukya, "'Delinquent Subjects'," 195–96.

58 For Madras see David Arnold, "Looting, Grain Riots and Government Policy in South India 1918," *Past and Present* 84 (1979): 111–45. On flight of people designated as criminal tribes in British India to Hyderabad, and particularly *jagir* territories, see Bhukya, "'Delinquent Subjects'," 196–97. Chapter 6 examines the Hyderabad–Bombay borderlands from the perspective of populations resident there.

59 "Fugitive Offenders Act 1881, Application to Indian States," OIOC L/P&S/13/523, 1924–1937.

60 "Deputy Secretary to the Government of India in the Foreign and Political Department to Resident at Mysore, dated 6 May 1930 Simla," OIOC L/P&S/13/523.

because such legislation was often "strongly opposed."[61] It was only in 1933 that Cochin became the first state to pass a version of the FOA.[62] Debates over its application simmered well into the twentieth century and reveal the systemic jurisdictional complexity of Greater British India, from Southeast Asia to East Africa.[63] Coordinating police and judicial institutions across greater British India remained a central concern of colonial officials until empire's end, and Hyderabad's frontier policy in particular was an enduring concern.

The jurisdictional difference produced by rolling back colonial extraterritorial powers, and fortifying sub-imperial legal sovereignty, produced unintended consequences. While leaving the Nizam to police the frontier may have cut colonial costs, it also gave free rein to Hyderabad officials and administrators of land grants with policing and judicial powers in critical border regions. These consequences continued to be constituted as security threats to neighboring British territory.

Hyderabad's western frontier zone served as a refuge for radical militant anti-colonialists, such as Balkrishna Chapekar, who, along with his two brothers, had been accused of assassinating British officers C. R. Ayerst and W. C. Rand in 1897.[64] In addition, the frontier remained a major source of anxiety owing to the passage of ordinary dacoits, smuggled commodities, and, notably, weapons used by criminals as well as radical militant anti-colonialists.[65] Hyderabad, especially from the 1930s, was an important locus for the articulation of radical Islamist political thought and practice. These developments happened alongside other trends that threatened the security of the colonial state and offered shelter to those whose interests went against those of the Raj.

Traffic in firearms in the early twentieth century stirred colonial concerns about the frontier. In a series of cases between 1928 and 1934,

61 D. T. Monteath to W. H. Lewis, Government of India, Reforms Office, New Delhi, 23 January 1936. The separation of Burma and questions over the colony's relation with "non-British India" elicited the suggestion that a uniform system across the princely states be developed. See also the great consternation in London over the procedure for extraditing a suspect from Panang (Malay states) to Pudukkotai (Indian princely state), 29 July 1937, At the Court at Buckingham Palace, OIOC L/P&S/13/523.

62 "Text of 2 January 1933 passing of the Cochin Fugitive Offenders Act," OIOC L/P&S/13/523.

63 "Fugitive Offenders Act 1881, Application to Indian States," OIOC L/P&S/13/523, 1924–1937.

64 Some of Veer Savarkar's collaborators in the Nasik Conspiracy and Jackson murder case of 1909 also crossed the frontier to plot schemes and source arms.

65 For an examination of horticultural Raj attempts to prevent the free flow of commodities between British India and sub-imperial states see Roy Moxham, *The Great Hedge of India* (London: Constable, 2001).

anti-colonial activists from Bombay, Bengal, and Punjab obtained revolvers from a network of arms dealers in Hyderabad. These "terrorists," "revolutionaries," "sedition-mongers," and "undesirable characters," and their suppliers, who were allegedly "in full sympathy with the cult of violence," constituted an arms network linking people across British India, sometimes via Indore and other sub-imperial states, to sources in Hyderabad City.[66] Hyderabad eventually agreed to deport the figures involved, three Muslim brothers and a Marwari, to British India or other states. Hyderabad's justification for delays in shutting down the network was protecting the official powers of the city *kotwāl* (police chief), who was in charge of criminal jurisdiction over the capital city, which led to colonial implications of the *kotwal*'s complicity in the smuggling ring. Hyderabad's defense of the prerogative of the *kotwal*, a trusted Asaf Jah official, is suggestive of a familiar political ethics. Loyal state officials and nobles were constitutent parts of the Hyderabad political system. The structural configuration and ethics of Moglai statecraft can be glimpsed in several of the cases considered above, and other state initiatives in Hyderabad.

## Across the frontier: statecraft in Moglai

Machineries of state worked differently on either side of Hyderabad–British India frontiers. Formidable obstacles to Raj projects and agencies posed by the intransigent and decentralized Asaf Jahi state apparatus limited the reach of a colonial discourse that wedded empirical and racialized forms of official knowledge to institutional power. The sometimes noncommittal, sometimes obstinate position of Hyderabad regarding colonial frontier initiatives accompanied a competing political vision, which created an anomalous institutional and economic structure. As shown above, Hyderabad administrators frequently referred to the decentralized nature of their political system when responding to Raj attempts to regulate flows of commodities or people in the frontier zone. Many different figures exercised legal and police power: holders of state land entitlements (*jagir*, *samāsthān*), provincial or local state employees (administrators of *ṣarf-i ḳhāṣ* crown lands, lower-level officers and functionaries).[67] Hyderabad's political scenario, owing in part to its internally fragmentary character, sheltered a variety of popular economic practices and livelihoods by frontier people, whether agrarian or itinerant. Raj projects

[66] "The retirement of the Commissioner of the City Police, Hyderabad State, in connection with illicit arms traffic in the State," OIOC R/1/1/2568, 252-P (Secret), 1934.

[67] On Hindu-ruled *samasthan* statelets in Hyderabad see Benjamin B. Cohen, *Kingship and Colonialism in India's Deccan, 1850–1948* (New York: Palgrave Macmillan, 2007).

sought to expand and protect a vision of a demobilized, and thus secure, peasantry yoked into taxation regimes and an economy oriented to maximizing British profits in global markets. Hyderabad's formal territorial legal sovereignty, and a fragmentary internal political structure premised on the loyalty and autonomy of land grantees and frontier officials, produced a political terrain that did not easily bend to colonial designs. This decentralized political structure, emphasis on the preservation of state sovereignty, and the ethics of patrimonial loyalty and autonomy accompanied the articulation of a positive political vision focused on protection and support of the subject population. The rhetorical development, and institutional implementation, of Hyderabad's patrimonial political ethics is visible in late nineteenth-century state famine policy, and policies related to marginalized populations – Dalits and Adivasis – in the twentieth century. Some of the impact of these developments can be surmised by the degree and significance of cross-border flows of people into Hyderabad.

### *Famine relief*

From the 1860s into the early twentieth century, South Asia suffered numerous devastating famines. While several regions in the subcontinent experienced food scarcity during these periods, the Deccan Plateau and Central India were struck by particularly lethal famines. In examining the causes, social effects, and ineffective nature of Raj relief efforts with regard to famines in British India, scholars have emphasized the central roles of capitalist agricultural transformations, free-market ideologies, and fiscal prudence. Reports on the Hyderabad State response to the worst of the Deccan famines – that of 1876–78 – reveal a famine policy founded on a political ethics distinct from that of British India.[68]

Officials invoked the Mughal legacy, particularly Shah Jahan's policies, in advocating the state's obligation to place the survival and prosperity of the subject population ahead of state revenues.[69] Hyderabad's famine policy entailed expenditure for material relief and remission of revenue demands. This assumption of responsibility for providing a safety net to the Nizam's subjects and other deprived populations in the frontier zone was a key manifestation of Asaf Jah patrimonial political ethics. Officials emphasized providing effective relief without disrupting strained

[68] Saiad Mahdi Ali, *Report on the History of the Famine in His Highness the Nizam's Domains in 1876/77, 1877/78* (Bombay: Exchange Press, 1879) (hereafter *RHFHHND*).

[69] Ibid., 18–19. The Report's authors are more ambivalent on the role of Aurangzeb and his efforts to manipulate grain markets through state importation and sale at fixed prices.

rural Deccani social ecologies. Mass migration from British India into Hyderabad suggests that famine policy produced a distinct social terrain there.

Famines in colonial South Asia increased in intensity after 1860 as an effect of the Raj's rural economic policy. Agrarian capitalism entailed commercialization of agriculture, emphasis on cash-crop cultivation, rent offensives to draw more revenue from rural producers, and integration of production into regional or global markets.[70] These economic mechanisms had ecological impacts, and more intensive cultivation often resulted in environmental damage, soil exhaustion, and decreased productivity, which combined with droughts or heatwaves.[71] Famines had structural and empirical causes, and entitlement crises (Raj failures to distribute grain stocks) intensified their effects.

Agrarian capitalism shaped social relationships and contexts, and broke down existing rural patrimonial networks of reciprocity. The Raj discontinued longstanding policies of maintaining grain reserves for public relief that served as local safety nets in times of drought or shortfall.[72] A new rural class system, informed by "capitalistic attitudes" of landholders, triggered a larger breakdown of structures of village solidarity.[73] Accordingly, in times of want, landholders, under pressure from revenue officials to raise cash for payments, refused to employ or feed rural laborers, as had previously been a presumed obligation.[74] Revenue pressures and the need for credit to make payments or obtain necessities often left both landholders and laborers in debt.[75] Landholders in turn frequently alienated holdings to officials or moneylenders for non-payment of revenues.[76] The rural poor often began to commit crimes, such as cattle theft, or to enter into direct conflicts with their immediate antagonists (merchants, rich peasants, and moneylenders). These conditions resulted in

[70] On 1860–1900 as the era of famines see David Ludden, *An Agrarian History of South Asia* (Cambridge University Press, 1999), 167. On commercialization of agriculture see B. R. Tomlinson, *The Economy of Modern India*, 2nd edn. (Cambridge University Press, 2013), 48–49. On the integration of Central India into the market economy from 1860 see D. E. U. Baker, *Colonialism in an Indian Hinterland: The Central Provinces, 1820–1920* (Delhi: Oxford University Press, 1993), ch. 3.

[71] Laxman D. Satya, *Cotton and Famine in Berar, 1850–1900* (New Delhi: Manohar, 1997); Mike Davis, *Late Victorian Holocausts: El Niño Famines and the Making of the Third World* (London: Verso, 2001).

[72] Davis, *Late Victorian Holocausts*, 26; Ludden, *Agrarian History*, 200.

[73] David Arnold, "Famine in Peasant Consciousness and Peasant Action: Madras, 1876–8," in *Subaltern Studies III: Writings on South Asian History and Society*, ed. Ranajit Guha (Delhi: Oxford University Press, 1984), 62–115, see esp. 75–85, here 79; Satya, *Cotton and Famine.*

[74] Arnold, "Famine in Peasant Consciousness," 79. [75] Ibid., 81–82.

[76] Baker, *Indian Hinterland*, ch. 3; Satya, *Cotton and Famine*, 237–38.

intensive intervention on the part of colonial police, primarily targeting rural underclasses, many of whom were marked as criminal tribes and placed under surveillance.[77]

In the context of famine conditions and breakdown of village solidarities, colonial relief efforts did little to ameliorate, and often exacerbated, deprivation and social disarticulation. Prior to late 1870s reforms, Raj relief efforts followed a rigid laissez faire ideology. Accordingly, the colonial state eschewed state-subsidized aid, grain distribution, and price regulation since they were thought to produce dependency and hamper the operation of the free market and economic recovery.[78] As the Deccan famine worsened in 1878, the Raj began to implement relief efforts. These, however, were designed to support capitalist agriculture and limit state expenditure. They proposed increased commercialization as a solution, and ran 'relief works' through public works departments as a means of focused labor extraction, limiting aid to those who were able-bodied enough to do intensive labor.[79]

The often coercive nature of labor, regimentation and incarceration in relief camps, and lack of official accommodation for cultural boundaries related to eating and social contact generated a high level of suspicion between peasant and state.[80] Further, colonial relief efforts, belated though they were, did not incorporate arrangements for remission of loans, forgoing of revenue demands, or restriction on grain exports or pricing.[81] As such, famine-sufferers in British India were left to rely upon private aid, remaining patrimonial networks, or migration elsewhere, often as indentured labor overseas.[82] Key resources for peasant survival during the 1876–78 Deccan famine were the British philanthropic Mansion House Fund, and what was left of disintegrating rural reciprocity networks.[83] In addition to temples, scattered zamindari estates,

77 Arnold, "Famine in Peasant Consciousness," 90–91, 95; Gordon, *Marathas, Mauaders*, ch. 7; Bhukya, "'Delinquent Subjects'."

78 Davis, *Late Victorian Holocausts*, ch. 1; Gorachand Patnaik, *The Famine and Some Aspects of the British Economic Policy in Orissa, 1866–1905* (Cuttack: Vidyapuri, 1980), ch. 2; Arnold, "Famine in Peasant Consciousness," 106.

79 Tomlinson, *The Economy of Modern India*, 48–49; Davis, *Late Victorian Holocausts*, 35–36; Ludden, *Agrarian History*, 182–84. The latter suggests that post-1870s imperial famine relief works were the origin of modern development discourse. For the formative role of free market ideology on famine relief in the World War I era see Arnold, "Looting, Grain Riots."

80 Arnold, "Famine in Peasant Consciousness," 103–9.

81 Ibid., 106. On continuing grain exports from famine regions to elsewhere in British India see Baker, *Indian Hinterland*, ch. 3, and internationally, Davis, *Late Victorian Holocausts*, ch. 3.

82 Arnold, "Famine in Peasant Consciousness," 97–103.

83 Ibid., 111 on the Mansion House Fund in the Deccan famine. On British non-state voluntary aid in colonial famine relief, Georgina Brewis, "'Fill Full the Mouth of Famine':

philanthropic merchants, and other sub-imperial states, Hyderabad was a refuge for famine-stricken South Asians, with huge numbers attempting to cross into Moglai.[84]

A state-published volume from 1879, just after famine's end, provides detailed coverage of Hyderabad's official famine relief efforts.[85] British Indian evidence reveals deepening capitalist agriculture, breakdown of the rural social ecology, and limited relief efforts that advanced these two conditions. By contrast, this account of Hyderabad's policy suggests both different prior conditions and alternative relief strategies that put providing relief to all sufferers over fiscal considerations.

Famine Relief Committee secretary Mehdi Ali's Report documented the brutal famine in the southern and western districts of the state between 1876 and 1878. The Report emphasized the relative prosperity of the Hyderabad agrarian system, comparing it implicitly with British India, and the careful planning and effectiveness of famine relief policy. In the introductory section the author drew a parallel between urban development (specifically, the street system) and agrarian prosperity in Hyderabad as critical evidence of progress in the state.[86] The view of social progress as a measure of state development prevails throughout the Report, noting that agrarian reforms, including redivision of districts and reworking of land settlement systems, protected peasants from exploitation while increasing productivity.[87] How well these claims reflected the agrarian condition is unclear, but the Report included substantiating data on the sufficiency of grain stores for famine relief in Hyderabad, and the export of surplus grain to British India during the famine.[88] Moreover, the central place of the peasantry's welfare, and emphasis on serving the needy by eschewing government profits, in Hyderabad's famine discourse reveals a distinctive ethic of state social responsibility. Scholarship on rural social relations in British India suggests that, by comparison, Hyderabad and other sub-imperial states experienced little or no land alienation to moneylenders during lean times. Further, this scenario bore a direct relation to relative prosperity of peasants and robustness of reciprocity networks.[89]

Voluntary Action in Famine Relief in India 1896–1901," *Modern Asian Studies* 44.4 (2010): 887–918.

84 Davis, *Late Victorian Holocausts*, 35–36. On migrants from Hyderabad during famines hoping to obtain work harvesting cotton in British-administered Berar being turned back at the border, Satya, *Cotton and Famine*, 278–79.

85 *RHFHHND*. 86 Ibid., 26–27. 87 Ibid., 53, 56–57. 88 Ibid., 64.

89 David Hardiman, *Feeding the Baniya: Peasants and Usurers in Western India* (Delhi: Oxford University Press, 1996), 198–99.

Whatever the material conditions, Asaf Jah famine discourse departs in critical regards from the Raj example. Rather than merely providing labor for the able-bodied, Hyderabad famine planners made distinctions between if and how much work the affected could be expected to perform. Accordingly, they developed multiple relief modalities, from specific public works and special relief works for those able to provide full or light labor to relief houses for those unable to work.

In public works, Hyderabad engineers were instructed to focus on forms of labor appropriate for a weakened workforce and helpful in providing basic needs, thus avoiding road work and focusing on building water-storage tanks and irrigation channels.[90] In requiring work of able-bodied people in famine relief projects, Hyderabad officials made reference not to fiscal concerns (as in British India), but argued that the intention was to allow people to develop a "spirit of self-reliance" in times of deprivation. Further, this rhetoric was a way to forward claims about the improved agrarian conditions of the country.[91] The idea of the state providing paid labor when "ordinary channels of gaining a livelihood are dried up" was a strategy for drawing affected people into state relief schemes who were wary of accepting outright charity, such as members of "respectable classes."[92]

Aside from work schemes, relief houses were set up on the outskirts of towns in famine areas for those unable to work, or who could only do certain kinds of light work.[93] Organizers allotted funds to defray or assume the cost of transporting and victualing people who were unable to get themselves to relief houses.[94] They assigned doctors to the houses, and reportedly, as a result of their work, illness was minimal.[95] In addition to the infirm and incapacitated, several categories of able-bodied people were exempted from work schemes and placed in relief houses: women attending children (considered light work), women with infants, women in purda (collectively supported by public subscriptions from Hyderabadi Muslims), men who led the blind to poor houses, and managers of the houses themselves.[96] The Report's authors paid particular attention to arrangements for orphan children, noting the provision of feeding bottles and green spaces for play within relief houses, and detailing children's multiple social origins

90 *RHFHHND*, ch. 5 on PWD, Appendix 3, 5 on avoiding road work.
91 Ibid., 157–58. 92 Ibid., A. 4, 4–5, 14.
93 On outskirts of town location and basic set-up and provisions see ibid., A. 4. On light cotton processing in relief houses, ibid., A. 1, 11.
94 Ibid., A. 1, 7–8. 95 Ibid., A. 1, 11. 96 Ibid., A. 1, 2–3.

and efforts to return them to their families or communities after the famine.[97]

Details on relief houses indicate the cultural accommodations Hyderabad officials sought to make in famine policy. In keeping with the rhetorical focus on the state's rural underclass, the Report envisioned relief house inmates as people of "the poorest and most helpless classes."[98] However, famine relief committees developed schemes for a variety of people. They described "faquirs and mashaikhs" (ascetic mendicants) who subsisted on charity by vocation as particularly vulnerable and important relief targets.[99] Officials planned means to keep in place boundaries observed between different communities of Hindus, Muslims, and Dalits (here, "pariahs"), by maintaining separate cooking, eating, and sleeping facilities.[100] Beyond accommodations for cultural practices, arrangements for food in relief houses included consideration of the tastes of famine-sufferers in addition to concerns about basic nutrition. The Report outlined the need to provide food in accordance with local grain preferences and seasonal vegetables and preparations, and included a recipe for a "chutni" (salt, chillies, tamarind, onion) necessary "to make the food [boiled jowari, or sorghum] palatable."[101]

The Report referred several times to mass immigration from British Indian districts and the treatment famine migrants received in Hyderabad. Officials seem to have taken great pride in the fact that migrants were treated "in the same manner as the Nizam's subjects" in relief matters.[102] Statistics provided show that immigrants to Hyderabad outnumbered emigrants to British India roughly four to one, and data on specific relief houses and inmates indicates that nearly 10 percent of relief recipients in Hyderabad came from British India, initially Bombay Presidency, and later Madras Presidency.[103] Anecdotes describe mass migration of peasants with their cattle from certain places, leaving localities in Sholapur and Ahmednagar districts on the Bombay side of the frontier largely depopulated.[104]

Hyderabad officials sought to meet the "backward wave of distress" that led British Indian subjects to the Nizam's territory after the famine lessened by maintaining and expanding networks of reciprocity in the

97 Ibid., A. 4, 14. The Report indicated that many of the "orphan children" obtaining relief were falsely placed in relief houses under that category by famine-stricken parents or guardians, often from British India.

98 Ibid., A. 1, 12. 99 Ibid., A. 4, 14. 100 Ibid., A. 1, 2, 4, 11.

101 Ibid., A. 1, 4. 102 Ibid., 9.

103 Figures on relief houses show 97,806 total people in relief houses, of whom 9,066 came from British India: ibid., 6–7. On origins of migrants, 67.

104 Ibid., 66, 149. See also Davis, *Late Victorian Holocausts*.

rural frontier world. Policies toward immigrants were designed to prevent many of the problems of British Indian famine relief and the capitalist agricultural scene described above. Hyderabad levied no customs on goods, including cattle; charged no grazing cess; provided waste lands for cultivation by migrants; required state police to prevent the plunder of immigrants and assist them in safe passage; and called upon villagers to employ immigrants for farm labor and otherwise assist them, including by sharing housing.[105] Asaf Jah famine policy envisioned a culture of social cohesion and mutual obligation in the countryside, even for new migrants, to offer land for grazing and cultivation as commons, and to prevent deprivation and criminalization of rural populations.

A considerably later text, a 1938 Hyderabad State Manual on scarcity and famine, suggests a continuation and refinement of state relief to distressed populations.[106] Like the 1879 famine Report, the Manual emphasized the self-reliant and secure state of Hyderabad's rural masses. Supplementing references to the relatively prosperous agrarian scene there, it noted that the rise of industrial employment, irrigation improvement, and communications facilities had decreased risk of scarcity or famine.[107] State-provided relief continued to be conceived as a demonstration of political ethics, and one that could be instructive to subject populations: "[An] essential object of State intervention is to prevent physical deterioration and dispiritedness among the people and so to place them in a position easier to resume their ordinary pursuits on the advent of better times."[108] The Manual rehearsed priorities familiar from the Report: employment of capable people in appropriate endeavors at a reasonable distance from their homes, "gratuitous relief" to those unable to work, non-interference with trade, aid to cultivators by suspension of revenue demands and loans, requirement of local cooperation, and provision of relief on the same terms to immigrants from British India.[109]

Hyderabad famine policy and implementation included specific measures for some of the most vulnerable groups in South Asia during this period: Dalits, Adivasis, and other communities that were often defined as criminal in colonial sociology. In the British Indian context

105 *RHFHHND*, 67, 149. On British Indian practices see discussion above. Specifically on cattle grazing rights see Baker, *Indian Hinterland*; Bhukya, "'Delinquent Subjects'," 190. The latter also provides detail on police persecution during famine times.

106 Hyderabad, Revenue Department, *The Hyderabad Scarcity and Famine Manual* (Hyderabad: Government Central Press, 1938) (hereafter *HSFM*).

107 Ibid., iii. 108 Ibid.

109 Ibid., iv. See also 24 on exemption from debt-related seizure of agricultural produce needed for sowing or support of cultivators and dependents. On arrangements for British Indian migrants, 82. The Manual also outlined procedures for informing Raj officials about potential scarcity.

famines provided alibis for increased surveillance, criminalization, police persecution, and forced sedentarization and peasantization of many communities.[110] As noted above, the 1879 Report noted specific arrangements for accommodating Dalits in relief houses. Both the Report and the 1938 Manual suggest that the bulk of famine employment in Hyderabad was through the Public Works Department, which featured Dalits in key positions since at least the early twentieth century.[111] Banjaras, often persecuted as a criminal community, had been closely involved with the carrying trade before the development of railway transport. The 1870s Report described employment of Banjara bullock-based transportation specialists as both recipients (paid labor) and providers (deliverers of grain and other goods) of famine relief.[112] The 1938 Manual detailed specific arrangements for providing affected Adivasis ("Forest Tribes") with appropriate work through the Hyderabad Forest Department, or supplying gratuitous relief for those unable to work.[113]

Hyderabad famine policy, rather than criminalizing state subjects or British Indian immigrants, conceived the police as an agency for distributing relief effectively to those in need. The 1879 Report assigned police to assure safe passage of migrating people to relief houses or smooth integration into agrarian employment, and celebrated the complete absence of reports of dacoity, plunder of property, or cattle theft.[114] The 1938 Manual charged police with reporting on conditions indicating deprivation (unemployment, scarcity, wandering and starving persons, high emigration or immigration, increase in mortality) and facilitating relief efforts (relieving wanderers and distressed people or directing them to nearby villages with available relief, establishing relief depots on heavily trafficked routes, providing grain or fodder to migrants), in addition to enjoining regular and special efforts for keeping the peace (reporting on crime, protecting grain markets).[115] If deprivation or destruction of livelihood of vulnerable communities instigated mass criminalization and persecution in British India, the evidence from Hyderabad suggests a different picture. Famine discourse expressed a political ethics founded on protection of state subjects along with newcomers in times of need, and particularly the most vulnerable segments of the population.

110 Bhukya, "'Delinquent Subjects'."

111 Simon Charsley, "Evaluating Dalit Leadership: P. R. Venkatswamy and the Hyderabad Example," *Economic and Political Weekly* 37.52 (2002): 5237–43, here 5241.

112 *RHFHHND*, 93.

113 *HSFM*, 68. This is not to say these plans were uniformly implemented. For evidence of state exploitation of Adivasi labor during famines on the Hyderabad–Central Provinces frontier see Bhukya, "'Delinquent Subjects'."

114 *RHFHHND*, 149. 115 *HSFM*, 70–71, 82.

Twentieth-century Hyderabad State policies regarding Dalits, Adivasis, and other marginalized groups during ordinary times invoked a similar rhetoric of protection and integration into patrimonial networks of loyalty and reciprocity.

### *Dalits and Adivasis*

When it came to the status of marginalized populations, Nizam–Raj borders divided jurisdictional spaces that became increasingly distinct in the early twentieth century. As shown above, late nineteenth-century Hyderabad administrators sought to protect the state's legal sovereignty, and employed tactics of delay, impeding realization of British Indian frontier policies related to commerce and security.[116] Ineffective Raj legislative attempts to criminalize vulnerable groups on an extraterritorial basis suggest similar jurisdictional friction. Hyderabad famine discourse developed an agenda for protection of vulnerable populations through state aid and integration into frontier reciprocity networks. In the twentieth century the Asaf Jah state undertook initiatives for Dalit and Adivasi social and economic advancement.

Historical scholarship on marginalized populations in Hyderabad State provides crucial detail on the complexity of political agendas between state imperatives and Raj pressures.[117] The Raj sought to force the Nizam's hand in areas such as forest management and criminal caste and tribe policing that had critical implications for marginalized communities. In British India forestry and criminal identification were institutions deployed explicitly to work Dalits and Adivasis into the Raj economic vision for South Asia, or to move them out of its way. Many peripatetic communities were either forcibly settled in villages (sedentarized) and pushed into agricultural labor (peasantized) or defined as hereditary criminals through the 1860 CTA and other legislation. Adivasi livelihoods often depended on free use of forests. Raj officials sought to exploit forest products, especially hardwood stocks, for profit, or bring these regions under settled cultivation, which entailed moving populations out of forest areas and attempting to peasantize them.[118] These processes resulted in continuing cycles of marginalization, criminalization, armed anti-colonial

116 On the temporal practice of slowness as a mode of anti-colonial critique in Egypt see Barak, *Time Technology*, ch. 5.

117 Bhukya, *Subjugated Nomads*; S. Abdul Thaha, *Forest Policy and Ecological Change: Hyderabad State in Colonial India* (Delhi: Foundation, 2009).

118 On uneven peasantization of Adivasi communities in British India see Shashank Kela, "Adivasi and Peasant: Reflections on Indian Social History," *Journal of Peasant Studies* 33.3 (2006): 502–25.

opposition, and state violence. The friction produced by jurisdictional difference with the Moglai frontier, however, produced incomplete or delayed generalization of colonial schemes.[119] Further evidence suggests the emergence of a distinct state policy toward marginalized communities in twentieth-century Hyderabad.

By the late 1930s Dalits were a significant and increasingly politicized group in Hyderabad and beyond. State officials sought to cultivate a Nizam–Dalit alliance for several internal and subcontinent-wide strategic reasons: to develop domestic political support; to offset colonial stereotypes about the provincial, despotic, and elitist character of Muslim rule in Hyderabad; and as a counter-balance to increasing pressures of majoritarian nationalist movements. In 1945 the Nizam provided land for a Dalit college in the Marathwada region of Hyderabad.[120] The Nizam also courted B. S. Ambedkar, British India's most prominent Dalit political leader, to enjoin his followers to convert to Islam as a means of publicly disavowing the Hindu caste system.[121] Ambedkar chose to advocate Buddhism for Dalit conversion, and his position further split an already factionalized Dalit movement in Hyderabad.[122] Nevertheless, in the mid-1940s, with decolonization on the horizon, several Hyderabadi Dalit leaders promoted the state's continued independence despite Ambedkar's late advocacy for integration of all sub-imperial states into a unified and centralized India. Hyderabadi Dalit leaders, contrarily, tended to see India as inevitably upper-caste dominated and Hindu majoritarian.[123]

During the last decade of Hyderabad's sovereignty several Dalit leaders professed loyalty to the Nizam, operated organizations with official support, and enjoyed influence in state policy discussions. Key figures in the movement such as B. Shyam Sunder (an Aurangabad-born Dalit leader) and B. S. Venkatrao (a high Asaf Jah Public Works Department official born in the capital city) were powerful advocates of the

[119] See in particular Bhukya, *Subjugated Nomads*. It is worth noting that both this source and Thaha, *Forest Policy*, put forth arguments that the Raj effectively dictated criminal tribe, forestry, and Adivasi policy in Hyderabad, though the detailed evidence these works cite suggests considerable uneveness in these domains.

[120] Anupama Rao, *The Caste Question: Dalits and the Politics of Modern India* (Berkeley: University of California Press, 2009), 206–7.

[121] Christopher S. Queen, "Dr. Ambedkar and the Hermeneutics of Buddhist Liberation," in *Engaged Buddhism: Buddhist Liberation Movements in Asia*, ed. Christopher S. Queen and Sallie B. King (Albany: State University of New York Press, 1996), 45–71, here 51.

[122] On Dalit politics in Hyderabad State see Gail Omvedt, *Dalits and the Democratic Revolution: Dr. Ambedkar and the Dalit Movement in Colonial India* (New Delhi: Sage, 1993), chs. 3, 9, 10.

[123] Taylor C. Sherman, "Migration, Citizenship and Belonging in Hyderabad (Deccan), 1946–1956," *Modern Asian Studies* 45.S1 (2011): 81–107, here 88.

Nizam–Dalit alliance.[124] Sunder and Venkatrao cast the alliance within the framework of Hyderabadi patrimonial culture of loyalty and reciprocity. Venkatrao lauded "cosmopolitan Hyderabad culture and expression of lasting harmony between the different races and creeds who have flourished here happily for ages together."[125] Sunder described the Nizam as a "benign ruler who is not a foreigner but is one among us," and contrasted the centrality of "egalitarian[ism] and justice" in Hyderabadi Muslim values to "chauvinistic, class conscious and highly individualistic" caste Hindu politics outside the state.[126] In this fashion, Hyderabadi Dalit leaders cast the Nizam's regime as more conducive to Dalit advancement than the social and political spaces of either neighboring British India or an anticipated decolonized nation-state in the region.

Compared to Dalit movements, Adivasi movements in British India were less politically consolidated on a subcontinent-wide basis. As such, the Nizam had little to gain politically by making the status of these groups a priority. Nevertheless, evidence from 1940s Hyderabad reveals a series of official efforts at improving Adivasi living conditions, particularly on frontiers, and integrating them into networks of reciprocity and loyalty in the Nizam's state.

In British India Adivasis were subjected to intensive pressures by colonial policies and conflicts with various communities that were integrated into the dominant economic or agrarian picture. Raj policies from the mid-nineteenth century tended, first, to cast Adivasi communities as encroachers on the forest lands upon which they often depended for their livelihoods, and second, to push them into marginal positions in the agrarian economy.[127] The British Indian Forest Department, founded in 1864, drove this process in defining forest lands as sources of colonial commodities, such as timber, or via expanding agrarian settlement. Legislation along these lines of 1878, 1894, and 1927 also tended to cast Adivasis as trespassers on forest lands.[128] Even if the nineteenth century

124 On Sunder and Venkatrao in the Hyderabadi Dalit political scene, see Omvedt, *Dalits and the Democratic Revolution*, 295–98, 304–7. Omvedt tends to portray these figures (whom she terms "pro-Muslim," which she opposes to "Ambedkarite") as complicit with both the Nizam's regime, which she describes as "feudal," "backward," and "autocratic," and rising "militant and semi-fascistic" Muslim chauvinist politics of mid-1940s Hyderabad: 305. For a brief biography of Venkatrao see Sanjay Paswan and Pramanshi Jaideva, *Encyclopaedia of Dalits in India*, vol. IV: *Leaders* (Delhi: Kalpaz, 2002), 216.

125 Quoted in Omvedt, *Dalits and the Democratic Revolution*, 306.

126 Quoted ibid., 205–6.

127 On competing visions of tribals as 'encroachers' versus 'natural inhabitants' of forest lands see Bert Suykens, "The Tribal–Forest Nexus in Law and Society in India," *Critical Asian Studies* 41.3 (2009): 381–402.

128 Ibid., 385–87.

in British India was the era of "the great sedentarization," Adivasi groups peasantized slowly and unevenly, often being pushed progressively deeper into more inaccessible forest tracts, further from disciplinary or economic pressures.[129] Those Adivasi communities who pursued agrarian livelihoods tended to do so without formal title to lands, or were progressively stripped of property rights during the late colonial period. The conditions of Adivasis that prevailed in British India – pressure to peasantize, little formal land control, criminalization – were broadly similar to those in Hyderabad during the late nineteenth and early twentieth centuries.[130] However, the later start and limited scope of state intervention in agrarian transformation, and the development of twentieth-century government policies specifically advocating Adivasis, produced a significantly different context on Hyderabad's side of territorial frontiers.[131]

Policies on Gonds, one Adivasi group centered by the nineteenth century around Hyderabad's northeastern borders with British India and several smaller sub-imperial states, reveal divergences between Raj and Nizam Adivasi administration. In the British Indian Central Provinces several Gond groups held zamindari land settlements by the mid-nineteenth century, but later policies led to Gonds being stripped of these rights.[132] These developments were combined with colonial education of Gond heirs to zamindari holdings and encouragement of integration into caste society. Situating developments in this era as part of "coercive and reformative" attempts to make Gonds "productive subjects of a modernizing state," Bhukya shows how Raj policy excluded Gonds from access

129 Kela, "Adivasi and Peasant," 506. Kela also points out that the transition from tribesman to farmer also often occurred in reverse. On meanings and geographies of state avoidance, often through integration into 'tribal' ethnic groups, see Scott, *The Art of Not Being Governed.*

130 On extensive Adivasi land alienation in northeastern Hyderabad State, especially Adilabad, following the penetration of colonial capital into the region *c.* 1920–40, see Ramdas Rupavath, "The Persistence of Land Alienation: The Experience of Tribal People of Andhra Pradesh," *Journal of Asian and African Studies* (2014): 1–17, here 3.

131 The argument here departs from explicit or implicit positions of several scholars of Adivasis or forest policy in the region. For an argument that Hyderabadi and British Indian forest policies were essentially identical, but which does not distinguish between Adivasis and the agrarian peasantry or take account of key mid-1940s administrative changes in Hyderabad, see Thaha, *Forest Policy*. Other works cited here focus largely on Adivasi experiences under the Raj and in the postcolonial era, and often do not clearly distinguish between British Indian and Hyderabad policies in their narratives. One source explicitly does not explore Hyderabad policy based on the claim that British Indian policy was the basis for postcolonial India legislation: Suykens, "Tribal–Forest Nexus," 392, n. 71. On continuities between Asaf Jahi and post-1948 Indian policy see below.

132 Bhangya Bhukya, "The Subordination of the Sovereigns: Colonialism and the Gond Rajas in Central India, 1818–1948," *Modern Asian Studies* 47.1 (2013): 288–317, here 305–6.

to political sovereignty in colonial or national formations by granting limited yet highly restricted self-rule.[133]

Gond experiences in Adilabad district in twentieth-century Hyderabad were considerably different, with formal land entitlements coming later, but situated within the prevailing dicourse of loyalty, reciprocity, and protection of marginal groups. The 1864 ryotwari revenue settlement in Hyderabad resulted in Gonds losing *jagir* tenures and being granted few formal land-holdings compared to British India, though many Gonds were appointed as *mokhasis* (chieftains with police powers).[134] Following British Indian schemes, late nineteenth- and early twentieth-century Hyderabad policies sought to maximize revenue through the expansion of agricultural settlement. Forest legislation of 1890 and 1900 asserted state control over Adivasi lands, ostensibly for preservation and improvement.[135] Previously practicing shifting cultivation under a revenue arrangement that did not entail territorial holdings, implicit Gond communal entitlements were abrogated by the new policy.[136] Further, when Hyderabad officials sought to increase the revenue base in Adilabad district during the early twentieth century, many non-Adivasi groups were granted land titles over heretofore Gond community lands in exchange for establishing stable cultivation.[137] Loss of land rights experienced by Adilabad Gonds tended to push them deeper into inaccessible forest and hill regions.[138] Up to this point the scenario in Hyderabad was similar in many regards to that in British India.

A major Gond insurgency, combined with the presence of a key European anthropologist and Adivasi advocate, precipitated the development of a distinct Hyderabad Adivasi policy. Kūmāram Bhīm, a Gond leader in Adilabad, led a movement for Adivasi land and forest rights from 1938 to 1941.[139] Suppressed at the time, conditions of Gonds in Hyderabad were to change considerably following the arrival and employment of Christoph von Fürer-Haimendorf. The Austrian anthropologist initially came to South Asia in 1936, where he undertook fieldwork among the Nagas, an Adivasi community of the extreme northeast of the South Asia subcontinent. Von Fürer-Haimendorf was defined as an "enemy

[133] Ibid., 316–17. [134] Ibid., 304.

[135] M. Gopinath Reddy and K. Anil Kumar, *Political Economy of Tribal Development: A Case Study of Andhra Pradesh* (Hyderabad: Centre for Economic and Social Studies, 2010), 20.

[136] Ibid., 22; J. M. Girglani, "Tragedy of Tribals in Telangana" (B. Janardhan Rao Memorial Lecture, Kakatiya University, Warangal, 2007); Christoph von Fürer-Haimendorf, *Tribes of India: The Struggle for Survival* (Berkeley: University of California Press, 1982), 56.

[137] Girglani, "Tragedy of Tribals." [138] Ibid.

[139] Reddy and Kumar, *Tribal Development*, 24.

alien" upon the outbreak of World War II and the introduction of policies in British India enjoining confinement of nationals of Axis countries. By 1940, however, he had obtained permission from the Nizam to do ethnographic work among Adivasi communities of Hyderabad State and reside there. Despite obtaining special permission to return to his work in British India, von Fürer-Haimendorf, anxious about his national status, remained in Hyderabad, and in 1944 took up a government appointment in the state's new Social Service Department.[140] After the end of the war and the reinfusion of state funds into economic and social development in the Nizam's state, von Fürer-Haimendorf spearheaded an extensive Tribal Welfare initiative.

Informed by von Fürer-Haimendorf's recommendations, post-World War II Hyderabad devised policies to improve the livelihoods of Adivasi groups by granting formal landholdings, preventing alienation of Adivasi land to outsiders or non-Adivasis, and creating a parallel legal structure for what were designated as tribal lands. Scholars and subsequent Adivasi rights advocates have emphasized the effectiveness, for a time at least, of the policies for improving Adivasi conditions, some describing Hyderabad's as the first ever "special measures . . . for the welfare of the adivasis" in South Asia.[141]

Specific elements of Hyderabad Adivasi policy under von Fürer-Haimendorf suggest deliberate state protection of Adivasi groups, attempts to maintain existing loyalty networks and social practices, and moves to integrate these into the state's patrimonial political structure. Von Fürer-Haimendorf described a decades-long tendency toward Adivasi loss of settled tenure, and the decision to settle and stabilize these groups rather than risk their "continued deterioration."[142] The policy of granting *patta* (formal land titles) to Adivasis began in Adilabad in 1944, and was extended to the neighboring district of Warangal shortly after.[143] Described as "Haimendorf patta," land titles affirmed Adivasi

[140] Christoph von Fürer-Haimendorf, Interview by Alan Macfarlane, "Interview with Christoph von Fürer-Haimendorf at Lode, Cambridge" (1983), available at www.dspace.cam.ac.uk/handle/1810/28.

[141] E. A. S. Sarma, "The Adivasi, the State and the Naxalite: Case of Andhra Pradesh," *Economic and Political Weekly* 41.15 (2006): 1434–37, here 1436. See also Girglani, "Tragedy of Tribals." For a comparison of late Asaf Jah Hyderabad's policy with that of British Madras Presidency, where no formal land rights were granted, see D. Parthasarathy, "Law, Property Rights, and Social Exclusion: A Capabilities and Entitlements Approach to Legal Pluralism," in *Proceedings of the XIIIth International Congress of the Commission on Folk Law and Legal Pluralism, 7–10 April 2002, Chiang Mai, Thailand*, ed. Rajendra Pradhan, 3 vols. (Kathmandu: International Centre for the Study of Nature, Environment and Culture, 2003), vol. I, 295–322.

[142] Von Fürer-Haimendorf, *Tribes of India*, 55–56.

[143] Ibid., 65.

entitlement to lands long occupied by their communities, and were prominent in local lore and later social memory.[144]

In granting Adivasi land and rights, Hyderabad aroused opposition from existing landlords and some business concerns. Officials, operating as a "benevolent autocracy," dismissed competing non-Adivasi land entitlements as vested interests, and opposed land and labor exploitation such as that carried out by large timber contractors on Konda Reddi Adivasi groups in Khammam district near the border with Madras Presidency.[145]

Hyderabad policy sought to maintain or reconstruct older Adivasi political networks, and to accommodate them to the Nizam's administrative structure. Von Fürer-Haimendorf noted enduring political importance and popular influence among the Nizam's Gond subjects of historical sovereigns known as Gond Rajas in Chanda (Central Provinces, British India) and Utnur (Adilabad, Hyderabad).[146] Some newly Adivasi-titled lands in Hyderabad became centers of economic prosperity and bases of new community leaders. Large numbers of landless Adivasis migrated to Utnur (Adilabad), attracted by the charisma of Gond religious leader Kotnaka Suru (also known as Suruji Maharaj), and the availability of *patta* holdings for the settlement and development of agriculture on lands there.[147]

As with Dalits, policies for state protection and assistance resulted in a significantly different status for Adivasis in Hyderabad from what entailed across colonial frontiers. Policies and projects indicate an integration of Adivasi communities and leaders into the expansive Asaf Jahi patrimonial network, fortifying the networks of loyalty and reciprocity that characterized the state's political system. Even after Hyderabad's 1948 integration into India, elements of the Nizam's Adivasi policy seem to have remained in place for several decades in the region.[148] State initiatives for fostering social and economic integration in Hyderabad are visible in famine relief policies, as well as the state's proposed relationship with the most marginalized segments of the rural population. These policies are suggestive of the ways state sovereignty, and resulting jurisdictional and political difference, framed different social possibilities across the frontier.

144 Suykens, "Tribal–Forest Nexus," 395–96; Sarma, "The Adivasi, the State and the Naxalite," 1436.

145 Von Fürer-Haimendorf, *Tribes of India*, 48, 116.

146 Ibid., 152. 147 Ibid., 173.

148 On continuity of Asaf Jahi Adivasi policies in some places through the 1950s and 1960s and even into the 1980s, ibid., 42–45, 74.

## The political ethics of disorder

In the 1889 Malapur Survey of India case discussed above, theodolite officer Rodrigues described in detail the confrontation between the British Indian officer and the local Hyderabad functionary: "Mr Dickinson said 'if you a Government servant won't render assistance, who will?' and rose towards him [the Hyderabad *chaprasi*]. He likewise approached and said 'I am not your father's servant.'"[149] Rodrigues's documentary account, as pointed out above, did not take a stance on the righteousness of Raj or Nizam officials here, but the *chaprasi*'s statement that he repeats indicates emphatically his firm loyalty to the Hyderabad system. The Raj, cast as imperial patriarch, was located outside the patrimonial networks of affiliation and reciprocity that constituted the Hyderabad government. Asaf Jahi official strategies of insisting on autonomy of loyal officials in discharging judicial and policing functions destabilized colonial projects, and facilitated the maintenance of an alternative political space on the Hyderabad side of the border.

According to Guha's picture, resistant British Indian subjects were coerced into pacification by the formidable machinery of a political system that united colonialist knowledge and material power into a self-justifying dominant state form. The reluctance on the part of the Nizam's officials to surrender Hyderabadis accused of committing dacoity in British India was a way to assert sovereign authority over Asaf Jahi subjects. Integral to claiming this authority, however, was an implicit rejection of colonial knowledge's notion of 'civilization' that criminalized itinerant groups on the basis of their community membership.

As the next chapter will examine in detail, Hyderabad, like other internal and external frontier zones of the Raj, provided a resource for those who sought to defy the commands of the program for geopolitical and economic domination euphemistically dubbed the 'civilizing mission.' While only fragmentary evidence for Hyderabad's role as a beacon of anti-colonial resistance is available, it is worth noting that figures criminalized by the colonial state – such as so-called dacoits and members of itinerant castes and tribes – continued to find refuge in the domains of Moglai from the expanding reaches of the colonial state apparatus.

The Hyderabad frontier served to limit and challenge the extension of colonial knowledge and governance in South Asia, and as such it provides

[149] "Written Statement of A. Rodrigues, Sub-Surveyor, submitted to Colonel Ludlow" (undated), appended to Hutchinson (Deputy Superintendent, Survey of India of the No. 10 Bombay topographical party) to Warren (secretary to Bombay Government Political Department), dated Camp I dar, Gujarat Dist, 11 February 1889, MSA Political Department, Hyderabad, vol. II, 64/298, 1889.

an important departure-point for rethinking the juncture between knowledge and power in modern South Asian governance. The Raj responded to these limitations by the articulation and circulation of a black legend, and deploying extra-legal police forces extraterritorially into Moglai internal borderlands. Such attempts to extend colonial illegalities into the formally sovereign space of Hyderabad were of limited success owing to the state's capacity to shield internal political actors empowered by the Nizam's sovereignty from British encroachment.

The decentralized patrimonial state structure, and autonomy of land-grant holders and local or regional Asaf Jah officials, provided conditions for alternative state projects and social possibilities. Ostensibly feudal or backward zones of disorder such as Hyderabad served to fuel colonial extraterritorial encroachments, which, however, were never sufficient to rein in the destabilizing potential of lands across the 'Moglai' frontier and the political and social worlds therein.

# 6 Frontier as resource: law, crime, and sovereignty on the margins of empire

In March 1887 the Ahmednagar District Superintendent of Police, R. H. Vincent, requested sanction to offer a special reward to capture a bandit, "the notorious Bhil dacoit Daji walad Malhari," who was wreaking havoc in his district. Daji had escaped from police in his native Hyderabad State the previous May after being extradited from British-ruled Bombay Presidency. He had already absconded from the Nizam's or the Raj's police thrice previously. According to the commissioner of the Criminal Department, Daji's activities threatened to undo colonial progress in remaking agrarian society in the frontier district: "The outlaw had actually recommenced his depredations in the [Ahmed]Nagar District. The Bhils on the British frontier, as he lately found have fairly settled down as labourers and cultivators, but the presence of a reckless leader will soon unsettle them, and Government may have endless trouble in the monsoon if the man is not caught speedily by the offer of a substantial reward."[1]

Dacoit activity was constructed as a direct affront to British colonial policies of peasantization and sedentarization. As such, Bombay sought to induce Hyderabad to imprison figures such as Daji, a subject of the Nizam over whom the Raj had no jurisdiction. Daji, to whom we shall

1 "Ahmednagar, Daji Walad Malhari. Offer of a reward of Rs 500 for the capture of the dacoit. Recapture of – by the Ahmednagar Police," Bombay Judicial Department, 21 March 1887. MSA Political Dept., Hyderabad, 55/924. British colonial texts used the term "dacoit" to cast certain South Asian groups as hereditary thieves. Acute colonial concerns and policies for addressing dacoity, and related modes of criminality known as thagi, were central to the early nineteenth-century colonial project. Whether hereditary criminality was an effect of the social and economic history of colonialism or an imaginative figure of colonial discourse is a matter of continuing scholarly debate (see Chapter 5, 162–3, n. 46 above). On the colonial use of monetary rewards to capture criminals, and their limited effectiveness during the early nineteenth century, see Martine van Wœrkens and Catherine Tihanyi, *The Strangled Traveler: Colonial Imaginings and the Thugs of India* (University of Chicago Press, 2002), 51–52; Tom Lloyd, "Acting in the 'Theatre of Anarchy': The Anti-Thug Campaign and Elaborations of Colonial Rule in Early Nineteenth-Century India," *Edinburgh Papers in South Asian Studies* 19 (2006): 1–50, here 2–3; Lloyd, "Thuggee, Marginality," 208. Bhils were a non-settled community, primarily of central and western South Asia, which colonial sociology regarded as dacoits.

return, continued for the next several years to dog colonial police with his border-hopping antics. His case underscores the indeterminate character of colonial legal sovereignty in frontier regions and the fragmented nature of sovereignty in an imperial era.

The liminal spaces of modern empires were many. They represented major challenges to officials and provided invaluable resources for people subjected to imperialism. The turn of the nineteenth century is often associated with the culmination of imperial consolidation in Asia and Africa, but in fact empires remained heterogeneous entities unsettled by contested external frontiers and subordinated by sovereign polities within their domains. The fragmenting of sovereignty and proliferation of jurisdictions produced possibilities for marginal people across imperial space.[2] Extraterritorial judicial initiatives of colonial empires were limited by subordinated states' attempts to safeguard their legal sovereignty. The legal history of the frontier between sub-imperial Hyderabad and British Bombay Presidency illuminates the productivity of fissures within imperial space during the height of European global political dominance. The productivity of the frontier depended on the incompleteness of states' control over space. Contestations over jurisdiction between the Nizam of Hyderabad and the British Raj, and the Nizam's assertion of legal sovereignty over his subjects, rendered the frontier zone a critical social and political resource for officials of both the Raj and the Nizam and, crucially, for populations in the frontier zone. People in the region availed themselves of the possibilities produced by the proximity of borders to pursue livelihoods despite imperial pressure. Although I draw examples primarily from the last two decades of the nineteenth century, a period characterized by extensive extraterritorial colonial policing, the historical scope of these developments was considerably longer. Jurisdictional tensions between British India, Hyderabad, and other imperial territories or sub-imperial states spanned the nineteenth century and continued well into the twentieth.[3]

The formulation 'frontier zone' serves as both an empirical description and an analytical concept that indicates the ambivalent and productive character of particular spaces. Empirically, frontier means a borderline separating two countries (Hyderabad and British India).[4] It also signifies

[2] By 'marginal' I refer both to the geographical location and political irregularity of the frontier zone, as a margin between two states, and the social and economic statuses of the populations considered here.

[3] On the ambivalence of sovereignty in international law see Chapter 2 above.

[4] This departs from a view of "frontiers as *borderless* lands" or "empty" terrain. See Jeremy Adelman and Stephen Aron, "From Borderlands to Borders: Empires, Nation-States,

a limitation or edge, marking what is beyond the purview of the dominant (in this case colonial) state, and this second meaning is often connected to the frontier as a source of creativity and power.[5] In prominent historical accounts of places from North America to eastern Asia, however, the productivity of frontier zones disappears by a particular time, owing to successful political consolidation and other factors.[6]

Against prevailing models that emphasize closure of frontiers, I contend that the Hyderabad–Bombay frontier both remained open and retained its productive capacity well into the twentieth century, and indeed, the frontier zone's differential character endured throughout the high colonial period and beyond. While it had some characteristics of areas scholars have described and theorized as "borderlands," such as enabling negotiations and framing cross-border mobility, the frontier zone was not centered on an impregnable border.[7] In normative legal and institutional terms the frontier represented a clearly demarcated edge rather than a space of fluidity, but in social and political practice the proximity of multiple, often conflicting, judicial authorities made the frontier a 'zone': a particular space differentiated from nearby areas in terms of the rules that applied or were suspended there. The Hyderabad–Bombay frontier resembles the "zones of anomaly" that K. Sivaramakrishnan described as "blank spots in the cultivated vistas of British sovereignty."[8] In the context examined here, and in many other places in a world where expansive imperial geographic visions masked configurations of fragmented sovereignty, jurisdictional complexity made the frontier zone a vital resource for marginal people. Key here were sovereign states, and peoples' ability to play them against one another; in other words, the frontier zone was neither a "zomia" outside state authority nor a patch of

and the Peoples in between in North American History," *American Historical Review* 104.3 (1999): 814–41, here 816; and Michel Baud and Willem van Schendel, "Towards a Comparative History of Borderlands," *Journal of World History* 8.2 (1997): 211–42, here 213–14.

5 Frederick Jackson Turner, "The Significance of the Frontier in American History," in *The Frontier in American History* (New York: Holt, 1920 [1894]), 1–38.

6 On the United States, ibid.; William Cronon, *Nature's Metropolis: Chicago and the Great West* (New York: Norton, 1991); White, *The Middle Ground.* On Asia, Perdue, *China Marches West*; Tagliacozzo, *Secret Trades.*

7 On the borderlands concept in historical scholarship see Adelman and Aron, "Borderlands to Borders" and Baud and van Schendel, "Towards a Comparative History." For an application of the concept to South Asian 'princely states' as "arenas of multi-tiered negotiations among a variety of actors," see Chitralekha Zutshi, "Rethinking Kashmir's History from a Borderlands Perspective," *History Compass* 8.7 (2010): 594–608, here 597.

8 Sivaramakrashnan, *Modern Forests*, 38.

"lumpiness" hierarchically integrated within a dominant, unitary colonial state sovereignty.[9]

Shifting legal arrangements between Nizam and Raj shaped the social and political world of the frontier. This empirical setting provides a lens through which we can examine meanings of sovereignty in colonial South Asia, not only for competing states but also, crucially, for people living on the frontier. I begin by sketching the complicated relationship between the two governments over policing and legal jurisdictions. I develop the picture by examining cases involving people who used the frontier as a resource to pursue livelihoods. Finally, engaging with scholarship on the question of "social banditry," I reflect on the implications of lawlessness for states and subjects along the frontier. Existing scholarship on the relationship between legal consolidation and the making of modern states on the global scale is useful for framing some of these concerns.

## Crime, law, and state sovereignty

In a comparative history of law in the colonial world, Lauren Benton described a global trajectory in which consolidating empires leveled early modern legal flexibility over the nineteenth century, and "formally plural legal orders were transformed into state-dominated legal orders."[10] At the core of Benton's argument is the notion – cast as irony – that colonized individuals seeking to advance their own agendas in court contributed to the liquidation of legal pluralism and imperial consolidation. In a key example, litigants at East India Company courts in early colonial Bengal "helped to create a space for the colonial state." Reifying the notion of colonizers' "special relationship to truth" by participating in these forums, subjects unwittingly precipitated colonial legal hegemony, culminating in increasingly aggressive British claims to paramountcy during the nineteenth century.[11]

9 Zomia refers to the areas of highland Southeast Asia defined by lack of effective integration into states. For an elaboration of the concept see Willem van Schendel, "Geographies of Knowing, Geographies of Ignorance: Jumping Scale in Southeast Asia," *Environment and Planning D: Society and Space* 20.6 (2002): 647–68. For a detailed argument about zomias as a result of deliberate avoidance of state power, Scott, *The Art of Not Being Governed*. On the "peculiar and enduring lumpiness of imperial legal space" produced by "the layering of overlapping, semi-sovereign authorities within empires," Benton, *A Search for Sovereignty*, xiii, 290.

10 Benton, *Law and Colonial Cultures*, 209. Benton's study attempts to describe thoroughgoing global changes in the working of legal regimes, not merely colonial contexts.

11 Ibid., 129, 131.

For Benton the ascent of state-ordered legal regimes elaborates the meteoric rise of consolidated sovereignty during the long nineteenth century. What was visible in late eighteenth-century British India was manifest in Africa, Australia, and the Americas by the twentieth. In late nineteenth-century Uruguay, she argues, Brazilian and imperial European claims to extraterritorial jurisdiction gave rise to the formalization and aggressive assertion of state law over alternative forums. "Constructing sovereignty" and asserting control over national territory, as in colonial settings, meant establishing and upholding state law against other authorities: "The challenge to the state was not so much repressing 'lawlessness' as controlling 'other' law – the legal authority of caudillos [local strongmen], other states' claims to extraterritoriality, and litigants' recourse to legal strategies that placed them outside state control."[12]

Benton's history describes similar processes constitutive of imperial consolidation and nation-state development. In both cases the state, viewed through the lens of the legal institution, became the sole sovereign entity in any given place. The victory of the centralized state with its consolidated and hierarchical legal order meant the loss of multiple forums that subjects could employ. As this chapter will show, Benton's tidy trajectory, in which legal regimes are consolidated worldwide by 1900, is questionable if the scenario is viewed from any of a number of frontier cases, such as the one considered here. One of her central methodological insights, however, is useful in pushing further the analysis here.

The relationship between sovereignty and law in imperial contexts, as Benton points out, is often clearest when viewed in terms of the experience of subordinated people: "This process [transformation of 'formally plural' into 'state-dominated' legal orders] involved everywhere an extended historical moment in which the question of the legal standing of the most marginal people in the colonial order became symbolically central to the developing legal culture and the broader realignment of the political order."[13] Corresponding to this dynamic, the regulation of marginal populations was a primary concern of the Raj throughout the nineteenth century. Colonial officials suggested that endemic banditry had a deleterious effect on settled peasants, and in doing so they presumed a fundamental difference between criminals and an ostensibly normative, law-abiding peasantry. This presumed relationship was invoked to justify cross-border policing in Hyderabad and other non-colonized regions of the subcontinent from the early part of the century. Bombay Presidency and Hyderabad State archives bear ample evidence

[12] Ibid., 210, 216. [13] Ibid., 209.

of colonial attempts to encourage cooperation. In spite of, and partly due to, the multiplication of legal authorities in the area, resourceful subjects managed to manipulate the legal scenario on both sides of the Bombay–Hyderabad frontier.

The political context of the frontier zone was a product of the complex historical process of early modern state-building in South Asia and the steady but geographically uneven expansion of the British colonial state *circa* 1750–1850. Starting in the early eighteenth century with the political dissolution of the centralizing Mughal Empire, the subcontinent began an era of decentralization in which smaller, regional states proliferated. Wide-ranging social ties were central to the articulation of political authority.[14] Establishing the loyalty and security of subject populations, wielding authority over agrarian and commercial revenues, and patronage of specific sites of symbolic power and material accumulation were all constitutive elements of state-building and governance. These characteristics of South Asian state practice made borders between states fluid. The spread of British power entailed a distinctly territorialized geography of sovereignty, as reflected in the centrality of surveying and mapping projects to colonial governance.[15] Raj officials demarcated precise boundaries around their territories and sought to pacify fluid frontier zones.

Colonial political consolidation was undermined by the recognition, and post-1857 reaffirmation, of sub-imperial states such as Hyderabad as formal sovereign entities. Distinctions between conceptions of political sovereignty in South Asia were dramatized by the means and limits of colonial political expansion.

The broader, subcontinental (and empire-wide) condition of fragmented sovereignty during the colonial period provided the stage for a productive engagement between a British project and conception of territorialized sovereignty, and other notions of state practice.[16] The cases I present below from Hyderabad are suggestive of this encounter. Decentralized and patrimonial features of Hyderabad governance – official intransigence with respect to colonial frontier policy, the enduring political importance of bonds of personal loyalty, insistence on the responsibility of the state to safeguard the livelihoods of the subject population – frame and underscore the story below of frontier-dwellers' use of the resources of the frontier zone.

[14] Dirks, *Hollow Crown*; Norbert Peabody, *Hindu Kingship and Polity in Precolonial India* (Cambridge University Press, 2003).

[15] Edney, *Mapping an Empire*.

[16] On comparable developments in Southeast Asia see Winichakul, *Siam Mapped*.

## Policing imperial borders

Colonial officials employed ideas of civilizational hierarchy to justify extra-legal cross-border interventions. The Raj, functioning largely by coercion in directly ruled areas, was circumscribed by the formal sovereignty of sub-imperial states. In this context, Hyderabad officials presented themselves as responsive to the same concerns as a colonial state increasingly vigilant about maintaining 'law and order.' An early twentieth-century Urdu narrative celebrated the advanced character of the Nizam's police force:

> The treasurer of Mysore [a large sub-imperial state near Hyderabad], Sev Rāo . . . committed a great embezzlement and hastily fled . . . but for a great while he evaded capture. Since this man had great riches and was under the protection of influential people, his capture was widely considered impossible. However, it was completely impossible to evade . . . Nawāb Akbar Jang Bahādur [the *kotwal* of Hyderabad]. . . . One day in 1886 after Sev Rao took on a new disguise, he was captured . . . [Prime Minister] Sālār Jang pronounced a *farmān* [declaration]: "For the part he played in the detection, capture and pacification of the famous dacoit, I am honoring Nawab Akbar Jang with this sword and seals of honor, given as a reward by my own hand." The sovereign's reassurance planted seeds of courage and manliness in Akbar Jang Bahadur's heart. He . . . brought the importance of the office of the *kotwal* and responsibility to its precepts onto par with British India. Akbar Jang Bahadur's courage and reassurance grew owing to the sovereign's esteem of his work and heartfelt liberality.[17]

This section from a Hyderabad police chief's biography emphasizes the great prestige to be gained by assisting the Raj in combating dacoity. As the text put it, such work by officials put Hyderabad "onto par with British India" in terms of policing.[18]

It is somewhat incongruous, however, that the treasurer of nearby Mysore would be referred to as a dacoit. Indeed, colonial officials invoked the designation 'dacoit,' like 'thug,' an earlier term for alleged hereditary criminals, to describe putatively lawless, economically marginal mobile groups.[19] Moreover, the celebration of Nawab Akbar Jang Bahadur's capture of "a famous dacoit" belied the fact that dacoity policing was a major bone of contention between the Raj and the Nizam around the turn

[17] "Ek mashhūr ḍākū kī giriftārī a'lā-ḥażrat bandigān-'ālī kā aẓhār khūshnudī" [The capture of a famous dacoit and the visible pleasure of the sovereign], in Aḥmadullāh Ḳhāṅ, *Savāniḥ-yi 'umrī*, 57–58.

[18] See Chapter 5 above for a view of the making of the frontier from the perspectives of the two states, and a detailed consideration of state policies on thagi, dacoity, and criminal tribes.

[19] Ibid.

of the twentieth century. Nevertheless, this incident was situated alongside accounts of the late *kotwal*'s life of accomplishments in Hyderabad and overseas.[20] Contributions to law and order on behalf of the Nizam and the empire were interwoven in the policeman's biography, implying that the methods and goals of both polities were broadly in confluence. However, extant evidence contradicts this portrayal of extraterritorial policing, and reveals instead much friction between the state apparatuses of Hyderabad and British India.

Frontier political relations were characterized by moments of limited collaboration amidst protracted Nizam–Raj disagreements. The legal scene was fragmented and pluralist around the frontier: splintered between different forums within Hyderabad, and between the Nizam's and the Raj's territory. This legal indeterminacy was in large part engendered by Hyderabad's strategic 'failure' to consolidate state sovereignty, often through the tactic of interminable delays in following up on Raj requests. While the ambivalence of the frontier zone was also a resource for the Nizam's officials at the central and local levels, the fragmentary character of the Nizam's disciplinary institutions served to justify colonial cross-border interventions. Beneath the story of states and their claims to sovereignty, frontier conditions served as a vital political and social resource for people who ran afoul of the colonial legal regime, such as 'hereditary criminals,' fugitives, sex workers, bootleggers, and carrying traders. Their lives were bound up with contestations between the two governments, and ongoing institutional unevenness. A tangled configuration of fragmented sovereignties framed the frontier, but states and their policies did not completely circumscribe developments there.

## "Very difficult to obtain any clue": the limits of collaboration

Exchanges between Bombay and Hyderabad testify to colonial expectations of collaboration in frontier policing. The Raj often found Hyderabad a reluctant partner in this endeavor, and initiative for policing the frontier zone came largely from Bombay, whose police captured Hyderabad subjects under suspicion and provided Hyderabad with information on fugitives in Bombay. The Nizam's officials tended to respond only after long delays, and they rarely pursued colonial initiatives and requests,

[20] Aḥmadullāh Ḳhāṅ, *Savāniḥ-yi 'umrī*, ch. 4 (trip to Arabistan to procure horses), ch. 5 (suppression of the 1857 uprising), chs. 6–8 (Abyssinia campaign), chs. 15, 16, 21 (pacifying urban and rural gangs and local toughs), and ch. 22 (organizing public meetings).

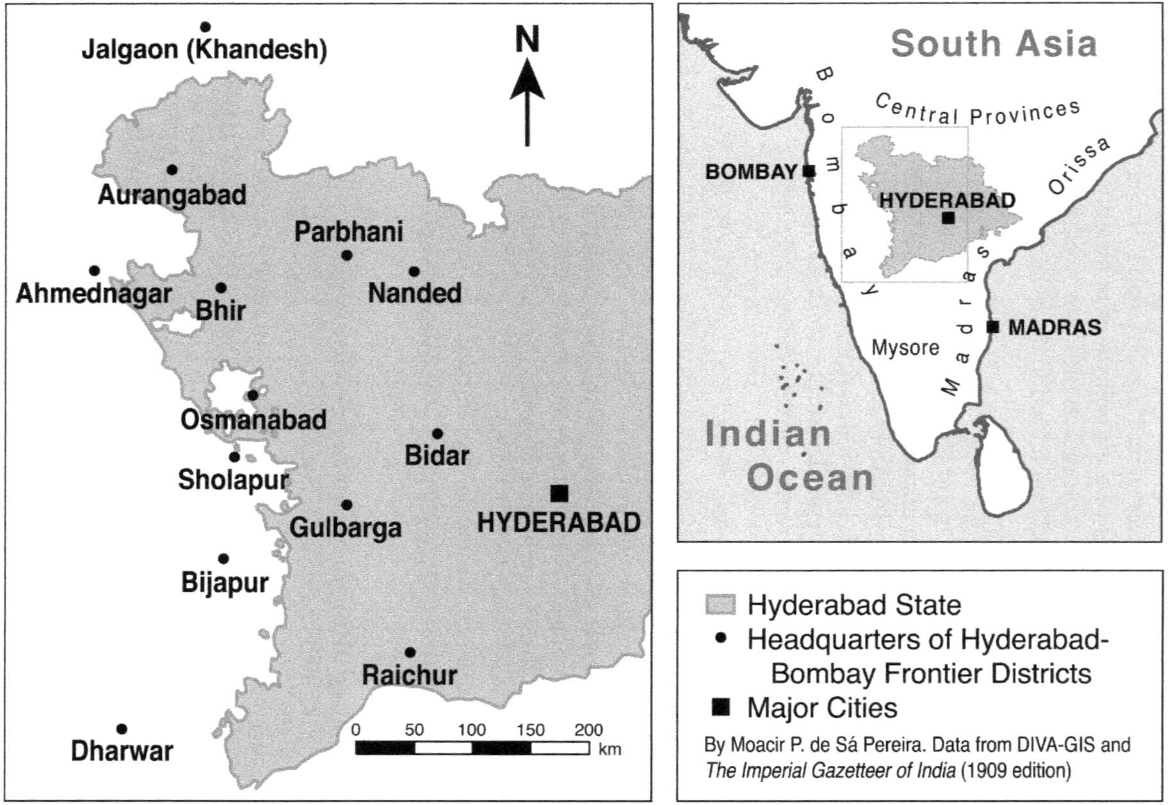


Map 3 Hyderabad State–Bombay Presidency frontier zone, *c.* 1900.

citing alleged lack of evidence or problems identifying fugitives. Frequently, suspects apprehended by Bombay and extradited to Hyderabad were released upon arrival.

In 1887 some unnamed subjects of the Nizam were captured and tried for dacoity in Ahmednagar (Bombay).[21] However, since the crime in question was committed in Hyderabad territory they were acquitted, "because the Court has no jurisdiction over Foreign subjects for an offense committed in Foreign territory."[22] In another case, colonial authorities demanded rapid extradition of ten accused persons, witnesses, and stolen property from a theft committed in the frontier district of Sholapur.[23] Hyderabad complied with the demand after great delay, ostensibly because the suspects resided within the jurisdiction of a noble's estate that was under indirect Hyderabadi administration. The Nizam's criminal jurisdiction over state subjects, and delays related to internal legal pluralism, impeded the efficient exercise of colonial justice.

Bombay authorities were generally vigilant in capturing and extraditing Hyderabadi subjects on the British side of the frontier, ranging from jail-breakers to petty thieves to dacoits.[24] Often in such instances Hyderabad was neither grateful for assistance nor prompt in responding. In 1900 the district magistrate of Sholapur offered to extradite Bali *walad* [son of] Gangu Mahar, for a theft committed in Lohara in Hyderabad's Osmanabad District.[25] Hyderabad's Judicial Secretary, M. Aziz Mirza, requested further information, since it appeared to him "very difficult, in the absence of fuller details, to obtain any clue in the case."[26] The district magistrate replied the next month to clarify that "some clothes were found which he (the accused) admitted to have obtained by theft at Lakdeshwar Borgaon [in Lohara]. These clothes, he said, belonged to a chati (cloth merchant) of that place."[27] The following January Mirza replied that an investigation had revealed that "no case of theft was committed in Boregaon in Lohara."[28] Numerous case files record

21 MSA Political Department, Hyderabad 55/633, 1887.

22 Secretary, Government of India to Chief Secretary, Government of Bombay, 22 March 1887, MSA Political Department, Hyderabad 55/633, 1887.

23 "Extradition. Delay in the extradition of certain persons accused of having committed theft in Sholapur," MSA Political Department, Hyderabad, vol. III, 59/141, 1888.

24 For the Raichur jailbreak see APSA 71/31/1, 1886. Citations for other cases are below.

25 "Bali wald Gangu Mahar (theft)," Judicial, Political, and General Secretary (M. Aziz Mirza) to Private Secretary, 17 October 1900, APSA 71/32/34, 1901.

26 His Highness' Minister (Private Secretary) to Mr. Jardine (Resident's Office), 18 October 1900, APSA 71/32/34, 1901.

27 District Magistrate, Sholapur to Assistant Resident, Secunderabad, 15 November 1900, APSA 71/32/34, 1901.

28 Judicial Secretary M. Aziz Mirza to the Private Secretary of the Minister, 10 January 1901, APSA 71/32/34, 1901.

similar communications from the British, with reminders to Hyderabad of extradition offers and, almost invariably, complaints regarding delays.

Tukaram Jiwaji's 1900 case illustrates coordination problems between colonial and Hyderabad officials. Jiwaji, a Kunbi (low-caste Maratha agriculturalist), was arrested at Khandesh (Bombay) for cattle theft in Aurangabad (Hyderabad).[29] Two complainants, Budhan and Gaupat, informed Bombay police that he had stolen their cattle and fled across the border to sell them. Jiwaji was captured by Bombay officials and held pending transfer to Hyderabad for trial. During the six months before Hyderabad replied, Tukaram Jiwaji managed to escape and fled "to his native place in His Highness' [the Nizam's] territory."[30] There, as in other places, irrespective of actual jurisdiction, Bombay did most of the frontier policing. Despite colonial expectations of rapid extradition or prosecution of suspects, cases frequently broke down after being passed to Hyderabad. From Bombay's perspective, the Nizam's claim to legal authority over his subjects and territories was an impediment to the smooth and efficient operation of colonial justice. In Jiwaji's case this caused a delay of several months, but in others, such as that of Bali referred to earlier, trials never occurred at all.

The proximity of multiple sovereign territories to one another, and the ease of crossing borders to flee the long arm of the law (or to bring rustled cattle to market), created leeway for subjects of either state whose livelihoods involved crime. If Tukaram Jiwaji could cross the border to delay his imprisonment, established figures in the rural scene, such as the cattle-owners Budhan and Gaupat, could direct complaints to multiple police forces and increase chances of regaining property and punishing offenders. Frontier legal pluralism provided structures that enabled some subjects to outwit the law and others to call it into play. Hyderabad–Bombay collaboration was hindered by both the flexibility of the legal situation and impediments such as Hyderabadi delays or refusals to prosecute. This institutional situation enabled a high capacity for lawlessness, which Hyderabad's staunch claims to legal sovereignty exacerbated.

## Interests of justice versus the protection of sovereignty

In May 1869 three Banjara women, all Hyderabad subjects, were taken into custody in British Bombay on a charge of stealing cattle. They were held for eight months, and British officials neither brought them to

29 "Tukaram Jiwaji Kunbi (Theft of Bullocks)," APSA 71/32/36, 1901.

30 District Magistrate, Khandesh to First Assistant Resident, 24 November 1900, Resident W. Haig to Vikarul Umara Bahadur, 18 April 1901, both in APSA 71/32/36, 1901.

trial nor addressed the Nizam's government, to whose jurisdiction they belonged.[31] When one woman became "very ill and in a dying state" the others managed to get a petition to Hyderabad requesting that action be taken. The incident precipitated a lengthy correspondence between the two governments in which Hyderabad railed against lengthy imprisonment without trial of subjects "arrested at the instances of Authorities in the British Government":[32] "British Authorities in many instances cause the apprehensions of persons and take no notice of them afterwards for lengthened periods, and the cost of their subsistence falls upon His Highness' Government while these unfortunate wretches after suffering prolonged imprisonment, in some instances die."[33] Hyderabad insisted that detaining prisoners on suspicion cease immediately, and that if state subjects were imprisoned, "the requisite evidence of criminality from the British Authorities" be immediately forwarded to the Nizam's minister.[34] While they objected to state funds being spent on prisoners languishing in British Indian jails, Hyderabad officials underscored colonial mistreatment of the Nizam's subjects as a significant problem. Hyderabad's concern to protect their legal sovereignty provided the context for such exchanges, and was decisive in the making of the frontier scene.

In Benton's account, extraterritoriality in Uruguay and elsewhere was seen "as an attack on state sovereignty," and such jurisdictions were opposed. In Uruguay "exclusive control of the administration of justice in the country was a condition of sovereignty."[35] For the Nizam the stakes were high, and he continually reasserted his legal sovereignty against colonial encroachment. Frontier problems were an empire-wide concern for the British, who dealt with intra-imperial flight from jurisdiction across the Indian Ocean region and beyond. The protection of state sovereignty was a key factor that shaped the legal landscape, and in turn the social world, on the frontier and across imperial space. The

31 "Complaint of instances having occurred in which subjects of His Highness have been arrested and have been suffered to remain for indefinite periods in prison," MSA Political Department, Hyderabad, 26/277, 1870–1. On the unnamed Banjara women see "Purport of Roobakaree to the Talookdar NW Division at the 14th Ramzan, 1286 H," 18 December 1869, MSA Political Department, Hyderabad, 26/277, 1870–1.

32 First Assistant Resident to Chief Secretary, Government of Bombay, 4 February 1870, MSA Political Department, Hyderabad, 26/277, 1870–1.

33 "Purport of Roobakaree to the Talookdar NW Division at the 14th Ramzan 1286 H," 18 December 1869, MSA Political Department, Hyderabad, 26/277, 1870–1.

34 Translation of letter from His Highness the Nizam's Minister to Resident, 17 February 1870, MSA Political Department, Hyderabad, 26/277, 1870–1. The last item in this file, an internal communication between Bombay officials, suggested that the case be subjected to inquiry, but it is unclear whether this took place. Political Department to Resident, 2 March 1870, MSA Political Department, Hyderabad, 26/277, 1870–1.

35 Benton, *Law and Colonial Cultures*, 245, 251, and 240.

high politics of law in the late British Empire demonstrate the ongoing fragmentation of sovereignty and colonial attempts to address it.

In Benton's formulation the end of the nineteenth century signaled the victory of state sovereignty in empires (British, French, Ottoman) and fledgling nation-states (Uruguay). The evidence from South Asia suggests, however, that colonial and formally sovereign polities possessed different degrees of influence and autonomy.[36] Subordinated states such as Hyderabad, despite British paramountcy, exercised legal authority and discretion. As one exchange over the constitution of the T&DD in Hyderabad State suggested, the Nizam's jurisdiction could be overstepped in certain instances by negotiation: "It may be assumed that the British authorities would apply for extradition [of Hyderabadi dacoits captured in British territory], and the Hyderabad Government, though undoubtedly chary of surrendering Hyderabad subjects, have agreed to surrender them if *the interests of justice* so require."[37]

Notwithstanding colonial expectations, the Nizam retained sovereignty over Hyderabadi subjects, even if colonial persuasion or coercion could occasionally wrest it away. Nonetheless, the power to mete out justice was jealously guarded and remained a primary condition of sovereignty in Hyderabad well into the twentieth century. The complex legal architecture of South Asia during the height of British colonial dominance suggests a more heterogeneous scene than Benton's picture of victorious colonial state sovereignty and legal consolidation.[38] Although imperial hierarchies sought to subjugate alternative law forums, subordinated yet sovereign states fragmented the political terrain of greater British India. Such cases were not merely exceptions, but rather served to unsettle the entire imagined edifice of imperial 'law and order.' Colonial attempts to

[36] This scenario also worked in reverse. Britain assumed territorial control in the subcontinent based on agreements with established sovereigns, such as the Mughals. Colonial military cantonments in Hyderabad and elsewhere were granted on temporary leases, and remained under non-colonial sovereignty until the end of the empire.

[37] Resident Trevor Chichele-Plowden, Esq., CSI to Secretary of Government of India, Foreign Department. Hyderabad Residency, 16 November 1897, "Working of the Rules in the Manual of the Thagi and Dakaiti Dept and Trial of Cases Prosecuted by the Dept in Hyderabad," Letters from India 1898, 153–423, OIOC L/P&S/7/381, my emphasis. Debates over the application of the 1881 Fugitive Offenders Act (FOA) in Greater British India, including Hyderabad, use identical language, invoking the need to safeguard "the interests of justice," "Memorandum explanatory of Agendum No. 6. Extension of the provisions for the Fugitive Offenders Act, 1881, to Indian States and Administered Areas," 1923, OIOC L/P&S/13/523, 1924–1937. See discussion in previous chapter of FOA.

[38] Benton accounts for "legal anomalies" in empires as part of a colonialist geographical logic of enclaves and corridors within a larger sovereign imperial terrain. Within her framework, the likes of 'princely states' and inaccessible mountainous regions under colonial rule are analogous: Benton, *A Search for Sovereignty*, ch. 5.

force the hand of sub-imperial states and other polities on extradition policy continued into the twentieth century, with only limited success. We cannot take the end of the nineteenth century as the moment when imperial or national entities eclipsed all other legal forms in their ascent to state sovereignty.

C. H. Alexandrowicz's depiction of an earlier period is useful for framing the multifarious character of high colonial sovereignty. In pre-1800 international law the "Family of Nations" was not the European and Christian configuration it was to become – Ceylon, Burma, Siam, and the Marathas stood "to a considerable extent on a footing of equality" with Portugal, the Netherlands, and England.[39] Alexandrowicz concluded his study of the foundations of international law with the eighteenth century, since the beginning of the nineteenth brought the contraction of the law of nations: "European egocentricity left the Sovereigns of the East Indies, which had largely contributed to the prosperity of the European economy, outside the confines of 'civilization' and international law shrank to regional dimensions though it still carried the label of universality."[40] Had Alexandrowicz extended his timeframe he might have noted the continuing tension between recognition of formal sovereignty of non-European states and the fact of brute colonial power. This fragmentary global framework produced frontier zones that allowed people at many levels of society to wield power within, across, and between, and not necessarily contained by, state sovereignties. On frontiers that were never fully consolidated, multiple legalities and temporalities jostled one another. Ensembles of overlapping institutions provided access to state power for those able to navigate complex legal terrain.

## Yellamma's flight: frontier as field of possibility

If the frontier was a transitional space crosscut by multiple jurisdictions, it was also a destination for flight from patriarchal legal and social structures in Bombay Presidency. This is not to say that patriarchal institutions were absent in Hyderabad territory,[41] but rather that the jurisdictional externality, and physical distancing, to be achieved by border-crossing opened

[39] Alexandrowicz, *Law of Nations*, 1. On postcolonial implications of this alternative legal history see Charles Henry Alexandrowicz, "New and Original States: The Issue of Reversion to Sovereignty," *International Affairs* 45.3 (1969): 465–80.

[40] Alexandrowicz, *Law of Nations*, 2.

[41] On the official legal recognition, and in some cases regulation and sponsorship, of some varieties of sex work in nineteenth-century Hyderabad State see Karen Leonard, "Political Players: Courtesans of Hyderabad," *Indian Economic and Social History Review* 50.4 (2013): 423–48.

up a field of possibility for women marginalized within the domestic world of the Bombay Deccan.

This was particularly so for women marginalized within the domestic world of the Bombay Deccan. In one 1886 case, which I will consider in detail, colonial authorities demanded the arrest and extradition of a woman accused of kidnapping a child bride in Bombay and absconding with her to Hyderabad territory. Nagapa, a resident of Sholapur, petitioned the Bombay police, demanding action to recover his wife and her possessions and punish her abductor. The district magistrate communicated the situation to the Hyderabad Resident:

> In about January last a woman named Narsa Saji, who was living near Nagapa's house at Sholapur, enticed away his wife by name of Yelama [Yellamma] about 11 years old out of the keeping of her lawful guardian [Nagapa] and carried her with property consisting of ornaments of the values of Rs 33-8-0 to a village Kongale [Kodangal] in the Gulbarga District in H. H. the Nizam's territory and thereby committed the offences of theft and kidnapping punishable under Sections 379 and 366 of the Indian Penal Code.

Whether her departure was voluntary or not, Yellamma figured in the case as her ornaments did: as property. The district magistrate went on to suggest that they had a sound prima facie case against Narsa Saji, a British subject, and prevailed upon the Resident to put the wheels of justice in motion in Hyderabad so that Saji might be apprehended and sent to Sholapur for trial.[42]

Throughout the nineteenth century, in colonial and metropolitan locations, the role of the law in enforcing wives' obligations to their husbands was hotly debated. This was particularly controversial in South Asia in the decades leading up to the incident in question. The 1884 Rukhmabai case in Bombay two years before, which reified the role of wives as property of their husbands, would have served as an important legal precedent here.[43] Yellamma's young age would have made the case also relevant to another, contemporaneous, controversy in Bombay: the region's conservative upper-caste elites staunchly opposed attempts to raise the marriage age for females in British India, culminating in widespread opposition to the 1891 Age of Consent Act.[44] In Yellamma's case, Bombay officials,

[42] J. F. Fleet, District Magistrate to First Assistant, Resident of Hyderabad, 16 June 1886, "Complaint by the District Magistrate of Sholapur of delay in surrendering accused persons on the part of His Highness the Nizam's Govt," MSA Political Department, Hyderabad 55/1676, 1887.

[43] Sudhir Chandra, *Enslaved Women: Colonialism, Law and Women's Rights* (Delhi: Oxford University Press, 1998), 15–41.

[44] Janaki Nair, *Women and Law in Colonial India: A Social History* (New Delhi: Kali for Women, 1996), 73–75; Radha Kumar, *The History of Doing: An Illustrated Account of*

under pressure to defend patriarchal prerogatives, acted at the behest of her husband, Nagapa, to see that she was returned and that Narsa Saji felt the full force of the law.[45] The colonial legal system was stacked against Narsa from the start, but other elements of the case made her position still more difficult.

The abstract of evidence consisted of a number of brief testimonies from various parties, some of whom had significant stakes in the case:

> Sayana wd. Sayana of Pacha peith Sholapur states: I know the complainant; his house is near mine; I know Narsa who lived in Timana's house. She was a public woman; about 3 1/2 months ago I and Chinaya saw Narsa with Yelama go out in the evening; Yelama had ornaments on her person.... Yelama had been living with her husband since her marriage up to the time she was taken away. Narsa was in the habit of frequently visiting the house of the complainant and had a great intimacy with Yelama. 2. Chinaya wd. Sayana, a neighbor of the complainant, states as above. 3. Sayana wd. Timana, also a neighbor of the complainant, states to the same effect. 4. Basaya wd. Bapaya who lives in the same peth [urban locality] in which the complainant resides, states the same as above. 5 and 6. Narsapa wd. Yelapa and Jaglapa wd. Yelapa, brothers of Yelama, of Maugalya peith, state: Narsa had been living in the house of Sayana and was a public woman. Narsa enticed away our Sister Yelama, who has been living with her husband.[46]

The testimony reveals the social and physical proximity of each of the testifying males – the first four resided in the same locality, including a father (Sayana) and his two sons (Sayana Jr. and Chinaya), and the latter two were brothers of the missing child wife. More striking still is that all of the statements, many of which were identical, referred to Narsa as a "public woman." This would have been the Victorian English equivalent of "whore" (*raṇḍī*) or "courtesan" (*ba'ījī*, *ṭawā'if*) in the vernacular depositions (not preserved in the record). While the deposed did not attach a clear stigma to Narsa's profession – indeed, she resided in the house of the first four – clearly all of them thought it highly relevant. I shall consider the potential meanings of Narsa Saji's occupation below.

Raj officials sent a request for cooperation and an abstract of evidence, and six months later Hyderabad replied that arrests had been made. The Nizam's judiciary, however, released the detainees, based on "difficulty in

*Movements for Women's Rights and Feminism in India, 1800–1990* (New Delhi: Zubaan, 1993), 24–27.

45 On collusion between the colonial state and established patriarchies see Prem Chowdhry, "Private Lives, State Intervention: Cases of Runaway Marriage in Rural North India," *Modern Asian Studies* 38.1 (2004): 55–84.

46 Abstract of Evidence, enclosure in Fleet to Assistant to Resident, 2 July 1886, MSA Political Department, Hyderabad, 55/1676, 1887.

identifying the accused, who, it is said, seems to have no connection with the information furnished by you, and has, therefore, been released on bail."[47] As in other cases, communication and policing across borders were hindered by delays and requests for additional information from Hyderabad. A subsequent communication by the district magistrate of Sholapur, who had sent a police constable on Narsa's trail, clarified the situation:

> Narsa Saji was arrested by the Tahsildar of Kalinjal [Kodangal, Gulbarga District, Hyderabad]; she had with her the wife of the complainant who has been kidnapped; both these persons were identified by the complainant and a Police Constable who has visited the place on purpose. Narsa Saji was then released on bail by the said Tahsildar. It will thus be seen that there is no difficulty in identifying the accused. I therefore request that you will be good enough to issue order for her surrender together with the girl kidnapped and the property stolen.[48]

Despite being identified in Hyderabad by the husband, Nagapa, and the British Indian police, Narsa Saji and her "captive," Yellamma, remained at large in Hyderabad State, sheltered from the long arm of the Raj's law.

The women remained at large owing in part to the obstinacy of the Hyderabad police and judiciary. Evidently, the word of a Bombay constable was insufficient to convince the Nizam's officials to extradite Narsa Saji and repatriate Yellamma and her property. The case file ends with a note from colonial official M. S. Wadia consisting of a timeline of what he called "a really bad case." Wadia noted with clear frustration, "More than 14 months delay has therefore taken place in the case which seems very simple and in which only one accused person is concerned."[49] Records of the case do not reveal whether Yellamma was ever returned to her husband, or what became of the kidnapper, with whom she shared "great intimacy."[50]

The subjectivity of a figure such as Yellamma, whose voice is absent in these materials, is impossible to definitively reconstruct. She is mentioned only after her passage into Hyderabad occasioned official communication across borders and legal systems. The archive speaks clearly in the voice of the colonial state, certain segments of Sholapur society, and more indirectly the machinery of state in Hyderabad. What this archival

47 A. H. Martindale, First Assistant Resident to District Magistrate, Sholapur, 11 February 1887, MSA Political Department, Hyderabad, 55/1676, 1887.

48 Fleet to First Assistant to Resident, 28 March 1887, MSA Political Department, Hyderabad, 55/1676, 1887.

49 Note by M. S. Wadia, 16 October 1887, MSA Political Department, Hyderabad, 55/1676, 1887.

50 Abstract of Evidence, enclosure in Fleet to Assistant to Resident, 2 July 1886, MSA Political Department, Hyderabad, 55/1676, 1887.

fragment does indicate are the alternative social worlds made possible by the proximity of the frontier, which divided the Raj's judicial regime from the externality of Hyderabad. The intervening space of the frontier zone presented a field of possibility for Narsa Saji and Yellamma, and the remainder of this section will elaborate on what this may have meant.

Sholapur Maratha and British colonial moral and legal codes defined Yellamma's liberation as state-initiated return (as property) to her socially mandated position as child bride of Nagapa. There are other discourses of liberation that Yellamma's flight, and possible initiation as sex worker under the tutelage of Narsa Saji, could be seen to enact. What it meant to be a "public woman" in South Asia changed considerably during the colonial period. The erudite social value ascribed to the *tawa'if* (courtesan) in South Asian Islamicate culture was at loggerheads with the view implied by paradigms of regulation and prohibition of "immoral activity."[51] There was no evident initiative by Hyderabad officials to safeguard the livelihoods of prostitutes, but the productivity of the frontier zone provided conditions for Narsa Saji's successful "abduction" of Yellamma. If one of Yellamma's possible social worlds was as a child bride, beholden to her husband and invested in the patriarchal social expectations that characterized much of South Asia, another would have been the life of a "public woman."[52]

Veena Talwar Oldenburg has argued that, for many women, taking up the occupation of a *tawa'if* was a path to liberation from oppressive social structures: "It would be no exaggeration to say that their 'life-style' *is resistance to rather than a perpetuation of patriarchal values.*"[53] She further claimed that stories about women entering the profession via abduction were largely fabrications traceable to the stigmatization of prostitution in British Indian and Urdu literature, discourse, and social practice. Oldenburg contends that sex work in South Asia signified a novel form of womanhood offering liberation from the oppressions of community, gender roles, and class.

Other factors suggest that the specter of sex work in the depositions masked what may have seemed an even greater threat to Bombay

51 On the demeaning of the courtesan figure in colonial law and Urdu literary imagination see Sarah Waheed, "Women of 'Ill Repute': Ethics and Urdu Literature in Colonial India," *Modern Asian Studies* 48.4 (2014): 986–1023.

52 On gender relations in Maratha country see Rosalind O'Hanlon, *A Comparison between Women and Men: Tarabai Shinde and the Critique of Gender Relations in Colonial India* (Delhi: Oxford University Press, 2000).

53 Veena Talwar Oldenburg, "Lifestyle as Resistance: The Case of the Courtesans of Lucknow, India," *Feminist Studies* 16.2 (1990): 259–87, original emphasis. Oldenburg's data comes primarily from fieldwork carried out in the 1970s and 1980s, but encompasses both the colonial and postcolonial periods.

Deccan patriarchal structures: Narsa Saji and Yellamma's possible status as *devadāsīs*. Referred to in colonial sources as "dancing girls" or temple prostitutes, *devadasis* are females dedicated to a temple and its deity, who forsake human marriage. The *devadasi* status of the characters in this case is implied by the name of the abducted child wife, since Yellamma is the name of the patron deity at whose temple *devadasis* are dedicated and also a common name for initiates.[54]

Distinctive features of the institution made *devadasis* a prime target of colonial and Brahminical reform movements.[55] Legislation placed increasing pressure on the institution in British India, starting with the 1860 derecognition of *devadasi* social institutions, and continuing with the criminalization of the community from 1880 onward.[56] According to the British Indian courts' codified version of Hindu law, *devadasis*, unlike most women in patriarchal caste Hindu society, had the right to adopt children, own property, and inherit matrilineally.[57] The common mode of initiation – adoption of girls – provided continuity to women without female offspring, but also made *devadasis* particularly susceptible to colonial legislation. A clause in the 1861 Indian Penal Code banning "procurement" of minors for prostitution was frequently used to persecute

[54] Ashwini Tambe suggested to me that the name Yellamma would imply a connection with the *devadasi* institution (2009, personal communication). For a consideration of the empowerment of women dedicated to the goddess Yellamma within an alternative sexual order see Lucinda Ramberg, "Magical Hair as Dirt: Ecstatic Bodies and Postcolonial Reform in South India," *Culture, Medicine and Psychiatry* 33.4 (2009): 501–22. Ramberg notes in particular the prominence of the institution in the present states of Karnataka and Maharashtra, and Telangana. Hyderabad State comprised adjacent portions of each of these regions.

[55] On anti-*devadasi* developments see Kay Jordan, "Devadasi Reform: Driving the Priestess of the Prostitutes out of Hindu Temples?" in *Religion and Law in Independent India*, 2nd enlarged edn., ed. R. D. Baird (Delhi: Manohar, 2005), 325–45; Kalpana Kannabiran, "Judiciary, Social Reform and Debate on 'Religious Prostitution' in Colonial India," *Economic and Political Weekly* 30.43 (1995): WS59–69; Janaki Nair, "The Devadasi, Dharma and the State," *Economic and Political Weekly* 29.50 (1994): 3157–67 and "'Imperial Reason,' National Honour and New Patriarchal Compacts in Early Twentieth-Century India," *History Workshop Journal* 66.1 (2008): 208–26; Kunal M. Parker, "'A Corporation of Superior Prostitutes': Anglo-Indian Legal Conceptions of Temple Dancing Girls, 1800–1914," *Modern Asian Studies* 32.3 (1998): 559–633; Amrit Srinivasan, "Reform and Revival: The Devadasi and her Dance," *Economic and Political Weekly* 20.44 (1985): 1869–76; M. Sundara Raj, *Prostitution in Madras: A Historical Perspective* (Delhi: Konark, 1993), ch. 6; Priyadarshini Vijaisri, "Sacred Prostitution and Reform in Colonial South India," *South Asia: Journal of South Asian Studies* 28.3 (2005): 387–411.

[56] Parker, "'A Corporation of Superior Prostitutes'," 589, 607.

[57] Jordan, "Devadasi Reform"; Nair, "The Devadasi"; Parker, "'A Corporation of Superior Prostitutes'." Raj, *Prostitution in Madras*, 117, notes that in early nineteenth-century Madras "education of females was only known among devadasis."

*devadasis* who adopted females.[58] In applying this law, officials invoked the rhetoric of "enticement into prostitution" to describe *devadasi* adoptions, and this appears in testimonies about Narsa Saji and Yellamma.[59] The language of the 1861 law allowed judges to apply criminal penalties in ambiguous situations, and strengthened the tools patriarchal society and the state used against *devadasis*.[60]

The legal and social offensive in British India against *devadasis* put women who sought to maintain control of property and adopt female heirs in a difficult situation. To carry out adoptions they often crossed borders beyond Raj jurisdiction into sub-imperial states and other non-British territories such as French Pondicherry.[61] This, along with the fact that the anti-*devadasi* movement in Hyderabad remained relatively weak into the twentieth century, suggests that flight to the Nizam's territory would have provided refuge to Narsa Saji and her young protégée if they chose to live as *devadasis*.[62]

As scholars of colonialism and nationalism have pointed out, South Asian women tended to be cast as instrumental objects rather than active subjects of liberation and improvement.[63] The history of *devadasi* legislation proves no exception: a confluence of interests between colonial officials and upper-caste patriarchies, and a tendency to value textual precept over practice, helped normalize regimes of sexuality and marriage, patrilineal inheritance, and male property ownership.[64] In the process, *devadasis* were stripped of property rights and "reduced to the status of proletarianised sex workers."[65] In a process spanning much of the nineteenth century, *devadasis* were disempowered and pushed to the margins of British Indian society, the latter quite literally since they fled to frontier zones and utilized them as resources to continue their livelihoods.

58 Kannabiran, "Judiciary," WS59.

59 On post-1861 legal references to "enticement" or "carrying away" of girls or women into prostitution see Ashwini Tambe, *Codes of Misconduct: Regulating Prostitution in Late Colonial Bombay* (Minneapolis: University of Minnesota Press, 2009), 28. On the language of "seduction" in 1819 statutes see Singha, *Despotism of Law*, 146–47.

60 Jordan, "Devadasi Reform," 328.

61 Parker ("'A Corporation of Superior Prostitutes'," 627) notes that many were accused of taking minors outside colonial territory for initiation. On flight to "native states" and European territories from Madras Presidency, see Raj, *Prostitution in Madras*, 123.

62 On the anti-*devadasi* movement in Hyderabad, see Vijaisri, "Sacred Prostitution," 406–8.

63 Lata Mani, "Contentious Traditions: The Debate on Sati in Colonial India," in *Recasting Women: Chapters in Colonial History*, ed. K. Sangari and S. Vaid (New Delhi: Kali for Women, 1989), 88–126.

64 Kannabiran, "Judiciary"; Nair, *Women and Law*; Parker, "'A Corporation of Superior Prostitutes'." On colonial law's strengthening of caste Hindu property claims in early twentieth-century Bombay Presidency, see Rao, *The Caste Question*, ch. 2.

65 Nair, "The Devadasi," 3165.

Available sources provide little sense of the perspectives of either longtime *devadasis* or recent inductees. In British India "there was no instance of a court examining whether a minor had acted as a 'free agent' in consenting to dedication as a temple dancing girl."[66] The case at hand bears out this point; both the depositions and the initial case description by the district magistrate, quoted above, describe Narsa's "enticement" of her intimate friend Yellamma rather than specifying coercion. The word choice would have been deliberate, and the depositions were probably pruned in the process of translation and compilation to assure an effective prosecution.

While scholarship on *devadasis* and courtesans suggests that these practices could provide women relief from patriarchal structures in British India, I do not mean to imply that Yellamma's departure to Gulbarga with Narsa necessarily represented freedom from the bondage of domesticity. We have no clear evidence detailing their experiences after crossing the frontier. Patriarchal colonial and upper-caste Hindu discourses constructed Yellamma's necessary return to her husband as liberation. Her potential participation in sex work or *devadasi* initiation could just as well be cast as liberation from other, perhaps more profound, forms of oppression.[67] Throughout all of this, young Yellamma – whether figured as bride–property, prostitute–criminal, or *devadasi*–victim – is rendered instrumental by colonial officials seeking to uphold justice, her kinfolk attempting to recover her, and perhaps by Narsa Saji seeking to induct her into a different livelihood.

The case does, however, bring into view the field of possibilities that the proximity of colonial and Hyderabad territory offered British subjects such as Narsa and Yellamma. The nascent state system Raj officials sought to consolidate ordered social worlds just as it produced pressures for flight and geographies of alterity. In the frontier zone the reach and applicability of various canons of law and modes of social practice were indeterminate. This flexibility was a potential resource for those who could cross the frontier, perhaps to participate in alternative regimes of labor and sexuality.[68] If legal ambivalence allowed some,

66 Parker, "'A Corporation of Superior Prostitutes'," 625.

67 Work on the Partition of British India has suggested that the violence and rupture created by the abduction of women has been overemphasized, and that the state's acts to 'return' women to their previous communities fortified patriarchal structures. See Urvashi Butalia, *The Other Side of Silence: Voices from the Partition of India* (Delhi: Penguin, 1998); Veena Das, *Critical Events: An Anthropological Perspective on Contemporary India* (Delhi: Oxford University Press, 1996).

68 Ramberg, "Magical Hair," 518, describes "Yellamma women," or *devadasis*, as being "implicated in a different sexual order," and Oldenburg, "Lifestyle as Resistance," 271, suggests that courtesans taught community members a "new meaning of being an aurat [woman]."

such as Yellamma and Narsa, to avoid colonial law, the proximity of jurisdictions also provided opportunities for rural people to invoke state power for their own purposes.

## Beyond state sovereignty: informers and thieves in rural society

The year 1888 saw a proliferation of requests for remission of sentence from Hyderabad subjects imprisoned for dacoity in the notorious British Indian prison of Yerawada in Pune, nearly a hundred miles from the Hyderabad frontier. These materials – English translations of vernacular letters addressed to Bombay officials – reveal extensive extraterritorial T&DD activity in late nineteenth-century Hyderabad. Colonial policing was based on a treaty that required the Nizam to surrender suspects in "the interests of justice."[69] The petitions document contestations within marginal Hyderabadi social groups, and state tactics that employed denizens of the frontier zone.

The 1887 remission request of Bhika Jamal and Sultan Dewa illuminates the workings of the Hyderabad T&DD. The petitioners' claims can be summarized as follows:

> The actions of the Resident were unjust. They were innocent of the charges. Two *gurundas* ['approvers,' or informants], Rupchand and Balram, fabricated evidence. The gurundas were members of the same [Multani] caste as the petitioners, and themselves convicted of dacoity and sentenced to transportation for life and/or imprisonment. In exchange for their freedom, the gurundas turned witness for the T&DD, and caused the wrongful conviction of their fellow community members.[70]

69 Hyderabad Resident Trevor Chichele-Plowden to Secretary of Government of India, Foreign Department, 16 November 1897, "Working of the rules in the Manual of the Thagi and Dakaiti Dept and trial of cases prosecuted by the Dept in Hyderabad," Letters from India 1898, 153–423, OIOC L/P&S/7/381.

70 This summary paraphrases the following documents: "Bhika Jamal and Sultan Dewa, prisoners in the Central Jail Yerrowda, Praying for the remission of the sentence passed upon them on a charge of dacoity," 21 April 1888, Oriental Translation Department "translation of the vernacular petition" submitted by appellants 6 April 1888 to Governor-General of India in Council, MSA Political Department, Hyderabad, vol. I, 57/214, 1888. The term *gurunda* (informant, or approver) is most likely a variant of the Persian term *goinda* or *goyanda* (literally, "one who talks") commonly used in the subcontinent. On the Central Indian use of *goranda* for *goyanda* see Robert V. Russell and Rai Bahadur Hira Lal, *The Tribes and Castes of the Central Provinces of India*, vol. I (London: Macmillan, 1916), 365. The social roles of these convicts-turned-informers in Hyderabad will be considered in detail presently. On *goindas* in the early nineteenth century, Lloyd, "Thuggee, Marginality," 208; Singha, "Providential Circumstances," 110.

Jamal and Dewa concluded their indictment of the corrupt system with what was an important structural element in remission requests: appeal to superior British justice: "Our belief is that no oppression is exercised under British rule in connection with the administration of justice. We do not know, however, whether any special laws besides those in force in British India are made for the use of the Hyderabad Residency. We pray that your Excellency-in-Council will be pleased to call for all the papers in our case, to ascertain whether there was any other evidence against us besides the statement of the Gurundas and whether any stolen property was found with us, and to remit the sentence which we, innocent persons, have been unjustly undergoing." These petitioners overestimated Bombay's willingness to regulate extraterritorial Raj jurisdiction in Hyderabad, and officials declined to intervene in their case, but the source nonetheless documents savvy frontier-dwellers navigating a plural legal terrain.[71]

Another petition from the same era provides further detail on the social conditions marginal people negotiated. In April 1888 three Hyderabadis in Yerawada Central Jail (Sekh Gutki, Sekh Lal, and Sekh Chand) requested remission of sentence. The petitioners implied corruption on the part of the Residency and the approvers who had offered evidence, caustically inquiring as to whether the colonial government had ordered the Thagi Department at Hyderabad "to act independently of the law and purely on the statements of Gurundas irrespective of any other evidence." They described their circumstances:

> We are Multanis by caste. We used to support ourselves by traveling from place to place and dealing in wood. Rupchand and Balram [the same informants named in Jamal and Dewa's petition], two men belonging to our caste had been convicted and sentenced for some offence committed by them. To benefit themselves they accepted places of Gurundas. They falsely mention the names of poor people in connection with any dacoities that may have been committed, admitting at the same time that they were their own accomplices in those dacoities.[72]

These *gurundas*, the same pair involved in the previous case, were apparently quite busy incriminating members of their caste. As itinerants, Multanis neatly fitted colonial sociology's profile of dacoits by

[71] Assistant Secretary, Government of India to Resident, Hyderabad, 14 June 1888, MSA Political Department, Hyderabad, vol. I, 57/214, 1888.

[72] "Petition to the address of the Government of India. From Sekh Gutki walad Sekh Mahabub and two other convicts in the Central Jail at Yerrowda, praying for the remission of the sentence passed upon them by the Sessions Court at – on a charge of dacoity," 7 April 1888, from Oriental Translation Department, MSA Political Department, Hyderabad, vol. I, 57/1068, 1888.

dint of their mobility and lack of integration into the settled agrarian economy.[73] The machineries of colonial justice criminalized these marginal populations, and the imprisonment of members of any given community tended, through the institution of the *gurunda*, to produce cycles of incrimination.[74]

The T&DD penetrated deep into Hyderabad rural society, and its victims employed a variety of tactics to gain the upper hand.[75] Another 1888 petition, from Kamiya walad Tuliya, says that he served the Nizam's government as a watchman, and had been convicted based on *gurunda* testimony despite the intervention of the village *kulkarnī* (rural accounting officer).[76] Even low-level state employees were not exempted from dacoity persecution. Kamiya claimed he did not know his accuser, but other dacoity cases reveal *gurundas* taking revenge on rivals. Ravya walad Balya Mang claimed he was imprisoned in Nanded District with his fellow villagers Chinya, Pochu, and Garibya (all Kaikadis), and subsequently:

> A quarrel took place between these persons and myself in connection with our work, and they bore a grudge against me for this. On [Pochu's] going to Hyderabad he became gurunda (approver) and at a time when there were only ten months wanting to complete the period of my sentence, he to take revenge upon me came to the jail and on the expiry of the period of my sentence arrested me and took me to Hyderabad.[77]

[73] A roughly contemporaneous colonial text glosses Multanis as Muslim Banjaras (also known as Kanjars) as "professional dacoits, highway robbers, and cattle-lifters, but not burglars" who ranged from Rajputana and Gujarat to the northern reaches of Hyderabad State. The text describes how two distinct groups of Multanis: the just-noted itinerant criminal tribe; and a settled non-criminal group that dealt in timber and firewood. The people considered here seem to combine elements of both groups. See E. J. Gunthorpe, *Notes on Criminal Tribes Residing in or Frequenting the Bombay Presidency, Berar and the Central Provinces* (Bombay: Times of India, 1882), ch. 7.

[74] On the "approver" figure in colonial law see Shahid Amin, "Approver's Testimony, Judicial Discourse: The Case of Chauri Chaura," in *Subaltern Studies V: Writings on South Asian History and Society*, ed. Ranajit Guha (New Delhi: Oxford University Press, 1987), 166–202.

[75] "Hyderabad. Petitions from Kamia walad Tuljia, Bijou Chandy walad Arjoon Bania Batia and Bhagia walad Bapu, convicts in the Yerrowda Central Jail praying for the remission of the sentences passed on them by Criminal Courts in – on charges of dacoity," Oriental Translator's Department, 26 June 1888, MSA Political Department, Hyderabad, vol. II, 58/1494, 1888.

[76] "Translation of a petition from Kamiya valad Tuliya [of] Bandhallir, Taluka Udgir, zilla Bedar in His Highness the Nizam's territory, to His Excellency the Viceroy and Governor-General of India-in-Council," dated 30 April 1888, received for translation 19 June 1888, MSA Political Department, Hyderabad, vol. II, 58/1494, 1888.

[77] "Translation of a petition from Ravya valad Balya Mang, inhabitant of Dongargaon, Taluka Halgaon, Zilla Nanded, in His Highness the Nizam's territory, to His Excellency the Viceroy and Governor-General of India-in-Council," dated 30 April 1888, received

The position of *gurunda* was an important resource for criminalized members of frontier society. Not only could they exchange information for commutation of sentences, they could also settle grudges with fellow villagers by initiating dacoity persecutions. Ravya, a Mang, and Pochu, a Kaikadi, were members of castes on the margins of Hyderabadi rural society.[78] It was Ravya's misfortune that his offer "to produce [criminal] evidence of my fellow villagers" came only after Pochu had fingered him as a dacoit.[79]

Like Rupchand and Balram Multani, Pochu Kaikadi was prolific in his informant work. According to another petition, Chandu walad Arjuna Kaikadi was arrested by Pochu, tried over the course of a year, found innocent, and released. Some time later he was arrested again by Pochu for the same crime, found guilty after a two-year trial, and sentenced to ten years' rigorous imprisonment at Yerawada.[80] Chandu questioned the veracity of the *gurunda*'s testimony and the legality of trying him on the same charge twice, since double jeopardy was illegal in British Indian law. Operating as a parallel legal order, T&DD in Hyderabad functioned by providing institutional shelter for state illegality. This means of splintering colonial sovereignty subjected marginal frontier figures to arbitrary and corrupt colonial judicial practices. But it also allowed members of rural society, as *gurundas*, to enact the colonial state's extraterritorial sovereignty. They did so by manipulating the very instruments of governmentality that criminalized them in the first place: social identification of depressed or mobile castes and tribes.[81] However, the power that approvers possessed to carry out vendettas by informing on their enemies was not without its costs.

for translation 19 June 1888, MSA Political Department, Hyderabad, vol. II, 58/1494, 1888.

78 Mangs are described as an unclean and superstitious caste with "a tendency towards crime," in Siraj ul Hassan, *Castes and Tribes*, vol. II, 462. The Kaikadis are glossed as a "wandering tribe" of "notorious highway robbers," in Great Britain, India Office, William Wilson Hunter, James Sutherland Cotton, Richard Burn, and William Meyer, *Imperial Gazetteer of India*, vol. VII (Oxford: Clarendon Press, 1908), 149.

79 "Translation of a petition from Ravya valad Balya Mang, inhabitant of Dongargaon, Taluka Halgaon, Zilla Nanded, in His Highness the Nizam's territory, to His Excellency the Viceroy and Governor-General of India-in-Council," dated 30 April 1888, received for translation 19 June 1888, MSA Political Department, Hyderabad, vol. II, 58/1494, 1888.

80 "Translation of a petition from Chandu valad Arjuna Kaikadi at present a convict at the Yerrowda Central Jail, to His Excellency the Viceroy and Governor-General of India-in-Council," dated 30 April 1888, received for translation 19 June 1888, MSA Political Department, Hyderabad, vol. II, 58/1494, 1888.

81 On similar trends in British India see Amin, "Approver's Testimony"; Nigam, "Disciplining and Policing."

Frontier society in Hyderabad responded to *gurunda* activity by drawing lines between good and bad neighbors. Pilu walad Raghu Mahar described his case in a petition:

> The Resident at Hyderabad passed upon me a sentence of five years on a charge of robbery. I pray that the sentence may be remitted for the following reasons. I did not commit the offence with which I was charged. No stolen property etc was found in my possession. Sidu Dhangar, one of the Gurundas (approvers), has a quarrel with me under the following circumstances: The Dhangar [shepherd caste] Gurunda had once come to our village for drinking *Shindi* liquor. Knowing him to be a Gurunda, myself and some others told him not to come any more to our village. For our having said this to him, the Gurunda some days afterwards arrested and took me [to Hyderabad] and caused the sentence to be passed upon me.[82]

If turning *gurunda* allowed the accused to empower themselves using the frontier's political resources, this act came at a certain social price: as Sidu Dhangar found, his status as a colonial informer rendered him unwelcome in Hyderabadi rural society. It is unclear from the record whether his banishment from the village and access to its liquor ceased after he incriminated Pilu, but it is likely that the *gurunda* stigma remained.

As the above examples demonstrate, *gurundas* used their powers to imprison marginal rural people (often of their own castes), agriculturalists, and even state employees.[83] Those who became representatives of extraterritorial colonial sovereignty were in response ostracized in the rural social world of Hyderabad. For all parties – from petitioners in Yerawada who cast aspersions on informers and the T&DD to *gurundas* themselves – and for frontier society at large, the legal pluralism of the borderlands was a vital resource for negotiating the circumstances in which they found themselves.

## Banditry, society, and statecraft

The Hyderabad–Bombay frontier's jurisdictional complexity reveals the lasting incompleteness of colonial attempts to consolidate legal

82 "Translation of a petition from Pilu valad Raghu Mhar, inhabitant of Hunasval, Taluka Dubalgandi, zilla Hyderabad (Deccan) and at present a convict in the Central Jail at Yerrowda, to His Excellency the Viceroy and Governor-General of India-in-Council," dated 30 August 1888, Oriental Translations Department, 3 October 1888, MSA Political Department, Hyderabad, vol. II, 58/1749, 1888.

83 For petitions from Koli agriculturalists accused by the *gurunda* Sidu Dhangar see "Petitions from Mansing walad Malhari Koli and Marpali, son of Saheboo, convicts in the C. J. at Yerrowda, praying for the remission of the sentences passed upon them by the Sessions Court at Hyderabad on a charge of dacoity," MSA Political Department, Hyderabad, vol. II, 58/1559, 1888.

sovereignty. Frontier developments elaborate the productive relationship between political authority and crime and lawlessness in modern South Asia. Following Eric Hobsbawm's work on "social banditry," historians have attempted to understand how putative criminals fit into rural societies. Hobsbawm's argument ran as follows:

> Social bandits . . . are peasant outlaws whom the lord and state regard as criminals, but who remain within peasant society, and are considered by their people as heroes, as champions, avengers, fighters for justice, perhaps even leaders of liberation, and in any case as men to be admired, helped and supported. This relation between the ordinary peasant and the rebel, outlaw and robber is what makes social banditry interesting and significant. It also distinguishes it from two other kinds of rural crime: from the activities and gangs drawn from the professional "underworld" or from mere freebooters ("common robbers"), and from communities for whom raiding is part of the normal way of life.[84]

He further specified that these brigands and the visions of liberation they gave to peasants embodied the last gasp of a precapitalist agrarian world in which extant modes of social ordering (kinship, tribal loyalties) were rapidly disintegrating. Social bandits – or "primitive rebels," as he called them elsewhere – belonged to the realm of the pre-political and were nostalgic figures upon whom peasants projected political desires.[85]

In contesting the teleological language that framed Hobsbawm's presentation, critics have questioned the liberatory implications he ascribed to social banditry. Anton Blok argued that brigandage in peasant societies advanced agendas of nobles and officials by keeping peasants docile.[86] Assessing banditry in nineteenth-century Egypt, Nathan Brown argued, "The *idea* of a crisis of banditry was a powerful tool, though not one that peasants could use." Rather, "Banditry as a national problem was invented as a political weapon by Egypt's rulers as a part of the process of creating a stronger, centralized state apparatus and as an effort to keep that apparatus out of British hands."[87] Contrary to the Egyptian state's intentions in making banditry policing an autonomous institutional domain outside the purview of the encroaching British, the

84 Eric J. Hobsbawm, *Bandits* ([New York]: Delacorte, 1969), 13–14.
85 For a critique of the concept of "pre-political" in Hobsbawm see Ranajit Guha, *Elementary Aspects of Peasant Insurgency in Colonial India* (Delhi: Oxford University Press, 1983).
86 Anton Blok, "The Peasant and the Brigand: Social Banditry Reconsidered," *Comparative Studies in Society and History* 14.4 (1972): 495–503; Eric J. Hobsbawm, "Social Bandits: Reply," *Comparative Studies in Society and History* 14.4 (1972): 503–5.
87 Nathan Brown, "Brigands and State Building: The Invention of Banditry in Modern Egypt," *Comparative Studies in Society and History* 32.2 (1990): 258–81, here 259–60. The parallel with Hyderabad is striking, where a similar panic over dacoity authorized British cross-border policing in the sub-imperial state.

perceived epidemic of brigandage precipitated colonial conquest. For Brown, banditry in this context was not a practice supported by the rural masses, but rather part of the tripartite plague visited upon the Egyptian peasantry of "bandits, rulers, and occupiers."[88]

All of these accounts share the presumption that banditry, or criminality in general, was a domain related to, but analytically distinct from, stable categories of peasantry, nobility, and state. Hobsbawm, Blok, and Brown strove to clarify the relationship between the idea and practice of lawlessness and other discrete domains.[89] Evidence from the Hyderabad–Bombay frontier suggests, however, that criminality – whether figured as dacoity, simple theft, kidnapping, or otherwise – was deeply intertwined with frontier peasant society. Rather than categorically distinguishing bandits from peasants, evidence here suggests that lawlessness was a constituent feature of rural society. What the Raj treated as criminality was in fact coterminous with the everyday life and livelihoods of many marginal people in the frontier zone.

Lawlessness was not only an integral aspect of peasant society, but also bore a close relationship with political sovereignty. The connection between, first, raiding, crime, and what appeared as anti-state insurgency, and second, the process of state building, has been elaborated in scholarship on politics in early modern South Asia. Stewart Gordon's work on eighteenth-century Malwa argued that the raiding that later colonial commentators criminalized as "thugee" was an effective strategy to mobilize the popular support and resources necessary to establish political authority. In his estimation, banditry and state-formation occupied the same continuum.[90]

If raiding was a path to political authority in South Asia, particularly in the Deccan and Central India, just before the rise of the Raj, then an imperative of the expansive colonial state was to shut down these avenues to power. This was an essential stage in the British move to liquidate competition and seize political authority. The early stages of the T&DD campaign during the first half of the nineteenth century can be seen in this light.[91] In the century's second half the Raj began to represent the consolidation of its authority by framing British paramountcy within

88 Ibid., 279, 280.

89 On social banditry in modern South Asia see Malavika Kasturi, *Embattled Identities: Rajput Lineages and the Colonial State in Nineteenth-Century North India* (New Delhi: Oxford University Press, 2002), ch. 6; Shail Mayaram, "Kings versus Bandits: Anti-Colonialism in a Bandit Narrative," *Journal of the Royal Asiatic Society of Great Britain and Ireland* 13.3 (2003): 315–38; Kim A. Wagner, "Thuggee and Social Banditry Reconsidered," *Historical Journal* 50.2 (2007): 353–76.

90 Gordon, *Marathas, Marauders*, ch. 1.

91 Singha, "Providential Circumstances" and *Despotism of Law*, ch. 5.

a doctrine of suzerainty, an integrative political language that carved out domains of power for sub-imperial states within a hierarchy of sovereign polities. This image both masked and fed jurisdictional tensions. Colonial state sovereignty was consistently undercut by alternative legalities of sub-imperial states such as Hyderabad, amidst territories that comprised British India. Lauren Benton's argument suggests an untrammeled rise of unitary state sovereignty through the global consolidation of legal regimes by the end of the nineteenth century. In South Asia, however, contradictions posed by sub-imperial states and other sovereign polities, or anomalous zones, reveal a contingent trajectory in which flexible and multifarious legal arrangements were incorporated into high-colonial political geography.

## Fragmented sovereignties, unruly states

C. H. Alexandrowicz and Lauren Benton both detailed legal arrangements prior to the nineteenth century where legal authority was not yet concentrated in European hands. Benton describes the simultaneous presence of multiple legalities in any given place, before the rise of state sovereignties linked to clearly demarcated territories by 1900.[92] Alexandrowicz's complementary argument emphasizes the multifarious character of political sovereignty before the nineteenth century.[93] Both histories end with the consolidation of European colonialism and the consequent end of legal and political sovereignty for non-European states and subjects. The scenario I have described here is difficult to fit into such a teleology.

In a world of splintered and often functionally overlapping sovereignties such as that of South Asia in the colonial period (and much of the world circa 1900), the putatively early modern global legal order, with all of the resources it offered to subjects, was never completely liquidated. Bombay territory may have been under a cohesive colonial legal regime, while the Raj penetrated Hyderabad through extraterritorial illegalities. But the frontier provided access to jurisdictional difference and spatial distance from the colonial state's disciplinary apparatuses. As Yellamma's alternative roles as child bride, sex worker, or *devadasi* suggest, these political and social resources were not necessarily liberating. Nevertheless,

92 "The familiar fluidity of legal orders in the early modern world provided institutional continuity that itself gave legal politics a certain similarity across widely disparate legal systems. The territories for which this condition of jurisdictional fluidity was true are so vast and diverse that they can be described as encompassing a *global* legal regime": Benton, *Law and Colonial Cultures*, 261.

93 Alexandrowicz, *Law of Nations*.

the frontier zone was productive of possibilities, different in degree if not in kind from those available in spaces firmly within British Indian terrain.[94]

The legal environment of the Hyderabad–Bombay frontier was distinct from the early modern scenario in two decisive ways. First, early modern legal pluralism often occurred in the same places at the same time. In the modern context, multiple legal orders were in close proximity with some overlap, but jurisdictional maps theoretically corresponded to clear territorial demarcations. Second, the modern period witnessed increasingly systemic attempts by dominant states, such as the Raj, to regulate social worlds by means of disciplinary apparatuses such as policing and surveillance. This point is borne out by colonial forays into Hyderabad – a foreign territory – in the form of cross-border policing, often relying on local informers, and extraterritorial jurisdictional arrangements such as the T&DD. Even as the Raj refined its techniques for transgressing frontiers, subjects practiced creative and effective tactics to manipulate the contradictions of colonial sovereignty and stay one step ahead of the law.

This chapter began with the late 1880s confrontation between Daji the notorious Bhil and the Bombay frontier police official R. H. Vincent. It is to Daji that I now return by way of conclusion. In a letter of April 1887, Vincent summarized Daji's history, starting with his rise to notoriety in 1883 and continuing with his flight across the border into Bombay, and his apprehension the next year by colonial police in Ahmednagar (Bombay). Daji escaped, but was caught by a joint Raj–Nizam task force in Gangapur (Aurangabad District, Hyderabad). However, "He again escaped from custody some months afterwards and . . . several [Bombay] Detectives were deputed to search for him and one of them found him, *dressed in the uniform of the Nizam's Police*, near the village of Holkar [Rahuri Taluka, Ahmednagar District, Bombay Presidency]. The detective was unarmed and Daji Bhil perceiving this agreed to quietly accompany the Police officer but suddenly drew a sword, which he had hidden behind him, rushed at the Head Constable and made good his escape."[95] In addition to border-hopping, then, Daji masqueraded as a member of the Nizam's police to outwit the joint task force. This tactic not only

[94] Benton elaborates the key role of geography in producing anomalous legal spaces within empire. For her consideration of South Asian 'princely states' within this framework see *A Search for Sovereignty*, 236–64.

[95] R. H. Vincent (DSOP [District Superintendent of Police], Ahmednagar) to A. T. Crawford (Commisioner, CD, Poona), 4 April 1887, MSA Political Department, Hyderabad 55/924, my emphasis.

endowed him with the cloak of officialdom but also provided him a ready excuse for carrying a weapon.

After escaping, Daji went on to commit more crimes in Ahmednagar, and was once more captured by British Indian police, who intended to pass him to the Nizam's authorities for trial. While still in Vincent's custody he agreed to give evidence on previous crimes, and implied a familiarity and allegiance with a Bombay police Patil. The promised evidence was never provided, however, since without a guarantee of pardon Daji "would never come to the point." Lacking a sound case to pass over to Hyderabad police, a regretful Vincent was compelled to set Daji free. In classic outlaw fashion, the notorious Bhil assured the police officer that he would "soon hear from him again."[96] Bombay returned to Daji Malhari's case in 1889, and officials criticized Hyderabad for the "inadequacy of [his] punishment."[97] Apparently, after all of Bombay's efforts in apprehending Daji and the many crimes he allegedly committed, the Hyderabad judiciary sentenced him to a mere three months' imprisonment.[98] According to the police docket on the matter, the only possible solution was to press Hyderabad officials to mete out stricter punishment.[99] The docket also diagnosed the root problem: "The position is quite clear! The Bhil is in league with the officials. He gets caught when a large reward is offered and he gets off to recommence his tricks."[100] Jurisdiction over such figures – "now on this, now on that side of the frontier" – lay with the state of which they were subjects; in Daji's case, Hyderabad.[101] And if Daji and his ilk could continue their activities and avoid significant legal consequences, this was in part a result of their ability to forge allegiances with police officials in Bombay, and no doubt some in Hyderabad. This was not a simple matter of corruption – the multiple sovereignties

96 Vincent to Crawford, 4 April 1887, MSA Political Department, Hyderabad 55/924.

97 J. G. Moore, Officiating Commissioner to the Secretary of Government, Poona, 15 January 1889, "Hyderabad. Dacoit Daji walad Malhari Bhil trial and punishment by the authorities of His Highness the Nizam's Government of," MSA Political Department, Hyderabad, vol. II, 64/541, 1889.

98 E. A. Bulkey, Acting DSOP, Ahmednagar to Waddington, 8 November 1888, MSA Political Department, Hyderabad, vol. II, 64/541, 1889.

99 Docket entry for 26 January 1889, MSA Political Department, Hyderabad, vol. II, 64/541, 1889.

100 Docket entry for 28 January 1889, MSA Political Department, Hyderabad, vol. II, 64/541, 1889. See also Vincent's gloss: "Daji Bhil has, I know, some very good friends among the Patils and Sowkars of this District and I strongly suspect that some of my own men are not over anxious either to catch him," 28 September 1888, MSA Political Department, Hyderabad, vol. II, 64/541, 1889.

101 See Vincent's description of Daji and his gang, in DSOP, Ahmednagar to G. Waddington, District Magistrate, Ahmednagar, 28 September 1888, MSA Political Department, Hyderabad, vol. II, 64/541, 1889.

clustered around the frontier splintered the reach and availability of state power.

As I have suggested, it was the proximity of multiple legal regimes that made possible the putatively illegal livelihoods of the "notorious Bhil" Daji Malhari, the "public woman" and kidnapper Narsa Saji, the cattle rustler Tukaram Jiwaji, various *gurundas*, and countless others. Near the frontier Raj officials (Bombay, Central Provinces, T&DD), the Nizam's police, and internal Hyderabadi authorities all exercised jurisdictions over different subjects in different places. Cross-border policing and judicial collaboration functioned to a degree, but were severely circumscribed by logistical matters. Moreover, the Nizam's claim to sovereignty over his own subjects made collaborations uneasy. All of these factors undermined the efficiency of colonial attempts to pacify the Hyderabad border.

In varied historical settings in South Asia and elsewhere, subjects manipulated the powerfully substantiated authority of colonial courts. In colonial Sri Lanka, as John Rogers has shown, British courts never functioned according to design, and through them subjects were able to summon state power to serve their needs. Indigenous legal cultures wherein subjects made instrumental use of putatively colonial institutions underscored courts' lack of popular moral authority.[102] On the Hyderabad–Bombay frontier, as in much of Greater British India, instrumental use of courts was supplemented by the resource of judicial difference across space. Both provided avenues for subjects within the enormous penumbra of empire to carry out livelihoods inimical to colonial visions. Hyderabad, and state officials such as Kotwal Nawab Akbar Jang Bahadur, clearly did not condone such livelihoods. Indeed, the Nizam's statist imperatives, together with colonial expectations, impelled Hyderabad to affect the appearance of emulating the British in identifying and stamping out 'crime.' However, persistent institutional underdevelopment in the frontier zone enabled the ways of life of Daji and others. Although conditions of lawlessness and sheltering of fugitives there were not a product of state design, Hyderabad's attempts to retain judicial and police sovereignty over subjects produced friction and played a major role in maintaining the situation. It is impossible to say with certainty how Daji the notorious Bhil obtained the Nizam's police uniform he wore on the day colonial officials tried to arrest him, but it is not inappropriate that he clad himself in a symbol of Hyderabadi sovereignty.

[102] John D. Rogers, *Crime, Justice and Society in Colonial Sri Lanka* (London: Curzon, 1987).

*Part III*

# Urban space

# 7 Remaking city, developing state: ethical patrimonialism, urbanism, and economic planning

## I

In 1876 the 'Adālat-i Bīrūn-i Baldah, or Suburban Court of Judicature, was established north of the Musa River in the vicinity of the British political headquarters in Hyderabad, the Chadarghat Residency.[1] The Court made judgments based on the British Indian legal canon in civil cases taking place in that part of the city. Europeans, their descendants, and native Christians could apply to have cases heard by the Court. Two decades after its foundation Hyderabad officials pushed for the Court's abolition, and it was closed in 1896.

## II

In 1911 the seventh Nizam of Hyderabad, Osman Ali Khan, went to Delhi for his coronation. During his trip a plague epidemic broke out in Hyderabad, affecting the area of the High Court on the south bank of the Musa River. The Nizam permitted the Court's temporary removal to the north of the river, but insisted it should be moved back to the Balad-i Ḥaidarābād (city proper) as soon as possible in accordance with a *ḥukm* (royal decree) of his late father.[2]

## III

In an era of urban crisis following cataclysmic 1908 floods, plague and cholera outbreaks, the Hyderabad City Improvement Board (CIB) was

[1] The Court's Persianate name means "court of the city's exterior." The Court was alternately called 'Adālat-i Aṭrāf-i Baldah or "court of the city's outskirts." Both the terms *bīrūn* and *aṭrāf*, when paired with *baldah* ("city," interchangeable with *balad*) were already associated with the suburban areas close to a city's urban core, as shown by the inclusion of "suburbs" in dictionary entries for the words: John T. Platts, *A Dictionary of Urdu, Classical Hindi, and English* (London: W. H. Allen & Co., 1884), 59, 208. Atraf-i Baldah was the official name for the suburban administrative division of Hyderabad State.

[2] Urdu farman from Jahangir Mansion, Delhi to Maharajah Kishen Pershad, 12 Zihaj 1329 H [3 December 1911] and APSA 37/1/339, Faridoonji Jamshedji, Camp Delhi to Mr Fazil Mooraj, Hyderabad, 5 December 1911, APSA 37/1/339.

founded in 1912. The CIB was charged with the "general improvement of the social, moral and physical conditions of the citizens." The majority of the body's extensive construction work was carried out north of the river, where the CIB laid out an infrastructure for decades of urban expansion and economic development.

These three moments indicate a northern turn in the city's orientation, and Hyderabad's movement from assertion of jurisdictional sovereignty over territory in the city to state-led technocratic transformation of urban space during the early twentieth century. Such developments manifested an enduring tension in Hyderabad between planning informed by economistic and technocratic principles, and the regime's ethical obligation to state subjects. I suggest here that the emergent global discourse and practice of *urbanism* served as a framework for integrating these ideas – producing an idiom that informed later state economic planning.

Hyderabad, fourth-largest city in South Asia during the colonial period, was remade between the 1870s and the decade following its 1948 integration into the postcolonial nation-state of India. Part of this chapter's task is to track the city's *empirical* changes, notably the northward movement of Hyderabad's urban core. This geographical shift corresponded to an ensemble of related infrastructural developments. These changes were entangled with key *analytical* transformations in the political meaning of space in the city, and eventually the state as a whole. In the nineteenth century Hyderabadi officials expressed sovereignty as moral and jurisdictional claim over territory and resident populations, in the city as in the countryside. From the early twentieth century in Hyderabad, as in many global locations, *the urban* signified a particular kind of abstract space, and the emergence of the modality of planning emerged as a technical means for its remaking. In time, the planning modality expanded beyond the capital. Planning provided a template for sketching out economic and social development in the state as a whole, encompassing provincial towns, industrial cities, rural areas, and connecting infrastructures. This productive analytical shift generated conceptual frameworks and specific institutions – as well as a new type of state intellectual – that remained significant in the articulation of state projects on regional and national levels in postcolonial India.

The particular context of Hyderabad City, and the sub-imperial state of which it was capital, shaped the workings of urbanist projects there. Hyderabad State was a key venue for political experimentation owing to formal sovereignty and autonomy from British India (which surrounded it), and connections to other places and intellectual currents (modernist Muslim states and statecraft, urbanist ideas and practices). However, the globally mediated shift to an urbanism envisioned as technical intervention into abstract space existed in tension with the prevailing patrimonial political rhetoric of the regime. Hyderabadi rulers and officials conceived their sovereignty in terms of moral authority over terrain and responsibility to subject populations. As deployed by Hyderabadi bureaucrat-intellectuals, urbanism and planning became vehicles for articulating two imaginaries of state: ethical patrimonialism expressing reciprocity between ruler and subjects in state territory, and interventionist technocratic planning effecting improvement through development of abstract space. Neither of these imaginations of space and power displaced or overcame the other; urbanism and planning became idioms for their integration.

In tracking empirical and analytical changes around Hyderabadi urbanism and planning, I begin by elaborating the concept of ethical patrimonialism in relation to state urbanism and situating Hyderabad in comparison to other places (other sub-imperial states; British India). I continue by sketching the geographical and cultural context of a city split between Muslim dynastic and British colonial domains, and nineteenth-century Hyderabadi assertions of urban sovereignty within the city's territory, that set the stage for the deployment of interventionist planning activity. The subsequent section examines the work of the CIB (founded in 1912), and tracks the increasing industrial focus and expansion of the urbanist project into state-wide economic planning after World War II. I highlight the emergence of a new type of South Asian bureaucrat-intellectual, the planner-technocract, in this process. In closing, I account for the legacies of the trajectories of urbanism and planning examined here, which themselves expand temporally and geographically beyond the erstwhile sub-imperial state.

## Ethical patrimonialism, statecraft, and comparative frameworks

In Hyderabad State a rhetoric of ethical patrimonialism was invoked to legitimize state planning interventions, where it supplemented and destabilized technocratic and economistic developmentalist visions. Patrimonialist rhetoric emphasized a personalized mode of authority premised on relationships of reciprocity between ruler and ruled.[3] Such ideas drew on a long history in Hyderabad, and reflected the state's political structure founded on loyalty between rulers, nobles, officials, and subjects. Patrimonialist rhetoric resonated with legitimizations of state-led

[3] On the role of patrimonialism in Hyderabad's political modernity, see above, Introduction, 6–8.

planning in proximate contexts of British India, other sub-imperial South Asian states, and postcolonial India.[4] In Hyderabad, autocratic executive power insulated urbanists and planners from both internal political resistance and Raj opposition. Patrimonial ideology, emphasizing royal authority and ethical obligation to subjects, was extensively invoked by Hyderabadi urbanists and planners. Further, the autocratic configuration of state power and capacity of official planning bodies to invoke executive power and financial support to further their ends was also crucial. The formally autonomous character of sub-imperial states, and tendency toward unitary, often autocratic, forms of rule facilitated largely unencumbered operation by urbanist and planning bodies.

The context of urbanism and planning in British India had important parallels with the Hyderabad scenario, but also key divergences. Several specific connections, institutional similarities, and common figures linked urbanism and planning in South Asian states and regions. Some urbanists and bodies in British India also worked with relative insulation from political opposition, such as Lutyens and Baker in planning New Delhi. The situation in Hyderabad (and some other sub-imperial states) was different in degree, though not in kind, from that in British India. In Hyderabad, state-level political authority was concentrated in the hands of the Nizam rather than, as in British India, shared between various entities (provincial or municipal politicians, mercantile or industrial capital interests, or competing state-level entities at different levels of colonial government). As such, while comparable to British Indian and other imperial contexts, the Hyderabadi planning domain was distinct in its high degree of insulation from direct popular or political pressure enabled by the particularity of the state form. Rather than placing Hyderabadi urbanism and planning within a strict teleology or typology of political forms, this chapter attempts to situate this case in comparison to other proximate contexts and amidst varied legitimizing idioms (ethical patrimonialism, technocratic developmentalism).

## Nineteenth-century contexts and contestations

### *Geographical and political orientation*

Hyderabad City, seat of the Nizams, was centered around an early modern walled capital on the south bank of the Musa River. British authorities

[4] See below on parallels with planning in Mysore, and legacies of Hyderabadi urbanism and planning in postcolonial India.

exercised control over military and civil areas – the Secunderabad Cantonment and the British Residency in Chadarghat – and their surroundings. In practical terms this amounted to most of the area north of the river (the trans-Musa).[5] The Nizam's capital housed core state institutions and groups from across South Asia and beyond linked to Hyderabad State's government or society. This included bureaucrats from North India with knowledge of administrative languages (Persian, Urdu, and, increasingly, English), military entrepreneur groups, and intellectuals enjoying state patronage or expanding Muslim political networks. Hyderabad's Islamicate cosmopolitanism contrasted the trans-Musa colonial military and civil areas of Secunderabad and Chadarghat. The latter featured a commercially oriented legal framework which attracted British Indian and European merchants and bankers, and entrepreneurial or professional communities from elsewhere in Hyderabad state. The Secunderabad Cantonment was located to the north and northeast of Hussain Sagar, a large artificial lake constructed in the early modern period. Chadarghat Residency sat on the north bank of the Musa, directly south of Hussain Sagar, and in close proximity to the walled city southeast across the river.

From the 1870s Hyderabad officials began to assert sovereignty over urbanizing lands around British military and political establishments under de facto colonial authority. This changing focus was partly a result of population growth and expanding commerce following the 1874 opening of Secunderabad and Hyderabad Railway Stations trans-Musa.

Hyderabad administrators began to develop explicitly urban policies in the wake of two crises. First, massive Musa flooding in 1908 submerged nearly half of the old city.[6] The foremost Indian civil engineer, M. Visvesvaraya, was hired to devise a water-management system. He constructed reservoirs and developed plans for urban drainage. Second, a plague outbreak in 1911 struck the old city and areas around Hyderabad Railway Station, reducing the urban population by one fifth (what had been a city of about half a million lost roughly 100,000 residents). Officials sought to remake the space of the city, which entailed state consolidation of urban lands. Claims to legal jurisdiction over the trans-Musa city provided a basis for broader transformations. The dramatic shift of royal capital and

[5] The key exception here is the suburb of Afzal Gunj, located on the north bank of the river just northeast of the urban core. This area was developed starting in the second quarter of the nineteenth century and integrated with the Nizam's city during the 1850s and 1860s. See Shah, "Constructing a Capital," ch. 2.

[6] Benjamin Cohen, "Modernising the Urban Environment: The Musi River Flood of 1908 in Hyderabad, India," *Environment and History* 17.3 (2011): 409–32.

state institutions later in 1911 out of the walled city and across the river continued a longer trajectory of urban assertion.

### *Jurisdictional sovereignty, moral authority, and territory*

Hyderabad's move to abolish the Suburban Court of Judicature in 1896 was a key moment in the shift of political focus to the trans-Musa. Despite being located in Hyderabad territory, the Suburban Court was established in 1876 north of the river and served colonial imperatives. It functioned to facilitate market-oriented economic activity in the city, and was the judicial component of the colonial capitalist economic zone the British established in trans-Musa Hyderabad. A British Indian judge empowered to settle civil cases involving Europeans, Anglo-Indians, and native Christians presided over it.[7]

The Court served as a judicial component of the establishment of the British colonial store-front in Hyderabad. The original judge – H. E. Trevor of Lincoln's Inn and Oxford University – was well qualified for colonial judicial service, but was wanting in the eyes of Hyderabad officials.[8] Salar Jang I, the prime minister, suggested to Trevor that in preparing for his post he ought to "acquire some knowledge of the Country and its languages," and sent English translations of Hyderabad legal codes. It is clear from the duties entrusted to Trevor, however, that deciding cases based on 'native' legal principles was not within the sphere of his responsibilities. Indeed, the judge applied "the same law as would have been administered by a British Court if the case had arisen in British India."[9] Accordingly, the Court followed the Letters Patent of the High Court of Fort William in Calcutta, dating to the late eighteenth century, and a foundational document for British rule in South Asia.

Cases from the Hyderabad Suburban Court indicate that it served at times as a forum for merchants in the state to avail themselves of comparatively liberal colonial laws regulating commerce. In an 1878 case, for

[7] "Abolition of the Suburban Court and Distribution of its Work," 9 March 1896, and "Resolution for the Abolition of the Suburban Court," APSA 37/1/148, 1896. See also Khan, *Tarikh-i 'Adalat-i Aṣafī*, 35–6; Muttalib, *Administration of Justice,* 153–55, 265–66. Khan notes that Syed Mahmood, son of the famed British Indian Muslim educationist Sir Syed Ahmed Khan, presided very briefly over the Court, in 1881, before he returned to Allahabad in British India where he became the first Muslim High Court Judge in British India. Aside from this brief period, the Court's judges were British. H. E. Trevor, who will be discussed below, presided in the early period. In its later years the Court came to be known as "Campbell's Court" after Trevor's successor. Khan and Muttalib give different dates (respectively 1877–94 and 1881–95) for the Court's lifespan from those indicated in the archival documents that inform the account here.

[8] Salar Jung to Trevor, 15 March 1876 in "Establishment of Suburban Court (Volume 2)," APSA 37/1/27.

[9] Ibid.

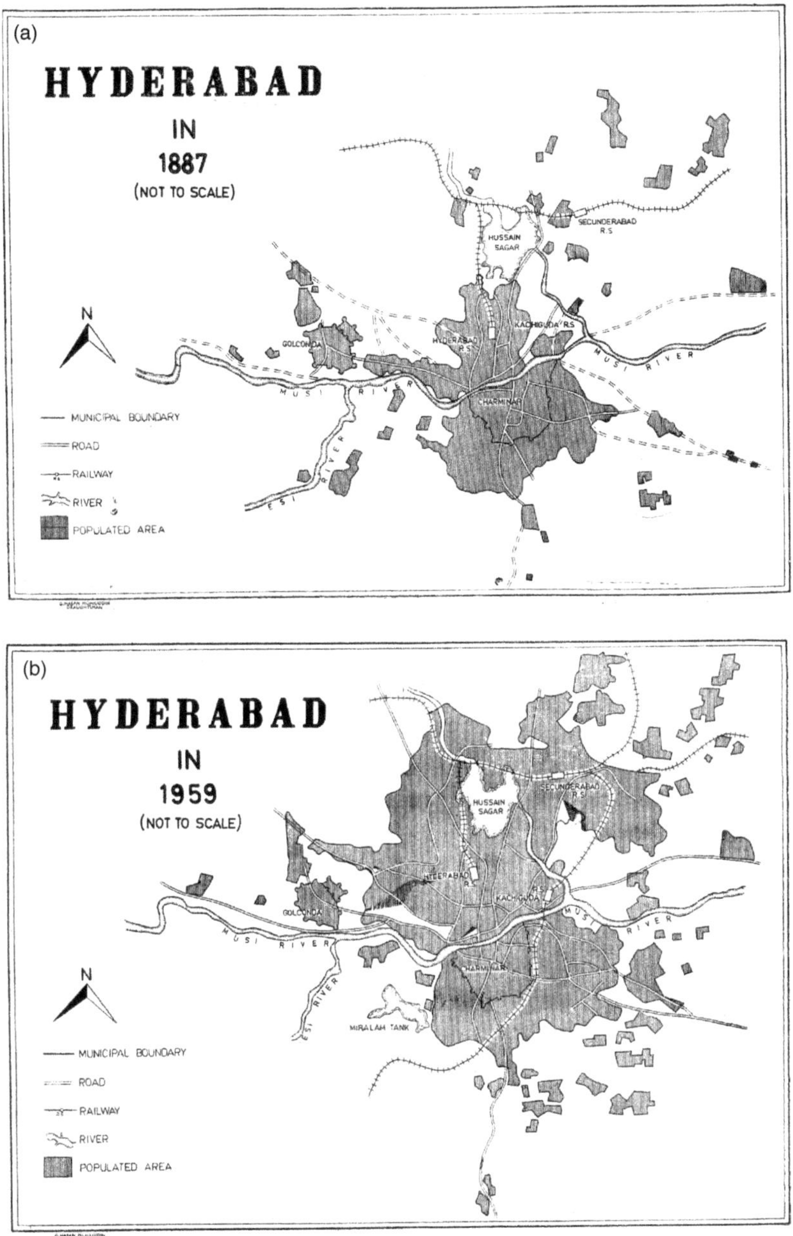


Map 4 The maps above show geographic expansion of Hyderabad City during the period under study. This chapter tracks population shifts from the old city (just south of the river on the map; the old city wall is drawn on the map in the area around the Charminar) to the trans-Musa areas north of the river centered on the Hyderabad Railway Station.
*Source:* Maps by Ghulam Hasan Mohiuddin, *Hyderabad in 1887* (Hyderabad: n.d.), and *Hyderabad in 1959* (Hyderabad: n.d.). Images courtesy of MIT Libraries

example, two merchants resorted to the Court in an attempt to recoup fines levied by an Abkari officer of Hyderabad State for unpaid duties on liquor sale.[10] The merchants, Pestonji Jihangir and Dorabji Lakkadawala, presented themselves as "British traders from Bombay and British subjects." In their numerous petitions they appealed to everyone from the judge of the Suburban Court to the Resident of Hyderabad, all the way up to the Viceroy and Governor-General of India, for exemption from what they portrayed as the oppressive laws of a "Foreign Prince." In the case documents Jihangir and Lakkadawala invoke language common to established colonial discourses on corrupt Muslim rule and righteous British intervention. They describe the Hyderabadi *ābkārī* (alcohol excise) official as "malicious and sinister," and invoke the "higher authority" of the British via the "learned, impartial and painstaking" Judge Trevor of the Suburban Court to proceed "with the characteristic uprightness of all English and British gentlemen." When the Hyderabadi *divan*, Sir Salar Jang, allegedly intervened in an "extra-judicial" manner to stop proceedings, the merchants derided his "all-powerful interference," and called upon colonial officials to push the Court to protect their "property and liberty" and ability to "carry on free trade" in Hyderabad. As this incident shows, the Suburban Court was seen as a vehicle for advancing the intervention of enlightened British rule in a benighted, Muslim-ruled state on the internal borderlands of empire. Jihangir and Lakkadawala's racialized account suggests that the Court represented the juridical instantiation of colonial economic penetration that sought to create in Hyderabad territory a British market zone. In political-conceptual terms, however, the extraterritorial claim the Court represented was crucial.

Hyderabad officials saw the presence of a court administering colonial law to an ambiguously defined range of people as an unwelcome transgression of sovereignty in the capital. The trans-Musa city was peripheral to administrative concerns during this period, but the state's decisive move to abolish the Court in the 1890s suggests a growing vigilance over affairs outside the walled city. The Suburban Court's abolition represented a defense of abstract judicial authority over diverse city populations. The Court's existence was premised on the notion that the Hyderabad judiciary was not competent to dispense justice to Europeans or Christians. The proceedings to abolish the Court reveal an expansive claim to Hyderabad officials' moral authority over the city's populace:

10 "Jihangir and Lakkadawala's Petition to Marquis of Ripon, G.C.S.I., Viceroy and Governor-General of India," 6 October 1880, OICO, 4 L/P&S/7/358, file 35, OIOC. Subsequent quotations in this paragraph are taken from this file.

> It is hardly just that, while the residents of one part of the City of Hyderabad have the advantage of the legal knowledge and experience of the learned judges of the High Court . . . those of another part should be deprived of such benefits . . . Considerable difficulty is occasioned in executing proceedings by reason of one town being under separate jurisdiction of two courts.[11]

If the Suburban Court was an affront to Hyderabadi judicial sovereignty, its abolition represented the unification of two heretofore discrete spaces of the expanding capital city.

Debates over an infrastructure project underscore the Nizam's designs for the trans-Musa city. In 1888 a joint Hyderabadi–English group proposed to build a tramway in the city under a state concession. A key selling-point of the project was that it would allow Hyderabad subjects, "especially the poorer classes," to travel quickly and cheaply, perhaps to facilitate construction workers' transit across the expanding city. The railway employees who had backed the project withdrew the following year, but their place was taken by Balkrishna Gopaljee, a "well-known contractor" in Hyderabad.[12] The proposal languished for a decade after British military officials insisted on road-widening in the areas of Secunderabad the tramway was meant to pass through. Upon its being taken up again in 1897, colonial officials again attempted to block the scheme by objecting to passage though areas over which the Raj exercised "full jurisdiction," namely, the Residency Bazars and Secunderabad Cantonment.[13] Hyderabad administrators maintained both their autonomy in managing relations with "any capitalists with a view to financial transactions" and their enduring sovereignty over the trans-Musa city. Officials pointed out that, while the Raj might operate courts of law under Residency orders, they did so based on the consent of the Nizam. Hyderabad, they argued, had neither ceded territory and full jurisdiction, nor had the British obtained it by other means.[14] In principle, as was the case in rural areas along Hyderabad–British India borders such as those considered in the foregoing chapters, sovereignty over urban space as *territory* was sacrosanct. Hyderabad's officials justified the exercise of sovereign power over the city as a component of their ethical obligations to the state's subjects as

[11] "Abolition of the Suburban Court and Distribution of its Work," 9 March 1896, APSA 37/1/148.

[12] Shortly after the Nizam's government and the British authorities in Hyderabad approved the tramway plan the Hyderabad Railway Company board of directors refused to allow its employees to take part. "Projects for the Construction of Tramway between Hyderabad and Secunderabad," 1887–1888, Hyderabad Residency Records, NAI F.16-1888, Political Department.

[13] "Proposed Tramway between Hyderabad and Secunderabad," 1897, Hyderabad Residency Records, NAI J.332–1897, Judicial Branch.

[14] Nawab Sir Vikar-ul-Umra Bahadur to Residency, 24 May 1897, ibid.

noted above. But concerted attempts to effect infrastructural consolidation in the trans-Musa city would not come to fruition until after the turn of the century and the death of the sixth Nizam.

## From sovereign terrain to urban space

The old city's association with political authority in Hyderabad impeded expansion of the capital city north of the river into the early twentieth century. Even after the 1908 floods devastated the old city, walled areas south of the Musa remained the firm boundaries of the ceremonial and administrative capital. At the time of his coronation in 1911 the seventh Nizam symbolically enacted his late father's decree to maintain the walled city as the seat of royal power. Accordingly, the High Court – moved trans-Musa temporarily during the 1911–12 plague outbreak – was relocated to the old city following completion of its new building.[15] Notwithstanding the symbolic import of the old city, the new Nizam moved the palace trans-Musa after his coronation. Significant population and economic shifts had already begun following the arrival of railways in the north, and flood and pestilence in the south. The movement of institutional spaces accompanied state-sponsored urban planning projects that facilitated and rendered permanent a northward population shift.

### *Planning city improvement*

The City Improvement Board was founded in 1912 – a year after the new Nizam's coronation – and was to shape urban Hyderabad over the following decades. Around this time improvement bodies were becoming critical entities in the remaking, expansion, and creation of cities and towns in South Asia and beyond. The Bombay Improvement Trust was founded in 1898, and similar bodies emerged across British India, sub-imperial states, and other entities in British Asia. City or town improvement bodies, primarily trusts, were formed in Mysore (1903), Calcutta (1911), Rangoon (1920), Singapore (1927), Secunderabad (1929), Lahore (1935), Nagpur (1936), Delhi (1937), Bangalore (1945),

[15] "Temporary transfer of the High Court to the Public Gardens," 1911, APSA 37/1/339. The Hyderabad High Court complex (1914–21) was initially designed by Vincent Esch, a British architect active in British India since the 1890s, associated with the Indo-Saracenic colonial style. Esch was also responsible for the monumental Errannagutta Railway Station (1914, now Kacheguda Station). See G. H. R. Tillotson, "Vincent J. Esch and the Architecture of Hyderabad, 1914–36," *South Asian Studies* 9.1 (1993): 29–46. For a consideration of the construction of the High Court (and some of the CIB projects discussed below) from the perspective of architectural history see Shah, "Constructing a Capital," ch. 6.

and other locations.[16] 'Improvement' work was an explicitly urban developmental idiom for remaking the physical space of cities and towns.

Improvement bodies in South Asia, as well as British and other European empires, are often seen as a modality for asserting state control. Whether as a vehicle for transplantation of European spatial ideas, assertion of racialized control, class or caste ordering, or deepening of biopolitical power, urban planning in pre-1947 South Asia appears as a vector of colonial power.[17] In Hyderabad the CIB provided a means of intervening via planning into urban space, much of which had been seized back from colonial control.

In interwar Hyderabad the CIB became the driving force behind housing precarious trans-Musa populations and infrastructure development on both sides of the river. Regular progress reports covering the period

[16] Janaki Nair, *Mysore Modern: Rethinking the Region under Princely Rule* (Minneapolis: University of Minnesota Press, 2011), 158–59; Aya Ikegame, "The Capital of Rajadharma: Modern Space and Religion in Colonial Mysore," *International Journal of Asian Studies* 4 (2007): 15–44; Janaki Nair, *The Promise of the Metropolis: Bangalore's Twentieth Century* (New Delhi: Oxford University Press, 2005). See Stephen Legg, *Spaces of Colonialism: Delhi's Urban Governmentalities* (Malden, MA: Blackwell, 2007), 162–63, 164–82. William J. Glover, *Making Lahore Modern: Constructing and Imagining a Colonial City* (Minneapolis: University of Minnesota Press, 2007), 149, 224 n58; Nikhil Rao, *House, But No Garden: Apartment Living in Bombay's Suburbs, 1898–1964* (Minneapolis: University of Minnesota Press, 2013); S. Manzoor Alam, *Hyderabad–Secunderabad, Twin Cities: A Study in Urban Geography* (Bombay: Allied, 1965); Sandip Hazareesingh, *The Colonial City and the Challenge of Modernity: Urban Hegemonies and Civic Contestations in Bombay City 1900–1925* (New Delhi: Orient Longman, 2007); Prashant Kidambi, *The Making of an Indian Metropolis: Colonial Governance and Public Culture in Bombay, 1890–1920* (Aldershot: Ashgate, 2007); Brenda S. A. Yeoh, *Contesting Space: Power Relations and the Urban Built Environment in Colonial Singapore* (Kuala Lumpur: Oxford University Press, 1996). The emergence of improvement bodies often followed legislative acts enabling town-planning activity across colonial administrative units, such as the 1922 Punjab Town Improvement Act and the 1919 United Provinces Town Improvement Trusts Act. See Glover, *Making Lahore Modern*, for Punjab; Nandini Gooptu, *The Politics of the Urban Poor in Early Twentieth Century India* (Cambridge University Press, 2001) for UP. Much of this legislation followed from Great Britain's 1909 Housing and Town Planning Act. See Gooptu, *Politics of the Urban Poor*, 77, and Walter Addington Willis, *Housing and Town Planning in Great Britain, Being a Statement of the Statutory Provisions Relating to the Housing of the Working Classes and to Town Planning Including the Housing, Town Planning, etc., Act, 1909* (London: Butterworth & Co., 1910).

[17] Gooptu, *Politics of the Urban Poor*; Legg, *Spaces of Colonialism*; Nair, *Mysore Modern* and *The Promise of the Metropolis*. On the prevalence of the "British model" in planning in small sub-imperial states in peninsular Gujarat, see Howard Spodek, "Urban Politics in the Local Kingdoms of India: A View from the Princely Capitals of Saurashtra under British Rule," *Modern Asian Studies* 7.2 (1973): 253–75. On planning as a mode of colonial and neo-colonial subordination to Europe of colonized or 'developing' countries, see Anthony D. King, "Exporting Planning: The Colonial and Neo-Colonial Experience on Planning," in *Shaping an Urban World: Planning in the Twentieth Century*, ed. Gordon Emanuel Cherry (London: Mansell, 1980), 203–26. For a comparative account of British and French planning in colonial Africa, see Ambe J. Njoh, *Planning Power: Social Control and Planning in Colonial Africa* (London: UCL, 2007).

Image 1 Hyderabad City slum area targeted for improvement work, 1938–39. This area, located on the south bank of the Musa on the north-western edge of the old city, was a site of intensive CIB intervention. *Source: RPHCIB* 1938–39.

from 1914 to 1941 explain the key principles, mode of operation, and major projects the Board undertook.[18] The reports describe the rapid, unplanned expansion of the city, and resulting problems. They present the CIB as a panacea for emerging urban issues. The plague-related population decline during the 1910s was a central concern. Congestion – described as lack of light, air, and open space – was identified as the primary culprit and a menacing urban problem. The CIB set itself to removing slums and other unsanitary areas and expanding drainage and transportation infrastructure.

[18] For the first report see Hyderabad, City Improvement Board, *Report on the Progress of the Hyderabad City Improvement Board for the years 1322–1327 Fasli (1914–1919 A.D.)* (Hyderabad: Government Central Press, 1919). The author, location, and publisher are the same for subsequent reports. The second report covers a ten-year period (1327–1336 F, or 1919–28 CE), and the subsequent ten reports cover one Fasli year each (from 1930–31 to 1940–41 CE). Henceforth, I will refer to all reports as *RPHCIB* and specify CE years in to which their coverage corresponds.

The first report described the formation and early years of the CIB.[19] Following the Board's 1912 constitution and staffing, the first head engineer, P. A. Bhavnani, was sent to Bombay to consider "sanitary improvements" there in the wake of the 1896 plague epidemic.[20] Beyond British India, the CIB's urbanist program was informed by planning initiatives elsewhere in the world. Looking to municipal bodies in Germany, the United States, England, and Italy, the Board set for itself a planning horizon of twenty to fifty years, within a minimum zone of seven miles beyond the current expanse of the city.[21] Berlin, cited as an example of "a City which is getting closed in by surrounding towns," was invoked to advocate planning for a twenty-mile radius. Standards for road width, and plans for razing the old city walls and developing a ring road based on their path, were based on precedents in contemporaneous European cities.[22]

CIB work began in 1914, and despite wartime delays it acquired land and developed a comprehensive plan for urban improvement in its first five years. The planning process included a statistical assessment of plague outbreak that presented it as direct result of density and drainage problems following from slum expansion. In identifying areas in need of improvement, the CIB surveyed Hyderabad City's changing geography and demographics. The first report identified three zones: "Androon Balda," inside the old city walls (holding 38 percent of the population and a density over five times the city average); "Baroon Balda," suburbs outside the city walls (22 percent of the population); and "Chaderghat," the trans-Musa area around the British Residency (40 percent of the population).[23] Citing water and drainage problems, the "worst slums'" were located in the old city area, and the report noted lack of previous interest in improvement owing to "the trend of population being towards the northern suburbs where most of the offices and bungalows of the high officials of the State are situated." In effect the trans-Musa shift of palace and institutions was already causing a deterioration in living conditions for the state's subjects in the old city. But the situation was little better in their destinations. Other targets for sanitary intervention were the booming new areas of settlement between Hussain Sagar and the north bank of the Musa, and especially the Nampally locality near

19 *RPHCIB* 1914–19.

20 Bhavnani, initially sanitary engineer, quickly rose to superintending engineer, and served as the Board's chief technocrat until his death in 1927. On response to the plague and the Bombay Improvement Trust's 1898 formation, Kidambi, *The Making of an Indian Metropolis*, ch. 3.

21 *RPHCIB* 1914–19. The 1939–40 report describes a grant-in-aid paid to Sub-Engineer Muzafferuddin Ansari, "for one year's study in Town-planning in Edinburgh."

22 *RPHCIB* 1914–19.

23 Ibid. Statistics, however, indicate no substantial correlation of plague deaths to density.

Image 2 Panorama of emerging urban area before and after improvement work, 1930–31. Mallapally, along with neighboring Nampally, lay directly adjacent to Hyderabad Railway Station, and was rebuilt by the CIB as a dense new working-class neighborhood during the interwar era.
*Source: RPHCIB* 1930–31.

Hyderabad Railway Station where "plague first broke out."[24] These two insalubrious zones – the dense and deteriorating old city, and expanding trans-Musa areas – became focal points for improvement work.

The CIB's strategy was to acquire slum areas and "dishouse the people gradually as demolition proceeds and not all at once," then lay out roads, open spaces, drains, and housing plots. To adjust urban densities the Board proposed relocation of the dishoused onto "open pieces of ground which will be specially acquired for housing purposes'.[25] The CIB took on large-scale construction of a new residential architecture, accelerating and concretizing, figuratively and literally, the northward shift already underway.[26]

The CIB enjoyed major geographic scope and unstinting state support in carrying out projects. They worked in unison with the Municipal Corporation of Hyderabad (MCH), whose chair served as the Board's

[24] Ibid. [25] Ibid.
[26] On the CIB's role, and Hyderabad's prominence, in early use of reinforced cement–concrete in South Asia see Stuart Tappin, "The Early Use of Reinforced Concrete in India," in *Proceedings of the First International Congress on Construction History, Madrid, 20th–24th January 2003*, ed. S. H. Fernández (Madrid: Instituto Juan de Herrera, 2003), 1931–40, 1938 on the Hyderabad CIB.

director for much of the 1930s. Reports indicate that the CIB could compel the MCH to hand over areas, enforce or enact bylaws, and reassume administration of 'improved' urban lands once the CIB's work was done. The geographic extent of the municipality was 33.5 square miles – significantly larger in pure spatial terms than the five other cities in the subcontinent with greater population density than Hyderabad.[27]

Despite extensive funding and political support, the CIB faced impediments to property acquisition in the form of multiple urban land-tenure arrangements and an emerging property market. Delays in land acquisition reveal the profound implications of the changes to the urban fabric they set into motion. A 1908 post-flood policy restricting riverside construction proved a useful resource for wresting property from reluctant building owners.[28] In these "Restricted Areas" the Board undertook park, road, drainage, and wall projects, producing open and green spaces and integrating them into the new urban fabric. However, administrators of *sarf-i khas* (crown lands) frequently slowed projects by opposing slum clearance or the laying of roads.[29] In such cases, the CIB availed executive pressure to take control. As was the case with property held by the municipality, officials placed urban territory under land grant tenures (such as *sarf-i khas*) at the disposal of the CIB.

Acquisition for development stimulated a revaluation of urban space that led to conflicts with slum landlords seeking to protect incomes or use court decisions to increase assessed land values. Litigation brought to the High Court by affluent communities in some localities slowed work. But the CIB continued to make "good progress" on demolition and road construction, which succeeded in "brightening up the locality as new pucca [*pakkā*, permanent and solid, as opposed to *kachchā*, or improvised and temporary] buildings were constructed."[30] Urbanist projects proceeded in tension with an emerging land market, and the CIB experienced delays owing to "excess cost due to court awards for compensation of property."[31]

From the outset the CIB was wary of stimulating a capitalist land market: '"It was thought advisable to acquire these lands [940 acres] at once rather than wait till the owners, recognising their importance to the Board

27 *RPHCIB* 1919–28. Bombay, Madras, Bangalore, Baroda, and Mysore were denser large cities. The CIB also proposed to control development in open lands in a zone extending two miles beyond the municipal boundary.

28 *RPHCIB* 1914–19. 29 *RPHCIB* 1933–34; *RPHCIB* 1934–35.

30 *RPHCIB* 1935–36. For definitions of these South Asian terms for built structures, for South Asian English, see Henry Yule and A. C. Burnell, *Hobson-Jobson: A Glossary of Colloquial Anglo-Indian Words and Phrases, and of Kindred Terms, Etymological, Historical, Geographical and Discursive*, 2nd edn, ed. William Crooke (London: J. Murray, 1903), 287 for "cutcha, kutcha," 734 for "pucka"; for Hindustani, Platts, *Dictionary of Urdu*, 817–18 for "*kaćća*" 265 for *pakkā*.

31 Ibid.

(a)

Scheme 4, View 1 River Bank Akberjah side before improvement.

(b)

Scheme 4, View 2—Same as View No. 1 after improvement so far.

Image 3 Hyderabad City riverbank improvement work, 1914–19. Riverside areas, such as this one, were sites of extensive intervention, facilitated by the special status of riverside lands established by 1908 post-flood policies. Here, slum areas were replaced by public parks envisioned as "lungs of the City."
*Source: RPHCIB* 1914–19.

as suitable sites for extension, had raised the price."[32] The implications of land speculation, however, were managed by authoritarian interventions by state officials on behalf of the CIB. Costs and legal challenges were remedied through a combination of state financial support and official manipulation of courts. Targeted state support insulated the Board from both the emerging land economy and impediments raised by land grant holders. The CIB presented its work as an urbanist manifestation of the state's ethical–patrimonial obligation to the populace. Accordingly, the core component of the new urban environment was permanent housing for urban workers.

### *Trans-Musa urbanization and Model Houses*

Housing – slum demolition and the construction of low-cost dwellings – formed the mainstay of the CIB's work. The body's mandate was for "acquiring open lands round the City for housing the dishoused."[33] The Board redeveloped whole localities within a new logic of public urban space centered on assistance to laboring groups. While the Board constructed parks, urban institutions (schools, orphanages, hospitals), and drainage structures, its primary planning activity was in the areas of housing and infrastructure for transportation and economic development. For the early Board "slum clearance" was "the main feature": "The slum dwellers were to be housed in model colonies with a view to safeguard their health and indirectly the health of the whole population of Hyderabad; also to provide play-grounds for poor children. These are to be the lungs of the City."[34] Elimination of slums and construction of housing were centerpieces of an integrated scheme for developing a sanitary city. The CIB was ostensibly to house people in the same localities as the slums they had previously inhabited.

Records of Board schemes suggest that their housing work consolidated Hyderabad's demographic shift northwards. Board projects regularized housing for precarious populations, primaily around Hyderabad Railway Station. CIB work accelerated the major south–north urban population shift already underway, and advanced a secondary population shift to heretofore sparsely populated areas east of the old walled city. An examination of the statistics provided in CIB reports reveals the geography of residential relocations. Intensive CIB work took place in four broad zones:

1. Hyderabad Railway Station and adjacent areas, between Hussain Sagar and the Musa River (Nampally, Mallapally, Aghapura, Red Hill, Dhulpet, Feelkhana, Khairatabad, Afzal Gunj, Begum Bazar)

[32] Ibid. [33] *RPHCIB* 1914–19. [34] *RPHCIB* 1914–19.

2. The Musa's south bank, opposite Chadarghat Residency, east of the walled city (Azampura, Malakpet)
3. Trans-Musa areas near the Residency and east of Hussain Sagar (Sultan Bazar, Errannagutta, Bhoiguda, Lingampally)[35]
4. The old city proper, south of the Musa, within the city walls (Moghulpura, Bazar-e-Noorul Umra [formerly Noorkhan Bazar], Sultan Shahi, Purani Haveli, Darush-Shifa, Hussaini Alam, Ghansi Bazar, Rikab Ganj, Dabirpura, Gowlipura)[36]

A comparison of CIB figures for, first, "Slum Clearance and Development" (SC&D) and, second, "Model House" (MH) construction, demonstrates the geographical shift in the city's residential core that the Board's work consolidated.[37]

Table 1 *Hyderabad City Improvement Board work, 1914–1941*

| | SC&D acreage | SC&D % | MH units | MH % |
|---|---|---|---|---|
| Zone 1: Hyderabad RS and Environs | 624.88 | 47.60% | 2,317 | 59.40% |
| Zone 2: South Suburban (outside city walls) | 83 | 6.32% | 689 | 17.67% |
| Zone 3: Residency and Hussain Sagar East[38] | 127.52 | 9.71% | 399 | 10.23% |
| Zone 4: Walled City | 477.31 | 36.36% | 395 | 10.12% |

The first category, counted in acres, comprised locations where the CIB razed existing structures to free land for various purposes (housing, parks, drains, roads). The second category, counted in units of housing constructed, comprised new dwellings for working-class Hyderabadis. As Table 1 shows, viewing these two sets of statistics together allows for a comparison of inhabited areas that were demolished and depopulated, and locations of new urban habitations.

Imbalances between SC&D and MH figures reveal the geographic shift in Hyderabad's residential core that the CIB effected: 57 percent

35 Sultan Bazar was referred to as Residency Bazars until 1933. The areas referred to here as Errannagutta and Lingampally are now known, respectively, as Amberpet and Bagh Lingampally.

36 The last two of these localities intersected the city wall.

37 Here, the term "Model Houses" refers also to "Low-Rent Houses." The two were architecturally similar and designed for working-class residents, but had different funding structures.

38 Zone 3 was also the location of a significant internal shift. SC&D in the areas immediately adjacent to the Residency were met with extensive housing construction further north towards Hussain Sagar and east along the Musa bank. CIB work here effected a population shift away from the existing core area around the Residency.

of total SC&D acreage was in the trans-Musa area, where the capital and many state institutions were by this time located, and 70 percent of Model House units were constructed there. Conversely, the areas to the south of the Musa River comprised 43 percent of SC&D area, with only 28 percent of Model Housing being located there. The CIB, then, destroyed and created housing in a pattern that moved working-class state subjects from areas south of the river to the new trans-Musa urban core it was creating. The CIB-driven shift from the old city outwards appears even more dramatic when one compares its work in areas inside the walls to that in the rest of the city. The area inside the city walls experienced 36 percent of SC&D, but only 10 percent of Model House construction.[39]

CIB work created whole new residential landscapes and shifted populations on a large scale. Before the Board commenced work, Zone 1, around the railway station, was a sparsely populated region with pockets and ribbons of largely unplanned settlement. The CIB transformed it into a new urban residential core by constructing dense new neighborhoods around the station and north along the railway line.[40] The data above suggests that the CIB drove populations out of settlements inside the old city walls and rehoused them in suburban areas of the city – primarily trans-Musa, near the new political and commercial centers. This process continued with the extension of the Nizam's control over city lands.

Hyderabad's nineeteenth-century assertions of sovereign authority over heretofore colonially dominated suburban spaces in the trans-Musa city laid the groundwork for the urbanist interventions traced above. Consolidation of urban space under a single state authority was a gradual but steady process and gathered momentum through the mid-twentieth century. The geography of CIB work paralleled the slow process of Hyderabad's assertion of control over urban lands. Following the return by the British of the Residency Bazars (renamed Sultan Bazar) in 1933–34, the CIB commenced road-widening, slum demolition, and model house construction in the area.[41] After World War II the retrocession of the urban, non-military areas of the Secunderabad

39 Over a third of this housing was put up in neighborhoods that intersected the walls.

40 *RPHCIB* 1940–41.

41 On preparation for the handover see Nawab Mahdi Yar Jung Bahadur, Political Member, to Major GT Fisher, IA, Secretary to the Resident, 28 March 1933, "Rendition of the Hyd. Residency bazaars to His Exalted highness the Nizam's Government," APSA 71/32/88, 1933. See *RPHCIB* 1936–37, 1937–38, 1938–39 and 1940–41 on plans, apportioning of funds, housing development, and road work in Sultan Bazar.

(a)

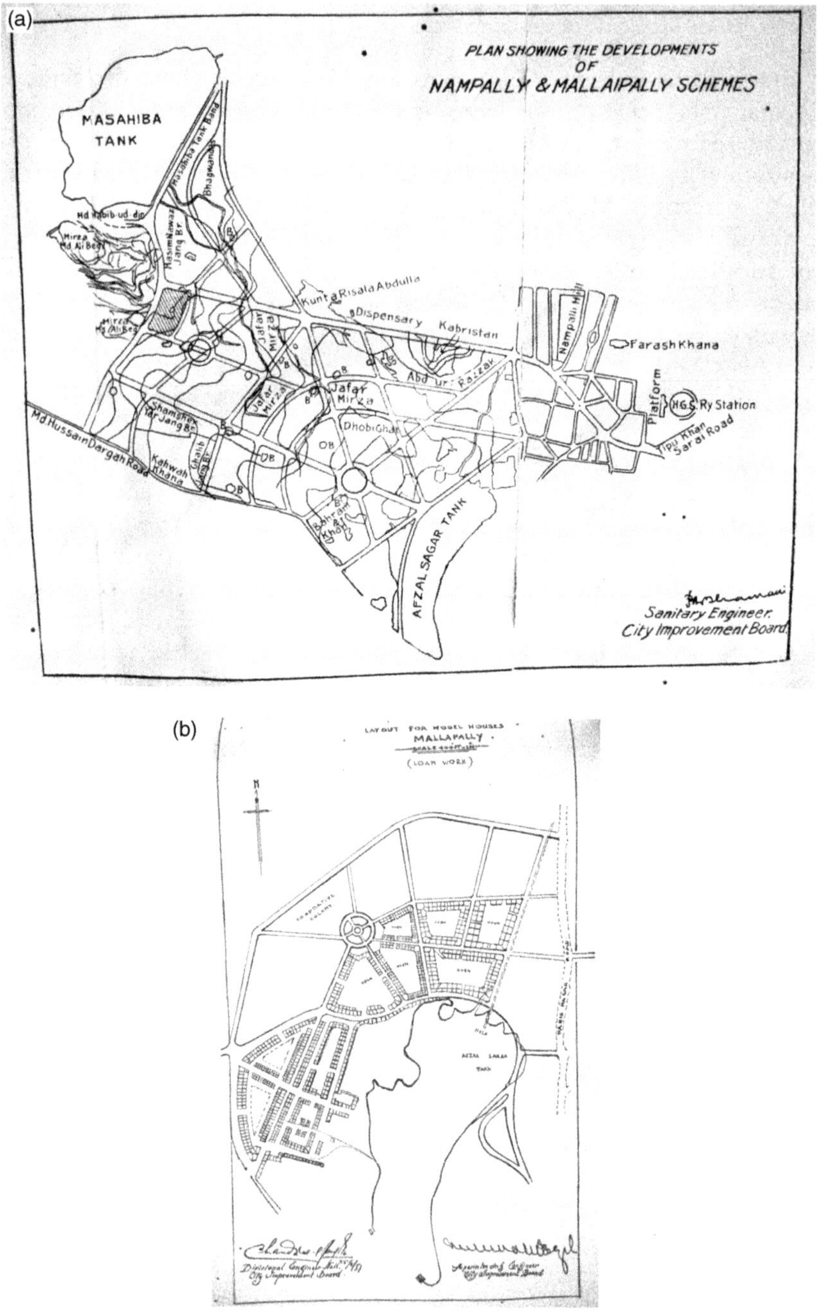


(b)

Image 4 Road and housing block plans for new urban neighborhoods, *c.* 1914–40. The CIB superimposed road schemes through the haphazardly settled areas around Hyderabad Railway Station, which in turn provided the infrastructure for blocks of Model Houses intended for the urban masses.
*Source: RPCIB* 1914–19, 1938–39.

Cantonment to Hyderabadi control expanded the scope for state-directed urban planning.[42]

Hyderabad's regaining of authority over formerly British-controlled urban areas, and the waning of colonial political and economic power in the subcontinent generally, had important implications for planning. States such as Hyderabad – as, later, the Republic of India – were able to launch comprehensive planning initiatives informed by their own political imperatives rather than those of colonial rulers.

The Hyderabad CIB's work, while generating the geographic shift in urban population outlined above, reflected a particular rhetoric where urbanism appeared as vehicle for the Nizam's patrimonial obligations to state subjects in the city. CIB housing development in some regards represented Hyderabadi deployment of the global idiom of technocratic urbanism, with Board officials consciously emulating European and American models. Accounts of improvement work in Hyderabad also invoked the ideology of ethical patrimonialism. Model Houses were designed to suit the needs of working-class families (and, in the instance of one development, bachelors), and communities such as Dalits and Muslims were explicitly included in plans for development. Excluded were Anglo-Indians and domiciled Europeans, groups associated with Britain's imperial project. Further, the quasi-environmentalist discourse around assuring city-dwellers "light and air," free circulation via "arterial" roads, and "lungs of the city" in urban parks allowed CIB officials to frame their work in a language of social improvement resonant both with global public health discourse and established patrimonial rhetoric. 'Improving' Hyderabad's residential landscape characterized the Board's early work. The period after 1930 saw an increasing focus on urban economic life.

## Commerce, industry, and urban planning

From the outset, the Hyderabad CIB cast commercial and industrial infrastructure expansion as integral to its work. This initially entailed development of market spaces within the city. By World War II large-scale

[42] Extensive documentation on the Cantonment's retrocession, some dating back to 1931, is to be found in "Secunderabad Cantonment: Proposed partial retrocession of jurisdiction to Nizam's Government," OIOC L/P&S/13/1230, 1937–1946. As with decolonization in British India, World War II altered the timeline of the retrocession. The return of Hyderabad's Cantonment to native sovereignty, along with similar areas in other major cities in sub-imperial states such as Bangalore, Indore, and Bhopal, preceded formal decolonization in the Raj's 'directly ruled' territories in South Asia.

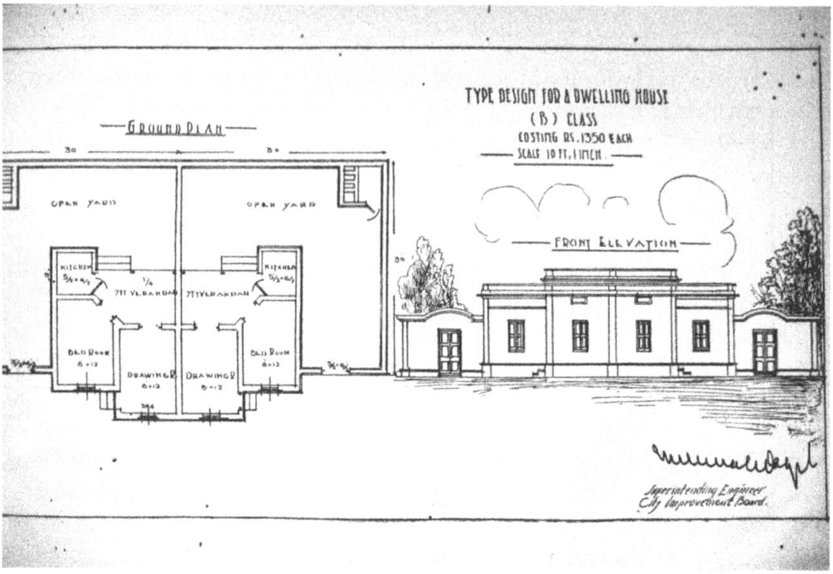


(a)

View of Khairatabad Model Houses

(b)

Image 5 Model House design (1931–32) and image of a new neighborhood (1939–40). Model Houses were designed, constructed, and represented as ideal dwellings for working-class families that would be constituent elements of new urban neighborhoods.
*Source: RPHCIB* 1931–32, 1939–40.

commercial and industrial projects had displaced interventions into the city's residential landscape as the primary work of the CIB.

CIB schemes included construction of both minor local and major central market spaces. This work was conceived to benefit business communities in the city and to integrate markets into the new urban fabric the CIB was developing. Several of the Board's Model House schemes incorporated markets within residential quarter plans. On a grander scale, two signature CIB projects centered on iconic urban market spaces: Pathergatti Bazar in the old city, and Moazzam Jahi Market near Hyderabad Railway Station.

The Pathergatti project was carried out in what was already a major shopping area, and entailed road widening and construction of paved walkways and shop-lined arcades in the center of the old city.[43] Moazzam Jahi Market was a new trans-Musa commercial space between Hyderabad Station and the Residency area, named for the ruler's second son, Moazzam Jah, who also served as president of the CIB.[44] These projects – both in major traffic areas – represented CIB attempts to integrate spaces of commerce into the changed urban fabric.

The CIB's first foray into large-scale state economic planning was a 1930–31 scheme to lay out an expansive industrial area on 120 acres in Musheerabad, a huge undeveloped swath east of Hussain Sagar. The estate was named the Azamabad Industrial Area after the Nizam's eldest son, Azam Jah. By 1940–41 plots had been allotted to factories for consumer goods (tobacco, matches, silk), and construction materials (cement-reinforced concrete 'hume' piping, iron, steel). Industrial development had stimulated a land speculation boom in the heretofore outlying area by the time connecting roads had been laid in the late 1930s.

CIB economic development planning reshaped the residential and social terrain of the city, built commercial spaces and infrastructures, and stimulated the urban land economy. And as a 1937 report put it, economic development would also provide Hyderabad with the infrastructure to compete with both British Indian manufactures and those of Japan, and even those of Britain itself.[45] In Hyderabad's large-scale economic development, technocratic planning expanded beyond urban spaces.

43 The CIB's Pathergatti work extended from World War I into the 1940s. See *RPHCIB* 1914–19 through 1940–41.

44 *RPHCIB* 1930–31 through 1934–35.

45 Hyderabad, *The Economic Life of Hyderabad* (Hyderabad: Government Central Press, 1937).

(a)

(b)

Image 6 Changing commercial spaces in the old city, *c.* 1914–28. The CIB remade key urban commercial spaces in Hyderabad, including the construction of arcaded shopping areas on the road leading to the iconic Charminar in the old city.
*Source: RPCIB* 1914–19, 1919–28.

(a)

PLATE 13. Industrial area (Azamabad)—View of main road through the area.

(b)

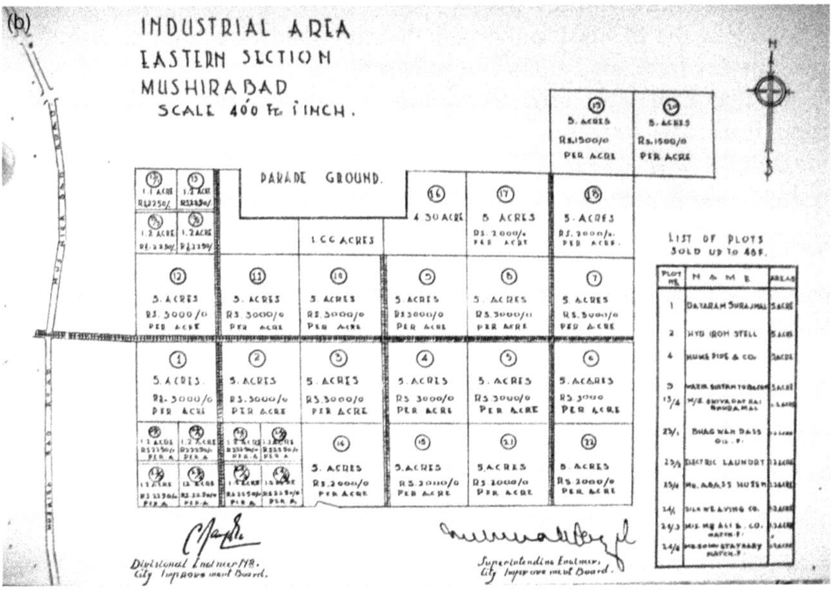


Image 7 Planning industrial spaces in Hyderabad City, 1930s. Industrial development on the fringes of the city was a key focus of later CIB planning work. Azamabad, in an undeveloped trans-Musa area east of Hussain Sagar, was the first major urban industrial space planned and constructed by the CIB.
*Source: RPCIB* 1932–33, 1938–39.

## From urbanism to state economic planning

After World War II the planning modality that had been instrumental in reshaping Hyderabad City emerged as a template for producing state-wide transformations.[46] The expanding scope of planning is visible first in industrial development on the city's fringes, and subsequently across the state in the postwar schemes of the Town Planning Department (TPD).

Industrial development became a major CIB imperative starting in 1930–31, and continued to be a priority into the 1940s.[47] Transcripts of CIB meeting proceedings from 1946, after a wartime lull, demonstrate renewed focus on industrial development. To combat the proliferation of small industrial workshops in the city, Board engineers proposed creating a designated industrial area west of the walled city and constructing housing for laborers and managerial staff there. CIB officials also noted the need to regulate private development around Azamabad, where industrial units were rising "unabated and uncontrolled."[48] The question of economy and infrastructure, taken up by the CIB in plans for the city, extended planning in Hyderabad beyond the urban terrain of the capital and into other areas of the state.

Following the 1930s development of Azamabad, a second major industrial cluster established along the railway line to the northwest of Hussain Sagar. Begun in 1941 after the outbreak of World War II, the Sanathnagar Industrial Area housed factories manufacturing munitions, various metalworks, and machine tools.[49] These facilities were developed by Hyderabad to support the British war effort, and became the core of a manufacturing hub after Hyderabad's 1948 integration into India. Other industrial areas were located on urban fringes along railway lines, such as Moula Ali northeast of Azamabad, and Patancheru northwest of Sanathnagar.[50] Monies from industrial development fed into commercial urban construction in the trans-Musa city, but development

[46] On the movement of planning discourses from urban to rural areas in British India and early postcolonial India, and a similar shift from improvement to development ideologies to the one traced here, see William J. Glover, "The Troubled Passage from 'Village Communities' to Planned New Town Developments in Mid-Twentieth-Century South Asia," *Urban History* 39.1 (2012): 108–27.

[47] *RPHCIB* 1940–41 details the continued acquisition of property for inclusion in Azamabad Industrial Area and construction of roads linking it to other parts of the city.

[48] "Proceedings of the Hyderabad City Improvement Board Meetings," 1946, Hyderabad Residency Records, NAI 127.A, Accounts Branch.

[49] K. N. Gopi, *Urban Growth and Industrial Locations* (New Delhi: Oxford and IBH, 1980), 6.

[50] Ibid., 21.

planning in Hyderabad soon pushed beyond the confines of the capital region.[51]

The TPD's extensive 1944 report demonstrates the anticipated rise of large-scale state-wide economic planning in the post-World War II era.[52] The report contained short essays by state officials on various topics (communication, public health, markets) by state officials and an exhaustive compilation of maps, plans for towns, photographs of sites and buildings, and designs for structures (factories, housing, markets). Narrative sections emphasized the need to provide workers' housing and sanitary layouts for mill and factory towns.[53] The Report enumerated improvements or new construction throughout Hyderabad state on textile and paper mills, a filter-bed facility (for purification of water from industrial byproducts), collieries, and a silk factory.[54] Other proposed works included infrastructure (railways, roads), social facilities, and workers' housing for provincial industrial towns. The TPD head, M. Fayazuddin, emphasized the imperative to draw up schemes "ready for immediate execution" at the end of World War II.[55] He described three types of necessary work: "replanning or improving of existing towns . . . planning of new towns . . . [and] planning of extension schemes for existing towns." Targets were to include administrative, industrial, and agricultural centers, as well as new model towns and soldier colonies.[56]

Narrative sections of the TPD report yoked state-led technocratic planning to social progress. Fayazuddin's programmatic chapter noted objectives similar to those in CIB reports considered above: open space in towns, housing for state subjects (especially workers), slum clearance, road improvements, and other infrastructures for transit and communication. The TPD's rhetoric of town improvement as social intervention also recalls the CIB's justificatory language of royal obligations

51 For example, Alladdin Buildings in Begumpet, just northwest of Hussain Sagar, was constructed by the original owner of Allwyn Metal Works in Sanathnagar industrial area: ibid.; Omar Khalidi, *A Guide to Architecture in Hyderabad, Deccan, India* (Cambridge, MA: Aga Khan Program for Islamic Architecture, 2008), 241.

52 Hyderabad, *Town Planning in H.E.H. the Nizam's Dominions* (Hyderabad: His Highness the Nizam's Government, 1944) (henceforth *TP*).

53 The Report also contained some proposals for maintaining healthy conditions in pilgrimage centers and provincial capitals.

54 Project sites were located in districts in the three main regions of Hyderabad: Telangana (Adilabad, Karimnagar, Warangal), Marathwada (Aurangabad, Bhir, Nanded, Osmanabad, Latur), and the Karnatak (Gulbarga, Raichur).

55 M. Fayazuddin, "Town and Country Planning in H.E.H. the Nizam's Dominions," *TP*, 7–12. For attribution of Fayazuddin as author of the report as a whole and an extended discussion of his planning work, see M. Ahmed Ali, *Historical Aspects of Town Planning in Pakistan and India* (Karachi: Al-Ata, 1971), 89–93.

56 *TP*, 8, 9.

to meet "public needs." Fayazuddin emphasized the need of "the present enlightened Government" to "provide the best possible conditions for development of the next generation." Parallel to these concerns was a technocratic, economistic argument about state imperatives to "conserve . . . Industrial and Financial resources," and facilitate "commerce and industries" through planning. In Fayazuddin's estimation these principles were inextricable. Better conditions for workers would result in "a high standard of efficiency."[57] As such, the patrimonial idiom was seamlessly integrated with the technocratic rhetoric of state planning.

The 1944 report shows the planning modality's expansion beyond urbanism in the capital. Bolstered by executive support from Hyderabad's rulers, TPD officials now envisioned the economic refashioning of the state as a whole. The rhetoric through which they communicated their vision combined older patrimonial political ethics with a technocratic rationality centered on development schemes informed by specialist knowledge. Presiding over the expansion of urbanism to state economic planning was a new brand of highly skilled, and increasingly powerful, state official.

## Planner-technocrat as engineer-statesman

Emerging technocratic modalities of intervention, such as urban and economic planning, engendered a new iteration of the Deccani bureaucrat-intellectual: the planner-technocrat.[58] Fayazuddin exemplified the increasing power such figures wielded as World War II drew to a close. This new Hyderabadi bureaucrat-intellectual – the planning engineer – was adept in deploying a form of power delegated by state executives. Generous government funding provided a secure resource base for initiatives such as the CIB and TPD, and empowered engineers in state government.

Planner-technocrats across South Asia moved from the urban improvement scene in the interwar period to positions of state power by the end of the colonial era. Civil engineer Mokshagundam Visvesvaraya (1860–1962) was an exemplary early planner-technocrat in South Asian politics. Working in another sub-imperial state, his native Mysore, and various locations in British India and the empire, he was called to Hyderabad in 1908 following major flooding that year. Visvesvaraya advised on the city's

[57] Ibid., 7–8.
[58] On the Hyderabadi bureaucrat-intellectual in general see Introduction; and as disseminator of the image of Hyderabad's modernity to a global public see Chapter 4.

reconstruction and developed comprehensive plans for flood protection and drainage for city and suburbs. His time in Hyderabad stimulated the expansion of state-led urbanism that resulted in the CIB's foundation.[59] His influence and legacy were critical in Hyderabad, as in numerous other places in South Asia. Following his long career as a civil engineer, Visvesvaraya went on to serve as *divan* of Mysore state, setting a precedent for the rise of the technocrat as politician in South Asia. He later authored several volumes on state-level economic planning that were to prove influential in postcolonial India.[60]

Zain Yar Jung (1889–1961), nephew of Syed Hossain Bilgrami, a key Hyderabadi bureaucrat-intellectual from an earlier era, entered state service during the period of intensive engineering activity following the 1908 Musa flood. After studying engineering at Crystal Palace in London he returned to Hyderabad to work on Visvesvaraya's post-flood water management projects. Jung went on to design important buildings in Hyderabad (such as the Nampally Bachelors' Quarters, built by the CIB) and elsewhere in South Asia and Europe. Engineering proved to be his entry point into politics. Zain Yar Jung served as Hyderabad's State Architect, Municipal Corporation Commissioner, Minister of Public Works and Railways, and finally as Agent-General in New Delhi for the Nizam in the last days of Hyderabad State (1947–48).[61] This "engineer-statesman," as his biography describes him, demonstrates the rising importance in Hyderabad of the planner-technocrat as politician. His career also illustrates the roles of planners in integrating technocratic modalities of intervention with the rhetoric of patrimonial ethics. His biographer emphasized the "sympathy and benevolence" with which he enjoined Public Works officers to look upon the poor, and his "hutment to hutment" consultation of occupants in government housing colonies.[62]

59 M. Visvesvaraya, *Memoirs of my Working Life* (Bombay: Burton, 1951), 36, 39–41 and *A Brief Memoir of my Complete Working Life* (Bangalore: Government Press, 1960), 4–5.

60 Vinod Vyasulu, "Nehru and the Visvesvaraya Legacy," *Economic and Political Weekly* 24.30 (1989): 1700–4; M. Visvesvaraya, *Industrializing India: Constructive Policies and Plan* (Bangalore: Bangalore Press, 1933), *Planned Economy for India* (Bangalore: Bangalore Press, 1934), *Nation Building: A Five-Year Plan for the Provinces* (Bangalore: Bangalore Press, 1937), *Prosperity through Industry, Move Towards Rapid Industrialization* (Bombay: All-India Manufacturers' Organisation, 1943), and *Reconstruction in Post-War India: A Plan of Development All Round* (Bombay: All-India Manufacturers' Organisation, 1944). On Visvesvaraya's engineering and political work in Mysore see Nair, *Mysore Modern*, introduction, and *The Promise of the Metropolis*, 14–16.

61 Dildar Husain, *Glimpses of an Engineer-Statesman of Hyderabad Deccan* (Hyderabad: Indian Institution of Engineers, 1961).

62 Ibid., 39.

As in other locations, twentieth-century Hyderabad saw the emergence of the engineer onto the political scene. In the CIB as well, engineers became increasingly prominent. The Board went from having one engineer actively employed as a CIB officer in 1914 to a half dozen such officers in an increasingly complex hierarchy by 1941. CIB reports from the 1930s emphasized particular engineers' work on specific projects and provide details of their career trajectories. Chandulal C. Dangoria, for example, rose from Divisional Engineer (1933–37) to Assistant Engineer and Executive Officer (1938–41), and finally to superintending engineer when the CIB resumed work after World War II.[63]

The formation and transformation of the CIB after World War I, and the emergence of the TPD during World War II, chart the ascent and dynamism of planning in Hyderabad, and the rise of the planner-technocrat in government. The planner's domain expanded beyond urban intervention in the capital city to state-wide economic development. In the process, the planner-technocrat emerged as a political actor in Hyderabad, characterized by autonomy and insulation from opposition resulting from official economic and executive backing. Such figures were instrumental in combining diverse political languages. In the context of Hyderabad, they elaborated an idiom integrating ideas of technocratic economic development, which were gaining currency worldwide, with an older ideology of the patrimonial ethical obligation of rulers to their subjects. The state-form changed when Hyderabad was integrated into the Republic of India, and the Nizam stripped of ruling authority. Planner-technocrat figures and institutions continued to be important, as did the fused technical and ethical languages of planning.

## Planning Hyderabad, planning India

The history of Hyderabadi urbanism and state economic planning continued after the state ceased to exist as an autonomous entity in 1948. Among the most significant resonances of this planning history are the enduring power of the planner-technocrat figure and the resilient discourse of planning as both technocratic project of economic development and ethical expression of state benevolence. The rhetorical idiom and elements of the structural constitution of planning developed in Hyderabad informed early postcolonial Indian developmentalism.

63 Dangoria was a graduate of the Iowa State College of Agriculture and Mechanical Arts. See Philip C. Fleming, "Low-Cost Housing in Hyderabad," *Journal of the American Institute of Architects* 6.2 (1946): 76–80.

In institutional terms, Hyderabad's urbanist and planning bodies remained important in the city and the broader region. The CIB continued their work in the capital city, as did the Secunderabad Town Improvement Trust (TIT), a body founded in 1929 that explicitly modeled its work after the CIB, borrowing Model House plans and building materials.[64] The 1956 breakup and linguistic reorganization of Hyderabad State, and Hyderabad City's inclusion in Andhra Pradesh, provided impetus for political reorganization. In 1960 the CIB and the TIT were combined and reconstituted as the Andhra Pradesh Housing Board (APHB). The APHB operated exclusively within the capital region through 1972.[65] It continued CIB initiatives in land acquisition, slum clearance, and construction of subsidized housing for workers.[66]

Hyderabadi planner-technocrats played major roles in early postcolonial Indian national institutions. Hyderabadi 'engineer-statesman' Zain Yar Jung served as president of the Indian Institution of Engineers in 1954, and helped establish specific scientific professional engineering standards for India.[67] The former TPD head, M. Fayazuddin, was a founder and the first president of the Institute of Town Planners, India (ITPI, founded in 1951). Their journal, published from 1955 onwards, indicates both the global engagements of the ITPI's work and the predominance of members from former 'princely' states, and particularly Hyderabad, in the new all-India body.[68]

The prominence of planners in the ITPI representing what had been non-colonial cities less than a decade earlier suggests that the particular governmental situations in these states may have lent itself to the development of planning institutions. Hyderabad's political framework, wherein planning bodies were empowered by executive measures, was conducive to the articulation and expansion of the planning modality. Similar

64 "Secunderabad Town Improvement Scheme," NAI Hyderabad Residency Records, 75–1929, Political Branch (index # 522).

65 Vijaya Bhole, *Housing and Urban Development in India* (New Delhi: Classical, 1988), 145, notes that 77 percent of APHB land acquisition in the twin cities was outside municipal limits. On the scope of the Board's work, and expansion beyond the capital area in 1973, see Andhra Pradesh (India), *A.P. Housing Board RTI Act* (2005), "Administrative and Accounts Manual," 33.

66 Bhole, *Housing and Urban Development*, 7, 135, 137–45.

67 Husain, *Engineer-Statesman*, 8, 18.

68 The first full listings of members (one-third of which are from former sub-imperial states) appears in the *Journal of the Institute of Town Planners, India* 9 (1957). For Fayazuddin's own account of his work in Hyderabad, which references the USA and UK as models, and draws considerable content from the 1944 TPD document discussed above, see M. Fayazuddin, "Planning in the States: Hyderabad," *Journal of the Institute of Town Planners, India* 2 (1955): 20–27.

scenarios seem to have existed in other large sub-imperial states such as Mysore, where regimes' internal sovereignty and autocratic structures of rule depoliticized development and facilitated state-initiated urbanism and later economic planning.[69] The Nizam's autonomous status and sovereign authority enabled the 'improvement' of the capital and its showcasing as staging-ground for globally informed urbanism. The movement from urbanism to comprehensive economic planning, and the enduring patrimonialist idiom, provided a template that was to prove crucial to postcolonial India's developmentalist vision. The trajectory of industrial development in Hyderabad helps elaborate this connection.

In his industrial history of Hyderabad, C. V. Subba Rao emphasized the particularity of Hyderabad's state-led social, economic, and industrial development, and the role of its autonomous nobility and administrative elite therein.[70] By contrast, British Indian industrial development was in the hands of private interests.[71] Hyderabad State's mid-nineteenth-century reforms streamlined fiscal administration and created new revenue sources, which "allowed the state to develop infrastructural facilities."[72] While providing a context for urbanist interventions (a topic Subba Rao does not discuss), state finance and the administrative set-up created conditions for industrialization in three stages: infrastructure (especially railways), agricultural expansion, and limited large-scale industry in the first stage (from 1870); intensive state support of industry in the second (1919–39); and finally continued state support, a shift away from agro-based industries, and integrated development planning (post-World War II through 1948).[73] These stages culminated in a rapid and massive expansion of the industrial economy.[74] But, according to Subba Rao, in the last years before Hyderabad's 1948 integration into India the "overarching role of the state prohibited growth" by preventing the rise of "autonomous capital capable of reproducing itself."[75] A key component

69 In discussing development in late subimperial Mysore under Visvesvaraya and others, Nair argues that Mysore's brand of modernity was a product of "governance in lieu of politics." See Nair, *Mysore Modern*, 16–18.

70 C. V. Subba Rao, *Hyderabad: the Social Context of Industrialisation, 1875–1948* (New Delhi: Orient Longman, 2007), ch. 2.

71 Subba Rao argues that in other sub-imperial states, such as Mysore, elites were creatures of colonial machinations: ibid.

72 Ibid., 29.

73 Ibid., 37–54, 69–70. Most of these developments were financed through a particular Hyderabadi institution, the Industrial Trust Fund, which provided heavy subsidies and tax relief.

74 Ibid., 144–47. The proportion of land revenue as total state revenue declined from roughly 50 percent in 1900–1 to 16 percent by 1947–48.

75 Ibid., 121.

of the moribund nature of Hyderabad's capitalism was the continuing power of the nobility who formed "states within the state," and whose revenues by and large remained tied to the agrarian sector, thus preventing the deepening of industrial capitalism and widespread social change in Hyderabad.[76] Social and economic trends in late sub-imperial Hyderabad contextualize the language of patrimonial ethics deployed there. Subba Rao's account also suggests the remarkable potential a centralized, autocratic state capable of guaranteeing economic input and autonomy for planners might have to effect industrial development.

In Hyderabad the preferred instrument for integrated economic planning was the Five Year plan.[77] Hyderabad's First Five Year Plan of 1945 was never completed, but several elements of Hyderabadi planning resurface in India's postcolonial planning regime. Hyderabad TPD plans date to 1944, the same year that the Indian "Bombay Plan" was drafted. Both identified intensive state investment as the central imperative for economic expansion, but the policy implications and alliances they represented were distinct. Hyderabad's TPD proposals provided an agenda for development that was followed closely after World War II, and through Hyderabad's integration into India. TPD plans cast social interventions (worker housing, urban parks) as integral to planning, and entailed state ownership (joint or exclusive) of industrial installations. The Bombay Plan informed India's postcolonial 'developmentalist' state. Recent scholarship suggests that the Bombay Plan represented an attempt by capitalists to define an economic agenda in tune with their interests. This entailed rhetorical advocacy of "social justice" while undercutting the power of labor unions, and support of mere government "control," rather than ownership, of industry.[78] In place of "disciplinary planning" the Bombay Plan and later the Planning Commission implemented a framework where government oversight to assure social progress was structurally constrained and "severely compromised by the state's concern to appease capitalists."[79] The mix of ethical patrimonialism and technocratic economistics that informed Hyderabadi planning, then, was distinct from the maneuvering of big industrial capital to define the terms

[76] Ibid., 72–75, 153. [77] Ibid., 50.

[78] Vivek Chibber, *Locked in Place: State-Building and Late Industrialization in India* (Princeton University Press, 2008), 30, 88–89, 103. For an earlier work that describes the Bombay Plan as reflective of industrialists' interest in protecting private capital see Benjamin Zachariah, *Developing India: An Intellectual and Social History, c. 1930–50* (New Delhi: Oxford University Press, 2005), ch. 5.

[79] Chibber, *Locked in Place*, 127, 129.

of the developmentalist state in postcolonial India. The suppression of the democratic process in both instances provides an important parallel.

Even as it emphasized postcolonial India's democratic nature, Nehru's Planning Commission was an autonomous executive body. While distinct, the patrimonial idiom deployed in Hyderabad has affinities with India's paternalistic–liberal state imaginary. The non-colonial planning experience in Hyderabad and elsewhere helps historicize 1950s Nehruvian developmentalism, the autonomy of his Planning Commission, and the enduring power of landed elites despite attempts at land reform. Crucially, both developmentalist idioms relied on the executive power of a centralized state to provide economic backing and protection from popular or political opposition. In Hyderabad, development planning in the post-World War II era followed directly from planning initiatives in the early twentieth century, integrating older idioms of sovereign authority with newer modalities of technocratic intervention.

## Hyderabadi urbanism and developmental trajectories

Writing in 1955, M. Fayazuddin, president of the ITPI, identified key problems facing planners in the young Indian nation-state by detailing the situation in Hyderabad. He pointed to "cancerous development" in what was now the capital of a province within India and the nation's fifth-largest city. Fayazuddin described new urban populations "encroaching over the most fertile lands and gardens of the suburban areas. This has happened in almost all the places, particularly where industries were established without any regard to the general structure of the town."[80] To solve these problems, he proposed state-directed comprehensive planning. As he had a decade earlier in the 1944 TPD report, Fayazuddin underscored the importance of industrial zoning and worker housing.[81] His account strove to integrate the historical specificity of Hyderabadi urbanism with the new national scene in India. His advocacy of planned development, the ethical obligations of government to workers, and critique of narrowly economistic thinking recalls the complexity of the urbanist and planning idioms in pre-1948 Hyderabad.

In tracing the discursive and material production of colonial India as economic entity, Manu Goswami notes that 'princely states' were clubbed with provinces of British India as part of the internal–domestic territorial economy (as opposed to the external–foreign economy).[82] Goswami in

80 Fayazuddin, "Planning in the States," 20. 81 Ibid., 25.
82 Goswami, *Producing India*, 82.

turn domesticates political and economic developments in sub-imperial states, by encompassing them within the produced economic 'state space' of India. In economic histories of South Asian state economic planning, relatively stable colonial–national trajectories dominate narratives, fitting particular developments in sub-imperial states (or in the numerous provinces and regions that constituted British India) into sweeping, flattened narratives of economic change.[83]

As the example of Hyderabad demonstrates, the polity's political autonomy during the colonial period facilitated state-led institutional intervention in shaping residential architecture, infrastructure, and industrial expansion in the capital city, and eventually the state as a whole. The expansive planning modality allowed Hyderabad officials to engage with and implement urban projects informed by global trends manifest in municipal governance elsewhere. State autonomy and autocratic power facilitated the emergence of the planner-technocrat as a key figure in Hyderabad City by World War I, and statewide by the end of World War II. During this period urbanists in British India negotiated a political terrain split between a reactionary colonial state and elite-dominated nationalist parties. The dominance of colonial elites, capitalists, and later nationalist leaders in shaping the British Indian urban domain was not paralleled in Hyderabad.[84] The scenario in Hyderabad traced here suggests that notions of ethical patrimonialism were central to legitimizing (and perhaps shaping) urbanist and planning projects.

The sovereign terrain of Hyderabad State and City facilitated experimental interventions into the urban domain engaged with both global trends (technocratic planning) and existing political values (ethical patrimonialism). This complex rhetoric provided a conceptual framework for a city expanding northwards. It then underwrote the expansion of urbanism into state economic planning in the sub-imperial state of Hyderabad. This dynamic planning idiom, at once ethical and technocratic, and the planner-technocrats who elaborated it continued to infuse

[83] Chibber (*Locked in Place*, 115) notes the existence of subimperial states only in passing. On 'princely' states as endemic of the general tendency toward enduring weakness of centralized state power in colonial and postcolonial South Asia (particularly India) and local or regional despotic power see Atul Kohli, *State-Directed Development: Political Power and Industrialization in the Global Periphery* (Cambridge University Press, 2004), 232, *inter alia*.

[84] On engagements between colonial rulers and Indian capitalists see Preeti Chopra, *A Joint Enterprise: Indian Elites and the Making of British Bombay* (Minneapolis: University of Minnesota Press, 2011). On colonial urbanism, see Kidambi, *The Making of an Indian Metropolis*; Hazareesingh, *The Colonial City*; Legg, *Spaces of Colonialism*; Glover, *Making Lahore Modern*; and Beverley, "Colonial Urbanism."

languages of development, urban and otherwise, even after the post-colonial Indian nation-state integrated Hyderabad into its domain. The histories of urbanism and planning in Hyderabad traced here also framed political negotiations between Raj and Nizam over urban spaces, and the social possibilities therein, which the next chapter examines through the question of public health.

# 8 Improvising urbanism: sanitation and power in Hyderabad and Secunderabad

## I

In 1866, less than a decade after the 1857 uprising, British Indian Army officer Edward Balfour prepared an extensive report on sanitation. The document covered one area of the Secunderabad Cantonment, the Raj's largest military establishment outside its territory, located in the Hyderabad metropolitan area. He emphatically described the city as "the filthiest I have seen in any country," and proposed extensive measures to eliminate rampant unsanitary conditions.[1] Among these were improving drainage, removal of unauthorized latrines, creating public squares from unused land, removal of encroachments on the streets as well as mud houses and walls, and enforcing strict regulations on work such as animal slaughter and sale of food. His report included detailed descriptions of problems in different localities, places in want of public latrines or open air spaces, and even provided sketches of the shapes he prescribed for drain-bottoms.

## II

Hyderabad State's 1944 official report on town planning, considered in the previous chapter, included a detailed section on urban public health. Uncannily echoing Balfour's text of eight decades earlier, the 1944 report expanded on the "evils and the dangers to public health" present in the city, and suggested means of alleviating them. The planning report called for "the improvement and opening up of existing insanitary

[1] Edward Balfour "Report on the sanitary state and prospects of Trimulgherry," 1866 IOR/V/27/840/22/1, 1866. His account of drainage in the city is particularly hyperbolic: "The vast bulk [of drains] were in every degree of filth; filth of every kind, everywhere; and, in many places, filthy puddles, filth and ordure, filth pits and houses spewing forth fermenting ordure. Refuse and rubbish heaps everywhere, every corner a refuse bin, many with ordure, and the masses of refuse such as to indicate their presence for years. Most towns have spots with objectionable features, but almost every part that was visited by me was in the above state."

areas" through slum-clearance, elimination of "offensive trades," and strict zoning laws in order to allow for proper drainage, light, and air.[2]

Viewed together, the two prescriptive texts cited above suggest a remarkable consistency to urban planning ideas: an unbroken discursive continuity across several decades between the imperial Raj and the minor state of Hyderabad. The rhetorical similarities, however, are misleading. As this chapter shall demonstrate, patterns of conflict and negotiation between Nizam and Raj reveal divergent, often competing, visions of the city. Shared urbanist idioms obscure productive departures in Hyderabad from a regulatory and organizing 'colonial urbanism.' Urbanism in sub-imperial Hyderabad was an experimental and improvised political language and practice shaped by engagements between state officials and urban dwellers. Indeed, the goal of fostering the lives and livelihoods of people in the city figured crucially into governance practices in the capital. Hyderabadi urbanism often incorporated putatively modernist internationally circulating ideals shared with colonial officials, but was informed by a patrimonial political ethics valuing protection of the public good. Accordingly, Asaf Jah officials defended popular entitlement to spaces of labor, dwelling, and worship in the city. These considerations suggest potential alternative genealogies of the urban in modern South Asia.

The previous chapter mapped the jurisdictional, demographic, territorial, and built expansion of the Nizam's capital, Hyderabad City, within a larger context of economic and infrastructural change. It provided a chronology of the dramatic remaking of urban space from a wide-angle view, in light of big state-led planning initiatives. If the city was the central locus of political experimentation and investment, the emergence of the urban political arena also shaped the possible social worlds of city-dwellers. To examine the implications of these developments, the current chapter zooms in on micropolitics in the peri-urban fringe, focused on the areas around the British military Cantonment of Secunderabad in the far north of the expanding metropolitan area.

I begin by considering some perspectives on the relationship between colonialism and urban modernity in the South Asian context, then examine a series of Raj–Nizam negotiations over governance of urban spaces and practices. In doing so I describe the workings of a materially grounded colonial aesthetic vision for the city and a competing, contingent, Hyderabadi urbanist discourse, both centered on the idea of

[2] Dr. M. Farooq, Deputy Directory of Public Health Department, "Public Health in Relation to Town Planning," *TP*, 2–4.

public health. I conclude by considering the implications of the divergent urbanist political programs of Hyderabad and Secunderabad.

## Colonialism and South Asia's urban modernities

As scholars Dipesh Chakrabarty and Sudipta Kaviraj have suggested in writings on public space in British India's erstwhile capital, Calcutta, urban modernity was not a homogeneous process manifest and experienced in equivalent terms across the globe.[3] Kaviraj argues that colonialists sought to discipline the everyday practices of the residents of cities such that they conformed to a "bourgeois conception of what it meant for a space to be a modern city."[4] Of course, in no location did the ideology of colonial modernity find perfect realization in built, lived, and governed urban spaces. Visions of the hygienic and civilized modern city were often reasonably consistent across various discursive forms ranging from planning documents to municipal debates. However, the urban ideal had a wide variety of parallel material lives in South Asian cities during the period of British colonial dominance, and left diverse legacies.[5] The prime staging-grounds for the modern urban project in South Asia were the capital city, Calcutta (after 1911 New Delhi) and the major colonial port cities of Bombay and Madras.[6] However, cantonments and civil stations across the empire replicated the ideal separation of functional zones from residential areas, and social groups from one another (along lines of race, religion, class, and so forth) that characterized colonial urban modernity.

At the core of the Raj's project of producing modern cities were the discourses of sanitation and medicine, combined in the language of public health. In Britain itself, other modernizing locations, and colonial South Asia, public health discourse and legislation became a core instrument for

[3] Dipesh Chakrabarty, "Of Garbage, Modernity and the Citizen's Gaze," *Economic and Political Weekly* 27.10/11 (1992): 541–47; Sudipta Kaviraj, "Filth and the Public Sphere: Concepts and Practices about Space in Calcutta," *Public Culture* 10.1 (1997): 83–113.

[4] Kaviraj, "Filth and the Public Sphere," 84.

[5] For visions of city planning that present significant departures from established colonial ideas of urban modernity in South Asia see the large corpus of city plans produced by Scottish planner Patrick Geddes. Citations of these plans and critical examinations of his life's work can be found in Meller, *Patrick Geddes* and Ramchandra Guha, "Patrick Geddes and Ecological Town Planning in India" (unpublished manuscript, 2006).

[6] A wealth of recent scholarship has illuminated different aspects of South Asian urban history during the colonial period. See, *inter alia*, Glover, *Making Lahore Modern*; Hazareesingh, *The Colonial City*; Kidambi, *The Making of an Indian Metropolis*; Legg, *Spaces of Colonialism*; Nair, *Mysore Modern* and *The Promise of the Metropolis*; Rao, *House, But No Garden*. For a thematic survey of historical scholarship on this topic, Beverley, "Colonial Urbanism."

bringing dwellers of cities into the statist modern project that colonialism sought to universalize.[7] Changing modes of colonial urban power bear out the rise of sanitary governance.

By the early twentieth century colonial urbanism entailed a modification of eighteenth- and nineteenth-century spatial politics premised on racial segregation. Supplementing an older 'dual city' imaginary, later colonial policies increasingly emphasized the importance of sanitation in the governance of cities. The city remained in large part segregated, but urban colonial subjects were increasingly subject to biopolitical surveillance regulating physical mobility and varied urban practices (labor, sexuality, entertainment, consumption). Changing colonial urbanist visions were often manifest in planning and governance models by which the city was to be organized into zones where certain activities could be carried out and certain groups of people could reside. This was framed within a discourse that placed high value on sanitary governance. Indeed, maintaining the 'sanitary city' served as a sweeping justification for building elements of surveillance and bodily policing into the city.[8]

If the Raj was the key player in the rise of urbanist discourse in South Asia, similar notions of modern urbanism were becoming prominent globally. Municipal movements in metropolitan, colonial, and uncolonized locations provided channels for productive global exchanges of ideas by intellectuals, activists, and administrators.[9] Indeed, as discussed in the previous chapter, the municipal arena, and city improvement bodies, became key venues of political exchange and intervention in South Asia from the late nineteenth century. The formally unitary character of colonial sovereignty, however, circumscribed the scope of municipal power in British India, and broader urbanist planning and governance remained largely the domain of the Raj until decolonization. The

[7] On sanitary technologies in the USA see Martin V. Melosi, *The Sanitary City: Environmental Services in Urban America from Colonial Times to the Present* (Baltimore: Johns Hopkins University Press, 1999). On sanitation and power in colonial Calcutta see Ishita Pande, *Medicine, Race and Liberalism in British Bengal: Symptoms of Empire* (London: Routledge, 2010), chs. 5, 6.

[8] Kenneth Ballhatchet, *Race, Sex, and Class under the Raj: Imperial Attitudes and Policies and their Critics, 1793–1905* (London: Weidenfeld & Nicolson, 1980); Legg, *Spaces of Colonialism* and Stephen Legg, "Governing Prostitution in Colonial Delhi: From Cantonment Regulations to International Hygiene (1864–1939)," *Social History* 34.4 (2009): 447–67; Svati P. Shah, "Producing the Spectacle of Kamathipura: The Politics of Red Light Visibility in Mumbai," *Cultural Dynamics* 18.3 (2006): 269–92; Tambe, *Codes of Misconduct*.

[9] Shane Ewen and Pierre-Yves Saunier, eds., *Another Global City: Historical Explorations into the Transnational Municipal Moment, 1850–2000* (New York: Palgrave Macmillan, 2008).

potential for the urban as an emergent sphere of non-colonial politics is visible all the more in Hyderabad City owing to the Nizam's sovereignty. Developments in the capital city – different in degree, if not in kind, from British Indian municipal developments – provide key evidence for rethinking genealogies of urban politics in South Asia.

## Polities and people in Hyderabad City: the Secunderabad fringe

The urban villages, or suburban neighborhoods, surrounding the British Cantonment at Secunderabad were a locus of rapid growth in terms of population and building activity starting in the last quarter of the nineteenth century. Migrants from surrounding British India and the Hyderabad countryside flocked here to take advantage of the economic boom in the twin cities, fueled by the opening of the Secunderabad and Hyderabad Railway Stations in 1874, and featuring expanding markets and potential employment in construction and later industrial production. Exchanges between sub-imperial Hyderabad and the British colonial establishment at Secunderabad suggest a developing conflict over the shape and appearance this emerging northern core of the city should take on. The assertion of legal control over city space was crucial to the Nizam's performance of power. However, in addition to being a struggle over symbolic and actual sovereignty between two polities, Nizam–Raj negotiations served to define the parameters of urban life in the rapidly developing northern portions of the city, a history that had a profound effect on the lives of residents of these areas.

The Secunderabad Cantonment and the Chadarghat Residency were placed under British control by treaties with the Nizam dating to 1798. Under colonial rule and planning regimes these areas came to resemble cantonments and civil lines across British India: a distinct urban typology characterized by a high level of segregation between functional and residential areas, people of different classes or social groups ('natives' and Europeans, elites and peasants), as well as specific patterns of urban form and governance.[10] The Raj sought to exert control over the spaces of labor, dwelling, and worship in the city. Justification was produced with reference to the notion of 'public space,' and the prevailing colonial

[10] Beverley, "Colonial Urbanism"; Anthony D. King, *Colonial Urban Development: Culture, Social Power and Environment* (London: Routledge, 1976), ch. 5 and *The Bungalow: The Production of a Global Culture* (London: Routledge, 1984); John Brush, "The Morphology of Indian Cities," in *India's Urban Future: Selected Studies from an International Conference sponsored by Kingsley Davis, Richard L. Park, and Catherine Bauer Wurster*, ed. Roy Turner (Berkeley: University of California Press, 1962), 57–70.

discourse on urbanism sought to normalize specific visions of how a city should be structured to be economically and administratively efficient, attractive, and salubrious.

The northern edge of the expanding city, near Secunderabad, was the terrain upon which the struggle to define the urban future of Hyderabad was fought. As important suburban 'villages' on the outskirts of the Cantonment such as Begumpet, Yusufguda, Chilkalguda, and Khairatabad began to emerge on the fringes of a burgeoning Secunderabad, the British increasingly insisted on their prerogative to regulate urban life in a radius drawn around the Cantonment's boundaries, variously defined between one-quarter and two miles. The question of administrative borders between sub-imperial and colonial areas was made all the more complex by the fact that – like much of the Nizam's state – the area around the Cantonment was a patchwork of *jagir* land grants under the direct administration of various aristocrats, Paigah estates jointly governed by a collective of high nobles, *sarf-i khas* lands providing revenues for the royal family itself and under the authority of a specially appointed official, and *dīvānī* lands that formed the mainstay of the Nizam's dominions and were under state control.[11] The variety of land tenures and jurisdictional arrangements endowed a structural ambivalence to the urban administrative scene, and provided Hyderabad with a consistently reliable alibi for resisting colonial fiats. While Raj officials in the state worked from a clear agenda for structuring and governing the city, Hyderabadi urbanism was very much an improvised emerging discourse. In the newly developing northern regions of the city in the Cantonment's sphere of influence, the urban vision of the Nizam's government took form in a series of interventions against initiatives of the British that targeted urban dwellers.

Those subjects of the Nizam residing in areas surrounding the Secunderabad Cantonment felt acutely the impact of the colonial establishment's urban policy on their everyday lives. Nizam–Raj contestations over urban policy were in part a struggle for sovereignty over a burgeoning area endowed with symbolic and economic value. They also provided an opening for the increased presence of marginal segments of the city's population in the archival record. Rarely do the subjects of the

[11] Establishing fixed land-tenure arrangements in rural areas was a central means by which Company Raj solidified political authority, as has been examined in a robust scholarly literature, *inter alia* Ranajit Guha, *A Rule of Property for Bengal: An Essay on the Idea of the Permanent Settlement* (Durham, NC: Duke University Press, 1996 [1963]); Burton Stein, *Thomas Munro: The Origins of the Colonial State and his Vision of Empire* (Delhi: Oxford University Press, 1989). There is less scholarship on urban lands under the Raj. On the varied land tenure arrangements in colonial Bombay City see Rao, *House, But No Garden*, ch. 1.

Nizam speak for themselves in the archive. Nevertheless, documentation of conflicts over space reveal that Hyderabadi officials frequently opposed colonial designs by making reference to the needs, established practices, and sometimes collectively authored petitions of city-dwellers.

Contestations between the Hyderabadi administration and the British establishment over the areas immediately surrounding the Cantonment encompassed several domains of urban life. Major differences emerged over the question of how the city should look and what spaces of labor, dwelling, and worship should constitute. Inextricably intertwined with the tussle over the appearance of the city was the colonial discourse on public health and sanitation, which was constantly invoked with reference to the military Cantonment. First, I will examine competing visions of the aesthetics of public space in Hyderabad, and then turn to consider the ways in which colonial urbanism was yoked to the notion of maintaining healthy and sanitary conditions.

## Prickly pears, house numbers, and ordering urban space

Fashioning Secunderabad into a suitable home for the large community of British soldiers and administrators who were stationed there, as well as even greater numbers of South Asian merchants seeking economic liberties, was a multifaceted process that involved not only ordering the Cantonment area itself, but also regulating urban form across the boundaries and into the Nizam's territories. As shown in the previous chapter, Asaf Jah officials were initially disinclined to assert jurisdictional claims in areas north of the Musa, with administration of urban settlements in that area largely left in British hands until the late nineteenth century. With the rapid expansion of the colonial commercial economy there, and the increased influx of people and goods made possible by the 1874 completion of the Hyderabad State Railway, however, the picture changed considerably. The urbanization of the 'villages' bordering the Cantonment was increasing apace as population density in Secunderabad continued to swell. In this context, the colonial establishment sought to exert greater control just as the Nizam's administration was beginning to direct more attention to the trans-Musa city.

Colonial officials set several projects in motion to bring the increasingly dense swaths of Hyderabadi territory surrounding the Secunderabad Cantonment into conformity with the colonial urban vision. Some initiatives were innocuous, such as the extended campaign in the first decade of the twentieth century initiated by the Cantonment Magistrate to eradicate prickly-pear cactus plants both inside the Cantonment and within in a two-mile radius of its boundaries.[12] Removal of the cacti entailed extensive measures to make sure the thorny and hardy plant did not grow back the following season. Records of the eradication campaign demonstrate the detail with which colonial authorities cataloged even the horticultural life of a large number of Hyderabadi urban villages, including an extensive listing of more than two dozen places around the Cantonment in which the prickly pear was to be removed.[13]

Colonial geographical knowledge was sometimes deployed to garden Secunderabad and its environs so that aesthetically offensive and potentially dangerous plants were not able to thrive. In other instances colonial designs for the area were explicitly linked to the British initiative to govern portions of the Nizam's territory. A series of correspondences from the same period, this time regarding the absent or irregular numbering system for houses in the areas around Secunderabad, includes a list of villages containing several of the same place names that appear on the prickly-pear project list.[14] In a 1905 letter to the *divan* of Hyderabad the Resident conveyed the Cantonment Magistrate's complaint that "Police and Municipal work is considerably hindered in the villages mentioned in the margin and within Cantonment jurisdiction owing to the houses in them being unnumbered or numbered in an irregular manner."[15] To ease the work of Secunderabad authorities, the Resident requested: "His Highness' Government may be moved to arrange for the regular

[12] "Ṣafā'i-yi zaqqūm-i khārdār-i iṭirāf-i chā'onī-yi sikandarābād dār ḥalqah-i do mīl – Arrangement to destroy the prickly pear shrub round the Secunderabad Cantonment," APSA 37/1/260, 1903–1906. The provenance of the prickly-pear cacti in the region is uncertain. The plant is not native to South Asia, but is a post-Columbian import, widely used for food purposes in the Americas and the Mediterranean, but not in South Asia. On a largely unsuccessful attempt to use parts of the plant as cattle feed during famine times see *RHFHHND*, 141–42. On use of prickly-pear hedges as a customs barrier between British India and sub-imperial states to the north, Moxham, *Great Hedge of India*. It is unknown whether such uses were made of the plant in the south in general or on the internal colonial frontier of Hyderabad–Secunderabad in particular: Roy Moxham, personal communication, 2005.

[13] The villages listed: Balamrai, Seetharampore, Boosaressy Guda, Hussain Ahmed Kancha, Thocutta, Dhanipoora, Russulpoor, Maredpally, Trimulgherry, Kakaguda, Chilkulguda, Koommeegutta, Sikh village, Bowenpally village, Hassan Ahmed Kancha, Ferozeguda, Hasmathpait, Mulkajgire, Hyderguda, Lothcunta, Doddier, Lallamean Hamlet, Mettoogoodah, Chilkulgudah, Mushirabad, Molack poor, Hussain sagar, Kavadiguda, Begumpett, Bhugareanta poore, Pattiguda. Spellings used in the source documents have been retained: APSA 37/1/260, 1903–1906.

[14] The villages listed: Pedda Tokatta, Chinna Tokatta, Rasalpur, Tawaipura, Sikh village, Trimulgherry village, Kakaguda village, Maredpalli, Sitarampur, Balamrai, Chakliguda. "Complaint of the Cantt Magistrate and Secretary Cantt Committee, Secunderabad, of hindrance of Police Municipal work, on account of the houses in certain villages within Cantt jurisdiction, not being properly numbered," APSA 37/1/274, 1905–1907.

[15] Haig [Resident] to Maharaja Sri Kishen Prasad Bahadur, KCIE [Prime Minister], 10 September 1905, APSA 37/1/274, 1905–1907.

numbering in English figures of the houses in the villages in question."[16] The villages straddled the boundary between the corridor of Secunderabad Cantonment area and the Asaf Jahi territory surrounding it, and Raj officials had to rely on Hyderabad to carry out projects. Correspondence continued on the matter throughout the next couple of years, as apparently the English numbering system insisted upon was not implemented. The posting of numbers on houses in the villages in question may well have had no perceptible effect on the subjects of the Nizam residing therein. Nevertheless, this trend suggests that colonial notions of urban order, such as a regular house numbering system to designate addresses, were seen as crucial to the work of Cantonment police and municipal authorities.

In and around Secunderabad the aesthetic project of colonial urbanism was intertwined with a British push to assert tighter control over the Cantonment and surrounding areas. Frequent initiatives to clearly define the limits of the Cantonment itself, as well as the supplementary radius drawn around it – which came to be referred to as "the outer cantonment boundary" – were designed to enhance the capacity of colonial officials to navigate and govern areas in the Nizam's territory.[17] Hyderabad often put such colonial 'recommendations' into effect with considerably delay, but none of the above practices of ordering urbanizing space around Secunderabad elicited objection from Asaf Jah officials.

## Civic contestation and the public good

Secunderabad's championing of a particular aesthetic vision of South Asian urbanism together with a colonial discourse on law and order did not in and of itself precipitate conflict with Hyderabad. Not so for Raj attempts to regulate the Nizam's subjects. Initiatives aimed at restricting the everyday lives of Hyderabadis incited strenuous and often effective resistance from Asaf Jah officials. British authorities, as we have seen, extended the apparatuses of colonial knowledge out from the imperial island of the Cantonment and into surrounding territories,

16 Ibid.

17 "Verification of the Secunderabad Cantonment Boundary by the Government of India Survey Department," APSA 37/1/294, 1909. The quotation is taken from this statement in Resident Howell to Maharaja Sri Kishen Prasad Bahadur, 1 November 1909: "The work has not begun and it is desireable that the 13 jagir villages, mentioned in the margin [*Pedda Tokatta, Chinna Tokatta, Sitarampur, Kakaguda, Maredpalli, Chakliguda, Tawaipura, Chandu Lal Bauli, Balamrai, Rasulpur, Trimulgherry village, Busareddiguda, Lalapett], and other areas under His Highness the Nizam's jurisdiction which lie within *the outer Cantonment boundary*, should have their limits clearly defined, so that they may be correctly shown in the new Cantonment Map [emphasis added and marginally noted villages inserted]."

mapping the terrain and ensuring that buildings were clearly marked. Secunderabad sought to mobilize this spatial knowledge and regulate lives and livelihoods, and sheer numbers, of Asaf Jahi subjects within the Cantonment's ambiguously defined 'outer boundary.' In such instances, Hyderabad contested the legitimacy of Secunderabad's projects. These negotiations posed limits on the penetration of colonial urbanism into northern Hyderabad and had important implications for the lives of the residents of these areas.

The archive abounds with incidents in which the Secunderabad colonial establishment raised objection against changes in the built form of neighboring and rapidly expanding suburban villages. In 1906, for example, the *kotwal* of Chilkalguda, a village within the Cantonment's quarter-mile radius, had arranged for a new police station to be constructed.[18] The Cantonment Magistrate insisted that Hyderabad "kindly cause early and stringent orders to be issued for the prevention of the erection of the building in question."[19] Devoid of any stated practical basis, this request was presented on the legalistic grounds that the police station's existence was in contravention of an 1893 treaty limiting construction in the Cantonment's quarter-mile buffer zone. Upon receiving this communication, Asaf Jah officials noted that the already completed construction had been undertaken "without any desire to go against the Settlement arrived at in 1893," and in light of these facts should be "permitted to remain a Police Station as a special case."[20] Cantonment authorities relented, and gave permission for the building to stand on the basis of this being a "special circumstance."[21]

18 "Complaint of the Cantonment Magistrate, ref: to the construction of a new building for a Police station in the village of Chilkulguda," APSA 37/1/262, 1906.

19 W. Haig, Resident to Sir Kishen Pershad Bahadur, KCIE, Yamin-us-Sultanat [Prime Minister], 27 January 1906, APSA 37/1/262.

20 Secretary to His Highness the Nizam's Government, Judicial, Police and General Departments to the Political Secretary of Government and the Private Secretary to His Excellency the Minister, 5 April 1906, APSA 37/1/262. The various correspondences here follow a complicated system of protocol for communication between British and Hyderabadi officials. The Cantonment Magistrate had to pass his requests on to the Resident, who communicated officially its substance the Prime Minister, Kishen Pershad, whose correspondence was handled by his private secretary, Faridoonji Jamshedji. The message would then be passed on to the relevant Hyderabadi official, in this case the Judicial, Police and General Secretary. And in responding the entire protocol was completed in reverse. This correspondence regarding this particular communication was all the more complex since confusion emerged over whether the location in question was part of a separately administered Paigah estate or under *divani* administration. The latter was eventually determined to be the case. See correspondence between Faridoonji Jamshedji, the Hyderabad Judicial Secretary, and Resident Haig from 7 April, 7 July and 9 July of 1906, APSA 37/1/262.

21 Resident to Prime Minister, 27 August 1906, APSA 37/1/262.

The Hyderabadi administration's argument to leave the newly constructed police station in place invoked the rhetoric of ethical patrimonialism – the Nizam's responsibility to oversee the welfare of his subjects – within the urban setting of the capital city. A key tactic for advancing this position was insistence on the centrality of intention and principle rather than the literal reading of a statute. While Secunderabad appealed to laws in force regulating urban construction, Hyderabad built a case on the basis of public utility: "The commissioner of Police, City and Suburbs, who was referred to on the subject reports that the new building has been constructed to be used as a police-station for the convenience of the general public, as the existing police station is far from habitations."[22] The notion of the "general public," figured here as Asaf Jahi subjects, was invoked frequently in correspondences between an increasingly assertive Hyderabad and the invasive colonial establishment over questions of urban governance around Secunderabad.

"The public good" as an abstract idea was so common in modern statist discourses of the late nineteenth century that it can be spoken of as a universal feature of the emerging urbanist lexicon.[23] Nevertheless, the concept had a particular valence in Hyderabad, both as part of an idiom shared with the emerging British Indian municipal political sphere and as an implicit reference to the Islamic legal concept of *maṣlaḥat* (public interest) within Hyderabadi patrimonialist discourse.[24] Taken together, the inclusion of the idea of the public good in the sources at hand represents an incorporation of the concepts of civic virtue and good governance from the language of colonial liberalism with Islamicate notions of political responsibility. These multiple resonances elucidate the improvised lexicon of Hyderabadi urban modernity. Of key significance in the lives of the populations of the urbanizing Secunderabad fringe is the fact that their own interests had become the substance of negotiations over the future of Hyderabad's urbanism.

[22] Secretary to His Highness the Nizam's Government, Judicial, Police and General Departments to the Political Secretary of Government and the Private Secretary to His Excellency the Minister, 5 April 1906, APSA 37/1/262.

[23] The regularization of Istanbul's urban fabric, via street standardization and construction of fire-resistant buildings, to "serve the public good (*menfaat-i umumiye*)" provides a parallel example: see Zeynep Çelik, *The Remaking of Istanbul: Portrait of an Ottoman City in the Nineteenth Century* (Berkeley: University of California Press, 1986), 50.

[24] On the increasing importance of the municipality in British Indian politics see Jim Masselos, *Towards Nationalism: Group Affiliations and the Politics of Public Associations in Nineteenth Century Western India* (Bombay: Popular Prakashan, 1974); Douglas E. Haynes, *Rhetoric and Ritual in Colonial India: The Shaping of a Public Culture in Surat City, 1852–1928* (Berkeley: University of California Press, 1991), ch. 2 traces the emergence of a political rhetoric in the municipal sphere around concepts such as "the public good."

Asaf Jah officials articulated opposition to colonial projects in the name of the subject population only in specific ways and certain contexts. Such apparently innocuous endeavors as keeping Hyderabadi territory in the Cantonment zone free of cacti or numbering buildings in a regular fashion did not raise objections, but colonial initiatives to move a public building such as the police station elicited staunch opposition. Likewise, when the Cantonment authority sought to regulate everyday lives of Asaf Jahi subjects, Hyderabad officials advocated on their behalf.

## Colonial aesthetics and the regulation of space

In August 1900 the Resident wrote to the Asaf Jah *divan* seeking to have some structures in the village of Thokatta removed:[25]

> The unauthorized erection of these walls is objectionable as they are calculated to afford cover for the unauthorized building of huts hereafter. Moreover clay walls of this description unless very frequently and carefully repaired will always present a dilapidated and unsightly appearance in the Cantonment. I am therefore to request that early and stringent orders may be issued for the removal of the walls in question and other walls which are said to have sprung up since the last report.[26]

This letter is one of many in a continuous exchange about the content and appearance of urban space in northern Hyderabad between colonial officials of the Residency and Secunderabad Municipality, *jagirdars*, and representatives of the Nizam's administration. Residency injunctions were primarily in reference to the 1893 Secunderabad–Hyderabad agreement that no new buildings would be erected within a certain radius of the Cantonment without special permission. The content of the 1893 regulation, assuming cantonment boundaries could be clearly determined, was unambiguous. The situation on the ground, however, was the outcome of political negotiations, shifts in how the Secunderabad radius was defined, and uses of space that straddled the boundary between licit and illicit. These processes combined to produce the improvisational urban fabric of these parts of the city.

The British attempt to maintain a cordon sanitaire around their establishment in the sub-imperial state was in keeping with established colonial practice of enforcing segregation between ruling class and subject

25 Thokatta is just north of Secunderabad's urban center, in the large suburban locality of Bowenpally.

26 Office of Resident Dennis Fitzpatrick to His Excellency Viqar al-Umra Bahadur, KCIE, 15 August 1900, "Prohibition of erection of buildings within a 1/4 mile of Secunderabad Cantonment limits," APSA 37/1/188, 1899–1902.

population. Such urban policies were current across British India and in numerous other colonial locations globally. In Hyderabad, however, there was an important difference: the sovereign authority over the populations affected by these urban planning fiats was the Nizam and not the encroaching British. While the municipal sphere in British India was at best a gradually emerging democratized space of native sovereignty, Hyderabad could back claims on behalf of state subjects with formal political authority. In cities under the Raj, the colonial state and subordinate planning bodies spoke on behalf of the people whose interests they purported to be serving. Colonial subjects empowered within the sphere of municipal governance contested projects – sometimes effectively – as aspiring participants in governance. They remained constrained by the legal framework dictated by the Raj and the idioms of colonial urbanism. The making of urban space on the Secunderabad fringe came to be a negotiated and improvised domain in which a wide range of ideas about the public good were expressed by Asaf Jah officials and by subjects in petitions to the Hyderabad government.

### *Spaces of labor*

The Resident's 1900 order to remove "dilapidated" and "unsightly" walls – an initiative which he had already put into effect via the Cantonment Magistrate – was rapidly opposed by the *nāẓim* of the Salar Jung Estate. The *nazim*, a *jagirdari* official in whose jurisdiction the village was located, objected on both legal and practical grounds:

> The prohibition to the erection of buildings within 1/4 mile of the cantonment limits without the permission of the cantonment authorities relates to the erection of houses or buildings of a permanent nature. The walls now raised by certain men of the Estate Elaka do not fall under the category of buildings, being made from clay for temporary use and having a height lower than the height of a man, and are intended only for the protection of fields from animals. These walls will, however, be pulled down as soon as the crops are harvested.
>
> Permission for the erection of such walls has been granted previously as will be well known to you . . . If the walls are to be pulled down then result will be a serious loss to the crops and the consequent ruin of the ryots [state subjects, especially agriculturalists].
>
> It would be desirable if the walls were allowed to remain for the protection of the fields, and I hope you will point out to the Resident (who desires their demolition on the ground of their being erected without proper permission) the desirability of allowing the walls to remain in the interest of the people.[27]

[27] Translation of Letter from Nazim of Salar Jung Estate to Secretary of Public Works Department, APSA 37/1/188, 1899–1902.

In his claim the *nazim* argued that the 1893 agreement did not apply in the case, but also invoked broader ethical and practical arguments. As he would have it, temporary clay walls were necessary for the peasantry of Thokatta to effectively carry out their livelihoods, and their erection in the area was a longstanding practice. The arguments from law, practice, and public utility marshaled by the *nazim* of the Salar Jung Estate in defense of urban spaces of labor were echoed and supplemented in other rejoinders from Hyderabad. Writing to the *divan*'s office, the Asaf Jah Revenue Secretary sketched out precisely how these walls fit into the larger economic picture of the state:

> The practice of having mud walls round their field has been carried out by the ryots of the village Thokatta since the past many years. The walls in themselves are not newly constructed but are renewed every year at the time of cultivation, which pays into the estate Treasury between five and six thousand Rupees. The local ryots say that as there is every danger of their crop being destroyed by the encroachment of the cattle of neighboring villages, the Honourable the Resident will be pleased to allow cultivation to go on under their defence as heretofore. Should it be deemed necessary to demolish these walls on account of their unsightly appearance the inhabitants of Thokatta in their petition to the Nazim have stated that the compound walls of many bungalows in the Cantonment of Secunderabad do not differ much from their own, and that they are quite willing to have them plastered over with chunam [quicklime].[28]

Following this line of argument: as went the fortunes of Hyderabad's peasant cultivators, so went the economic health of the state. In the Revenue Secretary's account the mud walls themselves stood as a guarantor of a flow of taxes into state coffers at the time of each harvest. Yearly wall construction in Thokatta was a longstanding practice, and facilitated smooth operation of the local agrarian economy. Urban villagers' practices ran against Secunderabad's initiative to segregate the military and residential areas of the Cantonment (as well as the polo and parade grounds, both a short distance from Thokatta) from agricultural production. As such, Hyderabad officials opposed realization of the colonial urban aesthetic vision. But the matter was not merely a question of appearances, as was borne out when the peasants' offer to plaster the walls fell upon deaf ears in Secunderabad. The Cantonment's initiative to tear down the walls was not to end with a bit of quicklime and whitewash.

The conflict continued to simmer. The Cantonment Magistrate issued notices and had numerous enclosure walls demolished in Thokatta,

[28] From Secretary of Board of Revenue to Private Secretary to His Excellency the Minister, 5 November 1900, APSA 37/1/188, 1899–1902.

while Hyderabad officials objected along the lines described above. The situation came to a head at year's end, when the *divan* appealed directly to the Resident to end the demolition of walls.[29] The Resident assured the *divan* that the disgruntled peasants were treated with "leniency and consideration." Niceties aside, his response to Hyderabad's objections was unequivocal: there were no similar unauthorized walls in Secunderabad, all of the walls in question were fresh construction, walls were not in fact necessary for agriculture, and allegations of special permissions given by a Cantonment officer were both false and wrong-headed ("... nor is it believed that a general sanction to overrun the cantonment with miles of mud walls was contemplated by that officer"). The Resident cited an additional reason, one that shifted the discourse away from the categories of ethics, established practice, and legal standing:

> That great difficulty is experienced by the Cantonment Authorities in causing the owners of Kutcha [*kachchā* temporary or in this case mud; as opposed to *pakkā*, permanent, or in this context, burnt brick] compound walls in Secunderabad to maintain them in good order as required by the Cantonment rules and that it is not desirable to augment it by permitting the erection of the walls in question, round the different areas of cultivated land within the Cantonment, which if suffered to be built will in time form a complete network over it and prove a serious task to supervise with the existing Sanitary establishment.[30]

The crux of Secunderabad's position against wall construction, then, was the need of Cantonment officials to effectively oversee the space of the city and ensure its cleanliness. The centrality of sanitation or public health in colonial urbanism here is a point to which I shall return. Another aspect of this conflict over mud walls indicates how tensions over urbanism ranged from work spaces to residential structures.

### *Spaces of dwelling*

In his initial complaint against the Thokatta walls' existence, the Resident expressed a marked anxiety over what might be going on behind their cover. Before the conversation was, perhaps conveniently, turned toward the question of agriculture by the *nazim* of the Salar Jung Estate (and no doubt initially by the peasants of Thokatta in their petition), the

[29] The Resident's order is recounted in the *divan*'s reply, From Faridoonji Jamshedji to Col. Barr, 20 December 1900, APSA 37/1/188, 1899–1902.

[30] From Resident (Jardine) to Sir Viqar ul-Umra Bahadur KCIE, 10 January 1901, APSA 37/1/188, 1899–1902. On *kachchā* and *pakkā*, see also Chapter 7, 235, n28.

Resident postulated that the walls in question were "calculated to afford cover for the unauthorized building of huts hereafter."[31] At stake here was not merely the visual aberration posed by an agricultural village amidst a rapidly urbanizing area near one of Britain's largest overseas military and civil establishments. The bone of contention was the ordering of urban space in the emerging northern core of Hyderabad City, the Secunderabad zone. All construction, production, and development should be rendered visible to the intrusive eye of Cantonment officials. Only this could ensure that no rules had been transgressed that might put Secunderabad at risk of being overrun by the teeming native city outside its boundaries.

An archival fragment about a roughly contemporaneous development in Bowenpalli makes this picture clearer. In 1898 the Cantonment Magistrate directed a similar appeal to Hyderabad to halt new construction near Secunderabad.[32] This time a Hyderabad health officer voiced opposition. M. A. Ghany wrote:

> I have also observed that the purdah walls of various Mohemedan houses have been falling down during recent rains and they were not allowed to be reconstructed. I would suggest that permission for reconstruction of their houses and walls should be given, but no new house should be allowed to be built within the limit, and it will be impossible for the inhabitants to live in dilapidated houses and lastly there are some families who are living in that village for more than one generation so it is difficult for them to leave the ground of their ancestors especially when they have their farms around the villages from which they derive profit for their livelihood.[33]

Ghany's insight underscores a defining contrast. Secunderabad's urbanist program was designed to prevent population increase in a buffer zone around the Cantonment. Competing interventions from Hyderabad centered around limiting restrictions on construction and improvement of certain existing structures. Construction was to be permitted when necessary to maintain the livelihoods, established practice (often described, as above, in the cultural language of community requirements and local networks), and viable residence of Asaf Jahi subjects in Hyderabad territory.

31 From Office of Resident Dennis Fitzpatrick to His Excellency Viqar al-Umra Bahadur, KCIE, 15 August 1900, "Prohibition of erection of buildings within a 1/4 mile of Secunderabad Cantonment limits," APSA 37/1/188, 1899–1902.

32 The conflict is recapped in From Resident to Nawab Sir Viqar al-Umra Bahadur KCIE, 11 January 1899, APSA 37/1/188, 1899–1902.

33 From M. A. Ghany, Health Officer, Chaderghat Municipality to The Secretary, Chaderghat Municipality, 17 September 1898, APSA 37/1/188, 1899–1902.

### *Spaces of worship*

Alongside spaces of labor and dwelling, the placement of temples and mosques sparked conflicts between Nizam and Raj urban officials. Cantonment authorities, responding to Abdul Sattar Khan's 1917 petition, sought to stop construction of a mosque in Picket village, near the military station's boundary. The Resident clarified his demographic concerns: "the situation of the village is such that any increase in it is highly undesirable, especially if the increase takes the form of a mosque and its attendant buildings."[34] The mosque figured in the colonial urbanist gaze as a harbinger of unwanted population increase in a sensitive area. Here, colonial pressure, and the presence of mosques in neighboring Karkhana and Kakaguda, compelled Hyderabad officials to revoke Sattar's permit.

A case from some decades earlier demonstrates Hyderabad's willingness to preserve public access to spaces of worship. Colonial officials sought in 1879 to expand a Protestant cemetery in Narayanguda, near the Chadarghat British Residency (well to the south of the Cantonment).[35] Asaf Jah officials cited reports from a *taluqdar* of the city's *atraf-i baldah* (suburbs) that there was a mosque on the land colonial officials sought. Accordingly, Hyderabad pressed for an alteration to the cemetery plans to accommodate a large space around the mosque to facilitate the needs of worshipers.[36] After examining the layout with the Hyderabadi suburban *taluqdar*, colonial officials devised a collaborative plan in which the mosque was left out of the new extension's limits.[37]

Hyderabad's concern for urban dwellers' access to spaces of worship sometimes had effects that reached beyond the space of the city. In two cases from the first decade of the twentieth century Asaf Jah officials sought to secure revenues from land grants in Berar to support a major urban temple, and maintenance of Hindu and Muslim pilgrim ascetics at another temple's *maṭh* (monastery) in the city.[38] Berar, Hyderabad

[34] Resident (HR Lynch Blom) to Nawab Sir Faridoon Jang Bahadur, KCIE, CSI, Assistant Minister, Political Department, His Highness the Nizam's Government, "Request to Build a Mosque in the Village of Picket," 8 January 1917, APSA 37/1/447, 1916.

[35] "Land acquisition for a Protestant cemetery at Chadarghaut," Political Office, Hyderabad Residency, OIOC R/2/80/163, 1869–79.

[36] Nizam's Minister to Resident, 18 February 1879, OIOC R/2/80/163.

[37] Secretary, Local Funds Committee, Chaderghat Municipality to First Assistant Resident, 1 April 1879, OIOC R/2/80/163.

[38] "Proper maintenance of the temple of Shri Sitaram Maharaj in Sitaram Bagh in the city of Hyderabad," Hyderabad Residency, Political Office, OIOC R/2/81/197, 1907, and "Annual money grant to Bhairathi Guru, to feed and support travelling Gosayees and fakirs at a monastery in Begam Bazar, Hyd, in lieu of the Jagir village of Dhanoda in Berar which was resumed in 1898," Hyderabad Residency, Political Office, OIOC R/2/82/203, 1908, continued in R/2/82/204, 1909.

territories seized by the British in lieu of questionable debts, was the location of two *jagir* land grants designated to maintain the noted urban spaces of worship. Assuring continuity of the grants and disbursement of revenues entailed Hyderabad officials pressing Raj administrators in Berar.

If the last instances broadened the geographic scope of Raj–Nizam engagements considered here, the cases discussed in this section had important implications for urban dwellers' abilities to use the space of the city. Juridico-legal contestation over sovereignty, negotiations, and collaborations resonated on the broader level of state politics. But Secunderabad's expansive urban aesthetics threatened to constrain everyday spaces accessible to Asaf Jahi subjects in the capital city. Hyderabadi officials advanced their own urbanist program by striving to protect spaces of labor, dwelling, and worship, shaping quotidian lives of people in an emerging city on the fringes of colonialism.

## "A standing menace": public housing as public nuisance

The language colonial officials marshaled to shape the areas around Secunderabad in accordance with their urban vision was shot through consistently with references to cleanliness, salubriousness, and sanitation. Addressing the *divan*, Residency officials listed a series of problematic "buildings on Moglai land within the Secunderabad Cantonment boundary [constructed] without reference to proper authority."Alongside complaints against the unauthorized erection of a new room in the "already overcrowded and unwholesome locality" of Maredpalli and a "regular eye-sore in the hamlet which is only a few yards off the road leading to the 2nd British Infantry lines," the Residency cited another major infraction:

> One Gangapershan, a liquor vendor, has been permitted by the Havildar of Kakaguda to re-erect an old disused privy to the rear of his house in Maridpalli. No plan with section of the proposed latrine has either been called for or submitted, and the work in consequence is being very ill-executed. There is no proper flooring or drain or cistern, and if the latrine is allowed to be used, it will, in a very short time, become a nuisance.[39]

The Resident cited protecting "the sanitation of the Cantonment" as cause for halting construction and demolishing the buildings in question.

[39] From Resident to Viqar al-Umara Bahadur KCIE, "Prohibition of erection of buildings within a 1/4 mile of Secunderabad Cantonment limits," 4 August 1900, APSA 37/1/188, 1899–1902. The areas noted in the letter were Maredpalli, on the northeast border of Secunderabad, and neighboring Chukliguda (Chillcalguda), located between the eastern border of Secunderabad and the railway lines at Lallaguda.

This was a particularly sensitive issue at the time owing to an outbreak of cholera in the Cantonment, which posed a considerable risk to the health of, among other groups, the large military regiment quartered there. In the language of colonial urbanism, the problem of "overcrowding of huts and hovels" was presented as part and parcel of a broader threat to public health posed by unregulated areas of Hyderabad in the north of the city.

The "ill-executed latrine" was not merely a "nuisance" in aesthetic terms, but placed the British Indian station at Secunderabad under the risk of contamination and illness. Cantonment officials emphasized the need for Hyderabad to rein in the Kakaguda suburban official, who had authorized the noted domestic construction projects underway in the area. Attempts to order the urban space of Moglai areas in the Cantonment zone were not limited to construction carried out by subjects of the Nizam, but also included official projects.

The late nineteenth and early twentieth centuries saw considerable residential migration of Asaf Jah nobility out of the old walled city to the south and into the areas north of the river, including the environs of Chadarghat Residency, several localities in the Cantonment zone, and Banjara Hills to its southwest. In keeping with this trend, the *divan* of Hyderabad, Viqār ul-Umarā Bahādur, oversaw the construction of a large palace for himself during the 1890s in the area of Begumpet.[40] Located just north of Hussain Sagar, which was at the time the main source of water for the northern portion of the city, the Minister's Begumpet palace was within view of Secunderabad's military and civil areas to its east and north. While the palace was under construction, Viqar ul-Umara arranged for housing nearby for the large work crews, consisting of several clusters of straw shanties. After the building's completion, however, the dwellings remained in place, now occupied by members of the *divan*'s large core of servants and retainers, and numerous others. The housing provided for the *divan*'s construction workers had become a small village in its own right. During the monsoon season of 1900 Cantonment authorities sought the removal of these residences of Begumpet's laboring classes on the basis that they were in close proximity to Secunderabad and its water supply:

> I have the honor to bring to your notice and request that very early and effectual action be taken with regard thereto – the rapid growth of the hamlets to the west of the Minister's Palace at Begumpett and in the near vicinity of the boundary of the Cantonment of Secunderabad.

[40] On the construction of "suburban palaces" by state nobles during this period see Shah, "Constructing a Capital," ch. 5.

These hamlets were originally isolated groups of straw shanties for the convenience of the large gangs of daily labourers employed on the Minister's Palace above mentioned; and it was tacitly understood that directly the buildings were completed and the work people no longer required, the huts would, one and all, be completely removed.

I have however noticed that such has not been the case, but on the contrary, since the commencement of the wet weather a considerable number of these temporary huts have given place to structures of a more permanent character with tiled roofs &c, and the whole place has therefore become into a regular village, or rather a series of villages.

In the interests of the health of this Cantonment to which this collection of huts is a standing menace, I am to request you to arrange for their prompt removal.[41]

Once again residences of the Nizam's subjects – direct employees of his highest minister – had run afoul of Secunderabad's urban vision. Their "standing menace" to the Cantonment's health dictated, according to the magistrate's logic, that they should be removed immediately.

Within a matter of days after Secunderabad's request Hyderabad officials had begun to plan for the construction of permanent housing and relocation of the *divan*'s employees to another part of Begumpet. Planners and architects in the state's employ, including Mr. G. Rangatham Naidu and Azeez Jung, were commissioned to devise a housing scheme, and over the following three months the Nizam's officials entered into talks with colonial officials to obtain approval for the plans.[42] By December the construction of the houses (between 200 and 300, according to Azeez Jung's count) was underway.[43] However, the Residency immediately raised objections, and dispute ensued between colonial officials in Hyderabad over risks the development might pose to public health:

From the papers before the Resident it would appear that the site selected for the location of the buildings together with the plan were approved by a Committee composed of the Deputy Assistant Adjutant-General, the Cantonment Magistrate, the Staff Surgeon Secunderabad and Nawab Aziz [Azeez] Jung on the 29th August 1900 and the construction of the quarters sanctioned by the General Officer Commanding under certain conditions as to an outfall drain being built.

41 From Captain O. G. Ievers, Cantonment Magistrate and Secretary to Cantonment Commission to Private Secretary to His Highness the Nizam's Minister, Hyderabad, 31 July 1900, "Rapid increase in the number of huts to the west of H.E.'s Palace at Begumpet," APSA 37/1/236, 1900–1903.

42 From Azeez Jung to Faridoonji Jamshedji, 11 August 1900, APSA 37/1/236, 1900–1903.

43 The plan is described in From Nawab Azeez Jung Bahadur, Secretary and Sudder Taluqdar, to His Excellency the Nawab Sir Vikar ul-Umra Bahadur, KCIE to Faridoonji Jamshedji, 3 October 1900. The progress of construction on four of the housing blocks is reported with disapproval in Ievers to Private Sectretary, 3 December 1900. Both files from APSA 37/1/236, 1900–1903.

This drain it appears has not yet been commenced – far less completed – and the danger of pollution to the Hussain Saugor Tank by the unchecked drainage therefore exists in a very *lively* and objectionable form . . . This Residency ought to have been consulted . . . [and] considers it of utmost importance that steps should be taken promptly to prevent the evil effects to be apprehended by the present condition of affairs and has accordingly suggested to the General Officer Commanding that another Commission to be appointed by this Residency, should assemble after consultation with you to consider, in connection with the report of 1899 on the conservancy of the Hussain Saugor tank and all orders bearing on the subject, what steps should be taken to prevent the pollution of the Hussain Saugor tank before the settling in of the rains. I am to express a hope that you will in the meanwhile be so good as to stop all work on the servants quarters until final arrangements are made and executed to prevent the pollution of the tank water.[44]

By the Residency's logic, water purity was critical to the maintenance of public health, and a housing colony without proper drainage posed a direct threat. Exchanges on the matter continued to circulate between Residency, Cantonment, and Hyderabad into late 1902. Asaf Jah officials maintained that providing nearby accommodation for servants was crucial to ensuring proper labor conditions and the smooth operation of the *divan*'s palace. Nevertheless, the completed portions of the housing project were either torn down or converted to non-residential use (as storage go-downs for grain) at the strong insistence of the Resident.

The episode of the Begumpet huts reveals little about the actual sanitary risk posted by servant housing, but much about the power dynamics surrounding sanitation. Colonial authorities' reference to concerns over public health shifted quickly into assertions of authority over the Nizam's sovereign domains (in fact, territories administered as *jagir* holdings of a state official, a point which will warrant further consideration). However, unlike the above instances of intransigence or outright resistance to colonial urbanist initiatives, this case played out with Hyderabad officials capitulating to, possibly accepting, the principle of maintaining a clean water supply through sanitary housing with effective drainage. Such ideas no doubt informed the later public housing initiatives carried out by the Hyderabad CIB considered in the previous chapter. The immediate result of this Raj–Nizam confluence of interests was an extensive, and no doubt expensive, project spearheaded by the Minister to provide convenient and well-equipped public housing to the laborers who stood to be displaced by Secunderabad's fiat.[45] The colonial urban

44 From Resident Haig to Sir Viqar al-Umara Bahadur KCIE, 25 March 1901, APSA 37/1/236, 1900–1903, emphasis in original.

45 One description gives accounts of the cattle-sheds and "kabutar-khanas" (pigeon houses) that were part of the housing development. These inclusions were probably in

vision in this instance centered on maintaining a clean water supply for soldiers and civil officers, as well as unsullied vistas for Europeans around the Hussain Sagar area. Hyderabadi urban officials seem to have accepted the first principle (if not necessarily the second), but also placed a premium upon providing livable housing to subjects of the state and employees of the *divan*. Following a logic described above in reference to agricultural revenues of the Nizam's subjects, acceptable labor and living conditions of the populace figured as a precondition to the health of the state and the comfort of its nobles. In rhetoric at least, Hyderabad officials opposed the abstract standards of public health owing to their ostensible concern for subjects' working and living conditions. Official advocacy of the urban working class would have served, perhaps crucially in the making of the case, to provide reliable labor to Hyderabad's highest minister. Nevertheless, the formation of a competing urbanist rhetoric with which to oppose colonial encroachment, however unstable and improvised, elucidates the emerging terms of urbanist discourse.

This incident provides a useful position from which to reconsider the relationship between sovereignty over space as an abstract political category and the role of states in determining the contours of everyday life of their subject populations. In a pithy report produced during the conflict over the huts in Begumpet, the chief engineer of the general branch of Hyderabad's Public Works Department stated:

> As regards [the] suggestion that the Cantonment Authorities should exercise sanitary jurisdiction in the Begampet village, I am afraid it cannot be adopted as Begampet is a Jagheer village belonging to the Minister, and Cantonment jurisdiction has never been exercised there. From what I know of the Minister, he will undoubtedly be very glad himself to take all measures to keep the village in a thoroughly sanitary condition. To my knowledge there is a sufficient conservance establishment employed in that village.[46]

This brief statement demonstrates several of the key means by which Hyderabad tended to present its positions to the colonial state. The report was authored by J. B. Buchanan, a European employee of Hyderabad, and he elucidated the complicated land-tenure situation in the state whereby

part to satisfy the *divan*'s dairy needs and aviary diversions (keeping passenger pigeons was a common pursuit for much of South Asia's Islamicate elite), but no doubt these would have also provided milk and amusement to the residents of the buildings. These elements of the housing development are noted in Resident to Maharaja Kishen Pershad Bahadur, Private Secretary to His Excellency the Minister, 30 September 1902, APSA 37/1/236, 1900–1903.

46 Copy of report sent to Private Secretary to His Excellency the Minister by [J.B.] Buchanan Chief Engineer, General Branch, Public Works Department of His Highness the Nizam's Government, 17 June 1901, APSA 37/1/236, 1900–1903.

the area in question was under the *divan*'s direct control. Buchanan noted the *divan*'s jurisdiction as a means to absolve Hyderabad of responsibility to implement a British initiative. Critically here, Buchanan pointed out that the principles of modern public health the colonial state sought to implement were also the brief of Hyderabad and the Asaf Jah *divan*, and that sanitary arrangements were already in place.

The underlying ends of modern urbanism – in this instance, maintaining a clean water supply – were a shared concern of both Raj and Nizam, according to Buchanan's report. As such, formalizing the transgression of Hyderabad's sovereignty in Begumpet by granting the Cantonment "sanitary jurisdiction" was not necessary or expedient. Hyderabad's claim to speak for the goals of public health in the city was a tactic to advance an Asaf Jahi iteration of modern urbanism without Raj interference. If the colonial assumption of sovereignty in this domain could be fended off, then Hyderabad could maintain control, and ostensibly ensure sanitary conditions without patrimonial obligations, such as housing for urban laborers. This kind of negotiation served to provide the state with sufficient autonomy to improvise its own urbanism on the fringes of colonial territory in the sub-imperial state. That retaining the Begumpet housing project for Viqar ul-Umara's employees was not a successful venture does not obviate the validity of Hyderabad's strategy, and in other instances these techniques were effective in providing a space for the state's own urban initiatives. Decades later, when decolonization was in the offing and the return of Secunderabad to the Nizam was being considered, the Resident himself expressed some misgivings regarding the often excessive transgressions of sovereignty:

> On the very few occasions when we have [returned territory to Hyderabad from the Cantonment], this Resident has usually resisted such requests, in order to avoid creating undesirable pockets of State jurisdiction in the midst of the Administered Areas, using the arguments that the land is still required for "subsidiary military purposes," i.e. strategic and sanitary. The argument has perhaps occasionally been somewhat unduly stretched.[47]

In the era of imperial dissolution, colonial officials conceded that sanitary arguments had been an alibi for asserting urban power over and against Hyderabad's sovereign claims to the city.

[47] Proposed rendition of a portion of the Secunderabad Cantonment to His Exalted Highness the Nizam's Government, 27 July 1938 Resident (Confidential) at Hyderabad "Secunderabad Cantonment: Proposed partial retrocession of jurisdiction to Nizam's Govt," Political (Internal) Department, Hyderabad, OIOC L/P&S/13/1230, 1937–1946.

## Conflict and collaboration over public health

The discourse of public health, emerging in the subcontinent during the late nineteenth and early twentieth centuries, served a number of different functions in Hyderabad. It was a way for the Raj to exert extraterritorial authority beyond the formal boundaries of the Cantonment itself and into neighboring suburban villages either controlled directly by the Nizam or in the hands of his nobles. Extraterritorial authority was claimed in some cases to guard against disease or pestilence in the Cantonment and threat to the cleanliness of water sources. In other cases, however, the Cantonment Authority's overtures to maintaining health and sanitation within a variously defined radius of Secunderabad suggests a developing struggle over the aesthetics and social implications of the twin cities' expanding peri-urban fringe. Secunderabad policy was designed to prevent increase in population, to maintain clear lines of separation between different types of people and activities, and to render the city legible to the colonial disciplinary gaze. Accordingly, Raj officials opposed construction of housing for marginal populations (spaces of dwelling such as huts, public housing), institutions around which city-dwellers would cluster (spaces of worship), or edifices needed for cultivation and harvest of agricultural produce (spaces of labor) near the Cantonment. The discourse of public health by Secunderabad officials authorized the extension of colonial power beyond the Cantonment and into the Nizam's domains. The resistance of Hyderabad officials, from local revenue or police functionaries up to top-ranking administrators, indicates an emerging contestation over both urban aesthetics in Hyderabad–Secunderabad and the position of government towards the city's population.

There were other instances where colonial public health initiatives in the city were taken as exemplary models by Hyderabad officials. In 1920 the Resident communicated to Hyderabad official Nizamat Jung Bahadur:

> I am desired to inform you that the Medical Officer in charge, Cantonment Hospital, Bolarum, reports that there is a woman in the village of Lothkunta in the Cantonment of Secunderabad suffering from leprosy and considers her likely to be a source of danger to the troops of the vicinity. As Lothkunta is one of the Hyderabad villages situated in the Secunderabad Cantonment, I am to request you kindly to arrange for the removal of the woman from the village to any place 5 miles outside the Cantonment boundary.[48]

[48] Resident (D.S. Mackenzie) to Nizamat Jung Bahadur, 10 August 1920, "Removal of a woman suffering from leprosy from the village of Loth Kunta to any place 5 miles outside the Cantonment boundary," APSA 37/1/475, 1920.

This was a case within the Cantonment, an area over which Hyderabad had long since ceded jurisdiction to the colonial establishment. Lothkunta, however, was one of the villages under Hyderabadi control within the precincts of the Cantonment, and accordingly the Resident was obliged to contact the Nizam's officials to obtain leave to remove the leper. Hyderabad immediately acceded to the Cantonment's request in this instance, and directed for her to be removed to an asylum for lepers in Dichpalli, some 100 miles distant, in the Nizamabad province of Hyderabad State.[49] In terms of the official exchange, this is an instance in which the public health imperatives of the Raj matched those of the Nizam, and indeed the notion of keeping a leper safely outside a dense urban settlement continuous with the non-colonial areas of the city was recognized as a shared concern. A marginal note, initialed by Nizamat Jung, reveals another telling element of the incident:

> What about lepers so often seen in Hyderabad? If the Government can take action at the behest of the Cantonment authorities, certainly they can with regards of the Hyderabad problem as well. Ask the Judicial what arrangements, if any, have been made for the removal of lepers from inhabited areas of the City and Suburbs.[50]

The Minister's line of questioning and subsequent planning reveal the extent to which colonial allopathic medical ideas about sanitary living conditions and how to regulate epidemic diseases were shared by the highest Hyderabad officials. In several other cases (such as those in Thokatta, Maredpalli, and Begumpet above) Hyderabad opposed demands that Raj officials put forward in the name of public health. The quarantining of lepers, however, the Asaf Jah state saw as worth pursuing.[51]

## "Sanitary jurisdiction" as urban power

The uneven extension of public health projects in South Asia has been understood by some as a product of imperial caution in an unstable empire. Writing on British India, Mark Harrison argued that before World War I public health measures were enacted only on a very limited basis in areas under colonial administration.[52] He argued that

[49] From Nizamat Jung to Evans at Residency, 25 October 1920, APSA 37/1/475, 1920.
[50] Handwritten note initialed "NJ" in the margins of Hyderabad's copy of ibid.
[51] On the later Hyderabad-funded expansion of the Mission Leper Home and Hospital in Dichpalli to accommodate over 700 patients see Hyderabad, *Economic Life of Hyderabad*, 153.
[52] Mark Harrison, *Public Health in British India: Anglo-Indian Preventive Medicine, 1859–1914* (Cambridge University Press, 1994).

enforcement of sanitary regulations was largely restricted to British-occupied areas and military cantonments. Harrison attributed what he suggests was a failure of the colonial state to extend public health regulations into native society to intransigence on the part of the British Indian public and reluctance of the British, in the wake of the events of 1857, to offend "deep-rooted religious and cultural practices."[53] Harrison downplayed the functioning of public health measures as a "tool of empire." The embattled and economically strained later Raj was in a position to deploy the instrument of sanitary power only to a limited extent.[54] Even as British Indian subjects were empowered to join the Indian Medical Services and increased their roles in municipal government during the interwar years, public health measures made only "slow progress."[55] Harrison concluded by suggesting that "improvements in public health depended on active co-operation between colonial officials and indigenous peoples," and limited state financial commitment combined with the broader racist underpinnings of the colonial project to undercut expansion of sanitary governance.[56]

As has been the line of argument throughout this book, it is necessary to analytically disaggregate sub-imperial states such as Hyderabad from British India as a whole. Comparison of the conflicts that emerged in both settings can result in fresh insights on British India as well. Harrison's emphasis on the broader economic and political contexts of colonial rule is instructive here. If the Raj's rigid racial hierarchy precluded sanitary collaboration between colonizer and colonized there, the divergent configuration of sovereignty in Hyderabad engendered other possibilities. Attention to the spatially diverse distribution of political authority in South Asia helps to identify the complex dynamics in Hyderabad, whereby Asaf Jah officials were keen to follow thorough on initiatives such as the quarantining of lepers from urban areas (Nizamat Jung's envy of the Cantonment initiative in this regard is striking here). An analysis of the structures of formal urban power in specific contexts (Hyderabad, British Indian cities) shows how public health fitted into the matrix.

Harrison claimed that the central focus of his book was the role of medicine as a "colonizing discourse" and "an instrument of 'social control' in the colony," but ultimately, "the desire to control and contain the indigenous population was checked by the political and economic imperatives of colonial rule."[57] This formulation follows from an overall

[53] Ibid., 87. [54] Ibid., 228–29. [55] Ibid., 233. [56] Ibid., 234.

[57] Ibid., 3. For a contrasting take on colonial health policy in South Asia as oriented toward British interests to the detriment of the subject population see Radhika Ramasubban, "Imperial Health in British India, 1857–1900," in *Disease, Medicine, and Empire: Perspectives on Western Medicine and the Experience of European Expansion*, ed. Roy Macleod and Milton Lewis (London: Routledge, 1988), 38–60.

understanding of the colonial state in South Asia as an insecure governing body struggling to maintain its position. Accordingly, efforts to assert power in various arenas (here, to make cities 'healthy' places) were circumscribed by the state's need to maintain popular consent. Other scholars have emphasized the extent to which the discourse of public health was itself a vector of colonial power. Medical and scientific discourses such as public health were central to the thoroughgoing attempts of the state to render populations into governable colonial subjects.[58] As Hyderabad makes clear, however, it is crucial to distinguish between instances where specific public health initiatives were seen as disruptive to established and necessary everyday practices, and moments in which projects were seen as largely progressive and on balance beneficial to the livelihood of communities. Detailing these contexts allows one to identify places and moments in which colonial medical knowledge served as a means to assert social control over populations, and other contexts in which these projects were less embroiled in contestations over control of South Asian bodies and lives, labor, dwelling, and worship.

Hyderabad City and its environs suggest a revealing alternative perspective on the role of colonial medical discourses in South Asia. The emergent political sphere of the urban was subject here to a 'native' state with a significant degree of sovereignty and ability to exercise considerable power in defense of its subjects, government interests, and their own visions of progress. In Harrison's estimation the British Indian scene was defined by a "modernizing" colonial state constrained by the idea or fact of popular opposition. South Asian municipal or medical officials appear as impediments to the expansion of crucial sanitary reforms rather than active players in the making of urban power, and interests cancel one another out in the urban scene.

The history of Hyderabad and Secunderabad provides examples of contestations between multiple sovereign bodies over who had the authority to oversee public health measures, even when their ends were often a matter of consensus. If British India were viewed from the perspective of the municipality, where South Asians had considerable political authority by the 1880s, perhaps multiple foundations of urban power would be visible as well. Such a picture is surely obscured by the enduring fact that, in colonial cities, only the Raj possessed formal political sovereignty and could mobilize a coherent urban vision and authoritatively legislate spatial practices. Within an urban world subject to this vision, sanitary power appears one-dimensional: as a vector of

[58] Prakash, *Another Reason*; David Arnold, *Colonizing the Body: State Medicine and Epidemic Disease in Nineteenth-Century India* (Berkeley: University of California Press, 1993) and *Science, Technology and Medicine in Colonial India* (Cambridge University Press, 2000).

colonial power. A view from a sovereign fragment suspended in the web of empire suggests alternative genealogies of urbanism.

Hyderabad State had its own urban vision – a contingent and improvised one that emerged on the margins of the project of British India's urbanism, to be sure – and if colonial ideas about how to shape a healthy city came in conflict with it, they were opposed.

## Urbanism improvised

In his provocative study of colonial urbanism in Morocco under the French Protectorate, Paul Rabinow sketched out a dynamic scenario by which a planned cordon sanitaire between the modern European city and the native medina in Rabat "served not only as a safety zone and segregative space, but as an intercultural meeting ground."[59] This improvisational urban space, according to Rabinow, allowed for a blurring of boundaries between social groups, and collaboration between French planners and Moroccan emperors. Casting his take on Morocco as a critique of what Janet Abu-Lughod had previously dubbed a "theater of apartheid," Rabinow's corrective maintains: "one could just as aptly call this space a theatralization of urban diversity."[60] If for Abu-Lughod the French colonial presence in Morocco meant restriction of native agency and economic marginalization, for Rabinow the socially and culturally productive character of the liminal spaces between the constituent European and native segments of the city was a key locus of the complexity of the colonial encounter there.

The history narrated here of modern Hyderabad City's formative period around the turn of the twentieth century presents a scenario where formal political sovereignty was held by either colonizers or non-colonial officials (or subordinate nobles) in different parts of the city. In treating this complex situation I have followed seeming contradictory critical paths, guided by evidence of Hyderabad or Secunderabad urbanist policy and practice. Accordingly, I have emphasized moments of conflict over emerging urban spaces between British Indian and Hyderabadi authorities, the ways in which ordinary residents of the area were affected, and the improvisational character by which spaces of urban diversity were negotiated in the expanding northern portion of Hyderabad City.

The discourse of colonial urbanism, often expressed in the language of public health, inscribed a circle of negotiated sovereignty around the

[59] Paul Rabinow, *French Modern: Norms and Forms of the Social Environment* (Cambridge, MA: MIT Press, 1989), ch. 9, here 299.

[60] Ibid.; Janet Abu-Lughod, *Rabat: Urban Apartheid in Morocco* (Princeton University Press, 1980).

Cantonment varying from quarter of a mile, to two miles for prickly pears, to five miles for lepers, to unknown distances when the purity of the water supply was in question. In doing so the colonial state planned a cordon sanitare that it sought to enforce in various ways, but ended up creating an "intercultural meeting ground." The context of the expanding peri-urban fringe on the frontier of colonial and Hyderabadi urban settlements was framed within the emergence of cities as loci for political negotiation globally, and in imperial contexts in particular. The space for negotiation within the British Indian municipal sphere was constrained by the continuing fact of racially ordered and formally unitary colonial sovereignty. Administration of Secunderabad's military Cantonment represented perhaps an extreme form of this dynamic. Raj officials there advocated a clear and consistent policy of colonial urbanism centered on an aesthetic valuing clear lines of separation between races, classes, and different activities within the city. The Nizam's officials often drew upon emerging global urbanist principles, such as public health, at times by collaborating in implementing colonial projects in the city. Hyderabad's own urbanist program entailed opposition to the Raj's demands if and when they came into conflict with the Nizam's sovereign control over part of the city. Core Hyderabadi urbanist principles also began to take shape. Herein, defending the public good meant protecting urban dwellers' access and control over spaces of labor, dwelling, and worship in the city. Conflicts and collaborations at the intersection of colonial and non-colonial physical spaces on the peri-urban fringe of Hyderabad–Secunderabad suggest that such meeting-grounds could be key spaces where overlapping but often incompatible visions of the modern South Asian city were negotiated and improvised.

# Conclusion: fragmented sovereignty in a world of nation-states

> If I understand the representative of the Netherlands rightly, he conceives of a State in an absolute, monistic sense – it is either a sovereign State or it is not a State at all. It is either black or white, in his view there are no greys. I believe that for modern needs we have to conceive of a State in a more elastic way; it may qualify as a State in certain respects, but not in others. – Ambassador Tsiang of China, 1947[1]

The years following World War II constituted a crucible moment for the making of the global state system, a process with dire consequences for Hyderabad and other minor states. This Conclusion tracks global political changes by which state sovereignty came to be conceived within a "monistic," zero-sum logic; the particular dynamics shaping political possibilities in South Asia; and contemplates ways around analytical barricades that these trends constitute.

As the Chinese ambassador's statement above suggests, UN debates circled around definitions of political sovereignty. His plea for more elastic conceptions of what constituted stateness succeeded in this instance: representatives of the Republic of Indonesia won the ability to present before the United Nations Security Council (UNSC) even before formal independence from the Netherlands. The UN's management of the worldwide post-imperial transition did much to shape the contours of the global state system. Stateness was coming to unambiguously mean territorial and independent nation-state status or reasonable expectation of rapid progress to that end (as with Indonesia). This rigid definition of sovereign statehood, which restricted participation in internationalist bodies, had a cataclysmic impact on the global configuration of fragmented sovereignty that this book has described.

After Hyderabad's 1948 integration into the Republic of India, remaining representatives of the Asaf Jah state sought to bring a case of violation

[1] Official Records, Security Council [ORSC], 2nd Year, 181st Meeting, 12 August 1947, UN S/PV.181, p. 1935. This statement came in a debate about whether Indonesia, at the time a Dutch colony, was qualified to appear before the Security Council.

of sovereignty before the UNSC, as discussed in Chapter 2. Hyderabad's representative Moin Nawaz Jung, from exile in Karachi, argued stridently that the Nizam's state was "an independent Government exercising normal governmental functions in all their plenitude."[2] In support of his petition Nawaz Jung cited Hyderabad's size and full complement of modern political institutions, and the contents of treaties with the Mughals and the British; referenced authorities such as Sir Henry Maine; invoked the 1933 Pan-American Convention; and drew comparisons to UNSC seating of representatives from Transjordan and Indonesia before these were recognized by UN member states as independent polities.[3] The 1948 UNSC debates echo some of these positions: the US representative criticized India for compelling Hyderabad's accession with violent military force, and Argentina compared these actions to fascist Italy's march on Addis Ababa.[4] In 1949 a defensive Netherlands, still combating anticolonial opposition in the Dutch East Indies, referenced India's disregard for Hyderabadi sovereignty in justifying theirs for Indonesia's, and drew a parallel between Indian dismissal of the Nizam's administrators and USSR suppression of dissenting officials.[5]

The postcolonial Indian position, that Hyderabad was "not a State in the international sense" before or after 1948, and was rather an integral part of India's domestic geography, prevailed in the UN.[6] The Hyderabad representative was never seated, and when in May 1949 Pakistan put forward the Nizam's claim for violation of sovereignty, "not a member of the Security Council said a word."[7] Subsequent appeals in the UN – Moin Nawaz Jung's December 1949 declaration of a Hyderabad government in exile, later Pakistani attempts to raise the case – were moot.[8] Hyderabad's claims to sovereignty and recent status as a formally autonomous state had no currency in the new world order's dominant international organization.

The legal geography of fragmented sovereignty that accommodated minor states, with their ambivalent autonomy and alternative temporalities, was phased out in the post-World War II consolidation of the global

2 Hyderabad, Delegation, *Hyderabad Question*, 2.
3 Ibid., 2, 13. See 48–51 for extensive data on the state, similar to some of the accounts of Hyderabad's modernization composed by state bureaucrat-intellectuals discussed in Chapter 4 above.
4 ORSC 3rd Year, 359th Meeting, 20 September 1948, UN S/PV.359, 4–5, 7–9.
5 ORSC 4th Year, 400th Meeting, 14 January 1949, UN S/PV.400, 6.
6 Eagleton, "The Case of Hyderabad," 280.
7 Ibid., 299. See transcript, UN S/PV.425. ORSC 4th Year, 425th Meeting, 19 May 1949.
8 ORSC 12th Year, 761st Meeting, 16 January 1957, UN S/PV.761, 5–6; ORSC 20th Year, 1244th Meeting, 22 September 1965, UN S/PV.1244(OR), 2.

state system. Other developments have rendered the story of Hyderabad told in the foregoing chapters an "unthinkable history," whose implications are difficult to imagine.[9] Retrieving obscured pasts – Trouillot's Haitian Revolution built on non-European intellectual foundations, Hyderabad as sovereign Muslim modernist state – is made difficult by powerful historiographical impediments.

In Hyderabad widespread violence from the end of World War II through 1948 (and after) has powerfully inflected historical and popular narratives. Bloodshed at the hands of the Razakar Muslim chauvinist militia (affiliated to the MIM, and claiming to represent the Nizam's interests), and Hindu majoritarian militia violence and official Indian military force (cast as retaliatory violence), have associated the Asaf Jahi past with an ahistorical image of Muslim despotism.[10] This image has made the everyday political workings of Hyderabad State difficult to visualize.

Accounts of buried pasts, such as that of Hyderabad presented here, provide a departure point for counter-histories that denaturalize received historical narratives or the concepts they are founded upon. As a sovereign state in a largely colonized South Asia, the Asaf Jah state incubated distinct intellectual, political, institutional, judicial, social, urban, spatial, and everyday worlds. In New Historicist scholarship the meticulously presented, obscure, cryptic historical anecdote represents a "miniature completeness . . . that necessarily interrupts the continuous flow of larger histories."[11] The anecdote constitutes an analytical position from which to undermine "epochal truths," first puncturing received narratives, then recontextualizing, and developing new rough teleologies informed by the contingency and diversity of historical experience in the minor. Similarly, the "compact wholeness" of late Asaf Jah Hyderabad, a 'minor' state compared to 'major' empires or nation-states, makes visible the textural heterogeneity in the South Asian and global political landscape. Reflection upon and recasting of South Asian and global histories

[9] See "An Unthinkable History: The Haitian Revolution as a Non-Event," ch. 3 in Michel-Rolph Trouillot, *Silencing the Past: Power and the Production of History* (Boston: Beacon, 1995).

[10] On failed political negotiations and violence in late Asaf Jah Hyderabad and integration into India see, *inter alia*, Benichou, *Autocracy to Integration*; Pernau, *Passing of Patrimonialism*, chs. 5–6; A. G. Noorani, *The Destruction of Hyderabad* (New Delhi: Tulika, 2013). For assessments of the violence of Hyderabad's integration attentive to postcolonial Indian political dynamics see Taylor C. Sherman, *State Violence and Punishment in India* (London: Routledge, 2010), ch. 9; Purushotham, "Internal Violence"; Sunil Purushotham, "Destroying Hyderabad and Making the Nation," *Economic and Political Weekly* 49.22 (2014): 29–33.

[11] Gallagher and Greenblatt, *Practicing New Historicism*, 49–50.

in the late imperial era requires revisiting the many aspects of the life of the state presented here to conceive Hyderabad as historical object.

In tying together the many threads elaborated in this book, this Conclusion surveys the historical and conceptual landscapes of the late imperial world of fragmented sovereignty as seen from Hyderabad. It starts with an account of the end of the Nizam's state and the dismantling of the sustaining global legal architecture, and goes on to consider the forms of South Asian political solidarity that have made the minor state's history difficult to conceive. I then present a summary description of the Hyderabadi political languages and practices visible in the Nizam's state (patrimonial, modernist, Muslim internationalist, polyglot, multi-religious, territorially ambivalent), and discuss their institutional and discursive legacies. Finally, opening up to broader terrains, I reflect on the book's historiographical implications for conceptualizing the political pasts, and futures, of Hyderabad, South Asia, and the world.

## Closures

Hyderabad's status as a state, and the political ideas and institutional practices that constituted it, depended on the late imperial geographies described in this book. The global political configuration of minor states in a world of fragmented sovereignty (Chapter 1) relied on an ambivalent legal architecture that created openings for claims to parity and the practice of political autonomy (Chapter 2). These flexible frameworks, which prevailed from the late nineteenth through mid-twentieth centuries, enabled state bureaucrat-intellectuals to establish a place within moral and conceptual geographies of South Asia (Chapter 3), and to develop widespread connections to protean internationalist networks (Chapter 4). In turn, the minor state became a site of political alterity and venue for institutional experimentation, manifest in distinctive political, material, and social worlds, located in rural areas beyond colonial frontiers (Chapters 5 and 6) and in urban Hyderabad (Chapters 7 and 8). Decisive mid-twentieth-century changes spelled the end of minor statehood, and with it the institutional practices, political discourses, and social worlds Hyderabad contained. This section traces global shifts that reconfigured geographies, and corresponding dynamics in South Asian and Muslim politics.

### *The legal framework of sovereignty disavowed*

Anti-colonial nationalists and postcolonial politicians promoted nation-states as avatars of virtuous bygone polities after illegitimate imperial rule.[12] Nevertheless, international bodies seldom recognized post-imperial statehood claims as "reversion" to "original sovereignty."[13] Advocates of Hyderabad's UN case contended that the Nizam had been sovereign before the emergence of the Raj, and hedged bets by referencing treaties ostensibly enacted between sovereign entities.[14] During the late imperial era such arguments provided Hyderabadi officials and activists with political leverage, and gave the state domains of autonomy. Following decolonization and the 1948 invasion of the Nizam's territories the Indian nation-state headed off such challenges and integrated Hyderabad.[15]

If military force was one component of India's takeover of Hyderabad, diplomatic power provided a decisive instrument for undermining legal claims and the competing visions of sovereignty they represented. The UN was one forum where India fortified its position as sole legitimate sovereign within their new borders. Other international configurations, such as the 1955 Bandung Afro-Asian States Conference and the Non-Aligned Movement after 1961, facilitated aggressive moves to consolidate postcolonial unitary state sovereignty. When faced with claims for regional autonomy or independence, India and other 'new states' deployed military force, then leveraged international support to undermine opposition.[16]

The new international order provided diplomatic support for state consolidation measures that had been impractical or impossible during late imperialism. After decolonization India used coercion to liquidate competing sovereign claims from former sub-imperial states such as Hyderabad, Junagadh, and Travancore.[17] The postcolonial state proceeded to iron out wrinkles in the national fabric by disregarding special constitutional provisions granted to Kashmir, and formally integrating regions under other legal or sovereign regimes (Goa was taken from the Portuguese in 1961, Sikkim's monarchy was abolished in 1975). Different trajectories are visible in other locations in Asia and Africa where minor states were incorporated into new nation-states. In Hyderabad

12 Anderson, *Imagined Communities*; Chatterjee, *The Nation and its Fragments*, chs. 4, 5.
13 Alexandrowicz, "New and Original States."
14 Hyderabad, Delegation, *Hyderabad Question.*
15 Purushotham, "Internal Violence."
16 With reference to mobilizations in Highland Asian regions including Kashmir, Northeast India, Highland Burma, and Tibet see John D. Kelly, "Nehru, Bandung, and the Fate of Highland Asia" (Mary Keating Das Lecture, Columbia University, New York, 2013).
17 For survey treatment see Ramachandra Guha, *India after Gandhi: The History of the World's Largest Democracy* (New York: Ecco, 2007).

military force combined with diplomatic support, and international law enabled India's disavowal then obliteration of the Nizam's sovereign claims. Political dynamics in postcolonial India have undermined the conceptual and structural foundations of state legitimacy that characterized sub-imperial Hyderabad.

### *Unitary nationalism, linguistic states*

The excision of a sovereign Hyderabad from South Asia's political landscape accompanied the disappearance of narratives of Asaf Jahi legitimacy. The Nizam's state had been a venue for articulating a range of political ethics grounded in regional and global geographical visions. Hyderabad's minor sovereignty was enabled by an overarching British imperial suzerainty that left room for internal spaces of formal political autonomy. The intensively centralized Indian national state, and the emergence of linguistic community as basis for provincial political solidarity, rendered many narratives about Hyderabad archaic or threatening.

The unitary idiom of governance that dominated the postcolonial context slotted alternative political narratives and practices into set places in hierarchically ordered national state space. Whereas Hyderabadi bureaucrat-intellectuals had conceived of the state within internationalist networks not necessarily mediated by British India, the nation-state required a uniform geography composed of subordinate and bounded territorial entities. The temporal heterogeneity and expansive web of connections that constituted Hyderabad's political structure had to be eliminated or consolidated into homogeneous and regular state spaces.

The violent nature of Hyderabad's integration, and the contours of the postcolonial political landscape, cut officials and elites of the erstwhile sub-imperial state out of the political scene. Some Hyderabadi officials and the institutional knowledges they embodied joined postcolonial national or provincial service, but most were disenfranchised. Many state officials were imprisoned upon India's conquest of Hyderabad, and military entrepreneurs tied into the patrimonial system were deported.[18] In the years after integration into ostensibly secular but Hindu-majority India, many of the Muslim intelligentsia – who had formed at least half

[18] On imprisonment of officials, Hyderabad, Delegation, *Hyderabad Question*, x, 298–99. On attempts to deport Arabs and Rohillas, Sherman, "Migration, Citizenship and Belonging."

of Hyderabad's administration following World War II – emigrated out of Hyderabad, as had been the case in North Indian cities such as Lucknow and Delhi.[19] The rise of majoritarian linguistic politics in defining India's internal political structure was also decisive in marginalizing the polyglot political legacy of Hyderabad.

Provincial spheres provided scope for the articulation of a variety of positions or agendas.[20] However, the linguistic community orientation of provincial politics foreclosed possibilities of Hyderabad's continuing salience. Cultural difference within the nation-state was permissible, even celebrated as diversity, but could only be politically enacted along defined lines. Linguistic states emerged by the 1950s and 1960s as a template for India's internal political structure, and existing or proposed provinces became idioms for expressing varied demands.

The rise to dominance of linguistic provincial idioms shaped the afterlife of what had been the Nizam's territories in multiple ways. On the rhetorical level, the polyglot, multi-religious, internationalist, cosmopolitan discourse of Hyderabadi legitimacy had little relevance in a framework where provincial autonomy claims were made in the name of linguistic majorities.[21] Territorially, Hyderabad State initially remained an administrative unit in India, but was broken down into linguistic components in the decade after India's creation. Andhra State became the first linguistic province in postcolonial India in 1953, formed from the majority Telugu-speaking districts of Madras State (formerly British India's Madras Presidency). This event preceded mobilizations across India for statehood status on the part of numerically dominant linguistic groups. The 1956 States Reorganisation Act carved out several new provinces in the Deccan. The Kannada-speaking majority districts of Hyderabad State joined an expanded Mysore (later renamed Karnataka). Marathwada, the Marathi-speaking majority districts of Hyderabad became

[19] Karen Isaksen Leonard, *Locating Home: India's Hyderabadis Abroad* (Stanford University Press, 2007); Syed Ali, "'Go West Young Man': The Culture of Migration among Muslims in Hyderabad, India," *Journal of Ethnic and Migration Studies* 33.1 (2007): 37–58. On Partition-era population shifts in the north, see *inter alia*, Vazira Fazila-Yacoobali Zamindar, *The Long Partition and the Making of Modern South Asia: Refugees, Boundaries, Histories* (New York: Columbia University Press, 2007); Neeti Nair, *Changing Homelands: Hindu Politics and the Partition of India* (Cambridge, MA: Harvard University Press, 2011).

[20] Guha, *India after Gandhi*, chs. 14–17. On "subnationalism" in the northeast see Sanjib Baruah, *India Against Itself: Assam and the Politics of Nationality* (Philadelphia: University of Pennsylvania Press, 1999).

[21] On cosmopolitanism in Hyderabad state and city see D. Parthasarathy, "Fasting, Mining, Politicking? Telangana and the Burdens of History," *eSocialSciences* (2010), available at www.esocialsciences.com/eSSResearchPapers/displayArticles.asp?aid=90.

part of polyglot Bombay State in 1956, then in 1960 a part of the linguistic state Maharashtra.[22]

In 1956 Telangana, the majority Telugu-speaking region of Hyderabad State, was combined with the ex-Madras districts to form Andhra Pradesh. Hyderabad became capital of this expanded Telugu-speaking province, which triggered a continuous influx to the city of professionals and agrarian capitalists from the ex-Madras, formerly British-ruled districts, and especially Coastal Andhra.[23] This immigration, combined with the earlier outflow or disenfranchisement of former Asaf Jah officials and elites, set in motion a transformation of Hyderabad's political culture. The globally mediated, polyglot, multi-religious, cosmopolitan imaginaries that characterized Asaf Jahi political culture were superseded by parochial idioms of solidarity between predominantly Hindu Telugu speakers.

### *Provincializing Muslim politics*

Even before linguistic majoritarianism emerged as the prime idiom of provincial politics, late colonial and early postcolonial politicians constructed the subcontinent's political architecture around the presumption that religious community units were the basis of political community. As Chapter 4 argued, late imperial and nationalist politics combined with global trends to contain Muslim internationalism within discrete territorial units. At the same time, Hyderabad's cosmopolitan and modernist affinities were superseded by increasingly exclusivist, conservative political aspirations aimed at Muslim political dominance in the subcontinent. The afterlives and transformations of Hyderabadi Muslim political thought were distinct in the two postcolonial nation-states that became home to bureaucrat-intellectuals from the erstwhile Nizam's state.

In India, Pakistan's presence as an 'Islamic state' and national antagonist put pressure on Muslim political mobilization. Politicians tended to be integrated within existing national or regional political parties, or operate minor opposition parties. Transregional Muslim political movements, marked as seditious and anti-national, were often radicalized or driven underground.

22 Guha, *India after Gandhi*, ch. 8; Joseph E. Schwartzberg, "Factors in the Linguistic Reorganization of Indian States," in *Region and Nation in India*, ed. Paul Wallace (New Delhi: Oxford University Press, 1985), 155–82.

23 D. Parthasarathy, "Rural, Urban, and Regional: Re-Spatializing Capital and Politics in India," in *Cleavage, Connection and Conflict in Rural, Urban and Contemporary Asia*, ed. Tim Bunnell, D. Parthasarathy, and Eric C. Thompson (Dordrecht: Springer Netherlands, 2013), 15–30.

Many Hyderabadi officials and elites migrated to Pakistan, as did other Muslim political thinkers from regions that became part of India. Much of Pakistan's postcolonial history has been characterized by attempts to quell dissension from marginalized regional or linguistic groups through heavy-handed state centralization, military deployment, and, by the late 1970s, highly conservative and exclusivist official definitions of Islam. The state's turn to the idea of 'Islamic' statecraft resulted in the canalization of Muslim politics to conform to official nationalist definitions. These dynamics alienated intellectuals in Pakistan, some Hyderabadi, who saw Muslim statecraft as conducive to an inclusive, diverse society based on cosmopolitan notions of citizenship.[24]

In both India and Pakistan changing scales and official constraints on effective political discourse left little space for globally mediated combinations of discursive elements. Hyderabadi political idioms – Asaf Jahi cosmopolitanism, patrimonialist modernity, Muslim internationalism, eclectic readings of Mughal or Deccani political legacies – and institutional practices did, however, have post-imperial afterlives.

## Legacies

Unlike rulers of some other former South Asian sub-imperial states, the Nizams played little active role in the postcolonial scene, either as symbolic figureheads, rich philanthropists, or provincial political figures.[25] Hyderabad's legacies are visible, rather, in the continuing salience of the modes of statecraft and the political ideas articulated by bureaucrat-intellectuals, and the social effects thereof. Even as the politics of nation-states have effaced the sovereignty and constrained the global intellectual circuits that constituted the Asaf Jah state, aspects of governance practice and political thought resonate in the postcolonial period.

### *State practice and institutional life*

Several Hyderabadi institutions remained intact on varying scales in the Indian republic. Regions of the Nizam's erstwhile state, and its capital city, continue to be shaped by alliances and styles of governance that developed over centuries of Asaf Jahi rule.

[24] Kamran Asdar Ali, "Communists in a Muslim Land: Cultural Debates in Pakistan's Early Years," *Modern Asian Studies* 57.4 (2011): 1068–95; Saadia Toor, *The State of Islam: Culture and Cold War Politics in Pakistan* (London: Pluto Press, 2011); Sarah Waheed, "Radical Politics and the Urdu Literary World in the Era of South Asian Nationalisms c.1919–1952," Ph.D. thesis, Tufts University, 2011, ch. 5.

[25] Ramusack, *Indian Princes*, epilogue.

Chapters 5 and 7 of this book provide accounts of governance practices and political experimentation in rural and urban Hyderabad, respectively, that distinguished the state from neighboring British India. The Republic of India inherited British India's broader political and economic organization.[26] However, institutions, techniques, or tendencies, and some specific figures, that shaped statecraft in Hyderabad continued to play national, regional, and local roles.

Famine relief and state assistance to Dalit and Adivasi communities were cast in a patrimonial framework that emphasized the regime's responsibility to the most economically marginalized sections of the population. Evidence from Hyderabad suggests post-1948 regional institutional continuity in Adivasi policy.[27] The general structure of state welfare projects anticipates postcolonial India's rising focus on developing political mechanisms for economic and political empowerment of marginalized communities.

Hyderabad's welfare projects were strategies for expanding the patrimonial base of state legitimacy or emphasizing the state's egalitarian ethics to observers. Dalit conversions to Islam, many carried out by the Majlis-i Ittihad al-Muslimin (MIM), can be seen as an attempt at building coalitions in support of the Nizam. The Indian Constitution, which integrated late imperial or sub-imperial governance practices, established reservation schemes for advancing Dalit and Adivasi groups within a changed republican, electoral political logic. The emergence since the 1980s of an MIM-led Muslim–Dalit coalition in Hyderabadi urban politics exemplifies the productive legacy of Asaf Jahi political alliances into the postcolonial present.[28]

The urban and state-wide planning regimes that reshaped Hyderabad during the early twentieth century have post-1948 institutional vestiges, as Chapter 7 noted. Former Asaf Jah officials played important roles in the making of Indian professional and government organizations related to urban development and larger-scale planning. Early postcolonial India exhibited a similar official focus on the importance and specific roles of technocrat-administrators, visible urban redevelopment paradigms, and five-year economic planning.

Construction and governance of urban terrain is one marked area of continuity between late Asaf Jah Hyderabad and postcolonial India. Chapter 7 described handovers, in 1935 and 1945, to Hyderabad of previously British-administered spaces of the city, including quarters

[26] Goswami, *Producing India*; Zachariah, *Developing India*; Chibber, *Locked in Place*.

[27] See Chapter 5 on the post-1948 work of von Fürer-Haimendorf's Tribal Welfare Board.

[28] Alam, "Composite Culture."

adjacent to the Raj's Residency and Cantonment establishments. These zones were quickly yoked into Hyderabad City Improvement Board (CIB) development schemes that were framed within a logic of state urban modernist development. Similar trends of the gradual decolonization of municipal power are visible in urban governance in British Indian cities. Transfers of urban areas in late Asaf Jah Hyderabad were, however, legal transactions between two sovereign entities, which were then assumed by the Indian state after 1948. Units of urban governance, such as the CIB and Hyderabad Municipal Corporation, retained administrative structures, agendas, and part of their personnel composition after the state's 1948 integration into India. As work on urban development in late twentieth-century Hyderabad suggests, there was also carryover in terms of logics of intervention.[29] Similar continuities between urbanism and other domains of politics are visible in formerly Raj-ruled places, though these follow global trends of urban change. Nevertheless, institutional connections in Hyderabad underscore the role sub-imperial paradigms played in shaping urban development and governance before and after 1948, and are suggestive of the heterogeneous sources of modern governance in South Asia.

Taken together, modes of institutional development – including elements of experimentation and improvisation – that characterized late imperial Hyderabad State shaped aspects of political life in postcolonial India. Labor connections and remittance of funds from the Persian Gulf, patrimonial links to East Africa and Yemen, and educational migration from Muslim countries to Hyderabad reveal continuing connections. Even as transnational Muslim flows have largely been marginalized on the official level, the cosmopolitan image of the Nizam's state has remained a figure in political discourse.

### *Historical memory in the postcolonial context*

Post-1948 national-level and Deccani regional movements have played on the notion that Asaf Jahi political culture was particularly inclusive when compared to that of the Raj. Representations along these lines use images of Hyderabad's past to make arguments about the nature of Muslim rule, and the status of Muslim populations in India. Another connected rhetorical idiom that invokes images of the Nizam's

[29] Anant Maringanti, "Neoliberal Inscriptions and Contestations in Hyderabad," Ph.D. thesis, University of Minnesota, 2007, ch. 2; Ratna Naidu, *Old Cities, New Predicaments: A Study of Hyderabad* (New Delhi: Sage, 1990); Bhole, *Housing and Urban Development*, 135–41; A. Malla Reddy, *Slum Improvement: The Hyderabad Experience* (Delhi: M.S., 1996).

state is the argument for separate statehood and political autonomy in Telangana.

As with the Mughals, Hyderabad functions as a figure of nostalgia for many South Asian left and secularist intellectuals. Descriptions of Hyderabad's shared Hindu–Muslim "composite culture" emphasize the accommodating and localized character of Muslim rule in the subcontinent. Such accounts serve to critique the historical justifications invoked by the conservative Hindu majoritarian right.[30] The latter cast Muslim rule as oppressive toward Hindus, and present this claim as a reason to question the legitimacy of Indian Muslims as full members of the national community.[31] In contrast, narratives about the Asaf Jah state as a collaborative Muslim–Hindu endeavor and 'progressive' regime situate Indian Muslims at the center of histories of coexistence. Nostalgic historical images of Hyderabad, which often link the early modern Qutb Shahi period with the Asaf Jahs, suggest the relevance of an abstracted version of the Nizam in the contemporary political imagination.

The movement leading up to the division of Telangana from Andhra Pradesh has also provided occasion for discussions of the legacy of the Nizam's rule. As noted above, 1956 saw the dissolution of Hyderabad as a provincial state, and the integration of Telangana, including Hyderabad City, into a linguistic province along with formerly British-ruled districts. Following migration to the new capital from ex-Raj districts, non-Telangana Telugus consolidated domination of state government employment and land and capital markets in Hyderabad City.

The marginalization of Telangana Telugus within Andhra Pradesh provided impetus for a series of mobilizations, starting in the 1960s, but defused through institutional mechanisms or state coercion. Following a new wave of provincial state creation in the subcontinent, the Telangana movement surged in the early 2000s, finally resulting in the formation of Telangana in June 2014.[32] Some pro-Telangana discourse takes on

[30] A recent book critical of the Indian military invasion of Hyderabad led by political leader Sardar Vallabhai Patel provides one example of this potent rhetoric. Note the admiring tone in describing Hyderabad's "composite culture" in Noorani, *The Destruction of Hyderabad*, and coverage of the book release "Sardar Patel a 'Hindu Nationalist' Hated Hyderabadi Culture, Says Noorani," *India Today* (November 30, 2013) and "Sardar Patel Hated Hyderabadi Culture: AG Noorani," *The New Indian Express* (November 30, 2013).

[31] On Hindu right political discourse see, *inter alia*, David Ludden, ed., *Contesting the Nation: Religion, Community, and the Politics of Democracy in India* (Philadelphia: University of Pennsylvania Press, 1996); Vasudha Dalmia and Heinrich von Stietencron, eds., *Representing Hinduism: The Construction of Religious Traditions and National Identity*, (New Delhi: Sage, 1995).

[32] Telangana was separated from Andhra Pradesh and became a separate provincial state on June 2, 2014, with Hyderabad to be joint capital of Telangana and residual Andhra Pradesh for the following decade.

a Hindu majoritarian, often anti-Nizam, tone.[33] Many advocates have emphasized, contrarily, that the cosmopolitan legacy of the Nizam's state and regional history of Muslim rule distinguish Telangana Telugus from more parochial groups from ex-Raj territories. Proponents cite demographic and cultural elements in support of this argument. Compared to other regions of Andhra Pradesh, Telangana has considerable Muslim and non-Telugu populations. Further, Telangana culture is said to draw significant elements (lingusitic, culinary, cultural) from Asaf Jahi Deccani cosmopolitanism (incorporating Persian, Urdu, Marathi, and Hindustani elements).[34]

Some strands of discourse in the Telangana movement present the Asaf Jahi legacy as a source for cosmopolitan regional cultural development, distinct from the parochial legacy of British rule in other regions.[35] Historical memory of the Nizam's state, and the push to preserve characteristic social and cultural resonances, function in the Telangana movement as a means for advancing contemporary political claims. The movement for a separate Telangana state is anomalous in a landscape where almost all new postcolonial Indian provinces to date have been defined on a linguistic or 'tribal' ethnic majoritarian basis. This fact, and the invocation of historical connections, alludes to Hyderabad state's role in illuminating paths not taken in South Asian and global political practice in the post-World War II era.

## The past and future of minor sovereignty

Despite the political and discursive closures of the mid-twentieth century various legacies of Hyderabad state remained institutional and conceptual features of the South Asian political landscape. The resonances of

33 On the creation of Telangana potentially serving Hindu right interests see Kancha Ilaiah, "Contrary Theories," *The Asian Age* (November 1, 2010). For the Telangana Rashtra Samithi's declaration of September 17, the date of the Nizam's surrender to the Indian military, as "Telangana Independence Day," see Purushotham, "Destroying Hyderabad," 32.

34 Parthasarathy, "Fasting, Mining, Politicking?"; Keshav Rao Jadhav, "'Backwardisation' of Telangana," *Economic and Political Weekly* 45.13 (2010): 15–20. On the ambivalent relationship of contemporary Telangana leaders towards the Asaf Jah past see H. Srikanth, "Construction and Consolidation of the Telangana Identity," *Economic and Political Weekly* 48.45/46 (2013): 39–45.

35 A recent controversy in which K. Chandrasekhar Rao, the Chief Minister of Telangana, praised the "secular" leadership and development work of the Asaf Jahi Nizams, and was criticized by the Hindu right political leadership for supporting a Muslim "autocrat," illustrates the dynamic and productive position of the subimperial Hyderabad in contemporary discourse. See "Nizam was great, secular ruler: Telangana CM," *Times of India* (January 1, 2015), "BJP criticises KCR for praising Nizam," *The Hindu* (January 3, 2015).

a transnationally linked sovereign state, and its intellectuals' blending of varied conceptual lexicons (Muslim, modernist, patrimonial, cosmopolitan), gesture toward alternatives to prevalent forms of postcolonial politics (unitary, majoritarian, parochial). The closure of Hyderabad's minor sovereignty represents a temporal and structural endpoint for the period and particular dynamics this book traced. As a discrete historical example of political practice, however, Asaf Jah Hyderabad provides a counter-history from which to recontextualize political concepts and historical trajectories for modern South Asia, the British Empire, and the world. This section reflects on key methodological impediments and interventions that the book's analysis of Hyderabad and the global condition of fragmented sovereignty bring into view.

### *Sovereignty and the nation-state*

Thinking from Hyderabad – a minor state that no longer exists either as a specific polity or a type of possible sovereign entity – renders visible key impediments to conceiving history in a transnational framework. Critical in shaping the categories and content of post-World War II politics is the generalization of the nation-state, both in the form of specific polities and the abstract unitary nation-state form as container for sovereignty. Nation-states shape thinking in several ways: organization of and structuring access to historical archives; production of national conceptual space through official and unofficial discourses; naturalization of geographical boundaries and ideas of inclusion and exclusion.[36]

Postcolonial dynamics in India, the region's largest nation-state, have shaped scholarly knowledge production about South Asia's historical past. India is a unitary, powerfully centralized nation-state that employs extensive state violence in relation to regional claims for a share in state sovereignty or complete independence. From the late British colonial period to economic liberalization and the consequent deepening of global capitalist connections in the 1990s, India has experienced a long period of enforced economic isolation and import substitution-oriented development planning. Ideas of Muslim solidarity, especially if on a transnational basis, have tended to be cast as a national threat rather than a basis for productive international alliance-building. Further, India has been locked into enduring political conflict with ostensibly 'Islamic' or

[36] Anderson, *Imagined Communities*; Trouillot, *Silencing the Past*, ch. 3; Nicholas B. Dirks, "History as a Sign of the Modern," *Public Culture* 2.2 (1990): 25–32; Ashis Nandy, "History's Forgotten Doubles," *History and Theory* 34.2 (1995): 44–66; Prasenjit Duara, *Rescuing History from the Nation: Questioning Narratives of Modern China* (University of Chicago Press, 1996).

'Muslim' Pakistan, and after 2001 has implemented policies and programs characteristic of the US-led, markedly Islamophobic 'Global War on Terror.'

While the effects of postcolonial India's historical trajectory have not produced a unitary grand narrative that squeezes out alternative perspectives entirely, histories such as Hyderabad's are nevertheless difficult to conceive. Divergent pasts of minor sovereign states push against the vision of India as historically unified terrain. Trans-regional connections along non-imperial circuits recede into the background in inward-looking nationalist historical imagination. Connections, such as those manifested in Hyderabad, that combined Muslim global solidarity and modernist political reforms appear contradictory and incongruous. Such conceptions, generalized within a massive nation-state and its institutions of knowledge production, have shaped historical ideas about South Asia and its connections to the world.

The example of Hyderabad provides a vantage point for rethinking the dominant historical narrative – and political structure – of India as a unitary, centralized nation-state. In the 1940s a wide array of social forces was unleashed in Hyderabad by the impending decolonization and nationalist transition. People debated and fought over whether Hyderabad should remain an independent state, or join India or Pakistan, and under what terms. As we have seen, Hyderabad became part of India. It is notable that, in addition to bureaucrat-intellectuals and officials, several groups there – state Dalit leaders, some communist organizations – advocated the state's continued independence or autonomy.[37] They perceived potential for (or in some cases evidence of) radical social or political restructuring within the relatively compact political unit.

Numerous thinkers and movements have proposed loosening the national center's hold on developments in the diverse cultural, geographical, and economic spaces that constitute India. These positions tend to be framed as debates over internal national political organization. However, the analytical standpoint implicit in the concept of fragmented sovereignty – divisible state power, ambivalent territoriality, scope for unmediated global connections articulated from constituent political units, potential for negotiation and improvisation of political

[37] Benichou, *Autocracy to Integration*, 181, 202. On the Dalit movement in Hyderabad, Omvedt, *Dalits and the Democratic Revolution*, chs. 3, 9, 10. For reassessments of Asaf Jah policy toward Dalits and Adivasis in the context of the impending creation of a Telangana state see Anveshi, "Nizam's Rule and Muslims: Truth and Fairy Tales about Hyderabad's Liberation," *Anveshi Broadsheet on Contemporary Politics* 1.1 (2010); Bhangya Bhukya, "Between Tradition and Modernity," *Economic and Political Weekly* 48.48 (2013): 120–25.

idioms – holds potential for a fresh reframing of these debates for India. In other contexts, divergent modes of state consolidation produced more fluid configurations of sovereignty.

### *Minor sovereignty in a world of nation-states*

The mid-twentieth-century emergence of the nation-state form as global standard modified the conceptual and institutional range of political possibilities. However, the post-World War II world's political geography remains textured and heterogeneous.

In India centralized national consolidation and anxieties of fragmentation make it difficult, for political and historiographical reasons, to conceive of minor states, now or in the past, as legitimate sovereign entities. Further, transnational connections in India not mediated by the national center often register as threats to the national fabric or security.

Political trajectories elsewhere have resulted in national units of varied scales arrayed in diverse relationships that imply other meanings of sovereignty. In Europe post-Cold War political fragmentation and the rise of the European Union have remade the landscape of sovereignty. Amidst a global ferment, divergent conceptions and critiques of sovereignty and related concepts are articulated and improvised.[38] Particular post-imperial transitions and trends leave open possibilities for minor states' enduring importance.

The various types of minor states considered in Chapter 1 reveal several trajectories of state-formation and sovereignty. Recent histories show the bundling and disaggregation of modes of sovereign power in continuous process. Political dynamics have also shaped historiography.

Uncolonized states, such as Siam (as Thailand) and the Qajar domains (as Iran), have largely retained sovereign statehood within similar territories. Global imperial pressures, either via ostensibly collaborative international institutions or post-World War II US economic or political imperialism, have continued to constrain domains of sovereignty (diplomatic, military, or economic relations; border control).[39] The Ottoman

[38] Hent Kalmo and Quentin Skinner, eds., *Sovereignty in Fragments: The Past, Present and Future of a Contested Concept* (Cambridge University Press, 2010); Jon Beasley-Murray, *Posthegemony: Political Theory and Latin America* (Minneapolis: University of Minnesota Press, 2010); Neil Walker, ed., *Sovereignty in Transition* (Oxford: Hart, 2003); Sally N. Cummings and Raymond A. Hinnebusch, *Sovereignty after Empire: Comparing the Middle East and Central Asia* (Edinburgh University Press, 2011); Arjun Appadurai, "Sovereignty without Territoriality: Notes for a Postnational Geography," in *The Geography of Identity*, ed. Patricia Yaeger (Ann Arbor: University of Michigan Press, 1996), 40–58.

[39] Similar arguments about imperial political or economic pressure could be made regarding other uncolonized states, such as Ethiopia, Nepal, or, most dramatically in recent decades, Afghanistan.

Empire gave way to the post-imperial Turkish Republic, which retained sovereign power in Anatolia at the cost of former imperial domains around the Mediterranean. In these instances, earlier histories, either as empire or minor state, have been appended to ostensibly continuous narratives of sovereignty that form official histories of twentieth-century nation-states.

Sub-imperial states have had widely varied post-imperial histories. In Hyderabad and other states that became Indian territory formal sovereignty was extinguished within a year or so after the end of the Raj, typically by treaty, but sometimes by military or diplomatic coercion.[40] This process was uneven in Pakistan, with sub-imperial states retaining certain sovereign powers or degrees of political autonomy decades after integration.[41] The loose political consolidation and centralization in Pakistan (relative to India) has made former sub-imperial states sites for articulations, or institutional manifestations, of alternative configurations of sovereignty. The Baluchistan province largely corresponds to the former sub-imperial state of Kalat. Since integration into Pakistan the erstwhile polity's putative legitimacy has been a rallying-point for regional autonomist and separatist movements, in which the Khan of Kalat and his family members have often participated.[42] A smaller former sub-imperial state, Swat, was the site of a 2009 Pakistani political experiment in empowering courts to exercise an ultra-conservative interpretation of Sharia law.[43] In both instances former sub-imperial states were departure-points for critiques of Pakistani sovereignty or institutional fragmentation of state power.

Beyond South Asia, locations once under sub-imperial regimes, such as parts of Nigeria and Malaysia, retain distinct elements of these pasts. The

40 The key exception, Kashmir and Jammu, retained elements of political autonomy, but its special constitutional articles were quickly disregarded in the context of territorial conflict with Pakistan.

41 Sultan-i-Rome, *Swat State (1915–1969) from Genesis to Merger: An Analysis of Political, Administrative, Socio-Political, and Economic Development* (Karachi: Oxford University Press, 2008). On the complicated and contested nature of the integration into Pakistan of states bordering India see Yaqoob Khan Bangash, "Three Forgotten Accessions: Gilgit, Hunza and Nagar," *Journal of Imperial and Commonwealth History* 38.1 (2010): 117–43. On proximate territories, the "Federally Administered Tribal Areas," that have, in contrast, been sites of intensive, destabilizing, often military, intervention from the colonial period into the present, Maira Hayat, "Still 'Taming the Turbulent Frontier'? The State in the Federally Administered Tribal Areas of Pakistan," *JASO-Online* 1.2 (2009): 179–206.

42 Shuja Nawaz, *Crossed Swords: Pakistan, its Army, and the Wars Within* (Karachi: Oxford University Press, 2008), 141; Manan Ahmed, *Where the Wild Frontiers Are: Pakistan and the American Imagination* (Charlottesville, VA: Just World, 2011), ch. 4.

43 Osama Siddique, "The Other Pakistan: Special Laws, Diminished Citizenship and the Gathering Storm" (Social Science Research Network, 2012), available at www.dx.doi.org/10.2139/ssrn.2185535.

postcolonial Malaysian political structure incorporates rulers of Malay states as constitutional monarchs, and as such retains the fragmented structure of formal sovereignty from the imperial era. Northern Nigeria, including Sokoto, was under the rule of sub-imperial Muslim emirs during the period of British dominance. The region has largely remained administratively distinct from other parts of Nigeria since decolonization in 1960. The history of Muslim rule in the region, including of sub-imperial sovereigns, has been a key component in arguments for the implementation of Sharia law there since the late 1990s. As in Swat, the interpretations of Sharia law that have been implemented tend toward the ultra-conservative, posing particular legal difficulties for non-Muslims and women. Legal structure and content of this kind tend to bear little relation to legal practice under sub-imperial sovereigns.

Sub-imperial states' integration as provinces of nation-states has had significant historiographical effects. With the naturalization of contemporary national boundaries much historical writing glosses over recent pasts when sovereignty was divided among political actors. In this anachronistic logic history becomes the genealogy of the nation-state. Accordingly, pasts of entities such as Hyderabad, Kashmir, Kalat, Swat, Sokoto, or Johor appear as ready-made stories of the transition from colonialism into nationalism in India, Pakistan, Nigeria, or Malaysia. This practice obscures histories of sub-imperial units uneasily integrated into post-colonial nation-states.[44] As above examples suggest, varied trajectories of sub-imperial states have produced distinct discursive environments. Where former states become articulation-points for political insurgency, new conceptual foundations for historical thinking come into view. Parallel trends are present in places that were not quite formally sovereign during the imperial era.

Improvised spaces of sovereignty, for geographical and geopolitical reasons, often continue to be sites of political friction with existing nation-states. Even if 'non-state spaces' have been systematically eliminated from the political landscape since World War II, borderlands remain destabilizing fissures in the global state system from which the meanings of sovereignty are reworked. Asian highlands and neighboring basins including the greater Himalaya region, western China plateaux and valleys, and highland Southeast Asia are prime sites for insurgencies against existing state forms.[45] Numerous sub-national movements with diverse goals

[44] The impoverishment of the political imagination produced by the silencing of minor sovereign pasts has been emphatically pointed out for Kashmir in recent scholarship. Similar moves would no doubt be instructive for contemporary understandings of political developments in Northern Nigeria or Pakistani border regions. On Kashmir see Zutshi, *Languages of Belonging*; Rai, *Hindu Rulers*. On Nigeria, Last, "'Colonial Caliphate'."

[45] Kelly, "Nehru, Bandung"; Scott, *The Art of Not Being Governed.*

(provincial status, regional or national autonomy) have been launched in the decades since World War II from northeast India and the borderlands between India, Bhutan, and Nepal. Kurdistan, now separate regions in Iran, Iraq, and Turkey, has since the Ottoman period been the location of protracted autonomy struggles. In recent decades it has hosted anti-state insurgency, some degree of devolution of provincial autonomy, or schemes for national independence.[46] Similarly, two ostensibly autonomous regions of China, Tibet and Xinjang (as East Turkestan), are sites of widespread, sometimes militant, movements for greater sovereign autonomy or full independence. Tibet, with a government in exile based in India, and East Turkestan, with key ties through Turkey and Turkic Central Asian countries, have used transnational resources to generate support and legitimacy for their claims to sovereignty. These borderlands of nation-states, often located at or beyond major natural boundaries, remain articulation points for sovereign claims, and often, as in the cases of Western China and Kurdistan, become zones for experimentation or improvisation with fragmentation of state sovereignty.

Alternative trajectories and concepts of sovereignty suggest a range of modes of stateness beyond the ostensibly normative, unitary, and territorial nation-state form (to which India largely corresponds). The consolidated institutional power of this form as a standard of sovereignty looms globally. The nation-state provides the dominant transactional idiom through which many of the entities considered above seek autonomy or independence. Nevertheless, they continue to exist as stages for performing sovereignty, and in some instances act as minor states. Examples of existing minor sovereign states illustrate the enduring process of disaggregation, recombination, and reconceptualization that constitutes stateness in the contemporary world.

### *Trajectories of Muslim politics*

Political dynamics in the decades around World War II resulted in provincialization of internationalist circuits, and particularly those founded on Muslim connections. Muslim political movements came to correspond to the boundaries of the nation-state, manifest global designs driven by dominant political and economic powers (such as Saudi Wahhabism),

[46] Events of the last year or so indicate a potential profound reshaping of sovereignty in Kurdistan and proximate regions. In the wake of US-led imperial intervention there, the frontier zone of Iraq, Turkey, and Syria are currently the site for an expanding radical Islamist polity known as the Islamic State in Iraq and Syria (ISIS). In 2014, ISIS expressed clear intentions, and developed networks, for expanding throughout the Muslim world. It remains to be seen what long-term effect, if any, the rise of ISIS will have on geographies and modes of state sovereignty in West Asia or globally.

or be driven underground by a post-imperial global security regime increasingly restrictive of Muslim connections.[47] Because of these dynamics it is difficult to historicize, or even identify, transformations of Muslim political thought that are both grounded in particular places and globally connected. Further, colonial disruptions of inclusive and cosmopolitan early modern Muslim political systems have obscured continuities into the colonial and contemporary eras. The history of sub-imperial Hyderabad reveals threads connecting times and places.

Muslim politics in Hyderabad, as shown in Chapter 4, was built upon transregional, often informal, diplomatic networks. Bureaucrat-intellectuals' writings develop accounts of Muslim modes of modernist internationalism, and situate Hyderabadi politics in multiple resonant canons of legitimacy. These included various explicitly modernist internationalisms, and older idioms of governance associated with South Asia in general and the Deccan in particular. These Hyderabadi political discourses, incorporative of ideas and subject populations of multiple and often non-Muslim origins, articulate connections between pre-colonial South Asian Muslim statecraft and postcolonial transformations. Unlike in British India, where intellectuals, as Faisal Devji put it, developed "a deterritorialized idea of Muslimhood," Hyderabad provided a territorially defined sovereign state from which to imagine politics.[48]

Key elements of the political culture Muzaffar Alam describes in his work on Indo-Persianate statecraft are visible in the rhetoric and practice of government in Hyderabad.[49] Under pre-colonial Muslim rule in South Asia, Alam argues, political legitimacy was envisioned as inclusive, and premised on consensual authority over state subjects of diverse origins. The Persian language, in the hands of Mughal textual specialists, provided an integrative framework for accommodating diverse lexicons of legitimacy and knowledge, both local non-Muslim (Hindu, Sikh) and global (Jesuit, European).[50] While the 'Moglai' roots of Asaf Jahi authority were a volatile legacy in the colonial historical imagination, as shown

47 On the globalization of radical militant anti-colonial and anti-imperial struggle, in contrast to the national provincialization of formal Islamist politics, see Engseng Ho, "Empire through Diasporic Eyes: A View from the Other Boat," *Comparative Studies in Society and History* 46.2 (2004): 210–46. On global security regimes, historical and contemporary, see Alavi, "'Fugitive Mullahs'"; Junaid Rana, *Terrifying Muslims: Race and Labor in the South Asian Diaspora* (Durham, NC: Duke University Press, 2011).

48 Devji, "Shadow Nation," 127.

49 Muzaffar Alam, *The Languages of Political Islam in India, 1200–1800* (University of Chicago Press, 2004).

50 Ibid.; Rajeev Kinra, "Handling Diversity with Absolute Civility: The Global Historical Legacy of Mughal Ṣulḥ-i Kull," *Medieval History Journal* 16.2 (2013): 251–95 and "Master and Munshī: A Brahman Secretary's Guide to Mughal Governance," *Indian Economic and Social History Review* 47.4 (2010): 527–61.

in Chapter 3 above, Hyderabadis often leveraged this heritage to underscore sovereign claims.

The British Raj used the Mughal political system to reframe their expansive imperial might in terms resonant in the region, but the British were not the only heirs to these rhetorics. Hyderabadi discourse fused and produced political languages by supplementing Mughal-style incorporative rhetoric with emphasis on global mediation and connection, as well as blending in other strategies and lexicons (political modernity, technocratic rule, international law, Muslim difference). This agglomerative political lexicon – emphasizing expansive and inclusive patrimonial connections, combining regional and global ideas – represents a transformation of idioms and practices of Mughal statecraft and their redeployment in a changed political present. Several historiographic factors have made such a trajectory difficult to trace. Sweeping Raj dominance over the political scene and historical representation in the subcontinent, including their seizure of the Mughal legacy, overshadows other genealogies of political practice. Late Asaf Jah Hyderabad appears in retrospect as an exclusivist dictatorship in light of the post-World War II rise of quasi-official Muslim chauvinism and the majoritarian orientation of integrationist nationalist discourse. However, traces of Mughal ideas in Hyderabad suggest continuities between pre-colonial South Asia and the late imperial era, before Muslim politics was canalized into majoritarian containers (as nationally in Pakistan, or regionally in Northern Nigeria) or caricatured and persecuted as anti-national sedition (as in India). Hyderabad's explicitly transregional and modernist supplement to Mughal Indo-Persianate rhetoric highlights regionally grounded internationalist connections that are obscured in the contemporary political landscape.

## *Many standards: reframing sovereignty*

Describing modes of power in the modern world, Engseng Ho extended Bernard Cohn's description of the colonial perspective as "the view from the boat" by suggesting that there were (and are) other boats, other vantage points than "the imperial ship of state."[51] Like diplomats, numerous and varied vessels docked in harbors and plying the seas displayed their credentials as representatives of sovereign states, flying flags signaling their allegiance. These standards provided access to different ports, passage through channels, and economic and political rights to people and

[51] Ho, "Empire through Diasporic Eyes," 213, n. 10.

objects they carried. Seeing the world from Hyderabad, and Hyderabad's world, underscores the possibilities of sovereignty.

This book has taken Asaf Jah Hyderabad's "ship of state" (a relatively minor vessel) as a position from which to gain perspective on late imperial political geography, both by looking outside at the world and inside at happenings within the state. These two perspectives and scales – external and internal, global and provincial – are deeply imbricated. Hyderabad's intellectual history reveals a flexible discourse interbraiding transnational circuits and internationalist visions with regional and local idioms of political legitimacy. The patrimonial relationships that formed the state's administrative structure provided a framework for this integration, and bureaucrat-intellectuals who constituted the state performed political experimentations that reshaped Hyderabad's institutional life. The resulting dynamics – flows of people, goods, and ideas across borders on varying scales; institutional change and enduring difference from British India – shaped the social worlds of Asaf Jahi subjects (or people who entered the state from British India and beyond).

The nesting and mutual constitution of intellectual, political, and social histories suggest continuities and connections on structural and everyday levels. Focusing, as this book has, on processes and emergences over several decades or longer, rather than on crisis moments, emphasizes the creative energies and productive effects of state sovereignty. Hyderabad's stateness appears as built forms, institutional structures, political cultures, social worlds, circuits of connection, and spatialized jurisdictional connections and absences. Taken together, the parts of this book suggest that intellectual, institutional, and spatial processes indeed constitute state sovereignty. The existence and power of the Nizam's standard produced a fuzzy territorial and political container for these developments. Looking at the state from the outside, British India and the late imperial world also appear differently.

The recasting of sovereignty suggested here has implications for South Asian, postcolonial, and global historiography on a number of levels. When it comes to sovereignty in South Asia, the Raj (followed immediately by a unitary territorial postcolonial state) is widely presumed to have carried the only legitimate standards in the land. But other, smaller boats also flew other flags. Hyderabad looked out upon the multiple faces of state sovereignty in the late imperial world. These forms of power inhabited different temporalities in the terrain of what is generally mapped as imperial space, and provided networks for the circulation of people, commodities, and ideas between, within, and beyond colonial space. The deep pink uniformity of the map of the British Empire (upon which the sun, putatively, never set) obscures minor states such as

Hyderabad, as well as informal political actors and entities on the external and internal fringes of empire that few maps are able to render.[52] Such visualizations still shape popular and scholarly notions of empire, and impoverish understandings of the geographies and politics of late imperial sovereignty. Histories written from the perspective of contemporary nation-states, conceived as inheritors of integrated political domains, are complicit in this vision.

Histories focused on South Asian regions or specific communities defined in varied terms (caste, class, religious group, gender, sexuality) have provided critical intermediate entry-points from which to rethink the process, and underscore the coercive violence, by which dominant colonial or national conceptual and political configurations were produced.[53] The view from Hyderabad provides a reminder of the contingency of both colonialism and nationalism (in any variety) as foundations upon which historical understandings were constructed. The discursive universe and transnational life of Hyderabad, and the Nizam's sovereign stateness, provided another conceptual and geographical temporality from which to produce histories. States flying other sovereign standards open vistas for rethinking political possibilities in imperial moments.

[52] Pippa Biltcliffe, "Walter Crane and the Imperial Federation Map Showing the Extent of the British Empire (1886)," *Imago Mundi* 57.1 (2005): 63–69; Felix Driver, "In Search of the Imperial Map: Walter Crane and the Image of Empire," *History Workshop Journal* 69.1 (2010): 146–57.

[53] Chatterjee, *The Nation and its Fragments*; Anjali R. Arondekar, *For the Record: On Sexuality and the Colonial Archive in India* (Durham, NC: Duke University Press, 2009); Antoinette M. Burton, *Dwelling in the Archive: Women Writing House, Home, and History in Late Colonial India* (New York: Oxford University Press, 2003); Mrinalini Sinha, *Specters of Mother India: The Global Restructuring of an Empire* (Durham, NC: Duke University Press, 2006).

# Bibliography

## ARCHIVES

Andhra Pradesh State Archives (APSA), Hyderabad
  Nizam's Government Records
    Administration Reports
    Administration (Secunderabad Cantonment)
    Excise (Abkari)
    Judicial (Extradition and Miscellaneous)
    Passport
    Political Department (Diplomatic and International Visits)
    Political Secretary's Office Files
    Private Secretary's Office Files
    Public Service (Hyderabad State Service, Europeans)
    Tour and Travel
Maharashtra State Archives (MSA), Mumbai
  Bombay Presidency Records
    Political Department (Hyderabad)
National Archives of India (NAI), New Delhi
  Government of India Records
    Foreign and Political Department
  Hyderabad Residency Records
    Accounts Branch
    Judicial Branch
    Political Department
Oriental and India Office Collections (OIOC), British Library, London
  Government of India Records
    Foreign and Political Department
  India Office Records
    Political and Secret (Hyderabad)
  Crown Representative Records
    Residency Records (Hyderabad)
United Nations, Official Documents System, www.documents.un.org/
  Official Records, Security Council (ORSC)

## PUBLISHED GOVERNMENT SOURCES

Andhra Pradesh (India), *A.P. Housing Board RTI Act* (2005).
Bombay (India), *Source Material for a History of the Freedom Movement in India (Collected from Bombay Government Records)*, vol. II: *1885–1920* (Bombay: Government Central Press, 1958).
Great Britain, India Office, William Wilson Hunter, James Sutherland Cotton, Richard Burn, and William Meyer, *Imperial Gazetteer of India*, vol. VII (Oxford: Clarendon Press, 1908).
Great Britain, Indian States Committee, and Harcourt Butler, *Report of the Indian States Committee, 1928–1929* (London: His Majesty's Stationery Office, 1929).
Hyderabad, *The Economic Life of Hyderabad* (Hyderabad: Government Central Press, 1937).
*Town Planning in H.E.H. the Nizam's Dominions* (Hyderabad: His Highness the Nizam's Government, 1944).
Hyderabad, City Improvement Board, *Report on the Progress of the Hyderabad City Improvement Board for the years 1322–1327 Fasli (1914–1919 A.D.)* (Hyderabad: Government Central Press, 1919).
*Report on the Progress of the Hyderabad City Improvement Board for the years 1327–1336 Fasli (1919–1928 A.D.)* (Hyderabad: Government Central Press, 1928).
*Report on the Progress of the Hyderabad City Improvement Board for the years 1340 Fasli (1930 to 1931)* (Hyderabad: Government Central Press, 1931).
*Report on the Progress of the Hyderabad City Improvement Board for the years 1341 Fasli (1931 to 1932)* (Hyderabad: Government Central Press, 1932).
*Report on the Progress of the Hyderabad City Improvement Board for the years 1342 Fasli (1932 to 1933)* (Hyderabad: Government Central Press, 1933).
*Report on the Progress of the Hyderabad City Improvement Board for the years 1343 Fasli (1933 to 1934)* (Hyderabad: Government Central Press, 1934).
*Report on the Progress of the Hyderabad City Improvement Board for the years 1344 Fasli (1934 to 1935)* (Hyderabad: Government Central Press, 1935).
*Report on the Progress of the Hyderabad City Improvement Board for the years 1345 Fasli (1935 to 1936)* (Hyderabad: Government Central Press, 1936).
*Report on the Progress of the Hyderabad City Improvement Board for the years 1346 Fasli (1936 to 1937)* (Hyderabad: Government Central Press, 1937).
*Report on the Progress of the Hyderabad City Improvement Board for the years 1347 Fasli (1937 to 1938)* (Hyderabad: Government Central Press, 1938).
*Report on the Progress of the Hyderabad City Improvement Board for the years 1348 Fasli (1938 to 1939)* (Hyderabad: Government Central Press, 1939).
*Report on the Progress of the Hyderabad City Improvement Board for the years 1349 Fasli (1939 to 1940)* (Hyderabad: Government Central Press, 1940).
*Report on the Progress of the Hyderabad City Improvement Board for the years 1350 Fasli (1940 to 1941)* (Hyderabad: Government Central Press, 1941).
Hyderabad, Delegation to the United Nations, *The Hyderabad Question before the United Nations: Documents and Other Materials* (Karachi: Civil and Military Gazette, 1951).

Hyderabad, Revenue Department, *The Hyderabad Scarcity and Famine Manual* (Hyderabad: Government Central Press, 1938).
India, Foreign Department and C. U. Aitchison, *A Collection of Treaties, Engagements, and Sunnuds, Relating to India and Neighbouring Countries*, 8 vols. (Calcutta: J. L. Kingham, Foreign Dept. Press, 1862–66).
India, Foreign and Political Department, C. U. Aitchison, and A. C. Talbot, *A Collection of Treaties, Engagements, and Sunnuds, Relating to India and Neighbouring Countries*, 2nd edn., 7 vols. (Calcutta: Foreign Office, 1876).
*A Collection of Treaties, Engagements, and Sanads, Relating to India and Neighbouring Countries*, 3rd edn., 11 vols. (Calcutta: Superintendent of Government Printing, 1892).
*A Collection of Treaties, Engagements, and Sanads, Relating to India and Neighbouring Countries*, 4th edn., 13 vols. (Calcutta: Superintendent of Government Printing, 1909).
*A Collection of Treaties, Engagements, and Sanads, Relating to India and Neighbouring Countries*, 5th edn., 14 vols. (Calcutta: Government of India, 1929–33).

## UNPUBLISHED SECONDARY SOURCES

Deshpande, Prachi, "Maratha-Marathi in Madras: Thanjavur and Beyond" (unpublished manuscript, 2012).
Girglani, J. M., "Tragedy of Tribals in Telangana" (B. Janardhan Rao Memorial Lecture, Kakatiya University, Warangal, 2007).
Guha, Ramchandra, "Patrick Geddes and Ecological Town Planning in India" (unpublished manuscript, 2006).
Kelly, John D., "Nehru, Bandung, and the Fate of Highland Asia" (Mary Keating Das Lecture, Columbia University, New York, 2013).
Maringanti, Anant, "Neoliberal Inscriptions and Contestations in Hyderabad," Ph.D. thesis, University of Minnesota, 2007.
Shah, Alison Mackenzie, "Constructing a Capital on the Edge of Empire: Urban Patronage and Politics in the Nizams' Hyderabad, 1750–1950," Ph.D. thesis, University of Pennsylvania, 2005.
Waheed, Sarah, "Islamic Thought and Travel in the Decolonizing World: Muhammad Asad's Orientalisms" (unpublished manuscript, 2013).
"Radical Politics and the Urdu Literary World in the Era of South Asian Nationalisms *c.* 1919–1952," Ph.D. thesis, Tufts University, 2011.

## PUBLISHED PRIMARY AND SECONDARY SOURCES

Abu-Lughod, Janet, *Rabat: Urban Apartheid in Morocco* (Princeton University Press, 1980).
Adelman, Jeremy and Stephen Aron, "From Borderlands to Borders: Empires, Nation-States, and the Peoples in between in North American History," *American Historical Review* 104.3 (1999): 814–41.
Adıvar, Halide Edib, *Inside India*, ed. Mushirul Hasan (Oxford University Press, 2009).

Agha, Sameetah and Elizabeth Kolsky, eds., *Fringes of Empire: Peoples, Places, and Spaces in Colonial India* (New Delhi: Oxford University Press, 2009).

Aḥmad, Naẓīruddīn, *Savāniḥ-yi Bahādur Yār Jang*, 3 vols. (Hyderabad: Bahādur Yār Jang Akaiḍīmī, 1986).

Aḥmadullāh Ḳhāṅ, Muḥammad, *Savāniḥ-yi ʿumrī: Navvāb Akbar Jang Akbarud-daulah Akbarulmulk bahādur marḥūm Sī. Es. Ī. Sābiq kotvāl-i Ḥaidarābād Dakan, jismeṅ kotwāl sāḥib marḥūm ke ḥālāt-i zindagī ibtidā se intihā tak daraj kiʾe gāʾe haiṅ* (Agra: Maṭbaʿ-yi Shamsī, 1907).

Ahmed, Aziz, "Afghani's Indian Contacts," *Journal of the American Oriental Society* 98.3 (1969): 476–504.

Ahmed, Manan, *Where the Wild Frontiers Are: Pakistan and the American Imagination* (Charlottesville, VA: Just World, 2011).

Ahmed, Zahir, *Life's Yesterdays: Glimpses of Sir Nizamat Jung and his Times* (Bombay: Thacker, 1945).

Aiyar, Sana, "Anticolonial Homelands across the Indian Ocean: The Politics of the Indian Diaspora in Kenya, *c.* 1930–1950," *American Historical Review* 116.4 (2011): 987–1013.

Alam, Javeed, "Composite Culture and Communal Consciousness: The Ittehadul Muslimeen in Hyderabad," in Dalmia and von Stietencron, eds., *Representing Hinduism*, 338–57.

Alam, Muzaffar, *The Languages of Political Islam in India, 1200–1800* (University of Chicago Press, 2004).

Alam, Muzaffar and Sanjay Subrahmanyam, eds., *The Mughal State, 1526–1750* (New Delhi: Oxford University Press, 1999).

*Writing the Mughal World: Studies on Culture and Politics* (New York: Columbia University Press, 2011).

Alam, S. Manzoor, *Hyderabad–Secunderabad, Twin Cities: A Study in Urban Geography* (Bombay: Allied, 1965).

Alavi, Seema, "'Fugitive Mullahs and Outlawed Fanatics': Indian Muslims in Nineteenth Century Trans-Asiatic Imperial Rivalries," *Modern Asian Studies* 45.6 (2011): 1337–82.

"Siddiq Hasan Khan (1832–90) and the Creation of a Muslim Cosmopolitanism in the 19th Century," *Journal of the Economic and Social History of the Orient* 54.1 (2011): 1–38.

Aleem, Shamim, *Personnel Management in a Princely State* (New Delhi: Gitanjali Publishing House, 1985).

Alexandrowicz, Charles Henry, *The European–African Confrontation: A Study in Treaty Making* (Leiden: Sijthoff, 1973).

*An Introduction to the History of the Law of Nations in the East Indies: (16th, 17th and 18th Centuries)* (Oxford: Clarendon Press, 1967).

"New and Original States: The Issue of Reversion to Sovereignty," *International Affairs* 45.3 (1969): 465–80.

Ali, Kamran Asdar, "Communists in a Muslim Land: Cultural Debates in Pakistan's Early Years," *Modern Asian Studies* 57.4 (2011): 1068–95.

Ali, M. Ahmed, *Historical Aspects of Town Planning in Pakistan and India* (Karachi: Al-Ata, 1971).

Ali, Saiad Mahdi, *Report on the History of the Famine in His Highness the Nizam's Domains in 1876/77, 1877/78* (Bombay: Exchange Press, 1879).
Ali, Syed, "'Go West Young Man': The Culture of Migration among Muslims in Hyderabad, India," *Journal of Ethnic and Migration Studies* 33.1 (2007): 37–58.
Althusser, Louis, "Ideology and Ideological State Apparatus (Notes Towards an Investigation)," in *Lenin and Philosophy* (New York: Monthly Review Press, 1971), 85–126.
Amanat, Abbas, *Pivot of the Universe: Nasir al-Din Shah Qajar and the Iranian Monarchy, 1831–1896* (Berkeley: University of California Press, 1997).
Amin, Shahid, "Approver's Testimony, Judicial Discourse: The Case of Chauri Chaura," in *Subaltern Studies V: Writings on South Asian History and Society*, ed. Ranajit Guha (New Delhi: Oxford University Press, 1987), 166–202.
Andaya, Barbara Watson, "From Rūm to Tokyo: The Search for Anticolonial Allies by the Rulers of Riau, 1899–1914," *Indonesia* 24 (1977): 123–56.
Anderson, Benedict R. O'G., *Imagined Communities: Reflections on the Origin and Spread of Nationalism*, new edn. (London: Verso, 2006 [1983]).
*Under Three Flags: Anarchism and the Anti-Colonial Imagination* (London: Verso, 2005).
Anderson, Clare, *Convicts in the Indian Ocean: Transportation from South Asia to Mauritius, 1815–53* (New York: St. Martin's Press, 2000).
*Legible Bodies: Race, Criminality and Colonialism in South Asia* (Oxford: Berg, 2004).
Anderson, Michael R., "Islamic Law and the Colonial Encounter in British India," in *Institutions and Ideologies: A SOAS South Asia Reader*, ed. Peter Robb and David Arnold (London: Routledge, 1993), 165–185.
Anghie, Antony, *Imperialism, Sovereignty and the Making of International Law* (Cambridge University Press, 2004).
Anonymous, *Hyderabad in 1890 and 1891: Comprising all the Letters on Hyderabad Affairs Written to the Madras "Hindu" by its Hyderabad Correspondent during 1890 and 1891* (Bangalore: Caxton Press, 1892).
Anveshi, "Nizam's Rule and Muslims: Truth and Fairy Tales about Hyderabad's Liberation," *Anveshi Broadsheet on Contemporary Politics*, special issue, 1.1 (2010).
Appadurai, Arjun, "Sovereignty without Territoriality: Notes for a Postnational Geography," in *The Geography of Identity*, ed. Patricia Yaeger (Ann Arbor: University of Michigan Press, 1996), 40–58.
Archambault, Hannah L., "Becoming Mughal in the Nineteenth Century: The Case of the Bhopal Princely State," *South Asia: Journal of South Asian Studies* 36.4 (2013): 1–17.
Arnold, David, *Colonizing the Body: State Medicine and Epidemic Disease in Nineteenth-Century India* (Berkeley: University of California Press, 1993).
"Famine in Peasant Consciousness and Peasant Action: Madras, 1876–8," in *Subaltern Studies III: Writings on South Asian History and Society*, ed. Ranajit Guha (Delhi: Oxford University Press, 1984), 62–115.
"Looting, Grain Riots and Government Policy in South India 1918," *Past and Present* 84 (1979): 111–45.

*Science, Technology and Medicine in Colonial India* (Cambridge University Press, 2000).
Arondekar, Anjali R., *For the Record: On Sexuality and the Colonial Archive in India* (Durham, NC: Duke University Press, 2009).
Aydin, Cemil, "Globalizing the Intellectual History of the Idea of the 'Muslim World'," in *Global Intellectual History*, ed. Samuel Moyn and Andrew Sartori (New York: Columbia University Press, 2013), 159–86.
*The Politics of Anti-Westernism in Asia: Visions of World Order in Pan-Islamic and Pan-Asian Thought* (New York: Columbia University Press, 2007).
Bahādur Yār Jang, *Bahādur Yār Jang kā safarnāmah: bilād-i islāmiyyah (1931)*, ed. Naẕīr al-dīn Aḥmad (Hyderabad: Qaʾīd-i Millat Akaiḍīmī, 1969).
Baker, D. E. U., *Colonialism in an Indian Hinterland: The Central Provinces, 1820–1920* (Delhi: Oxford University Press, 1993).
Ballantyne, Tony, "Rereading the Archive and Opening up the Nation-State: Colonial Knowledge in South Asia (and Beyond)," in *After the Imperial Turn: Thinking with and through the Nation*, ed. Antoinette Burton (Durham, NC: Duke University Press, 2003), 102–21.
Ballhatchet, Kenneth, *Race, Sex, and Class under the Raj: Imperial Attitudes and Policies and their Critics, 1793–1905* (London: Weidenfeld & Nicolson, 1980).
Bangash, Yaqoob Khan, "Three Forgotten Accessions: Gilgit, Hunza and Nagar," *Journal of Imperial and Commonwealth History* 38.1 (2010): 117–43.
Barak, On, *On Time: Technology and Temporality in Modern Egypt* (Berkeley: University of California Press, 2013).
Barkey, Karen, *Bandits and Bureaucrats: The Ottoman Route to State Centralization* (Ithaca: Cornell University Press, 1994).
Baruah, Sanjib, *India against Itself: Assam and the Politics of Nationality* (Philadelphia: University of Pennsylvania Press, 1999).
Baud, Michel and Willem van Schendel, "Towards a Comparative History of Borderlands," *Journal of World History* 8.2 (1997): 211–42.
Bawa, Vasant K., *The Nizam between Mughals and British: Hyderabad Under Salar Jang I* (New Delhi: S. Chand, 1986).
Bayly, C. A., *The Birth of the Modern World, 1780–1914: Global Connections and Comparisons* (Malden, MA: Blackwell, 2004).
*Empire and Information: Intelligence Gathering and Social Communication in India, 1780–1870* (Cambridge University Press, 1996).
*Indian Society and the Making of the British Empire* (Cambridge University Press, 1988).
"Representing Copts and Muhammadans: Empire, Nation and Community in Egypt and India, 1880–1914," in *Modernity and Culture: From the Mediterranean to the Indian Ocean*, ed. Leila Tarazi Faraz and C. A. Bayly (New York: Columbia University Press, 2002), 158–203.
Bayly, C. A., Sven Beckert, Matthew Connelly, Isabel Hofmeyr, Wendy Kozol, and Patricia Seed, "AHR Conversation: On Transnational History," *American Historical Review* 111.5 (2006): 1441–64.

Beasley-Murray, Jon, *Posthegemony: Political Theory and Latin America* (Minneapolis: University of Minnesota Press, 2010).
Benichou, Lucien D., *From Autocracy to Integration: Political Developments in Hyderabad State, 1938–1948* (Chennai: Orient Longman, 2000).
Benton, Lauren A., *Law and Colonial Cultures: Legal Regimes in World History, 1400–1900* (Cambridge University Press, 2002).
*A Search for Sovereignty: Law and Geography in European Empires, 1400–1900* (Cambridge University Press, 2010).
Berghahn, Volker R., *America and the Intellectual Cold Wars in Europe: Shepard Stone between Philanthropy, Academy, and Diplomacy* (Princeton University Press, 2002).
Berman, Marshall, *All That is Solid Melts into Air: The Experience of Modernity* (London: Verso, 1982).
Beverley, Eric L., "Colonial Urbanism and South Asian Cities," *Social History* 36.4 (2011): 482–97.
Bhagavan, Manu, *Sovereign Spheres: Princes, Education and Empire in Colonial India* (Delhi: Oxford University Press, 2003).
Bhole, Vijaya, *Housing and Urban Development in India* (New Delhi: Classical, 1988).
Bhukya, Bhangya, "Between Tradition and Modernity," *Economic and Political Weekly* 48.48 (2013): 120–25.
"'Delinquent Subjects': Dacoity and the Creation of a Surveillance Society in Hyderabad State," *Indian Economic and Social History Review* 44.2 (2007): 179–212.
*Subjugated Nomads: The Lambadas under the Rule of the Nizams* (New Delhi: Orient Black Swan, 2010).
"The Subordination of the Sovereigns: Colonialism and the Gond Rajas in Central India, 1818–1948," *Modern Asian Studies* 47.1 (2013): 288–317.
Bilgrami, Syed Hossain, *A Memoir of Sir Salar Jung, G.C.S.I.* (Bombay: Times of India Steam Press, 1883).
Bilgrami, Syed Hossain and C. Willmott, *Historical and Descriptive Sketch of His Highness the Nizam's Dominions*, 2 vols. (Bombay: Times of India Steam Press, 1883–84).
Biltcliffe, Pippa, "Walter Crane and the Imperial Federation Map Showing the Extent of the British Empire (1886)," *Imago Mundi* 57.1 (2005): 63–69.
Blake, Stephen P., "The Patrimonial-Bureaucratic Empire of the Mughals," *Journal of Asian Studies* 39.1 (1979): 77–94.
Blok, Anton, "The Peasant and the Brigand: Social Banditry Reconsidered," *Comparative Studies in Society and History* 14.4 (1972): 495–503.
Blumi, Isa, "Beyond the Margins of the Empire: Searching the Limitations of Ottoman Rule in Yemen and Albania," *MIT Electronic Journal of Middle East Studies* 3 (2003): 18–26.
Blunt, Wilfrid Scawen, *The Future of Islam*, ed. Riad Nourallah (London: Routledge Curzon, 2002 [1882]).
*India under Ripon: A Private Diary* (London: Unwin, 1909).
Bond, Patrick, "Bankrupt Africa: Imperialism, Sub-Imperialism and the Politics of Finance," *Historical Materialism* 12.4 (2004): 145–72.

Bose, Sugata, *A Hundred Horizons: The Indian Ocean in the Age of Global Empire* (Cambridge, MA: Harvard University Press, 2006).

"Nation as Mother," in *Nationalism, Democracy and Development: State and Politics in India*, ed. Sugata Bose and Ayesha Jalal (Delhi: Oxford University Press, 1997), 50–75.

Bose, Sugata and Ayesha Jalal, *Modern South Asia: History, Culture, Political Economy*, 2nd edn. (New York: Routledge, 2004).

Breckenridge, Carol A. and Peter van der Veer, eds., *Orientalism and the Postcolonial Predicament: Perspectives on South Asia* (Philadelphia: University of Pennsylvania Press, 1993).

Brewis, Georgina, "'Fill Full the Mouth of Famine': Voluntary Action in Famine Relief in India 1896–1901," *Modern Asian Studies* 44.4 (2010): 887–918.

Brown, L. Carl, *The Tunisia of Ahmad Bey, 1837–1855* (Princeton University Press, 1974).

Brown, Nathan, "Brigands and State Building: The Invention of Banditry in Modern Egypt," *Comparative Studies in Society and History* 32.2 (1990): 258–81.

Brush, John, "The Morphology of Indian Cities," in *India's Urban Future: Selected Studies from an International Conference Sponsored by Kingsley Davis, Richard L. Park, and Catherine Bauer Wurster*, ed. Roy Turner (Berkeley: University of California Press, 1962), 57–70.

Burbank, Jane and Frederick Cooper, *Empires in World History: Power and the Politics of Difference* (Princeton University Press, 2010).

Burton, Antoinette M., *At the Heart of the Empire: Indians and the Colonial Encounter in Late-Victorian Britain* (Berkeley: University of California Press, 1998).

*Dwelling in the Archive: Women Writing House, Home, and History in Late Colonial India* (New York: Oxford University Press, 2003).

Butalia, Urvashi, *The Other Side of Silence: Voices from the Partition of India* (Delhi: Penguin, 1998).

Buzpinar, Ş. Tufan, "Opposition to the Ottoman Caliphate in the Early Years of Abdülhamid II: 1877–1882," *Die Welt des Islams* 36.1 (1996): 59–89.

Campbell, A. C., *Glimpses of the Nizam's Dominions* (London: William Watson & Co., 1898).

Çelik, Zeynep, *The Remaking of Istanbul: Portrait of an Ottoman City in the Nineteenth Century* (Berkeley: University of California Press, 1986).

Chakrabarty, Dipesh, "Of Garbage, Modernity and the Citizen's Gaze," *Economic and Political Weekly* 27.10/11 (1992): 541–47.

*Provincializing Europe: Postcolonial Thought and Historical Difference* (Princeton University Press, 2000).

Chandra, Sudhir, *Enslaved Women: Colonialism, Law and Women's Rights* (Delhi: Oxford University Press, 1998).

Charsley, Simon, "Evaluating Dalit Leadership: P. R. Venkatswamy and the Hyderabad Example," *Economic and Political Weekly* 37.52 (2002): 5237–43.

Chatterjee, Partha, *The Nation and its Fragments: Colonial and Postcolonial Histories* (Delhi: Oxford University Press, 1995).

Chaudhuri, Nani Gopal, *British Relations with Hyderabad, 1798–1843* (University of Calcutta Press, 1964).

Cheragh Ali, [Moulavi], *A Critical Exposition of the Popular "Jihád" Showing That All the Wars of Mohammad Were Defensive; and That Aggresive War, or Compulsory Conversion, Is Not Allowed in the Koran* (Calcutta: Thacker, Spink & Co., 1885).

*Hyderabad (Deccan) under Sir Salar Jung*, 4 vols. (Bombay: Education Society, 1885).

*The Proposed Political, Legal, and Social Reforms in the Ottoman Empire and other Mohammedan States* (Bombay: Education Society, 1883).

Chibber, Vivek, *Locked in Place: State-Building and Late Industrialization in India* (Princeton University Press, 2008).

Chimni, B. S., "Third World Approaches to International Law: A Manifesto," *International Community Law Review* 8 (2006): 3–27.

Chopra, Preeti, *A Joint Enterprise: Indian Elites and the Making of British Bombay* (Minneapolis: University of Minnesota Press, 2011).

Chowdhry, Prem, "Private Lives, State Intervention: Cases of Runaway Marriage in Rural North India," *Modern Asian Studies* 38.1 (2004): 55–84.

Clark, Peter, "A Man of Two Cities: Pickthall, Damascus, Hyderabad," *Asian Affairs* 25.3 (1994): 281–92.

*Marmaduke Pickthall: British Muslim* (London: Quartet Books, 1986).

Clay, C. G. A., *Gold for the Sultan: Western Bankers and Ottoman Finance 1856–1881: A Contribution to Ottoman and to International Financial History* (London: I. B. Tauris, 2000).

Clunes, John, *An Historical Sketch of the Princes of India: Stipendiary, Subsidiary, Protected, Tributary, and Feudatory; with a sketch of the origin and progress of British Power in India* (Edinburgh: Shortrede, 1833).

Cohen, Benjamin B., *Kingship and Colonialism in India's Deccan, 1850–1948* (New York: Palgrave Macmillan, 2007).

"Modernising the Urban Environment: The Musi River Flood of 1908 in Hyderabad, India," *Environment and History* 17.3 (2011): 409–32.

Cohn, Bernard S., *An Anthropologist among the Historians and Other Essays* (Delhi: Oxford University Press, 1987).

"The Census, Social Structure and Objectification in South Asia," *Folk* 26 (1984): 25–49.

*Colonialism and its Forms of Knowledge: The British in India* (Princeton University Press, 1996).

"Representing Authority in Victorian India," in *The Invention of Tradition*, ed. Eric Hobsbawm and Terence Ranger (Cambridge University Press, 1983), 165–209.

Cooper, Frederick, *Colonialism in Question: Theory, Knowledge, History* (Berkeley: University of California Press, 2005).

Copland, Ian, "'Communalism' in Princely India: The Case of Hyderabad, 1930–1940," *Modern Asian Studies* 22.4 (1988): 783–814.

*The Princes of India in the Endgame of Empire, 1917–1947* (Cambridge University Press, 1997).

Coronil, Fernando, *The Magical State: Nature, Money, and Modernity in Venezuela* (University of Chicago Press, 1997).
Cronon, William, *Nature's Metropolis: Chicago and the Great West* (New York: Norton, 1991).
Croxton, Derek, "The Peace of Westphalia of 1648 and the Origins of Sovereignty," *International History Review* 21.3 (1999): 569–91.
Cummings, Sally N. and Raymond A. Hinnebusch, *Sovereignty after Empire: Comparing the Middle East and Central Asia* (Edinburgh University Press, 2011).
Dalmia, Vasudha and Heinrich von Stietencron, eds., *Representing Hinduism: The Construction of Religious Traditions and National Identity* (New Delhi: Sage, 1995).
Dalrymple, William, *The Last Mughal: The Fall of a Dynasty: Delhi, 1857* (New York: Vintage, 2008).
*White Mughals: Love and Betrayal in Eighteenth Century India* (London: HarperCollins, 2002).
Das, Veena, *Critical Events: An Anthropological Perspective on Contemporary India* (Delhi: Oxford University Press, 1996).
Datla, Kavita Saraswathi, *The Language of Secular Islam: Urdu Nationalism and Colonial India* (Honolulu: University of Hawaiʿi Press, 2013).
Davis, Kathleen, *Periodization and Sovereignty: How Ideas of Feudalism and Secularization Govern the Politics of Time* (Philadelphia: University of Pennsylvania Press, 2008).
Davis, Mike, *Late Victorian Holocausts: El Niño Famines and the Making of the Third World* (London: Verso, 2001).
DeGuzmán, María, *Spain's Long Shadow: The Black Legend, Off-Whiteness, and Anglo-American Empire* (Minneapolis: University of Minnesota Press, 2005).
Deleuze, Gilles and Félix Guattari, *Kafka: Toward a Minor Literature* (Minneapolis: University of Minnesota Press, 1986).
Deringil, Selim, "Legitimacy Structures in the Ottoman State: The Reign of Abdulhamid II (1876–1909)," *International Journal of Middle East Studies* 23.3 (1991): 345–59.
*The Ottomans, the Turks and World Power Politics: Collected Essays* (Istanbul: Isis, 2000).
"The Struggle against Shiism in Hamidian Iraq: A Study in Ottoman Counter-Propaganda," *Die Welt des Islams* 30.1/4 (1990): 45–62.
*The Well-Protected Domains: Ideology and the Legitimation of Power in the Ottoman Empire, 1876–1909* (London: I. B. Tauris, 1998).
Deshpande, Prachi, *Creative Pasts: History, Memory and Identity in Western India* (New York: Columbia University Press, 2007).
"Scripting the Cultural History of Language: Modi in the Colonial Archive," in *New Cultural Histories of India: Materiality and Practices*, ed. Partha Chatterjee, Bodhisattva Kar, and Tapati Guha-Thakurta (Delhi: Oxford University Press, 2014), 62–86.
Devji, Faisal, "A Shadow Nation: The Making of Muslim India," in *Beyond Sovereignty: Britain, Empire and Transnationalism, c. 1880–1950*, ed. Kevin

Grant, Philippa Levine, and Frank Trentmann (Basingstoke: Palgrave Macmillan, 2007), 126–45.
Dirks, Nicholas B., *Castes of Mind: Colonialism and the Making of Modern India* (Princeton University Press, 2001).
"History as a Sign of the Modern," *Public Culture* 2.2 (1990): 25–32.
*The Hollow Crown: Ethnohistory of an Indian Kingdom*, 2nd edn. (Ann Arbor: University of Michigan Press, 1993 [1987]).
Dorward, D. C., "British West Africa and Liberia," in *The Cambridge History of Africa*, vol. VII: *From 1905 to 1940*, ed. A. D. Roberts (Cambridge University Press, 1986), 399–459.
Driver, Felix, "In Search of the Imperial Map: Walter Crane and the Image of Empire," *History Workshop Journal* 69.1 (2010): 146–57.
Duara, Prasenjit, *Rescuing History from the Nation: Questioning Narratives of Modern China* (University of Chicago Press, 1996).
*Sovereignty and Authenticity: Manchukuo and the East Asian Modern* (Lanham, MD: Rowman & Littlefield, 2003).
Eagleton, Clyde, "The Case of Hyderabad before the Security Council," *American Journal of International Law* 44.2 (1950): 277–302.
Edney, Matthew, *Mapping an Empire: The Geographical Construction of British India, 1765–1843* (University of Chicago Press, 1997).
Eldem, Edhem, "Ottoman Financial Integration with Europe: Foreign Loans, the Ottoman Bank and the Ottoman Public Debt," *European Review* 13.3 (2005): 431–45.
Emrence, Cem, "Imperial Paths, Big Comparisons: The Late Ottoman Empire," *Journal of Global History* 3.3 (2008): 289–311.
Erdmann, Karl Dietrich, *Toward a Global Community of Historians: The International Historical Congresses and the International Committee of Historical Sciences, 1898–2000* (New York: Berghahn, 2005).
Ernst, Waltraud and Bishwamoy Pati, eds., *India's Princely States: People, Princes and Colonialism* (London: Routledge, 2007).
Esedebe, P. Olisanwuche, *Pan-Africanism: The Idea and Movement, 1776–1991*, 2nd edn. (Washington, DC: Howard University, 1994).
Esenbel, Selçuk, "Japan's Global Claim to Asia and the World of Islam: Transnational Nationalism and World Power, 1900–1945," *American Historical Review* 109.4 (2004): 1140–70.
Ewen, Shane and Pierre-Yves Saunier, eds., *Another Global City: Historical Explorations into the Transnational Municipal Moment, 1850–2000* (New York: Palgrave Macmillan, 2008).
EzzelArab, AbdelAziz, "The Experiment of Sharif Pasha's Cabinet (1879): An Inquiry into the Historiography of Egypt's Elite Movement," *International Journal of Middle East Studies* 36.4 (2004): 561–89.
Fahmy, Khaled, *All the Pasha's Men: Mehmed Ali, his Army, and the Making of Modern Egypt* (Cambridge University Press, 1997).
Fayazuddin, M., "Planning in the States: Hyderabad," *Journal of the Institute of Town Planners, India* 2 (1955): 20–27.
Feener, R. Michael, "New Networks and New Knowledge: Migrations, Communications and the Refiguration of the Muslim Community in the Nineteenth

and Early Twentieth Centuries," in *Muslims and Modernity: Culture and Society since 1800*, ed. Robert W. Hefner (Cambridge University Press, 2010), 37–68.

Ferris, John, "'The Internationalism of Islam': The British Perception of a Muslim Menace, 1840–1945," *Intelligence and National Security* 24.1 (2009): 57–77.

Firishtah, Muḥammad Qāsim Hindū Shāh Astarābādī, *Tārīkh-i Firishtah* (Lucknow: Navil Kishore, 1864).

Fisher, Michael Herbert, *Indirect Rule in India: Residents and the Residency System, 1764–1858* (Delhi: Oxford University Press, 1991).

Fleming, Philip C., "Low-Cost Housing in Hyderabad," *Journal of the American Institute of Architects* 6.2 (1946): 76–80.

Forster, E. M., *The Hill of Devi* (San Diego: Harcourt Brace Jovanovich, 1953).

*A Passage to India* (San Diego: Harcourt Brace Jovanovich, 1954 [1924]).

Fortna, Benjamin C., "The Reign of Abdülhamid II," in *The Cambridge History of Turkey*, vol. IV: *Turkey in the Modern World*, ed. R. Kasaba (Cambridge University Press, 2008), 38–61.

Freitag, Sandria, *Collective Action and Community: Public Arenas and the Emergence of Communalism in North India* (Berkeley: University of California Press, 1989).

"Sansiahs and the State: The Changing Nature of 'Crime' and 'Justice' in Nineteenth-Century British India," in *Changing Concepts of Rights and Justice in South Asia*, ed. Michael R. Anderson and Sumit Guha (Delhi: Oxford University Press, 1998), 82–113.

Freitag, Ulrike, "Hadhramis in International Politics c.1750–1967," in Freitag and Clarence-Smith, eds., *Hadhrami Traders*, 112–30.

Freitag, Ulrike and W. G. Clarence-Smith, eds., *Hadhrami Traders, Scholars, and Statesmen in the Indian Ocean, 1750s–1960s* (Leiden: Brill, 1997).

Gallagher, Catherine and Stephen Greenblatt, *Practicing New Historicism* (University of Chicago Press, 2001).

Gallagher, John, and Ronald Robinson, "The Imperialism of Free Trade," *Economic History Review* 6.1 (1953): 1–15.

Gates, Henry Louis, *The Signifying Monkey: A Theory of Afro-American Literary Criticism* (New York: Oxford University Press, 1988).

Giddens, Anthony, *The Consequences of Modernity* (Cambridge: Polity Press, 1990).

Glover, William J., *Making Lahore Modern: Constructing and Imagining a Colonial City* (Minneapolis: University of Minnesota Press, 2007).

"The Troubled Passage from 'Village Communities' to Planned New Town Developments in Mid-Twentieth-Century South Asia," *Urban History* 39.1 (2012): 108–27.

Gooptu, Nandini, *The Politics of the Urban Poor in Early Twentieth Century India* (Cambridge University Press, 2001).

Gopi, K. N., *Urban Growth and Industrial Locations* (New Delhi: Oxford and IBH, 1980).

Gordon, Stewart, *Marathas, Marauders, and State Formation in Eighteenth-Century India* (Delhi: Oxford University Press, 1994).

Goswami, Manu, "Imaginary Futures and Colonial Internationalisms," *American Historical Review* 117.5 (2012): 1461–85.
*Producing India: From Colonial Economy to National Space* (University of Chicago Press, 2004).
Green, Nile, *Bombay Islam: The Religious Economy of the Western Indian Ocean, 1840–1915* (Cambridge University Press, 2011).
"Forgotten Futures: Indian Muslims in the Trans-Islamic Turn to Japan," *Journal of Asian Studies* 72.3 (2013): 611–31.
Gribble, J. D. B., *A History of the Deccan*, edited and completed by Mary Gribble Pendlebury, vol. I (London: Luzac, 1896).
Groenhout, Fiona, "The History of the Indian Princely States: Bringing the Puppets Back onto Centre Stage," *History Compass* 4.4 (2006): 629–44.
Guha, Ramachandra, *India after Gandhi: The History of the World's Largest Democracy* (New York: Ecco, 2007).
Guha, Ranajit, "Dominance without Hegemony and its Historiography," in *Subaltern Studies VI: Writings on South Asian History and Society*, ed. Ranajit Guha (Delhi: Oxford University Press, 1989), 210–309.
*Dominance without Hegemony: History and Power in Colonial India* (Cambridge, MA: Harvard University Press, 1997).
*Elementary Aspects of Peasant Insurgency in Colonial India* (Delhi: Oxford University Press, 1983).
"The Prose of Counter-Insurgency," in *Subaltern Studies II: Writings on South Asian History and Society*, ed. Ranajit Guha (Delhi: Oxford University Press, 1983), 1–42.
*A Rule of Property for Bengal: An Essay on the Idea of the Permanent Settlement* (Durham, NC: Duke University Press, 1996 [1963]).
Guha, Sumit, "Serving the Barbarian to Preserve the *Dharma*: The Ideology and Training of a Clerical Elite in Peninsular India *c.* 1300–1800," *Indian Economic and Social History Review* 47.4 (2010): 497–525.
Gunthorpe, E. J., *Notes on Criminal Tribes Residing in or Frequenting the Bombay Presidency, Berar and the Central Provinces* (Bombay: Times of India, 1882).
Hall, Catherine, *Civilising Subjects: Colony and Metropole in the English Imagination, 1830–1867* (University of Chicago Press, 2002).
Hardiman, David, *Feeding the Baniya: Peasants and Usurers in Western India* (Delhi: Oxford University Press, 1996).
Harootunian, Harry D., *Overcome by Modernity: History, Culture, and Community in Interwar Japan* (Princeton University Press, 2000).
Harrison, Mark, *Public Health in British India: Anglo-Indian Preventive Medicine, 1859–1914* (Cambridge University Press, 1994).
Harvey, David, *The New Imperialism* (Oxford University Press, 2003).
Hayat, Maira, "Still 'Taming the Turbulent Frontier'? The State in the Federally Administered Tribal Areas of Pakistan," *JASO-Online* 1.2 (2009): 179–206.
Haynes, Douglas E., *Rhetoric and Ritual in Colonial India: The Shaping of a Public Culture in Surat City, 1852–1928* (Berkeley: University of California Press, 1991).

Hazareesingh, Sandip, *The Colonial City and the Challenge of Modernity: Urban Hegemonies and Civic Contestations in Bombay City 1900–1925* (New Delhi: Orient Longman, 2007).

Herzfeld, Michael, "The Absent Presence: Discourses of Crypto-Colonialism," *South Atlantic Quarterly* 101.4 (2002): 899–926.

Ho, Engseng, "Empire through Diasporic Eyes: A View from the Other Boat," *Comparative Studies in Society and History* 46.2 (2004): 210–46.

*The Graves of Tarim: Genealogy and Mobility across the Indian Ocean* (Berkeley: University of California Press, 2006).

Hobsbawm, Eric J., *Bandits* ([New York]: Delacorte, 1969).

"Social Bandits: Reply," *Comparative Studies in Society and History* 14.4 (1972): 503–5.

Hong, Young-sun, *Cold War Germany, the Third World, and the Global Humanitarian Regime* (Cambridge University Press, 2015).

Horowitz, Richard S., "International Law and State Transformation in China, Siam, and the Ottoman Empire during the Nineteenth Century," *Journal of World History* 15.4 (2004): 445–86.

Huber, Valeska, *Channelling Mobilities: Migration and Globalisation in the Suez Canal Region and Beyond, 1869–1914* (Cambridge University Press, 2013).

Husain, Dildar, *Glimpses of an Engineer-Statesman of Hyderabad Deccan* (Hyderabad: Indian Institution of Engineers, 1961).

Ḥusain, Munavvar, *Maulavī Chirāġh 'Alī kī 'ilmī Ḳhidmāt* (Patna: Ḳhudā Baḳhsh, 1997).

Hussain, Nasser, *The Jurisprudence of Emergency: Colonialism and the Rule of Law* (Ann Arbor: University of Michigan Press, 2003).

Hussin, Iza, "The Pursuit of the Perak Regalia: Islam, Law, and the Politics of Authority in the Colonial State," *Law and Social Inquiry* 32.3 (2007): 759–88.

"Textual Trajectories: Re-Reading the Constitution and Majalah in 1890s Johor," *Indonesia and the Malay World* 41.120 (2013): 255–72.

Ikegame, Aya, "The Capital of Rajadharma: Modern Space and Religion in Colonial Mysore," *International Journal of Asian Studies* 4 (2007): 15–44.

Ikegame, Aya and Andrea Major, eds., "Princely Spaces and Domestic Voices: New Perspectives on the Indian Princely States," *Indian Economic and Social History Review*, special issue, 46.3 (2009).

Ilaiah, Kancha, "Contrary Theories," *The Asian Age* (November 1, 2010).

Institute of Town Planners, India, *Journal of the Institute of Town Planners, India* 9 (1957).

Isaka, Riho, "Language and Dominance: The Debates over the Gujarati Language in the Late Nineteenth Century," *South Asia: Journal of South Asian Studies* 25.1 (2002): 1–19.

Jackson, Peter A., "Autonomy and Subordination in Thai history: The Case for Semicolonial Analysis," *Inter-Asia Cultural Studies* 8.3 (2007): 329–48.

Jadhav, Keshav Rao, "'Backwardisation' of Telangana," *Economic and Political Weekly* 45.13 (2010): 15–20.

Jalal, Ayesha, *Partisans of Allah: Jihad in South Asia* (Cambridge, MA: Harvard University Press, 2008).

*Self and Sovereignty: Individual and Community in South Asian Islam since 1850* (London: Routledge, 2000).

*The Sole Spokesman: Jinnah, the Muslim League, and the Demand for Pakistan* (Cambridge University Press, 1985).

Jayaram, R., *Administrative System under the Nizams (1853–1935)* (Bangalore: Ultra, 1998).

Jordan, Kay, "Devadasi Reform: Driving the Priestess of the Prostitutes out of Hindu Temples?" in *Religion and Law in Independent India*, 2nd enlarged edn., ed. R. D. Baird (Delhi: Manohar, 2005), 325–45.

Juderías, Julián, *La leyenda negra y la verdad histórica* (Madrid: Revistade Archivos, 1914).

*Kālāpānī*, dir. Raj Khosla (India, 1958).

Kalmo, Hent and Quentin Skinner, eds., *Sovereignty in Fragments: The Past, Present and Future of a Contested Concept* (Cambridge University Press, 2010).

Kannabiran, Kalpana, "Judiciary, Social Reform and Debate on 'Religious Prostitution' in Colonial India," *Economic and Political Weekly* 30.43 (1995): WS59–69.

Kashani-Sabet, Firoozeh, *Frontier Fictions: Shaping the Iranian Nation, 1804–1946* (Princeton University Press, 1999).

Kasturi, Malavika, *Embattled Identities: Rajput Lineages and the Colonial State in Nineteenth-Century North India* (New Delhi: Oxford University Press, 2002).

Kaviraj, Sudipta, "Filth and the Public Sphere: Concepts and Practices about Space in Calcutta," *Public Culture* 10.1 (1997): 83–113.

*The Imaginary Institution of India: Politics and Ideas* (New York: Columbia University Press, 2010).

Keddie, Nikki, "Iran under the Later Qājārs, 1848–1922," in *The New Cambridge History of Iran*, vol. VII: *From Nadir Shah to the Islamic Republic*, ed. Peter Avery, Gavin Hambly, and Charles Melville (Cambridge University Press, 1991), 174–212.

Keddie, Nikki R. and Jamal al-Din al-Afghani, *An Islamic Response to Imperialism: Political and Religious Writings of Sayyid Jamal al-Din "Afghani"* (Berkeley: University of California Press, 1983 [1968]).

Kedourie, Elie, *Afghani and 'Abduh: An Essay on Religious Unbelief and Political Activism in Modern Islam* (London: Cass, 1966).

Keene, Edward, *Beyond the Anarchical Society: Grotius, Colonialism and Order in World Politics* (Cambridge University Press, 2002).

Kela, Shashank, "Adivasi and Peasant: Reflections on Indian Social History," *Journal of Peasant Studies* 33.3 (2006): 502–25.

Kelly, Saul, "'Crazy in the Extreme'? The Silk Letters Conspiracy," *Middle Eastern Studies* 49.2 (2013): 162–78.

Khalidi, Omar, *A Guide to Architecture in Hyderabad, Deccan, India* (Cambridge, MA: Aga Khan Program for Islamic Architecture, 2008).

"Indian Muslims and Palestinian Awqaf," *Jerusalem Quarterly* 10.40 (2009): 52–58.

Khalidi, Omar, ed., *Memoirs of Cyril Jones: People, Society and Railroads in Hyderabad* (New Delhi: Manohar, 1991).

Ḳhān, Mīr Bāsiṭ ʻAlī, *Tārīḳh-i ʻAdālat-i Āṣafī* (Hyderabad: Shams al-Islām, 1937).

Khan, Saad Omar, "The 'Caliphate Question': British Views and Policy toward Pan-Islamic Politics and the End of the Ottoman Caliphate," *American Journal of Islamic Social Sciences* 24.4 (2007): 1–25.

Khazeni, Arash, "On the Eastern Borderlands of Iran: The Baluch in Nineteenth-Century Persian Travel Books," *History Compass* 5.4 (2007): 1399–1411.

Khuri-Makdisi, Ilham, *The Eastern Mediterranean and the Making of Global Radicalism, 1860–1914* (Berkeley: University of California Press, 2010).

Kia, Mana, "Limning the Land: Social Encounters and Historical Meaning in Early 19th-Century Travelogues between Iran and India," in *On the Wonders of Land and Sea: Persianate Travel Writing*, ed. Roberta Micallef and Sunil Sharma (Boston: Ilex, 2013), 44–67.

Kidambi, Prashant, *The Making of an Indian Metropolis: Colonial Governance and Public Culture in Bombay, 1890–1920* (Aldershot: Ashgate, 2007).

King, Anthony D., *The Bungalow: The Production of a Global Culture* (London: Routledge, 1984).

*Colonial Urban Development: Culture, Social Power and Environment* (London: Routledge, 1976).

"Exporting Planning: The Colonial and Neo-Colonial Experience on Planning," in *Shaping an Urban World: Planning in the Twentieth Century*, ed. Gordon Emanuel Cherry (London: Mansell, 1980), 203–26.

Kinra, Rajeev, "Handling Diversity with Absolute Civility: The Global Historical Legacy of Mughal Ṣulḥ-i Kull," *Medieval History Journal* 16.2 (2013): 251–95.

"Master and Munshī: A Brahman Secretary's Guide to Mughal Governance," *Indian Economic and Social History Review* 47.4 (2010): 527–61.

Kipling, Rudyard, "The Strange Ride of Morrowbie Jukes," in *The Phantom 'Rickshaw and Other Eerie Tales* (New York: J. W. Lovell, 1890 [1888]), 76–125.

Knöbl, Wolfgang, "State Building in Western Europe and the Americas in the Long Nineteenth Century: Some Preliminary Considerations," in *State and Nation Making in Latin America and Spain: Republics of the Possible*, ed. Miguel Angel Centeno and Agustín Ferraro (Cambridge University Press, 2013), 56–75.

Kohli, Atul, *State-Directed Development: Political Power and Industrialization in the Global Periphery* (Cambridge University Press, 2004).

Kolff, Dirk H. A., *Naukar, Rajput and Sepoy: The Ethnohistory of the Military Labour Market in Hindustan, 1450–1850* (Cambridge University Press, 1990).

Koskenniemi, Martti, *The Gentle Civilizer of Nations: The Rise and Fall of International Law, 1870–1960* (Cambridge University Press, 2002).

Kühn, Thomas, "An Imperial Borderland as Colony: Knowledge Production and the Elaboration of Difference in Ottoman Yemen, 1872–1918," *MIT Electronic Journal of Middle East Studies* 3 (2003): 5–17.

Kumar, Radha, *The History of Doing: An Illustrated Account of Movements for Women's Rights and Feminism in India, 1800–1990* (New Delhi: Zubaan, 1993).

Laffan, Michael Francis, *Islamic Nationhood and Colonial Indonesia: The Umma below the Winds* (London: RoutledgeCurzon, 2003).

Lafi, Nora, "Mediterranean Connections: The Circulation of Municipal Knowledge and Practices at the Time of the Ottoman Reforms, *c.* 1830–1910," in *Another Global City: Historical Explorations into the Transnational Municipal Moment, 1850–2000*, ed. Pierre-Yves Saunier and Shane Ewen (New York: Palgrave Macmillan, 2008), 135–50.

Landau, Jacob M., *The Politics of Pan-Islam: Ideology and Organization* (Oxford: Clarendon Press, 1990).

Last, Murray, "The 'Colonial Caliphate' of Northern Nigeria," in *Le temps des marabouts: itinéraires et stratégies islamiques en Afrique Occidentale française,1880–1960*, ed. David Robinson and Jean-Louis Triaud (Paris: Karthala, 1997), 67–82.

Lāyia 'Alī Ḳhāṅ, Mīr, Sir Sālār Jang II, *Vaqāyi'-i musāfarat-i Navvāb-i mustaṭāb-i ashraf-i arfa'-i vālā Mīr Lāyiq 'Alī Khān 'Imād al-Salṭanah Sar Sālār Jang Kī. Sī. Āy. Ī. baṣawb-i Farangistān*, ed. Omar Khalidi and Sunil Sharma (Tehran: Nashr-iTārīḳh iIrān, 2008).

Legg, Stephen, "Governing Prostitution in Colonial Delhi: From Cantonment Regulations to International Hygiene (1864–1939)," *Social History* 34.4 (2009): 447–67.

"An International Anomaly? Sovereignty, the League of Nations and India's Princely Geographies," *Journal of Historical Geography* 43 (2014): 96–110.

*Spaces of Colonialism: Delhi's Urban Governmentalities* (Malden, MA: Blackwell, 2007).

Lelyveld, David, *Aligarh's First Generation: Muslim Solidarity in British India* (Princeton University Press, 1978).

Leonard, Karen [Isaksen], "Cultural Change and Bureaucratic Modernization in 19th Century Hyderabad: Mulkis, Non-Mulkis and the English," in *Studies in the Foreign Relations of India, from the earliest times to 1947: Prof. H. K. Sherwani Felicitation Volume*, ed. P. K. Joshi and M. A. Nayeem (Hyderabad: Government of Andhra Pradesh, 1975), 442–54.

"Hyderabad, the Mulki–Non-Mulki Conflict," in *People, Princes and Paramount Power: Society and Politics in the Indian Princely States*, ed. Robin Jeffrey (New Delhi: Oxford University Press, 1978), 65–106.

*Locating Home: India's Hyderabadis Abroad* (Stanford University Press, 2007).

"Political Players: Courtesans of Hyderabad," *Indian Economic and Social History Review* 50.4 (2013): 423–48.

*Social History of an Indian Caste: The Kayasths of Hyderabad* (Berkeley: University of California Press, 1978).

Levine, Philippa, *Prostitution, Race, and Politics: Policing Venereal Disease in the British Empire* (New York: Routledge, 2003).

Lloyd, Tom, "Acting in the 'Theatre of Anarchy': The Anti-Thug Campaign and Elaborations of Colonial Rule in Early Nineteenth-Century India," *Edinburgh Papers in South Asian Studies* 19 (2006): 1–50.

"Thuggee, Marginality and the State Effect in Colonial India, circa 1770–1840," *Indian Economic and Social History Review* 45.2 (2008): 201–37.

Low, D. A., *Lion Rampant: Essays in the Study of British Imperialism* (London: Cass, 1973).

Low, Michael C., "Empire and the Hajj: Pilgrims, Plagues, and Pan-Islam under British Surveillance, 1865–1908," *International Journal of Middle East Studies* 40.2 (2008): 269–90.

Ludden, David, *An Agrarian History of South Asia* (Cambridge University Press, 1999).

Ludden, David, ed., *Contesting the Nation: Religion, Community, and the Politics of Democracy in India* (Philadelphia: University of Pennsylvania Press, 1996).

Lysa, Hong, "'Stranger within the Gates': Knowing Semi-Colonial Siam as Extraterritorials," *Modern Asian Studies* 38.2 (2004): 327–54.

Malla Reddy, A., *Slum Improvement: The Hyderabad Experience* (Delhi: M.S., 1996).

Malleson, G. B., *An Historical Sketch of the Native States of India in subsidiary alliance with the British Government; with a notice of the Mediated and Minor States* (Longman: London, 1875).

Mamdani, Mahmood, *Citizen and Subject: Decentralized Despotism and the Legacy of Late Colonialism* (Princeton University Press, 1996).

Manela, Erez, *The Wilsonian Moment: Self-Determination and the International Origins of Anticolonial Nationalism* (Oxford University Press, 2007).

Mani, Lata, "Contentious Traditions: The Debate on Sati in Colonial India," in *Recasting Women: Chapters in Colonial History*, ed. K. Sangari and S. Vaid (New Delhi: Kali for Women, 1989), 88–126.

Mann, Kristin and Richard Roberts, "Law in Colonial Africa," in *Law in Colonial Africa*, ed. Kristin Mann and Richard Roberts (Portsmouth, NH: Heinemann, 1991), 3–60.

Mantena, Karuna, *Alibis of Empire: Henry Maine and the Ends of Liberal Imperialism* (Princeton University Press, 2010).

Marashi, Afshin, *Nationalizing Iran: Culture, Power, and the State, 1870–1940* (Seattle: University of Washington Press, 2008).

Martin, Robert K., ed., *Queer Forster* (University of Chicago Press, 1997).

Masselos, Jim, *Towards Nationalism: Group Affiliations and the Politics of Public Associations in Nineteenth Century Western India* (Bombay: Popular Prakashan, 1974).

Mayaram, Shail, "Kings versus Bandits: Anti-Colonialism in a Bandit Narrative," *Journal of the Royal Asiatic Society of Great Britain and Ireland* 13.3 (2003): 315–38.

Mazower, Mark, *No Enchanted Palace: The End of Empire and the Ideological Origins of the United Nations* (Princeton University Press, 2009).

McLeod, John, "Marriage and Identity among the Sidis of Janjira and Sachin," in *India in Africa, Africa in India: Indian Ocean Cosmopolitanisms*, ed. John C. Hawley (Bloomington: Indiana University Press, 2008), 253–72.

*Sovereignty, Power, Control: Politics in the States of Western India, 1916–1947* (Leiden: Brill, 1999).

Meller, Helen, *Patrick Geddes: Social Evolutionist and City Planner* (London: Routledge, 1990).
Melosi, Martin V., *The Sanitary City: Environmental Services in Urban America from Colonial Times to the Present* (Baltimore: Johns Hopkins University Press, 1999).
Metcalf, Barbara Daly and Thomas R. Metcalf, *A Concise History of Modern India*, 2nd edn. (Cambridge University Press, 2006).
Metcalf, Thomas R., *Ideologies of the Raj* (Cambridge University Press, 1994).
*Imperial Connections: India in the Indian Ocean Arena, 1860–1920* (Berkeley: University of California Press, 2007).
Milner, Anthony, *The Invention of Politics in Colonial Malaya: Contesting Nationalism and the Expansion of the Public Sphere* (Cambridge University Press, 1994).
Minault, Gail, *The Khilafat Movement: Religious Symbolism and Political Motivation in India* (New York: Columbia University Press, 1982).
Mir, Farina, *The Social Space of Language: Vernacular Culture in British Colonial Punjab* (Berkeley: University of California Press, 2010).
Mitchell, Lisa, *Language, Emotion, and Politics in South India: The Making of a Mother Tongue* (Bloomington: Indiana University Press, 2009).
Mitchell, Timothy, *Colonising Egypt* (Berkeley: University of California Press, 1991).
*Rule of Experts: Egypt, Techno-Politics, Modernity* (Berkeley: University of California Press, 2002).
Mongia, Radhika V., "Race, Nationality, Mobility: A History of the Passport," *Public Culture* 11.3 (1999): 527–56.
Moxham, Roy, *The Great Hedge of India* (London: Constable, 2001).
Mudiraj, K. Krishnaswamy, *Pictorial Hyderabad*, 2 vols. (Hyderabad: Chandrakanth Press, 1929–34).
Mufti, Aamir, "Auerbach in Istanbul: Edward Said, Secular Criticism, and the Question of Minority Culture," *Critical Inquiry* 25.1 (1998): 95–125.
*Enlightenment in the Colony: The Jewish Question and the Crisis of Postcolonial Culture* (Princeton University Press, 2007).
Muttalib, M. A., *Administration of Justice under the Nizams, 1724–1948* (Hyderabad: Andhra Pradesh State Archives, 1988).
Naidu, Ratna, *Old Cities, New Predicaments: A Study of Hyderabad* (New Delhi: Sage, 1990).
Nair, Janaki, "The Devadasi, Dharma and the State," *Economic and Political Weekly* 29.50 (1994): 3157–67.
"'Imperial Reason,' National Honour and New Patriarchal Compacts in Early Twentieth-Century India," *History Workshop Journal* 66.1 (2008): 208–26.
*Mysore Modern: Rethinking the Region under Princely Rule* (Minneapolis: University of Minnesota Press, 2011).
*The Promise of the Metropolis: Bangalore's Twentieth Century* (New Delhi: Oxford University Press, 2005).
*Women and Law in Colonial India: A Social History* (New Delhi: Kali for Women, 1996).

Nair, Neeti, *Changing Homelands: Hindu Politics and the Partition of India* (Cambridge, MA: Harvard University Press, 2011).

Nandy, Ashis, "History's Forgotten Doubles," *History and Theory* 34.2 (1995): 44–66.

Narayan, B. K., *Agricultural Development in Hyderabad State 1900–1956: A Study in Economic History* (Secunderabad: Keshar Prakashan, 1960).

Nawaz, Shuja, *Crossed Swords: Pakistan, its Army, and the Wars Within* (Karachi: Oxford University Press, 2008).

Nayeem, M. A., *Hyderabad, Philatelic History* (New Delhi: Philatelic Congress of India, 1980).

Nettl, J. P., "The State as a Conceptual Variable," *World Politics* 20.4 (1968): 559–92.

Nichols, Robert, *A History of Pashtun Migration, 1775–2006* (Oxford University Press, 2008).

Nicholson, Timothy A., "A Cold War Education: The Role of the Peace Corps in Creating a Tanzanian Identity," in *African Culture and Global Politics*, ed. Danielle Sanchez (New York: Routledge, 2014), 381–409.

Nigam, Sanjay, "Disciplining and Policing the 'Criminals by Birth,' Part 1: The Making of a Colonial Stereotype – The Criminal Tribes and Castes of North India" and "Part 2: The Development of a Disciplinary System, 1871–1900," *Indian Economic and Social History Review* 27.2 and 3 (1990): 131–64 and 257–87.

Njoh, Ambe J., *Planning Power: Social Control and Planning in Colonial Africa* (London: UCL, 2007).

Noorani, A. G., *The Destruction of Hyderabad* (New Delhi: Tulika, 2013).

Ochsenwald, William L., "The Financing of the Hijaz Railroad," *Die Welt des Islams* 14.1/4 (1973): 129–49.

O'Hanlon, Rosalind, *A Comparison between Women and Men: Tarabai Shinde and the Critique of Gender Relations in Colonial India* (Delhi: Oxford University Press, 2000).

"Letters Home: Banaras Pandits and the Maratha Regions in Early Modern India," *Modern Asian Studies* 44.2 (2010): 201–40.

Öke, Min Kemal, *The Turkish War of Independence and the Independence Struggle of the South Asian Muslims: "The Khilafat Movement" (1919–1924)* (Ankara: Republic of Türkiye Ministry of Culture, 1991).

Oldenburg, Veena Talwar, "Lifestyle as Resistance: The Case of the Courtesans of Lucknow, India," *Feminist Studies* 16.2 (1990): 259–87.

Omvedt, Gail, *Dalits and the Democratic Revolution: Dr. Ambedkar and the Dalit Movement in Colonial India* (New Delhi: Sage, 1993).

Onley, James, "The Raj Reconsidered: British India's Informal Empire and Spheres of Influence in Asia and Africa," *Asian Affairs* 40.1 (2009): 44–62.

Özbek, Nadir, "'Beggars' and 'Vagrants' in Ottoman State Policy and Public Discourse, 1876–1914," *Middle Eastern Studies* 45.5 (2009): 783–801.

"Policing the Countryside: Gendarmes of the Late 19th-century Ottoman Empire (1876–1908)," *International Journal of Middle East Studies* 40.1 (2008): 47–67.

"The Politics of Poor Relief in the Late Ottoman Empire," *New Perspectives on Turkey* 21 (1999): 1–33.

Özcan, Azmi, *Pan-Islamism: Indian Muslims, the Ottomans and Britain (1877–1924)* (Leiden: Brill, 1997).

Pande, Ishita, *Medicine, Race and Liberalism in British Bengal: Symptoms of Empire* (London: Routledge, 2010).

Pandey, Gyanendra, *The Construction of Communalism in Colonial North India* (Delhi: Oxford University Press, 1990).

Parker, Kunal M., "'A Corporation of Superior Prostitutes': Anglo-Indian Legal Conceptions of Temple Dancing Girls, 1800–1914," *Modern Asian Studies* 32.3 (1998): 559–633.

Parthasarathy, D., "Fasting, Mining, Politicking? Telangana and the Burdens of History," *eSocialSciences* (2010), available at www.esocialsciences.com/eSSResearchPapers/displayArticles.asp?aid=90.

"Law, Property Rights, and Social Exclusion: A Capabilities and Entitlements Approach to Legal Pluralism," in *Proceedings of the XIIIth International Congress of the Commission on Folk Law and Legal Pluralism, 7–10 April 2002, Chiang Mai, Thailand*, ed. Rajendra Pradhan, 3 vols. (Kathmandu: International Centre for the Study of Nature, Environment and Culture, 2003), vol. I, 295–322.

"Rural, Urban, and Regional: Re-Spatializing Capital and Politics in India," in *Cleavage, Connection and Conflict in Rural, Urban and Contemporary Asia*, ed. Tim Bunnell, D. Parthasarathy, and Eric C. Thompson (Dordrecht: Springer Netherlands, 2013), 15–30.

Paswan, Sanjay and Pramanshi Jaideva, *Encyclopaedia of Dalits in India*, vol. IV: *Leaders* (Delhi: Kalpaz, 2002).

Patnaik, Gorachand, *The Famine and Some Aspects of the British Economic Policy in Orissa, 1866–1905* (Cuttack: Vidyapuri, 1980).

Peabody, Norbert, *Hindu Kingship and Polity in Precolonial India* (Cambridge University Press, 2003).

Perdue, Peter C., *China Marches West: The Qing Conquest of Central Eurasia* (Cambridge, MA: Harvard University Press, 2005).

Pernau [-Reifeld], Margrit, *The Passing of Patrimonialism: Politics and Political Culture in Hyderabad, 1911–1948* (New Delhi: Manohar, 2000).

"Reaping the Whirlwind: Nizam and the Khilafat Movement," *Economic and Political Weekly* 34.38 (1999): 2745–51.

Pickthall, Marmaduke, "The Muslims in the Modern World," *Journal of the Royal Central Asian Society* 23.2 (1936): 221–94.

Pitcher, Anne, Mary H. Moran, and Michael Johnston, "Rethinking Patrimonialism and Neopatrimonialism in Africa," *African Studies Review* 52.1 (2009): 125–56.

Platts, John T., *A Dictionary of Urdu, Classical Hindi, and English* (London: W. H. Allen & Co., 1884).

Pollock, Sheldon, ed., *Literary Cultures in History: Reconstructions from South Asia* (Berkeley: University of California Press, 2003).

Powell, Eve Troutt, *A Different Shade of Colonialism: Egypt, Great Britain, and the Mastery of the Sudan* (Berkeley: University of California Press, 2003).

Prakash, Gyan, *Another Reason: Science and the Imagination of Modern India* (Princeton University Press, 1999).

Preckel, Claudia, "The Roots of Anglo-Muslim Co-Operation and Islamic Reformism in Bhopal," in *Perspectives of Mutual Encounters in South Asian History: 1760–1860*, ed. Jamal Malik (Leiden: Brill, 2000), 65–78.

Purushotham, Sunil, "Destroying Hyderabad and Making the Nation," *Economic and Political Weekly* 49.22 (2014): 29–33.

"Internal Violence: The 'Police Action' in Hyderabad," *Comparative Studies in Society and History* 57.2 (forthcoming [2015]).

Quataert, Donald, *The Ottoman Empire: 1700–1922*, 2nd edn. (New York: Cambridge University Press, 2005).

Queen, Christopher S., "Dr. Ambedkar and the Hermeneutics of Buddhist Liberation," in *Engaged Buddhism: Buddhist Liberation Movements in Asia*, ed. Christopher S. Queen and Sallie B. King (Albany: State University of New York Press, 1996), 45–71.

Qureishi, M. Naeem, *Pan-Islam in British Indian Politics: A Study of the Khilafat Movement, 1918–1924* (Leiden: Brill, 1999).

Rabinow, Paul, *French Modern: Norms and Forms of the Social Environment* (Cambridge, MA: MIT Press, 1989).

Radhakrishna, Meena, *Dishonoured by History: "Criminal Tribes" and British Colonial Policy* (Hyderabad: Orient Longman, 2001).

Rai, Mridu, *Hindu Rulers, Muslim Subjects: Islam, Rights, and the History of Kashmir* (Princeton University Press, 2004).

Raj, M. Sundara, *Prostitution in Madras: A Historical Perspective* (Delhi: Konark, 1993).

Raj, Sheela, *Mediaevalism to Modernism: Socio-Economic and Cultural History of Hyderabad, 1869–1911* (Bombay: Popular Prakashan, 1987).

Rajagopal, Balakrishnan, *International Law from Below: Development, Social Movements, and Third World Resistance* (Cambridge University Press, 2003).

Rama, Angel, *The Lettered City*, trans. John C. Chasteen (Durham, NC: Duke University Press, 1996 [Spanish 1984]).

Raman, Bhavani, *Document Raj: Writing and Scribes in Early Colonial South India* (University of Chicago Press, 2012).

Ramasubban, Radhika, "Imperial Health in British India, 1857–1900," in *Disease, Medicine, and Empire: Perspectives on Western Medicine and the Experience of European Expansion*, ed. Roy Macleod and Milton Lewis (London: Routledge, 1988), 38–60.

Ramaswamy, Sumathi, *Passions of the Tongue: Language Devotion in Tamil India, 1891–1970* (Berkeley: University of California Press, 1997).

Ramberg, Lucinda, "Magical Hair as Dirt: Ecstatic Bodies and Postcolonial Reform in South India," *Culture, Medicine and Psychiatry* 33.4 (2009): 501–22.

Ramnath, Maia, *Haj to Utopia: How the Ghadar Movement Charted Global Radicalism and Attempted to Overthrow the British Empire* (Berkeley: University of California Press, 2011).

Ramusack, Barbara, "The Indian Princes as Fantasy: Palace Hotels, Palace Museums and Palace on Wheels," in *Consuming Modernity: Public Culture in a South Asian World*, ed. Carol A. Breckenridge (Minneapolis: University of Minnesota Press, 1995), 66–89.

*The Indian Princes and their States* (Cambridge University Press, 2004).

*The Princes of India in the Twilight of Empire: Dissolution of a Patron–Client system, 1914–1939* (Columbus: Ohio State University Press, 1978).

Rana, Junaid, *Terrifying Muslims: Race and Labor in the South Asian Diaspora* (Durham, NC: Duke University Press, 2011).

Rao, Anupama, *The Caste Question: Dalits and the Politics of Modern India* (Berkeley: University of California Press, 2009).

Rao, Nikhil, *House, But No Garden: Apartment Living in Bombay's Suburbs, 1898–1964* (Minneapolis: University of Minnesota Press, 2013).

Ray, Bharati, *Hyderabad and British Paramountcy, 1858–1883* (Delhi: Oxford University Press, 1988).

Raza, Ali, Franziska Roy, and Ben Zachariah, eds., *The Internationalist Moment: South Asia, Worlds, and World Views, 1917–39* (New Delhi: Sage Publications, 2014).

Reddy, M. Gopinath and K. Anil Kumar, *Political Economy of Tribal Development: A Case Study of Andhra Pradesh* (Hyderabad: Centre for Economic and Social Studies, 2010).

Regani, Sarojini, *Nizam–British Relations: 1724–1857* (New Delhi: Concept), 1963.

Reid, Anthony, "Nineteenth Century Pan-Islam in Indonesia and Malaysia," *Journal of Asian Studies* 26.2 (1967): 267–83.

Reynolds, Jonathan, "Good and Bad Muslims: Islam and Indirect Rule in Northern Nigeria," *International Journal of African Historical Studies* 34.3 (2001): 601–18.

Robinson, Francis, "The Islamic World: World System to 'Religious International'," in *Religious Internationals in the Modern World: Globalization and Faith Communities since 1750*, ed. Abigail Green and Vincent Viaene (Basingstoke: Palgrave Macmillan, 2012), 111–36.

Roessel, David, "Live Orientals and Dead Greeks: Forster's Response to the Chanak Crisis," *Twentieth Century Literature* 36.1 (1990): 43–60.

Roff, Willam R., *The Origins of Malay Nationalism*, 2nd edn. (Kuala Lumpur: Oxford University Press, 1994 [1967]).

Rogers, John D., *Crime, Justice and Society in Colonial Sri Lanka* (London: Curzon, 1987).

Roy, Parama, "Discovering India, Imagining Thuggee," *Yale Journal of Criticism* 9.1 (1996): 121–45.

Rudolph, Lloyd I. and Susanne H. Rudolph, "Authority and Power in Bureaucratic and Patrimonial Administration: A Revisionist Interpretation of Weber on Bureaucracy," *World Politics* 31.2 (1979): 195–227.

Rudolph, Susanne H., Lloyd I. Rudolph, and Mohan Singh, "A Bureaucratic Lineage in Princely India: Elite Formation and Conflict in a Patrimonial System," *Journal of Asian Studies* 34.3 (1975): 717–53.

Rupavath, Ramdas, "The Persistence of Land Alienation: The Experience of Tribal People of Andhra Pradesh," *Journal of Asian and African Studies* (2014): 1–17.

Russell, Robert V. and Rai Bahadur Hira Lal, *The Tribes and Castes of the Central Provinces of India*, vol. I (London: Macmillan, 1916).
Said, Edward, *Orientalism* (New York: Pantheon, 1978).
Saikia, Yasmin, *Fragmented Memories: Struggling to Be Tai-Ahom in India* (Durham, NC: Duke University Press, 2004).
Sajdi, Dana, "Decline, its Discontents and Ottoman Cultural History: By Way of Introduction," in *Ottoman Tulips, Ottoman Coffee: Leisure and Lifestyle in the Eighteenth Century*, ed. Dana Sajdi (London: I. B. Tauris, 2007), 1–39.
Şakul, Kahraman, "Eastern Question," in *Encyclopedia of the Ottoman Empire*, ed. Gábor Ágoston and Bruce Masters (New York: Facts on File, 2009), 191–92.
Samson, Melanie, "(Sub)imperial South Africa? Reframing the Debate," *Review of African Political Economy* 36.119 (2009): 93–103.
Sarma, E. A. S., "The Adivasi, the State and the Naxalite: Case of Andhra Pradesh," *Economic and Political Weekly* 41.15 (2006): 1434–37.
Satya, Laxman D., *Cotton and Famine in Berar, 1850–1900* (New Delhi: Manohar, 1997).
Schwartzberg, Joseph E., "Factors in the Linguistic Reorganization of Indian States," in *Region and Nation in India*, ed. Paul Wallace (New Delhi: Oxford University Press, 1985), 155–82.
Scott, James C., *The Art of Not Being Governed: An Anarchist History of Upland Southeast Asia* (New Haven: Yale University Press, 2009).
Sen, Satadru, *Disciplining Punishment: Colonialism and Convict Society in the Andaman Islands* (New Delhi: Oxford University Press, 2000).
Sen, Sudipta, "Unfinished Conquest: Residual Sovereignty and the Legal Foundations of the British Empire in India," *Law, Culture and the Humanities* 9.2 (2013): 227–42.
Sengoopta, Chandak, *Imprint of the Raj: How Fingerprinting was Born in Colonial India* (London: Macmillan, 2003).
Shah, Svati P., "Producing the Spectacle of Kamathipura: The Politics of Red Light Visibility in Mumbai," *Cultural Dynamics* 18.3 (2006): 269–92.
Shaheen, Muhammad, "Forster's Salute to Egypt," *Twentieth Century Literature* 39.1 (1993): 32–46.
Shankar, Shobana, "Medical Missionaries and Modernizing Emirs in Colonial Hausaland: Leprosy Control and Native Authority in the 1930s," *Journal of African History* 48 (2007): 45–68.
Sharkey, Heather J., *Living with Colonialism: Nationalism and Culture in the Anglo-Egyptian Sudan* (Berkeley: University of California Press, 2003).
Sherman, Taylor C., "Migration, Citizenship and Belonging in Hyderabad (Deccan), 1946–1956," *Modern Asian Studies* 45.S1 (2011): 81–107.
*State Violence and Punishment in India* (London: Routledge, 2010).
Sherwānī, Harūn Ḳhāṅ, *Yūrup Jang Se Pahle* (Hyderabad: Idārah-yi Adabiyāt-i Urdū, 1944).
Sibṭ-i Ḥasan, *Shahr-i nigārān* (Karachi: Dāniyāl, 1984 [1966]).
Siddique, Osama, "The Other Pakistan: Special Laws, Diminished Citizenship and the Gathering Storm" (Social Science Research Network, 2012), available at http://dx.doi.org/10.2139/ssrn.2185535.

Simms, Brendan, "Temperley, Harold William Vazeille (1879–1939)," in *Oxford Dictionary of National Biography*, online edition, ed. H. C. G. Matthew, Brian Harrison, and Lawrence Goldman (Oxford University Press, 2004).

Singh, Frances B., "A Passage to India, the National Movement and Independence," *Twentieth Century Literature* 31.2/3 (1985): 265–78.

Singh, Hira, *Colonial Hegemony and Popular Resistance: Princes, Peasants, and Paramount Power* (New Delhi: Sage, 1998).

Singha, Radhika, *A Despotism of Law: Crime and Justice in Early Colonial India* (Delhi: Oxford University Press, 1998).

"The Great War and a 'Proper' Passport for the Colony: Border-Crossing in British India, *c.* 1882–1922," *Indian Economic and Social History Review* 50.3 (2013): 289–315.

"Passport, Ticket, and India Rubber-Stamp: 'The Problem of the Pauper Pilgrim' in Colonial India (c.1882–1925)," in *The Limits of British Colonial Control in South Asia: Spaces of Disorder in the Indian Ocean Region*, ed. Ashwini Tambe and Harald Fischer-Tiné (London: Routledge, 2009), 49–83.

"Providential Circumstances: The Thuggee Campaign of the 1830s and Legal Innovation," *Modern Asian Studies* 27.1 (1993): 83–146.

"Settle, Mobilize, Verify: Identification Practices in Colonial India," *Studies in History* 16.2 (2000): 151–98.

Sinha, Mrinalini, *Specters of Mother India: The Global Restructuring of an Empire* (Durham, NC: Duke University Press, 2006).

Siraj ul Hassan, Syed, *Castes and Tribes of H.E.H. Nizam's Dominions*, 2 vols. (Bombay: Times of India Press, 1920).

Sivaramakrishnan, K., *Modern Forests: Statemaking and Environmental Change in Colonial Eastern India* (Stanford University Press, 1999).

Skaria, Ajay, *Hybrid Histories: Forests, Frontiers and Wildness in Western India* (Delhi: Oxford University Press, 1999).

Smith, Simon C., "'Moving a Little with the Tide': Malay Monarchy and the Development of Modern Malay Nationalism," *Journal of Imperial and Commonwealth History* 34.1 (2006): 123–38.

Sohrabi, Naghmeh, *Taken for Wonder: Nineteenth-Century Travel Accounts from Iran to Europe* (New York: Oxford University Press, 2012).

Spear, Thomas, "Neo-Traditionalism and the Limits of Invention in British Colonial Africa," *Journal of African History* 44.1 (2003): 3–27.

Spodek, Howard, "Urban Politics in the Local Kingdoms of India: A View from the Princely Capitals of Saurashtra under British Rule," *Modern Asian Studies* 7.2 (1973): 253–75.

Srikanth, H., "Construction and Consolidation of the Telangana Identity," *Economic and Political Weekly* 48.45/46 (2013): 39–45.

Srinivasan, Amrit, "Reform and Revival: The Devadasi and her Dance," *Economic and Political Weekly* 20.44 (1985): 1869–76.

Stein, Burton, *A History of India*, 2nd edn., ed. David Arnold (Malden, MA: Wiley-Blackwell, 2010).

*Thomas Munro: The Origins of the Colonial State and his Vision of Empire* (Delhi: Oxford University Press, 1989).

Stephens, Julia, "The Phantom Wahhabi: Liberalism and the Muslim Fanatic in Mid-Victorian India," *Modern Asian Studies* 47.1 (2013): 22–52.

Stern, Philip J., *The Company-State: Corporate Sovereignty and the Early Modern Foundations of the British Empire in India* (New York: Oxford University Press, 2011).

Subba Rao, C. V., *Hyderabad: The Social Context of Industrialisation, 1875–1948* (New Delhi: Orient Longman, 2007).

Suleri, Sara, *The Rhetoric of English India* (University of Chicago Press, 1992).

Sultan-i-Rome, *Swat State (1915–1969) from Genesis to Merger: An Analysis of Political, Administrative, Socio-Political, and Economic Development* (Karachi: Oxford University Press, 2008).

Suykens, Bert, "The Tribal–Forest Nexus in Law and Society in India," *Critical Asian Studies* 41.3 (2009): 381–402.

Tagliacozzo, Eric, *Secret Trades, Porous Borders: Smuggling and States along a Southeast Asian Frontier, 1865–1915* (New Haven: Yale University Press, 2005).

Tambe, Ashwini, *Codes of Misconduct: Regulating Prostitution in Late Colonial Bombay* (Minneapolis: University of Minnesota Press, 2009).

Tappin, Stuart, "The Early Use of Reinforced Concrete in India," in *Proceedings of the First International Congress on Construction History, Madrid, 20th–24th January 2003*, ed. S. H. Fernández (Madrid: Instituto Juan de Herrera, 2003), 1931–40.

Tavakoli-Targhi, Mohamad, *Refashioning Iran: Orientalism, Occidentalism, and Historiography* (New York: Palgrave, 2001).

Taylor, Phillip Meadows, *Confessions of a Thug* (London: Bentley, 1839).

Teitelbaum, Joshua, "Sharif Husayn Ibn Ali and the Hashemite Vision of the Post-Ottoman Order: From Chieftaincy to Suzerainty," *Middle Eastern Studies* 34.1 (1998): 103–22.

"'Taking Back' the Caliphate: Sharīf Ḥusayn Ibn 'Alī, Mustafa Kemal and the Ottoman Caliphate," *Die Welt des Islams* 40.3 (2000): 412–24.

Thaha, S. Abdul, *Forest Policy and Ecological Change: Hyderabad State in Colonial India* (Delhi: Foundation, 2009).

Tillotson, G. H. R., "Vincent J. Esch and the Architecture of Hyderabad, 1914–36," *South Asian Studies* 9.1 (1993): 29–46.

Tilly, Charles, "War Making and State Making as Organized Crime," in *Bringing the State Back In*, ed. Peter B. Evans, Dietrich Rueschemeyer, and Theda Skocpol (Cambridge University Press, 1985), 169–91.

Tomlinson, B. R., *The Economy of Modern India*, 2nd edn. (Cambridge University Press, 2013).

Toor, Saadia, *The State of Islam: Culture and Cold War Politics in Pakistan* (London: Pluto Press, 2011).

Travers, Robert, *Ideology and Empire in Eighteenth Century India: The British in Bengal* (Cambridge University Press, 2007).

Trocki, Carl A., "Political Structures in the Nineteenth and Early Twentieth Centuries," in *The Cambridge History of Southeast Asia*, vol. II: *The Nineteenth and Twentieth Centuries*, ed. Nicholas Tarling (Cambridge University Press, 1992), 79–130.

*Prince of Pirates: The Temenggongs and the Development of Johor and Singapore, 1784–1885* (Singapore University Press, 1979).

Trouillot, Michel-Rolph, *Silencing the Past: Power and the Production of History* (Boston: Beacon, 1995).

Turner, Frederick Jackson, "The Significance of the Frontier in American History," in *The Frontier in American History* (New York: Holt, 1920 [1894]), 1–38.

Vaidik, Aparna, "Settling the Convict: Matrimony and Domesticity in the Andamans," *Studies in History* 22.2 (2006): 221–51.

Vaikuntham, Y., *State, Economy and Social Transformation: Hyderabad State 1724–1948* (New Delhi: Manohar, 2002).

van Schendel, Willem, "Geographies of Knowing, Geographies of Ignorance: Jumping Scale in Southeast Asia," *Environment and Planning D: Society and Space* 20.6 (2002): 647–68.

van Wœrkens, Martine and Catherine Tihanyi, *The Strangled Traveler: Colonial Imaginings and the Thugs of India* (University of Chicago Press, 2002).

Vijaisri, Priyadarshini, "Sacred Prostitution and Reform in Colonial South India," *South Asia: Journal of South Asian Studies* 28.3 (2005): 387–411.

Visvesvaraya, M., *A Brief Memoir of my Complete Working Life* (Bangalore: Government Press, 1960).

*Industrializing India: Constructive Policies and Plan* (Bangalore: Bangalore Press, 1933).

*Memoirs of my Working Life* (Bombay: Burton, 1951).

*Nation Building: A Five-Year Plan for the Provinces* (Bangalore: Bangalore Press, 1937).

*Planned Economy for India* (Bangalore: Bangalore Press, 1934).

*Prosperity through Industry, Move Towards Rapid Industrialization* (Bombay: All-India Manufacturers' Organisation, 1943).

*Reconstruction in Post-War India: A Plan of Development All Round* (Bombay: All-India Manufacturers' Organisation, 1944).

von Fürer-Haimendorf, Christoph, *Tribes of India: The Struggle for Survival* (Berkeley: University of California Press, 1982).

Interview by Alan Macfarlane, "Interview with Christoph von Fürer-Haimendorf at Lode, Cambridge" (1983), available at www.dspace.cam.ac.uk/handle/1810/28.

Vyasulu, Vinod, "Nehru and the Visvesvaraya Legacy," *Economic and Political Weekly* 24.30 (1989): 1700–4.

Wagner, Kim A., "The Deconstructed Strangler: A Reassessment of Thuggee," *Modern Asian Studies* 38.4 (2004): 931–63.

"Thuggee and Social Banditry Reconsidered," *Historical Journal* 50.2 (2007): 353–76.

Waheed, Sarah, "Women of 'Ill Repute': Ethics and Urdu Literature in Colonial India," *Modern Asian Studies* 48.4 (2014): 986–1023.

Walker, Neil, ed., *Sovereignty in Transition* (Oxford: Hart, 2003).

Walkowitz, Judith R., *City of Dreadful Delight: Narratives of Sexual Danger in Late-Victorian London* (University of Chicago Press, 1992).

Washbrook, David, "The Maratha Brahmin Model in South India: An Afterword," *Indian Economic and Social History Review* 47.4 (2010): 597–615.

"South Asia, the World System, and World Capitalism," *Journal of Asian Studies* 49.3 (1990): 479–508.

Wasti, Syed Tanvir, "The Political Aspirations of Indian Muslims and the Ottoman Nexus," *Middle Eastern Studies* 42.5 (2006): 709–22.

Webb, Alexander Russell, *Yankee Muslim: The Asian Travels of Mohammed Alexander Russell Webb*, ed. Brent D. Singleton ([Rockville, MD]: Borgo, 2007).

Weber, Eugen, *Peasants into Frenchmen: The Modernization of Rural France, 1870–1914* (Stanford University Press, 1976).

White, Richard, *The Middle Ground: Indians, Empires, and Republics in the Great Lakes Region, 1650–1815* (Cambridge University Press, 1991).

Willis, Walter Addington, *Housing and Town Planning in Great Britain, Being a Statement of the Statutory Provisions Relating to the Housing of the Working Classes and to Town Planning Including the Housing, Town Planning, etc., Act, 1909* (London: Butterworth & Co., 1910).

Wilson, Jon E., *The Domination of Strangers: Modern Governance in Eastern India, 1780–1835* (Basingstoke: Palgrave Macmillan, 2008).

Winichakul, Thongchai, "The Quest for 'Siwilai': A Geographical Discourse of Civilizational Thinking in the Late Nineteenth and Early Twentieth-Century Siam," *Journal of Asian Studies* 59.3 (2000): 528–49.

*Siam Mapped: A History of the Geo-Body of a Nation* (Honolulu: University of Hawaiʿi Press, 1994).

Wink, André, *Land and Sovereignty in India: Agrarian Society and Politics under the Eighteenth-Century Maratha Svarajya* (Cambridge University Press, 1986).

Yang, Anand A., "Indian Convict Workers in Southeast Asia in the Late Eighteenth and Early Nineteenth Centuries," *Journal of World History* 14.2 (2003): 179–208.

*The Limited Raj: Agrarian Relations in Colonial India, Saran District, 1793–1920* (Berkeley: University of California Press, 1989).

Yeoh, Brenda S. A., *Contesting Space: Power Relations and the Urban Built Environment in Colonial Singapore* (Kuala Lumpur: Oxford University Press, 1996).

Yimene, Ababu Minda, "Dynamics of Ethnic Identity among the Siddis of Hyderabad," *African and Asian Studies* 6.3 (2007): 321–45.

Yule, Henry and A. C. Burnell, *Hobson-Jobson: A Glossary of Colloquial Anglo-Indian Words and Phrases, and of Kindred Terms, Etymological, Historical, Geographical and Discursive*, 2nd edn., ed. William Crooke (London: J. Murray, 1903).

Zachariah, Benjamin, *Developing India: An Intellectual and Social History, c. 1930–50* (New Delhi: Oxford University Press, 2005).

Zamindar, Vazira Fazila-Yacoobali, *The Long Partition and the Making of Modern South Asia: Refugees, Boundaries, Histories* (New York: Columbia University Press, 2007).

Zarinebaf, Fariba, "From Istanbul to Tabriz: Modernity and Constitutionalism in the Ottoman Empire and Iran," *Comparative Studies of South Asia, Africa and the Middle East* 28.1 (2008): 154–69.

Zor, Sayyid Muḥīuddīn Qādirī, *Sair-i Golkunḍah* (Hyderabad: Idārah-yi Adabiyāt-i Urdū, 1940).
Zubaida, Sami, "Middle Eastern Experiences of Cosmopolitanism," in *Conceiving Cosmopolitanism: Theory, Context and Practice*, ed. Steven Vertovec and Robin Cohen (Oxford University Press, 2002), 32–41.
Zutshi, Chitralekha, *Languages of Belonging: Islam, Regional Identity and the Making of Kashmir* (New York: Oxford University Press, 2004).
"Rethinking Kashmir's History from a Borderlands Perspective," *History Compass* 8.7 (2010): 594–608.

# Index

Lightning Source UK Ltd.
Milton Keynes UK
UKHW02f0157020318
318748UK00008B/118/P

9 781107 463080